WRITING ON THE MARGINS

Essays on Composition and Teaching

WRITING ON THE MARGINS

Essays on Composition and Teaching

David Bartholomae
University of Pittsburgh

WRITING ON THE MARGINS: ESSAYS ON COMPOSITION AND TEACHING by David Bartholomae

The Library of Congress has catalogued the paperback editon as follows: 2004107878

First published 2005 by
PALGRAVE MACMILLAN™
175 Fifth Avenue, New York, N.Y. and
Houndmills, Basingstoke, Hampshire, England RG21 6XS.
Companies and representatives throughout the world.

PALGRAVE MACMILLAN is the global academic imprint of the Palgrave Macmillan division of St. Martin's Press, LLC and of Palgrave Macmillan Ltd. Macmillan® is a registered trademark in the United States, United Kingdom and other countries. Palgrave is a registered trademark in the European Union and other countries.

ISBN: 1-4039-6803-9 hardback

A catalogue record for this book is available from the British Library.

First edition: October 2004
10 9 8 7 6 5 4 3 2 1

Printed in the United States of America.

ACKNOWLEDGMENTS

Carolyn C. Ball. "Telling Secrets: Students, Readers, and Disciplinary Authorities" by Carolyn C. Ball, Laura Dice, and David Bartholomae. Published in *Developing Discourse Practices in Adolescence and Adulthood,* edited by Richard Beach and Susan Hynds, Volume XXXIX. From the series *Advances in Discourse Processes,* edited by Roy O. Freedie. Copyright © 1990 Ablex Publishing Corporation. Reprinted with the permission of Greenwood Publishing Group, Inc., Westport, CT.

Acknowledgments and copyrights appear at the back of the book on page 380, which constitutes an extension of the copyright page. It is a violation of the law to reproduce these selections by any means whatsoever without the written permission of the copyright holder.

THIS BOOK IS FOR JOYCE.

LA MUCHACHA DORADA
SE BAÑABA EN EL AGUA
Y EL AGUA SE DORABA.

PREFACE

I'm grateful to Bedford/St. Martin's for providing an opportunity to present this collection of essays. I've included published material that has been important to me and that, when gathered together, articulate the long-term projects that I believe to be central to my work over the last twenty-some years.

When I began writing about composition, the field was in its earliest stages of becoming a recognized discipline. The essays I wrote were scattered here and there — some in journals and others in volumes, many written at the specific request of an editor — and it is unlikely that anyone would have encountered them all or read them in anything like an order. The scatteredness of the work is partly a product of temperament but also a product of the times. There weren't that many of us in the 1970s and 1980s and so we were frequently writing on demand, and the state of the profession was such that the opportunities to publish in composition were few and oddly distributed among venues that were often short-lived and disconnected. It has been important to me to assemble these essays here and to present them as the record of a single career, a record that might be read as determined and coherent.

Although the title of this book, *Writing on the Margins*, is drawn from one of the essays, it is not meant to highlight that essay or to give it special prominence. I chose the title because I liked the ring of it, but also for the way it alludes to three areas of our professional life that have most concerned me. It refers immediately to the practice of teaching — where writing on the margins (over and over and over again!) is one of the ways we deliver instruction to students. It refers as well to the kinds of writing that have become the primary subject matter of scholarship in composition — the writing of students, writing in the community and the workplace, private writing, "unauthorized" writing that falls into the margins between literature and silence. And, finally, I have argued for and experienced composition as a professional field that is marginal rather than central or hybrid. It is not a part of rhetoric or philosophy; it is not a subdivision of literary study; and it is not one of the various projects of educational research or cognitive science. The journals and professional meetings, doctoral programs and dissertations, all of these have drawn from more established areas of research and teaching. But the most interesting work in composition, to my mind, continues to resist the temptation to affiliate itself or to act as though it were comfortably at the center.

The opening essay, "Living in Style," was written for this book and so is the most recent piece in the collection. Placed at the beginning, it serves (I know) as an odd introduction. It is not conventionally prospective or retrospective. It doesn't speak directly to the essays that follow, nor does it try to sum up their arguments or reflect on the stages or outlines of a career. But it seems to me to be an appropriate entry point. It was written while I was rereading my essays and deciding which to include, and it took its direction and inspiration from what I found most interesting in their style and method (and disparity). In this essay, I was interested in gathering together the people and the materials that had been important to me; I was curious about the recent unexpected presence of Gertrude Stein in my reading and teaching; and I wanted to say something about the origins, uses, and purposes of the writing I have done for the scholarly community. So I offer "Living in Style" as a current articulation of how I have learned to write and read and teach over time. It draws on past and present; it includes materials from several areas of my intellectual and professional life; it thinks from my students' writing as well as the writing of my colleagues; it demonstrates broad rather than strictly disciplined reading. In that sense, it is like the final essay we often ask students to submit at the top of their semester portfolio. It is a place marker.

The essays that follow "Living in Style" are grouped into three sections titled "The Study of Error," "Teaching Composition," and "The Profession." "The Study of Error" collects essays that represent a consistent concern of my research and writing, the relation of student writing to conventional and institutional expectation (where student writing is usually taken to be wrong, fraught, mistaken, or in error). "Teaching Composition" gathers essays that speak to the teaching of writing, not simply my teaching but also "our" teaching (if such a unity can be imagined) as seen from a variety of vantage points and perspectives. And the final section, "The Profession," speaks more generally to Composition (with a capital C) as an area of professional identification and professional opportunity within the current domains of English Studies, the humanities, and the university. Within each section, the order of the essays is roughly the order of their writing (and not necessarily their publication). Each section is followed by a postscript. The postscripts *are* meant to be both retrospective and prospective. They provide a context to the essays and some sense of how I view their trajectory.

A note about the cover: The book's cover presents three of the oil paintings in a quite remarkable series by Felix de la Concha, who painted 365 views of the Cathedral of Learning at Pitt over a two-year period, one on each calendar day and each from a different position. The series is titled, "One a Day: 365 Views of the Cathedral of Learning, 1997–99," and it can be seen in its entirety on the seventh floor of Alumni Hall on the University of Pittsburgh campus. Each painting is 9 × 11; each was painted outside (and not in a studio).

De la Concha sees his work as an extension of the Spanish realist tradition that includes Francisco de Zubaran and Diego Velázquez. Anyone who teaches knows the power and fascination of repetition and accumulation, the same thing over and over but with a difference and a sense of purpose. I love the series as an act of devotion and discipline and obstinacy. The Cathedral is where I have worked and taught for almost thirty years. You see its presence on the margins of each canvas, standing adjacent to the neighborhoods of our city.

ACKNOWLEDGMENTS

Again, I am grateful to Bedford/St. Martins for the occasion of this book. I want to thank, in particular, editors who over time have also become valued friends and colleagues — Chuck Christensen, Joan Feinberg, and (more recently) John Sullivan.

I would like to thank those reviewers who helped me in the preparation of this book: Patricia Bizzell, John Boe, Jean Carr, Richard Miller, Tony Petrosky, Mike Rose, Jacqueline Jones Royster, Christine Ross and Nancy Sommers. I am grateful to each of them.

One of the great pleasures of my career has been the opportunity to work with a remarkable set of colleagues. Scholars in composition often work alone; I have had the privilege of working as part of a faculty, a group with a shared commitment to composition, general education, and the undergraduate curriculum. We became friends. We shared courses, materials, and student papers. We talked about our teaching and our work, read each other's prose, and supported each other's careers. The longer I have been in this business, the more I realize how rare and special this is — to have colleagues in composition. I want to name and to thank those whose words and ideas are everywhere in the sentences I write. Bill Coles was there at the beginning. Jean Carr, Steve Carr, Nick Coles, Kathryn Flannery, Paul Kameen, Tony Petrosky, and Mariolina Salvatori have been there forever. More recently, Joe Harris (now at Duke) and Jim Seitz. And even more recently, Don Bialostosky and Jennifer Trainor. I have also shared students and courses with Jonathan Arac, Lynn Emanuel, Colin MacCabe, and Philip Smith, and each has been an important colleague in composition.

At the University of Pittsburgh, we have an odd and demanding PhD program, one in which composition has never been a separate track but part of a general project in "cultural and critical studies." When you work with graduate students, particularly on PhD projects, you get more than you give, and I have learned much from the remarkably talented students who have worked with me: Carolyn Ball, Ellen Bishop, John Champagne, Matt Cooper, Marilyn DeMario, Laura Dice, Jeff Galen, Gwen Gorzelski, Bill Hendricks, Karen Hjelmervik, Bruce Horner, Glynda Hull, Linda Jordan, Paula Kristofik, Joan Latchaw, Min-zhan Lu, Barbara McCarthy, Richard Miller, Donna Dunbar Odom, Steve Parks, Jim Parlett, Christine Ross, Pat Saunders, Julia Sawyer, Margaret Shaw, Lynn Buncher Shelley, Patricia Sullivan, Steve Sutherland, Susan Wall, Kathleen Welsch, and Matt Willen.

I couldn't begin to name everyone in the profession whose work has been important to me, but I would like to thank those whose friendship has been sustaining and who have given generous attention over time to projects, to problems, and to work in progress: Pat Bizzell, John Gage, Bruce Herzberg, David Laurence, Andrea Lunsford, Don McQuade, Susan Miller, Mike Rose, Jackie Royster, Chuck Schuster, Jim Slevin, and Nancy Sommers. During the period of the writing of these essays, I taught for three full years at the Universidad de Deusto in Bilbao, Spain, including the first courses in composition since the Spanish Civil War and the era of Franco. (Deusto is now on the tourist map since it is right across the river from the Frank Gehry Guggenheim museum.) I am grateful to my colleagues and students for making this association so rich and rewarding, particularly Manuel Breva Claramonte and Aitor Ibarrola Armendariz.

And, finally, I'd like to thank my parents, Warren M. and Dorothy S. Bartholomae, and my family — Joyce, Jesse, Dan and Kate — for all they have given, which is just about everything that matters.

CONTENTS

WRITING ON THE MARGINS

Essays on Composition and Teaching

Living in Style

For years I have kept a commonplace book — more recently in a computer file. It is a collection of passages drawn from my reading and teaching, and it includes passages from student papers. In my mind I am recording moments of striking eloquence. When I turn to them, they stand as quick reminders of what has captured my attention; for my writing they serve as points of reference to individual performances and positions in a larger field of ideas or debate. I often use epigraphs at the beginnings of essays, and I almost always use them in assignments I write for courses, and the commonplace book serves as a source for these.

I want to open with the set of passages currently at the head of the collection. There are too many to serve as epigraphs, and so I offer these as a kind of found poem. It is a poem with an argument, and the argument addresses a question that has been at the center of my work, and so I believe these passages serve as an appropriate introduction to the essays in this volume. The question they ask is this: How do we understand the relationship between our students and the languages of power and knowledge that circulate inside and outside the university? Or, from the position of the student, what might it mean to match wits with the language, to see yourself in sentences?

> 1. Every sentence has a truth waiting at the end of it and the writer learns how to know it when he finally gets there. On one level this truth is the swing of the sentence, the beat and poise, but down deeper it's the integrity of the writer as he matches with the language. I've always seen myself in sentences. I begin to recognize myself, word by word, as I work through a sentence. The language of my books has shaped me as a man. There's a moral force in a sentence when it comes out right. It speaks the writer's will to live. The deeper I become entangled in the process of getting a sentence right in its syllables and rhythms, the more I learn about myself.
>
> — BILL GRAY, IN DON DELILLO, *MAO II* (48)

1

2. Topic sentence. However; but; as a result. Blah, Blah, Blah. It follows from this. Concluding sentence.

—CHARLES BERNSTEIN, *"THE SECRET OF SYNTAX"* (25)

3. When you are at school and learn grammar, grammar is very exciting. I really do not know that anything has ever been more exciting than diagraming sentences. I suppose other things may be more exciting to others when they are at school but to me undoubtedly when I was at school the really completely exciting thing was diagraming sentences and that has been to me ever since the one thing that has been completely exciting and completely completing. I like the feeling the everlasting feeling of sentences as they diagram themselves.

—GERTRUDE STEIN, *"POETRY AND GRAMMAR"* (210–11)

4. A sentence is an interval in which there is a finally forward and back. A sentence is an interval during which if there is a difficulty they will do away with it. A sentence is a part of the way when they wish to be secure. A sentence is their politeness in asking for a cessation. And when it happens they look up. A sentence is an allowance of a confusion. There are different ways of making of, of course.

A sentence is really when they are allowed without their properly felt in feeling an exchange. How are hours felt in their allowance.

A sentence is why they take pains to do it twice. Twice they take pains to do it twice as often. A sentence is with their liking to do it slowly. With their liking to do it slowly they allow themselves to advance.

—GERTRUDE STEIN, *HOW TO WRITE* (133)

5. If a person feels that by getting a college degree would make him a better person although the jobs to fit his education might not be in demand of course it makes sense.

In my opinion I believe that you there is no field that cannot be effected some sort of advancement that one maybe need a college degree to make it.

—STUDENT SENTENCES FROM MINA SHAUGHNESSY,
ERRORS AND EXPECTATIONS (50, 62)

6. When a sentence is called senseless, it is not as it were its sense that is senseless. But a combination of words is being excluded from the language, withdrawn from circulation.

—LUDWIG WITTGENSTEIN, *PHILOSOPHICAL INVESTIGATIONS* (500)

———

When I was first getting started in the profession (this was 1975), I was interested in Basic Writing. It seemed like there, in the performance of unprepared students and in the spectacle (at its best) of the university's confused and conflicted welcome or (at its worst) the university's dismissive response to students who didn't do what they were expected to do, there seemed to be something fundamental to composition, a problem of language and value, of education and citizenship — a challenge, a job worth a person's time and effort. Or, it was there that composition became interesting as both a job and an area of study, something a young PhD (in my case, with a dissertation on Thomas Hardy) might take as a point of professional identification. Although composition was not yet established as a field, my choices came at a time when it seemed both uninteresting and unprofitable to spend a career promoting an already famous author.

Jim Slevin tells a similar story. He was teaching at Lincoln University, the oldest historically black college in the United States. He was unprepared for how his students read and wrote. There is a problem here, he decided, and this is a problem that resides with us (with the institution, with English Studies, with the preparation of young PhDs in English) and not with them, with the students. He says:

> From that position, from that dim recognition that I needed to explore the place of alternative discursive practices in my own teaching, I was able to start learning from my students. . . . The paradigm change for me was not from product to process (something I encountered and welcomed later, less as a theoretical apparatus for professional definition than as an illuminating set of practices that made the work I wanted to do better). Rather it was a shift from seeing student writing as marginal to seeing it as central to the purposes of higher education, as where the real action was taking place (or not). (30)

This is from one of the opening essays in his book, *Introducing English: Essays in the Intellectual Work of Composition,* a book I admire enormously. And Slevin concludes, "the writing of students, especially those often considered *least*-suited to prevailing modes of instruction, is important because it alters institutions."

I wish I could believe this — that student writing has altered institutions. I'm not sure I do. But I like to think about how it can or might.

In 1976, it was not uncommon for those of us working with basic writers to say of our colleagues, "If they can read Gertrude Stein and value what she does, why can't they read the work of basic writers — why can't they give it the same time and attention, why can't they value the work?" Like the basic writer, the Stein I've featured in my opening passages was well aware that the written sentence is a regulatory device that belongs to "Them."

A sentence is part of the way — when they wish to be secure.
A sentence is when they are allowed — without their properly felt-in feeling — an exchange.

And within the conditions of the sentence, she taught herself to write with a precise attention to the workings of parts; she made visible the "feeling of sentences as they diagram themselves."

The Basic Writing student writes:

> In my opinion I believe that you there is no field that cannot be effected some sort of advancement that one maybe need a college degree to make it.

The kernel sentence is simple and heartfelt: "One needs a college degree to make it." As the sentence diagrams itself, however, it enacts the drama of a student writer who knows that to "make it" in college one also needs to learn to write in forms that are more highly elaborated, where the writer is present not only as the locus of desire ("I want to make it") but as someone who thinks, who commands that role in the classroom and in the academy, a context the student can only begin to imagine by beginning to write, and so the sentence opens with a variety of performative excursions:

> In my opinion
> I believe that you
> THERE IS NO FIELD THAT CANNOT BE EFFECTED
> *Some sort of advancement that?*
> One — maybe? — needs a college degree to make it.

"A sentence is their politeness in asking for a cessation. And when it happens they look up. A sentence is an allowance of a confusion. There are different ways of making of, of course." This is Gertrude Stein, thinking about the sentence as something one enters, a path of trial and error — something one works in and works with and works against, but not as "natural" expression. "A sentence is why they take pains to do it twice. Twice they take pains to do it twice as often. A sentence is with their liking to do it slowly. With their liking to do it slowly they allow themselves to advance."

Terry Castle has said that in Stein's writing, "grammar and life become indistinguishable" (214). And this in a review of Ulla Dydo's collection, *A Stein Reader*, a book that asks us to read Stein carefully, word for word (it asks that we not just exhibit her work) and to read it as a primer. The *Reader*, Dydo says, "returns us to the schoolroom where Stein asks what the three Rs are and teaches us to read in ways more fundamental than we had thought possible, more literal than we had known" (3).

I understand and appreciate Castle's point, that grammar and life become indistinguishable in Stein's writing, but I think she's wrong. I would say, with Dydo, that Stein teaches readers to remember the *difficult* relationship between grammar and life (between words on the page and the identity of the writer). This difficult relationship, matching with the language, is surprisingly *distinguishable* — visible, manifest — in Stein's writing, as it is in student writing, where the taking-it-for-grantedness, the inevitability of the sentence, is not so present, regular, or immediate. In these sentences, we see and feel and understand the work of the writer in relation to the work of writing. Dydo says that in Stein's most interesting writing (in *Tender Buttons*, for instance):

The energy of a piece comes in part from the act of writing, which enters it as a value that can be read, just as hues and brush strokes can be read in a painting. A text must be transcribed with attention to the evidence of its making. Print, while it cannot always reproduce that process, need not wipe it out. Inside a text are the lines that carry the words, the hand moving on paper, line breaks and spaces dictated by notebook or leaf, size and folds of paper, pen or pencil forming words, the shape of a draft visible in the way it is copied into a notebook, and even the effort to end a work in the space of one notebook. (7)

The now accepted way of accounting for the difficulty or the oddity of Stein's style is to name it in terms of sexual politics: Her writing is a project to "[free] language from the hierarchical grammars of patriarchy" (DeKoven 9). "Her verbal configurations are set up precisely to manifest the arbitrariness of discourse" (Perloff 76).

In another of the essays in *Introducing English*, "Academic and Student Genres: Toward a Poetics of Composition," Jim Slevin showed how he and his colleagues learned to read (to understand, to value) the essay of a "basic writer" by casting it in the tradition of Walt Whitman. The student was asked to describe and respond to a painting. The essay was "unreadable" — or unrecognizable as a coherent piece of work — until the lines on the page were recast in the format of lines from Walt Whitman's *Song of Myself*. You see the shape below (you'll need to imagine it laid out as a paragraph), and I believe the point of the comparison will be clear:

> I see this picture by Peter Blume very creative and colorful.
> I see the picture as if the people was really trying to put the world back
> together again and
> I see some smoke from an old building they were tearing down and the
> sky look very winded on that day and
> I see people trying to hold up a round large object and
> I see people dig holes in the ground and nailing stones back down into
> the ground
> I see other in the back ground working on a building and
> I see old bones from and [*sic*] animal and
> I see smoke going into the sky and . . . . (170)

The student was not alone, in other words, in writing this way — this was what Slevin and his colleagues learned. And read this way, "the language and form of a Whitman is just dead-on better than the academic paper that Andrew is more likely to have been required to do" (177).

It would be comforting (and relatively easy) if our job, then, was to find the bit of Whitman or Stein (or anyone else whom we valued) in the work of student writers. Unfortunately we don't just assign value; we also assign work. Slevin defines that work as the work of translation. Slevin's student was named Andrew; having provided this way of placing Andrew's project and valuing what Andrew is doing and then imaging possible revisions (or Andrew's next lessons), Slevin raises the question of what happens when Andrew's paper becomes part of a program of instruction that translates this project into the genres of academic writing, a relatively limited menu that can include: "Topic sentence. However; but; as a result. Blah, Blah, Blah. It follows from this. Concluding sentence."

Slevin's conclusion is that we must be careful "not just to provide Andrew with options but also to clarify the kind of violence this process entails, even with all the choices imaginable" (180). As far as the generic range is concerned, Slevin puts the emphasis on "all the choices imaginable," including "oral and written, literary and nonliterary, privileged and unprivileged" (180).

This latter is the big leap since it assumes that the work of composition can expand the genres of academic writing across the campus, and that it can teach the academy to value written language drawing upon oral, nonliterary, and unprivileged discursive traditions. I actually would take these as the two most important pedagogical challenges facing composition today. (The other great challenge concerns the status of faculty in the workplace.)

Literary genres, Slevin argues, can provide available models. The question to ask, he says, is not about the "place of literature in the classroom" but the "place of the classroom in literature" — that is, in what ways might an assigned text be offered as a writing lesson? The advantage:

> By not restricting the generic focus of the course to the genres of academic writing, we open up more traditional literary genres to the same critical scrutiny, engaging them as cultural practices with political and social implications. (158)

Slevin's choices are always surprising. (In one of his classes, *Don Quixote* as well as the *Narrative of the Life of Frederick Douglass*.)

The disadvantage? The act of translation (this genre into that) is always (must always be) determined by the institution, which sets into relief the "symbolic violence exercised within the generic hierarchy at work and by the generic translations required." The student's work becomes, finally, ours; there is no way around that. But to think of our students in relation to Whitman or Stein or even Cervantes, to think of them in relation to the history of writing and to the values of the "literary" — to do this rather than to dismiss them as childish, as "student writers" — this is certainly an achievement. Composition has historically questioned, Slevin says, even resisted, the "taken-for-granted hierarchies that govern accessibility and inaccessibility" (180). As a site of practice, composition has always defined the place (managed the process) by which these hierarchies are articulated in immediate relationship to student writing.

In my composition course last fall I taught a book of poems I very much admire, Lynn Emanuel's *Then, Suddenly* — . It is a book, I believe, with much to teach students about writing — a composition textbook. In fact, I have begun to gather about me a wide range of novels and books of poetry that are better composition textbooks than most of what I can find on the market. (Books of poetry are the best way I have found to focus attention on the sentence, and on punctuation and timing and rhythm.) Emanuel's book includes a poem titled "inside gertrude stein." I'll provide just part of it:

inside gertrude stein

Right now as I am talking to you and as you are being talked to, without letup, it is becoming clear that gertrude stein has hijacked me and that this feeling that you are having now as you read this, that this is what it feels like to be inside gertrude stein. This is what it feels like to be a huge typewriter in a dress. Yes, I feel we have gotten inside gertrude stein, and of course it is dark inside the enormous gertrude, it is like being locked up in a refrigerator lit only by a smiling rind of cheese. Being inside gertrude is like being inside a monument made of a cloud which is always moving across the sky which is also moving. Gertrude is a huge galleon of cloud anchored to the ground by one small tether, yes, I see it down there, do you see that tiny snail glued to the tackboard of the landscape? That is alice. . . .

Because someone must be gertrude stein, someone must save us from the literalists and realists, and narratives of the beginning and end, someone must be a river that can type. And why not I? (13–14)

In an interview, Emanuel said,

And I think the way that she [Stein] . . . will linger upon, and define, and make into an object or an architecture, the issue of the subordinate clause, or the issue of the period or the semi-colon, I felt that incredibly freeing. She made the invisible visible. These were the materials that I was working with daily as a matter of course and yet doing so in a way that they were just kind of beasts of burden carrying the meaning of the poem around with them. I adored that. You know language poets talk about abrading the transparency of language, and I found her way of doing that very exciting and productive, and annoying. (Svalina 3)

Although we are old friends, without knowing that she was writing a poem about inhabiting Gertrude Stein, I was at about the same time teaching an undergraduate course where I was asking students, including freshmen, to do just that. An account of the course is memorialized in one of the MLA-sponsored radio programs, part of the series titled "What's the Word." The show was titled "Improving Your Writing." My answer was that a writer could take time to find and work in the manner of an exemplary stylist, that he or she might take some time to write inside Gertrude Stein. Two students from my course then read their work and talked with the interviewer, Sally Placksin. In the course I asked students to read *Tender Buttons*. They had three assignments: (1) To prepare to read a section out loud, where the phrasing and intonation would indicate a way of reading the unreadable. (2) To write a piece in similar style. (3) And to write a brief essay reflecting on what they had done.

When asked by the interviewer what they learned from the exercise, one student, Ben, said "working inside Gertrude Stein gave me a different way of looking at language and of thinking about the so-called limits, how Stein defied those limits but also created new ones, that language is so powerful it can take it." This echoes a line from Stein's notebooks: "Eastern colleges too damn anxious to be safe. They needn't be so afraid it ain't so easy to be hurt as they seem to think least at least not by getting hit hard on the head. . . . They needn't be so afraid of their damn culture, it'd take more than a man like me to hurt it." Ben's own written exercise, titled, "A Sudden Supposition," was an homage to what he saw as the core of the piece he had read, titled, "A Seltzer Bottle." He said: "All of the 'supposing,' the supposing, the suppose this, suppose in August, suppose that there was no middle to summer. Those sort of things are all like what you read in academic writing where there are a lot of suppositions made. Hence I called my piece, "A Sudden Supposition" and it has to do with not really poking fun but showing the transparency of some of these supposings" ("Improving Your Writing").

Here is the Stein passage Ben was working with. You'll see that he is exactly right in finding within this the moves that might be associated with a certain form of academic writing.

A Seltzer Bottle

Any neglect of many particles to a cracking, any neglect of this mix around it, what is lead in color and certainly discolor in silver. The use of this is manifold. Supposing a certain time selected is assured. Suppose it is even necessary. Suppose no other extract is permitted and no more handling is needed. Suppose the rest of the message is mixed with a very long slender needle and even if it could be any black border, supposing all this, all together made dress and suppose it was actual. Suppose the mean way to state it was occasional. If you suppose this in August and even more melodiously, if you suppose this even in the necessary incident of there certainly being no middle in summer in winter, suppose this, in an elegant settlement, a very elegant settlement is more than of consequence. It is not final and sufficient and substituted. This which was so kindly a present was constant. (Stein, *Tender Buttons* 8)

Ben was identifying what Robert Frost refers to as "sentence-sounds." From 1906 to 1912, Frost was teaching English, including writing and rhetoric, first at Pinkerton's Academy in Derry, New Hampshire, and then at the State Normal School in Plymouth. In 1912, Frost moved with his family to England to commit himself to poetry full time. He returned to the United States in 1915, and in 1916 he accepted a position at Amherst College. This is Frost in 1914, in between his teaching jobs, writing to John T. Bartlett:

> I give you a new definition of a sentence.
> A sentence is a sound in itself on which other sounds called words may be strung.
> You may string words together without a sentence-sound to string them on as you may tie clothes together by sleeves and stretch them without a clothes line between two trees, but — it is bad for the clothes. . . . The sentence sounds are very definite entities. (This is no literary mysticism I am preaching.) They are as definite as words. It is not impossible that they

could be collected in a book though I don't see on what system they would be catalogued.

They are apprehended by the ear. They are gathered by the ear from the vernacular and brought into books. Many of them are familiar to us in books. I think no writer invents them. The most original writer only catches them fresh from talk, where they grow spontaneously.

A man is all a writer if *all* his words are strong on definite recognizable sentence sounds. The voice of the imagination, the speaking voice must know certainly how to behave, how to posture in every sentence he offers. (675)

Another student, Natalie, read from her reflective essay for the radio show. Her piece is sweet, as student writing is often sweet. It is also very smart:

[Stein] is making a serious comment on the project of reading and writing while at the same time being both fun and funny, mocking and yet participating in what she mocks. While reading her work, I was reminded of being a child. When I was just old enough for my Mom to allow me to separate from her immediate presence while food shopping, I would always immediately head to the bakery. I was a fine, upstanding member of the Acme cookie club, which meant that if I had my membership card with me, I would receive a free cookie with every visit. Cookie in hand, I would race back to find my mom, searching each aisle. Except, one time I couldn't find my Mom. My heart began to race. Though the rule was not to run in the food store, when I saw my Mom's slight frame, her red jacket and her long dark hair, I had to run to get her. I trucked down the aisle, grabbed my mom's elbow and then she turned. "You're not my Mom," I exclaimed. The heat began to rise to my face as irritation turned to embarrassment. Eventually I found my mother in the frozen food section. Gertrude Stein sounds like it is. But it is not quite it. Feels like it, but leaves a space of disjunction. Is, in fact, it. Legitimately feels as though it makes sense, but in the end feels contrived. Grab as many red coat wearing, dark haired women's elbows as you want. There's no solace in the frozen food section when dealing with Gertrude Stein. ("Improving Your Writing")

In this case, the students were pretty good writers and Stein — Stein as felt on the tongue and through their fingers — this Stein put them in the unfamiliar position of feeling writing as a test and a problem and to feel themselves as simultaneously beholden to and above the testmakers. I think they found her way of doing that very exciting and productive, and, as Emanuel says, very annoying.

———

In my composition courses in the last few years, I have also taught Don DeLillo's *Mao II*, a novel I very much admire, one that has a sudden timeliness since it considers the place of writing and the writer in the era of terrorism.

Mao II provides the opening passage in my collage. The passage is spoken by Bill Gray, a novelist and the central character in this novel. I'll confess that I find this passage thrilling. I love what it says and I love it because it says what I would say if asked why I have made (and continue to make) a career in composition:

> Every sentence has a truth waiting at the end of it and the writer learns how to know it when he finally gets there. On one level this truth is the swing of the sentence, the beat and poise, but down deeper it's the integrity of the writer as he matches with the language. I've always seen myself in sentences. . . . The language of my books has shaped me as a man. There's a moral force in a sentence when it comes out right. (48)

I love this, I know, because it is the language of my formation as a professional — and, I believe, of many of my generation. The language carries the explanations I gave to myself and to others when I was asked why I chose to work in composition.

We said, in the 1970s, that we worked with writing and with writers because we felt that writing had a moral force, that work with writing was a way to improve ourselves, our students, and our world. We measured not only our students but also our colleagues by the quality of their sentences — the beat and poise, the integrity of the writer as he or she matched with the language. We cast this as struggle, as urgent and as agonistic. It seemed perfectly right to invite all students into that struggle, even those labeled "unprepared." In Bill Gray's speech, I hear my most powerful teachers.

Richard Poirier:

> If English studies is not in command of a field of knowledge it can be in command of a field of energy. . . . English studies cannot be the body of English literature but it can be at one with its spirit: of struggling, or wrestling with words and meanings. Otherwise English studies may go one of two ways: it can shrink, in a manner possibly as invigorating as that which accompanied the retrenchment of Classics departments; or it can become distended by claims to a relevance merely topical. Alternatively, it can take a positive new step. It can further develop ways of treating *all* writing and *all* reading as analogous acts, as simultaneously developing performances, some of which will deaden, some of which will quicken us. (84)

This excerpt is from "What Is English Studies, and If You Know What That Is, What Is English Literature?" whose title attaches a 1970s qualifier to Gertrude Stein's essay, "What Is English Literature."

Or Bill Coles, in his address to his students:

> I ask the questions I do, not because I know the answers to them, not even because I do not know the answers to them, but because, though I know that they do not have answers in the conventional sense of the word (what kinds of questions do?), it is only the dead who cannot be brought to see as alive a subject through which there is the possibility of self-definition. For this reason, though I have never repeated an Assignment, every Assignment I have ever worked with, every question I have ever asked, involves the same issues: Where and how with this problem do you locate yourself? To what extent and in what ways is that

self-definable in language? What is this self to judge from the language shaping it? What has this self to do with you?

I wish to make clear that the self I am speaking of here, and the one with which we will be concerned in the classroom, is a literary self, not a mock or false self, but a stylistic self, the self construable from the way words fall on a page. The other self, the identity of a student, is something with which I as a teacher can have nothing to do, not if I intend to remain a teacher. That there is a relation between these two selves, between writing and thinking, intellect and being, a confusing, complicated, and involving relation indeed — this is undeniable. This relation, in fact, is the center of both the course as a course and the course as more than that. (12)

For both Poirier and Coles, if a writer's education is to matter, if it is to be anything more than a conventional exercise in correctness, it must confront the question of style — the record of where and how the writer matches with the language. As I think of this, I think also of Susan Sontag's *Against Interpretation*, a book that traveled through my class of graduate students and whose force I still feel in my thinking and teaching. This is from the title essay:

> What is important now is to recover our senses. We must learn to *see* more, to *hear* more, to *feel* more.
>
> Our task is not to find the maximum amount of content in a work of art, much less to squeeze more content out of the work than is already there. Our task is to cut back content so that we can see the thing at all.
>
> The aim of all commentary on art [I read this as "all commentary on student writing"] now should be to make works of art — and, by analogy, our own experience — more, rather than less, real to us. The function of criticism should be to show *how it is what it is*, even *that it is what it is*, rather than to show *what it means*. (14)

And there is the conclusion of Sontag's "On Style," another pertinent essay lost to the reading lists in composition. I think it speaks directly to the situation of student writing, both then and today. (I don't need to add an interpolated translation, in other words.) The essay as a whole argues that sentences (for example) may be political and revisionary; and it argues for an understanding of the artist (or writer) as agent that is neither naive nor nostalgic for some lost notion of individual presence. The essay restates the theory of style behind Coles's *The Plural I*, where he speaks, as does Poirier, of a "performing self." Finally, I would argue that Sontag's essay indicates how and why a composition course can and should be a course in close reading:

> What I have said about style has been directed mainly to clearing up certain misconceptions about works of art and how to talk about them. But it remains to be said that style is a notion that applies to any experience (whenever we talk about its form or qualities). And just as many works of art which have a potent claim on our interest are impure or mixed with respect to the standard I have been proposing, so many items in our experience which could not be classed as works of art possess some of the qualities of art objects. Whenever speech or movement or behavior or objects exhibit a certain deviation from the most direct, useful, insensible

mode of expression or being in the world, we may look at them as having a "style," and being both autonomous and exemplary. (36)

———————

Mao II, however, is designed to make a reader feel very foolish (or very dated) for being thrilled by Bill Gray. Bill can no longer write: He's blocked; he's a failure; he's selfish; he's a jerk. But that's not the issue; the novel is interested in history, not character, and in Bill's world there is no one with the motive or attention to read novels. Books, in fact, have value only as commodities, collectibles. And history has changed the terms of authorship. Bill says, while posing for a photographer:

> There's a curious knowledge that binds novelists and terrorists. In the West we become famous effigies as our books lose the power to shape and influence. Do you ask your writers how they feel about this? Years ago I used to think it was possible for a novelist to alter the inner life of the culture. Now bomb-makers and gunmen have taken that territory. They make raids on human consciousness. What writers used to do before we were all incorporated. (41)

And the photographer, snapping photos, says: "Keep going. I like your anger."

Bill does, in fact, head out into the world to try to make something happen, but again he fails. The plot works out the absurd death of the author — he dies foolishly, not heroically. Not only the plot, but the characters in the novel (writers, editors, readers) all argue convincingly that writing is no longer a possible or appropriate intervention in history. And this, frankly, is the argument that now circulates not only through English departments but through composition programs. Writing, student writing, doesn't matter as writing; it stands as symptomatic; it is where we can get the goods on our rotten culture and our rotten politics; what matters are our abilities to reveal the system builders beyond the individual act and the individual imagination.

———————

> "Culture" no longer matters as an idea for the [liberal arts] institution. And along with culture goes the hero of the story, the individual intellectual. . . . It is no longer possible for an individual subject to claim to "embody" the life of the mind — which has major implications for humanities research and teaching. (qtd. in Sabin 84)

This is from Bill Readings, "The University Without Culture" (in anticipation of *The University in Ruins*), and it serves as the pushing-off point for an essay by Margery Sabin, "Evolution and Revolution: Change in the Literary Humanities, 1968–1995," in *What's Happened to the Humanities*. Her goal is to think about how and where the student might play the role of the individual intellectual in current programs of English Studies.

If Readings's essay provides Sabin a critical point of purchase, to think about the possibilities of such a curriculum she turns to the Amherst English department from the 1940s to the 1960s, and she refers to the curricular impact of "Robert Frost, Reuben Brower, and the redoubtable Theodore Baird" (86). She says, "I begin by naming names because the vitality of the old Amherst English, like that of virtually any coherent curriculum, depended on the inspiring conviction of particular individuals rather than on the university of enduring truth of their ideas" (86). Sabin compares the old Amherst curriculum to the new to mark what has been lost. And she turns to two contemporary programs that, she says, "sustain literary values" without ignoring critical challenges to the idea of a canon or primary authority of authorship: the English major at Williams College and (to my great surprise) the composition program at the University of Pittsburgh.

For Sabin, the program at Pittsburgh is represented by some of the essays reprinted in this book (along with the *CCC* exchange with Peter Elbow), but primarily through *Facts, Artifacts, and Counterfacts*, the book that represents our work (in the late 1970s and early 1980s) to develop a curriculum for basic writers. What she highlights in the course is the concern to develop materials and to design a pedagogy that figures the student as an intellectual (as writers who can make something happen, as readers and thinkers with something to say and something to add to the conversation), and that does this with an awareness of the precariousness (and the conceit or fancy) of that figuration. Students write as authorities and study their writing with an eye to the very problems of knowledge, precedence, independence, and authority that are, in fact, the pressing writing problems of our time. Sabin refers to the work of the course as "humanistic reading and writing" — that is, it situates students in relation to the past, to history and culture, and imagines possibilities of agency and authorship (101). The course, she says, places emphasis on "authorship in language: who chooses to speak certain words and why." The course regularly asks, "Who speaks such words" and, she notes, the course asks this of both published writers and students. She concludes, the course "develops a model of authority in language that is another version of postmodern pragmatism: eclectic, skeptical, practical, bent on using inquiry into the nature of authority in language for the purpose of developing the authority of students themselves as writers" (100). In a volume of essays that are sometimes narrowly conservative and polemical, Sabin's essay is careful and thoughtful — and, while I can't speak for my colleagues, I am pleased to have our work cast in her terms as "literary and humanistic."

––––––––––

Let me conclude by rehearsing what I take to be the points around which this introduction has been circulating:

1. If it is our job to make student writing visible and readable, to give it value in the academy, then we must begin, as Andrea Lundsford said long ago, by "listening carefully to what our students tell us in their writing, and by characterizing that writing as fully as we can" (288). The legacy of Shaughnessy, and I would add, of my own work with Basic Writing, has shown what it might mean to listen carefully to what our students tell us in their writing. It requires close reading, the kind of reading once central to a literary education. And to *characterize* that writing, I'm

arguing today, we should look for appropriate characters within the history of writing and, in particular, within the history of the writing we admire. It makes a fundamental difference to define students' work in relation to Stein or to Whitman (or Stephen Greenblatt or Mary Louise Pratt or Adrienne Rich or John Wideman, authors from *Ways of Reading*) rather than to characterize them, at best, in terms of developmental stages or their distance from some imagined (and bogus) ideal of good or bad behavior.

2. If, as Bill Coles says (and as I believe) that what teaches is style, "style enacted as a demand for style," then one way for student writers to develop their reach and range, to feel both the power and limits of written language, is to work inside the styles of others through close reading and through imitation or homage. It is incumbent on us to think long and hard about the appropriate exemplary stylists. Note, I am not arguing for finding the appropriate topics, subjects, or arguments. I am arguing for stylists. Our choices will reflect our disagreements about the value of writing — what it does and what it is good for. But so be it. These are the arguments we should be having at our conferences. I would say that the exemplary stylists are those who struggle to make the language do something outside of conventional expectation. The models Tony Petrosky and I have chosen are represented in the seven editions of *Ways of Reading*, an anthology that, according to Lynn Bloom, stands alone in defining an alternative canon for freshman composition (413).

3. And Bill Gray and the integrity of the writer? *Mao II* is about the death of an author. Don DeLillo, unlike Bill Gray, goes on writing, and the novel, *Mao II*, presents itself as though it could make a difference — even a difference in how we understand terror and its sources. DeLillo is not Bill Gray. You don't find DeLillo in his sentences; you wouldn't find him saying anything so grand as "The deeper I become entangled in the process of getting a sentence right in its syllables and rhythms, the more I learn about myself" (48). To be sure, many of the sentences in *Mao II* are extraordinarily beautiful and powerful. But a reader never has the security of identifying them with a "DeLillo" whose character and vision are a defining feature, a point of identification. The novel gathers characters, languages, discourses, and contemporary points of reference (Beiruit and Andy Warhol) and puts them in perspective. You find DeLillo, as a figure, at work in these sentences and at work among them. DeLillo said in an interview:

> I don't think a writer can allow himself the luxury of separating himself from the crowd, even if he is by definition a person who spends much of his life alone in a room in the company of a typewriter, paper and pen. It is indispensable to be fully involved in contemporary life, to be part of the crowd, or the class of voices. Just as I was finishing *Mao II* I was immersed in reading the John Cheever diaries. On one page, Cheever tells what he saw happen one evening in New York during a baseball game. A player hits the ball into the stands. Forty people go after the ball, all trying to grab it. Cheever says that the job of the writer is not to describe the thoughts of an adulterous woman standing at the window watching the rain streak the glass. The writer, he says, should understand those forty people trying to get the baseball, understand the other ten or twenty thousand people who leave the stadium when the game is over. "Moral judgments embodied in migratory vastness." For me it was strange. I mean, perhaps it was because I was finishing *Mao II* just then

that the words struck me so forcefully, above all perhaps because they came from a writer like Cheever who had spent his entire professional life trying to understand the adulterous woman. I suppose that somehow he gave voice to an intuition which I had simply followed, that is, an attempt to place myself in the midst of a crowd. (Nadotti 88)

I think that is the point, actually, of the most fundamental lessons in style. The language is not yours. That is the opening assumption of the varied stylists in my list of references — Bernstein, Coles, Poirier, Shaughnessy, Shaughnessy's students, Sontag, Stein, and Wittgenstein. You did not invent it; it is not yours and yet, ironically, it is one of the most crucial ways you have of being present — of being present in the world, in the workplace, in the academy. For the purposes of education, the most effective lesson for student writers is to see (to hear, to understand) themselves inside the languages of contemporary life, contemporary thought, and the contemporary academy — different discursive worlds, to be sure. The most effective lesson is to get inside and to work inside sentences, with the ambition to make writing work for you — to make it do good work, to make it thoughtful and compelling, to be noticed and heard, to establish a presence, a stylistic self, in Coles's words, "construable from the ways words fall on the page," and from this writing lesson to learn what it means to be part of history, expectation, desire, and convention. Style is agonistic. The writer is caught within and struggles to make use of the available materials. The cover of Poirier's *The Performing Self* features a photograph of one of Michelangelo's four *Captives*, a sculptured body struggling to emerge from stone, the head absent. The image, he says, speaks the point of the book,

> that any effort to find accommodation for human shapes or sounds is an act that partakes of political meaning. It involves negotiation, struggle, and compromise with the stubborn material of existence, be it language or stone. (xvi)

That is what style can teach and the only way to teach it, I have learned, is by teaching students to pay attention to sentences — an act of attention that has fallen away from composition.

Pittsburgh, August 2003

WORKS CITED

Bartholomae, David. "Writing With Teachers" and "Response to Peter Elbow," *CCC*, February 1995, pp. 62–72; 84–87.

Bernstein, Charles. "The Secret of Syntax." *Content's Dream: Essays, 1975–1984*. Evanston: Northwestern UP, 2001. 25.

Bloom, Lynn Z. "The Essay Canon." *College English* 61.4 (1999): 401–30.

Castle, Terry. "Very Fine Is My Valentine." *Boss Ladies, Watch Out: Essays on Women, Sex and Writing*. New York: Routledge, 2002. 214.

Coles, William E., Jr. *The Plural I — And After*. Portsmouth: Boynton/Cook, 1988. 12.

Dekoven, Marianne. "Gertrude Stein and the Modernist Canon." *Gertrude Stein and the Making of Literature*. Ed. Shirley Neuman and Ira B. Nadel. Evanston: Northwestern UP, 1988. 9.

DeLillo, Don. *Mao II*. New York: Penguin, 1992. 48.

Dydo, Ulla E., ed. *A Stein Reader*. Evanston: Northwestern UP, 1993. 3.

Elbow, Peter. "Being a Writer vs. Being an Academic: A Conflict in Goals," and "Response to David Bartholomae," *CCC*, February 1995, pp. 72–83; 87–92.

Emanuel, Lynn. *Then, Suddenly —* . Pittsburgh: U of Pittsburgh P, 1999. 13–14.

Frost, Robert. "Letter to John T. Bartlett." 22 February 1914. *Frost: Collected Poems, Prose and Plays.* New York: Library of America, 1995. 675.

"Improving Your Writing." What's the Word Series. Modern Language Association. <http://www.mla.org/radio_participants/radio_shows 1999#improving>.

Lunsford, Andrea A. "The Content of Basic Writers' Essays." *College Composition and Communication* 31.3 (1980): 288.

Nadotti, Maria. "An Interview with Don DeLillo." *Salmagundi* 100 (Fall 1993): 88.

Perloff, Marjorie. *The Poetics of Indeterminacy: Rimbaud to Cage.* Princeton: Princeton UP, 2000. 76.

Poirier, Richard. "What Is English Studies, and If You Know What That Is, What Is English Literature?" *The Performing Self: Compositions and Decompositions in the Languages of Contemporary Life.* New Brunswick: Rutgers UP, 1992. 84.

Sabin, Margery. "Evolution and Revolution: Change in the Literary Humanities, 1968–1995." *What's Happened to the Humanities?* Ed. Alvin Kernan. Princeton: Princeton UP, 1997. 84, 86.

Shaughnessy, Mina. *Errors and Expectations.* New York: Oxford UP, 1977. 62, 50.

Slevin, James F. *Introducing English: Essays in the Intellectual Work of Composition.* Pittsburgh: U of Pittsburgh P, 2001. 30.

Sontag, Susan. "Against Interpretation." *Against Interpretation and Other Essays.* New York: Picador, 1966. 14.

——. "On Style." *Against Interpretation.* 36.

Stein, Gertrude. *How to Write.* New York: Dover, 1975. 133

——. "Poetry and Grammar." *Lectures in America.* New York: Random, 1935. 210–11.

——. *Tender Buttons.* Mineola, New York: Dover, 1997. 8.

——. "What Is English Literature." *Lectures in America.* 11–55.

Svalina, Mathias. "An Interview with Lynn Emanuel." *Blackbird: An On-Line Journal of Literature and the Arts* 1.2 (2002): 3. 15 Feb. 2003 <http://www.blackbird.vcu.edu/v1n2/features/emanuel_I_021403/emanuel_I_text.htm>.

Wittgenstein, Ludwig. *Philosophical Investigations.* Trans. Elizabeth Anscombe. Oxford: Blackwell Publishers, 2001. 500.

PART ONE

The Study of Error

The Study of Error

I t is curious, I think, that with all the current interest in "Basic Writing," little attention has been paid to the most basic question: What is it? What is "basic writing," that is, if the term is to refer to a phenomenon, an activity, something a writer does or has done, rather than to a course of instruction? We know that across the country students take tests of one sort or another and are placed in courses that bear the title, "Basic Writing." But all we know is that there are students taking courses. We know little about their performance as writers, beyond the bald fact that they fail to do what other, conventionally successful, writers do. We don't, then, have an adequate description of the variety of writing we call "basic."

On the other hand, we have considerable knowledge of what Basic Writing courses are like around the country, the texts that are used, the approaches taken. For some time now, "specialists" have been devising and refining the technology of basic or developmental instruction. But these technicians are tinkering with pedagogies based on what? At best on models of how successful writers write. At worst, on old text-book models that disregard what writers actually do or how they could be said to learn, and break writing conveniently into constituent skills like "word power," "sentence power," and "paragraph power." Neither pedagogy is built on the results of any systematic inquiry into what basic writers do when they write or into the way writing skills develop for beginning adult writers. Such basic research has barely begun. Mina Shaughnessy argued the case this way:

> Those pedagogies that served the profession for years seem no longer appropriate to large numbers of students, and their inappropriateness lies largely in the fact that many of our students . . . are adult beginners and depend as students did not depend in the past upon the classroom and the teacher for the acquisition of the skill of writing.

If the profession is going to accept responsibility for teaching this kind of student, she concludes, "We are committed to research of a very ambitious sort."[1]

From *College Composition and Communication* (Oct. 1980): 253–69.

Where might such research begin, and how might it proceed? We must begin by studying basic writing itself — the phenomenon, not the course of instruction. If we begin here, we will recognize at once that "basic" does not mean simple or childlike. These are beginning writers, to be sure, but they are not writers who need to learn to use language. They are writers who need to learn to command a particular variety of language — the language of a written, academic discourse — and a particular variety of language use — writing itself. The writing of a basic writer can be shown to be an approximation of conventional written discourse; it is a peculiar and idiosyncratic version of a highly conventional type, but the relation between the approximate and the conventional forms is not the same as the relation between the writing, say, of a 7th grader and the writing of a college freshman.

Basic writing, I want to argue, is a variety of writing, not writing with fewer parts or more rudimentary constituents. It is not evidence of arrested cognitive development, arrested language development, or unruly or unpredictable language use. The writer of this sentence, for example, could not be said to be writing an "immature" sentence, in any sense of the term, if we grant her credit for the sentence she intended to write:

> The time of my life when I learned something, and which resulted
> in a change in which I look upon life things. This would be the period of
> my life when I graduated from Elementary school to High school.

When we have used conventional T-unit analysis, and included in our tabulations figures on words/clause, words/T-unit, and clauses/T-unit that were drawn from "intended T-units" as well as actual T-units, we have found that basic writers do not, in general, write "immature" sentences. They are not, that is, 13th graders writing 7th grade sentences. In fact, they often attempt syntax whose surface is more complex than that of more successful freshman writers. They get into trouble by getting in over their heads, not only attempting to do more than they can, but imagining as their target a syntax that is *more* complex than convention requires. The failed sentences, then, could be taken as stages of learning rather than the failure to learn, but also as evidence that these writers are using writing as an occasion to learn.

It is possible to extend the concept of "intentional structures" to the analysis of complete essays in order to determine the "grammar" that governs the idiosyncratic discourse of writers imagining the language and conventions of academic discourse in unconventional ways. This method of analysis is certainly available to English teachers, since it requires a form of close reading, paying attention to the language of a text in order to determine not only what a writer says, but how he locates and articulates meaning. When a basic writer violates our expectations, however, there is a tendency to dismiss the text as non-writing, as meaningless or imperfect writing. We have not read as we have been trained to read, with a particular interest in the way an individual style confronts and violates convention. We have read, rather, as policemen, examiners, gate-keepers. The teacher who is unable to make sense out of a seemingly bizarre piece of student writing is often the same teacher who can give an elaborate explanation of the "meaning" of a story by Donald Barthelme or a poem by e. e. cummings. If we learn to treat the language of basic writing *as* language and assume, as we do when writers violate our expectations in more conventional ways, that the unconventional features in the writing are evidence of intention and that they are, therefore, meaningful, then we can chart systematic choices, individual strategies, and characteristic processes of thought. One can read Mina Shaughnessy's *Errors and Expectations* as the record of just such a close reading.[2]

There is a style, then, to the apparently bizarre and incoherent writing of a basic writer because it is, finally, evidence of an individual using language to make and transcribe meaning. This is one of the axioms of error analysis, whether it be applied to reading (as in "miscue analysis"), writing, or second-language learning. An error (and I would include errors beyond those in the decoding or encoding of sentences) can only be understood as evidence of intention. They are the only evidence we have of an individual's idiosyncratic way of using the language and articulating meaning, of imposing a style on common material. A writer's activity is linguistic and rhetorical activity; it can be different but never random. The task for both teacher and researcher, then, is to discover the grammar of *that* coherence, of the "idiosyncratic dialect" that belongs to a particular writer at a particular moment in the history of his attempts to imagine and reproduce the standard idiom of academic discourse.[3]

All writing, of course, could be said to only approximate conventional discourse; our writing is never either completely predictable or completely idiosyncratic. We speak our own language as well as the language of the tribe and, in doing so, make concessions to both ourselves and our culture. The distance between text and conventional expectation may be a sign of failure and it may be a sign of genius, depending on the level of control and intent we are willing to assign to the writer, and depending on the insight we acquire from seeing convention so transformed. For a basic writer the distance between text and convention is greater than it is for the run-of-the-mill freshman writer. It may be, however, that the more talented the freshman writer becomes, the more able she is to increase again the distance between text and convention. We are drawn to conclude that basic writers lack control, although it may be more precise to say that they lack choice and option, the power to make decisions about the idiosyncrasy of their writing. Their writing is not, however, truly uncontrolled. About the actual distance from text to convention for the basic writer, we know very little. We know that it will take a long time to traverse — generally the greater the distance the greater the time and energy required to close the gap. We know almost nothing about the actual sequence of development — the natural sequence of learning — that moves a writer from basic writing to competent writing to good writing. The point, however, is that "basic writing" is something our students *do* or *produce*; it is not a kind of writing we teach to backward or unprepared students. We should not spend our time imagining simple or "basic" writing tasks, but studying the errors that emerge when beginning writers are faced with complex tasks.

The mode of analysis that seems most promising for the research we need on the writer's sequence of learning is error analysis. Error analysis provides the basic writing teacher with both a technique for analyzing errors in the production of discourse, a technique developed by linguists to study second language learning, and a theory of error, or, perhaps more properly, a perspective on error, where errors are seen as (1) necessary stages of individual development and (2) data that provide insight into the idiosyncratic strategies of a particular language user at a particular point in his acquisition of a target language. Enough has been written lately about error analysis that I'll only give a brief summary of its perspective on second language or second dialect acquisition.[4] I want to go on to look closely at error analysis as a method, in order to point out its strengths and limits as a procedure for textual analysis.

George Steiner has argued that all acts of interpretation are acts of translation and are, therefore, subject to the constraints governing the passage from one language to another.[5] All our utterances are approximations, attempts to use the language of, say, Frank Kermode or the language, perhaps, of our other, smarter, wittier self. In this sense, the analogy that links developmental composition instruction with second language learning can be a useful one — useful that is, if the mode of learning (whatever the "second" language) is writing rather than speaking. (This distinction, I might add, is not generally made in the literature on error analysis, where writing and speech are taken as equivalent phenomena.) Error analysis begins with the recognition that errors, or the points where the actual text varies from a hypothetical "standard" text, will be either random or systematic. If they are systematic in the writing of an individual writer, then they are evidence of some idiosyncratic rule system — an idiosyncratic grammar or rhetoric, an "interlanguage" or "approximative system."[6] If the errors are systematic across all basic writers, then they would be evidence of generalized stages in the acquisition of fluent writing for beginning adult writers. This distinction between individual and general systems is an important one for both teaching and research. It is not one that Shaughnessy makes. We don't know whether the categories of error in *Errors and Expectations* hold across a group, and, if so, with what frequency and across a group of what size.

Shaughnessy did find, however, predictable patterns in the errors in the essays she studied. She demonstrated that even the most apparently incoherent writing, if we are sensitive to its intentional structure, is evidence of systematic, coherent, rule-governed behavior. Basic writers, she demonstrated, are not performing mechanically or randomly but making choices and forming strategies as they struggle to deal with the varied demands of a task, a language, and a rhetoric. The "systems" such writing exhibits provide evidence that basic writers *are* competent, mature language users. Their attempts at producing written language are not hit and miss, nor are they evidence of simple translation of speech into print. The approximate systems they produce are evidence that they can conceive of and manipulate written language as a structured, systematic code. They are "intermediate" systems in that they mark stages on route to mastery (or, more properly, on route to conventional fluency) of written, academic discourse.

This also, however, requires some qualification. They *may* be evidence of some transitional stage. They may also, to use Selinker's term, be evidence of "stabilized variability," where a writer is stuck or searching rather than moving on toward more complete approximation of the target language.[7] A writer will stick with some intermediate system if he is convinced that the language he uses "works," or if he is unable to see errors *as* errors and form alternate hypotheses in response.

Error analysis begins with a theory of writing, a theory of language production and language development, that allows us to see errors as evidence of choice or strategy among a range of possible choices or strategies. They provide evidence of an individual style of using the language and making it work; they are not a simple record of what a writer failed to do because of incompetence or indifference. Errors, then, are stylistic features, information about *this* writer and *this* language; they are not necessarily "noise" in the system, accidents of composing, or malfunctions in the language process. Consequently, we cannot identify errors without identifying them in context, and the context is not the text, but the activity of composing that presented the erroneous form as a possible solution to the problem of making a meaningful statement. Shaughnessy's taxonomy of error, for example, identifies errors according to their source, not their type. A single type of error could be attributed to a variety of causes. Donald Freeman's research, for example, has shown that, "subject-verb agreement . . . is a host of errors, not one." One of his students analyzed a "large sample of real world sentences and concluded that there are at least eight different kinds, most of which have very little to do with one another."[8]

Error analysis allows us to place error in the context of composing and to interpret and classify systematic errors. The key concept is the concept of an "interlanguage" or an "intermediate system," an idiosyncratic grammar and rhetoric that is a writer's approximation of the standard idiom. Errors, while they can be given more precise classification, fall into three main categories: errors that are evidence of an intermediate system; errors that could truly be said to be accidents, or slips of the pen as a writer's mind rushes ahead faster than his hand; and, finally, errors of language transfer, or, more commonly, dialect interference, where in the attempt to produce the target language, the writer intrudes forms from the "first" or "native" language rather than inventing some intermediate form. For writers, this intrusion most often comes from a spoken dialect. The error analyst is primarily concerned, however, with errors that are evidence of some intermediate system. This kind of error occurs because the writer *is* an active, competent language user who uses his knowledge that language is rule-governed, and who uses his ability to predict and form analogies, to construct hypotheses that can make an irregular or unfamiliar language more manageable. The problem comes when the rule is incorrect or, more properly, when it is idiosyncratic, belonging only to the language of this writer. There is evidence of an idiosyncratic system, for example, when a student adds inflectional endings to infinitives, as in this sentence, "There was plenty the boy had to *learned* about birds." It also seems to be evident in a sentence like this: "This assignment calls on *choosing* one of my papers and making a last draft out of it." These errors can be further sub-divided into those that are in flux and mark a fully transitional stage, and those that, for one reason or another, become frozen and recur across time.

Kroll and Schafer, in a recent *CCC* article, argue that the value of error analysis for the composition teacher is the perspective it offers on the learner, since it allows us to see errors "as clues to inner processes, as windows into the mind."[9] If we investigate the pattern of error in the performance of an individual writer, we can better understand the nature of those errors and the way they "fit" in an individual writer's program for writing. As a consequence, rather than impose an inappropriate or even misleading syllabus on a learner, we can plan instruction to assist a writer's internal syllabus. If, for example, a writer puts standard inflections on irregular verbs or on verbs that are used in verbals (as in "I used to runned"), drill on verb endings will only reinforce the rule that, because the writer is over-generalizing, is the source of the error in the first place. By charting and analyzing a writer's errors, we can begin in our instruction with what a writer *does* rather than with what he fails to do. It makes no sense, for example, to impose lessons on the sentence on a student whose problems with syntax can be understood in more precise terms. It makes no sense to teach spelling to an individual who has trouble principally with words that contain vowel clusters. Error analysis, then, is a method of diagnosis.

Error analysis can assist instruction at another level. By having students share in the process of investigating and interpreting the patterns of error in their writing, we can help them begin to see those errors as evidence of hypotheses or strategies they have formed and, as a consequence, put them in a position to change, experiment, imagine other strategies. Studying their own writing puts students in a position to see themselves as language users, rather than as victims of a language that uses them.

This, then, is the perspective and the technique of error analysis. To interpret a student paper without this frame of reference is to misread, as for example when a teacher sees an incorrect verb form and concludes that the student doesn't understand the rules for indicating tense or number. I want, now, to examine error analysis as a procedure for the study of errors in written composition. It presents two problems. The first can be traced to the fact that error analysis was developed for studying errors in spoken performance.[10] It can be transferred to writing only to the degree that writing is like speech, and there are significant points of difference. It is generally acknowledged, for example, that written discourse is not just speech written down on paper. Adult written discourse has a grammar and rhetoric that is different from speech. And clearly the activity of producing language is different for a writer than it is for a speaker.

The "second language" a basic writer must learn to master is formal, written discourse, a discourse whose lexicon, grammar, and rhetoric are learned not through speaking and listening but through reading and writing. The process of acquisition is visual not aural. Furthermore, basic writers do not necessarily produce writing by translating speech into print (the way children learning to write would); that is, they must draw on a memory for graphemes rather than phonemes. This is a different order of memory and production from that used in speech and gives rise to errors unique to writing.

Writing also, however, presents "interference" of a type never found in speech. Errors in writing may be caused by interference from the act of writing itself, from the difficulty of moving a pen across the page quickly enough to keep up with the words in the writer's mind, or from the difficulty of recalling and producing the conventions that are necessary for producing print rather than speech, conventions of spelling, orthography, punctuation, capitalization and so on. This is not, however, just a way of saying that writers make spelling errors and speakers do not. As Shaughnessy pointed out, errors of syntax can be traced to the gyrations of a writer trying to avoid a word that her sentence has led her to, but that she knows she cannot spell.

The second problem in applying error analysis to the composition classroom arises from special properties in the taxonomy of errors we chart in student writing. Listing varieties of errors is not like listing varieties of rocks or butterflies. What a reader finds depends to a large degree on her assumptions about the writer's intention. Any systematic attempt to chart a learner's errors is clouded by the difficulty of assigning intention through textual analysis. The analyst begins, then, by interpreting a text, not by describing features on a page. And interpretation is less than a precise science.

Let me turn to an example. This is part of a paper that a student, John, wrote in response to an assignment that asked him to go back to some papers he had written on significant moments in his life in order to write a paper that considered the general question of the way people change:

> This assignment call on chosing one of my incident making a last draft out of it. I found this very differcult because I like them all but you said I had to pick one so the Second incident was decide. Because this one had the most important insight to my life that I indeed learn from. This insight explain why adulthood mean that much as it dose to me because I think it alway influence me to change and my outlook on certain thing like my point-of-view I have one day and it might change the next week on the same issue. So in these frew words I going to write about the incident now. My exprience took place in my high school and the reason was outside of school but I will show you the connection. The situation took place cause of the type of school I went too. Let me tell you about the situion first of all what happen was that I got suspense from school. For thing that I fell was out of my control sometime, but it taught me alot about respondability of a growing man. The school suspense me for being late ten time. I had accummate ten dementic and had to bring my mother to school to talk to a conselor and Prinpicable of the school what when on at the meet took me out mentally period.

One could imagine a variety of responses to this. The first would be to form the wholesale conclusion that John can't write and to send him off to a workbook. Once he had learned how to write correct sentences, then he could go on to the business of actually writing. Let me call this the "old style" response to error. A second response, which I'll call the "investigative approach," would be to chart the patterns of errors in this particular text. Of the approximately 40 errors in the first 200 words, the majority fall under four fairly specific categories: verb endings, noun plurals, syntax, and spelling. The value to pedagogy is obvious. One is no longer teaching a student to "write" but to deal with a limited number of very specific kinds of errors, each of which would suggest its own appropriate response. Furthermore, it is possible to refine the categories and to speculate on and organize them according to cause. The verb errors almost all involve "s" or "ed" endings, which could indicate dialect interference or a failure to learn the rules for indicating tense and number. It is possible to be even more precise. The passage contains 41 verbs; only 17 of them are used incorrectly. With the exception of four spelling errors, the errors are all errors of inflection and, furthermore, these errors come only with regular verbs. There are no errors with irregular verbs. This would suggest, then, that when John draws on memory for a verb form, he gets it right; but when John applies a rule to determine the ending, he gets it wrong.

The errors of syntax could be divided into those that might be called punctuation errors (or errors that indicate a difficulty perceiving the boundaries of the sentence), such as

> Let me tell you about the situation first of all what happen was that I got suspense from school. For thing that I fell was out of my control sometime, but it taught me alot about respondability of a growing man.

and errors of syntax that would fall under Shaughnessy's category of consolidation errors,

> This insight explain why adulthood mean that much as it dose to me because I think it alway influence me to change and my outlook on certain thing like my point-of-view I have one day and it might change the next week on the same issue.

One would also want to note the difference between consistent errors, the substitution of "situation" for "situation" or "suspense" for "suspended," and unstable ones, as, for example, when John writes "cause" in one place and "because" in another. In one case John could be said to have fixed on a rule; in the other he is searching for one. One would also want to distinguish between what might seem to be "accidental" errors, like substituting "frew" for "few" or "when" for "went," errors that might best be addressed by teaching a student to edit, and those whose causes are deeper and require time and experience, or some specific instructional strategy.

I'm not sure, however, that this analysis provides an accurate representation of John's writing. Consider what happens when John reads this paper out loud. I've been taping students reading their own papers, and I've developed a system of notation, like that used in miscue analysis,[11] that will allow me to record the points of variation between the writing that is on the page and the writing that is spoken, or, to use the terminology of miscue analysis, between the expected response (ER) and the observed response (OR). What I've found is that students will often, or in predictable instances, substitute correct forms for the incorrect forms on the page, even though they are generally unaware that such a substitution was made. This observation suggests the limits of conventional error analysis for the study of error in written composition.

I asked John to read his paper out loud, and to stop and correct or note any mistakes he found. Let me try to reproduce the transcript of that reading. I will underline any substitution or correction and offer some comments in parentheses. The reader might first go back and review the original. Here is what John read:

> This assignment calls on *choosing* one of my incident making a last draft out of it. I found this very difficult because I like them all but you said I *had* to pick one so the Second incident was decide*d on*. Because (John goes back and rereads, connecting up the subordinate clause.) So the second incident was decided on because this one had the most important insight to my life that I indeed learn*ed* from. This insight explains why adulthood *meant* that much as it dose to me because I think it always influence*s* me to change and my outlook on certain thing*s* like my point-of-view I have one day and it might change the next week on the same issue. (John goes back and rereads, beginning with "like my point of view," and he is puzzled but he makes no additional changes.) So in these *few* words *I'm* going to write about the incident now. My exp*er*ience took place *be*cause of the type of school I went to (John had written "too.") Let me tell you about the situation (John comes to a full stop.) first of all what happen*ed* was that I got *suspended* from school (no full stop) for thing*s* that I *felt* was out of my control sometime, but it taught me a lot about *responsibility* of a growing man. The school *suspended* me for being late ten time*s*. I had *accumulated* (for "accumate") ten *demerits* (for "dementic") and had to bring my mother to school to talk to a counselor and *the* *Principal* of the school (full stop) what *went* on at the meet*ing* took me out mentally (full stop) period (with brio).

I have chosen an extreme case to make my point, but what one sees here is the writer correcting almost every error as he reads the paper, even though he is not able to recognize that there *are* errors or that he has corrected them. The only errors John spotted (where he stopped, noted an error, and corrected it) were the misspellings of "situation" and "Principal," and the substitution of "chosing" for "choosing." Even when he was asked to reread sentences to see if he could notice any difference between what he was saying and the words on the page, he could not. He could not, for example, see the error in "frew" or "dementic" or any of the other verb errors, and yet he spoke the correct form of every verb (with the exception of "was" after he had changed "thing" to "things" in "for things that I *felt* was out of my control") and he corrected every plural. His phrasing as he read produced correct syntax, except in the case of the consolidation error, which he puzzled over but did not correct. It's important to note, however, that John did not read that confused syntax as if no confusion were there. He sensed the difference between the phrasing called for by the meaning of the sentence and that which existed on the page. He did not read as though meaning didn't matter or as though the "meaning" coded on the page was complete. His problem cannot be simply a syntax problem, since the jumble is bound up with his struggle to articulate this particular meaning. And it is not simply a "thinking" problem — John doesn't write this way because he thinks this way — since he perceives that the statement as it is written is other than that which he intended.

When I asked John why the paper (which went on for two more pages) was written all as one paragraph, he replied, "It was all one idea. I didn't want to have to start all over again. I had a good idea and I didn't want to give it up." John doesn't need to be "taught" the paragraph, at least not as the paragraph is traditionally taught. His prose is orderly and proceeds through blocks of discourse. He tells the story of his experience at the school and concludes that through his experience he realized that he must accept responsibility for his tardiness, even though the tardiness was not his fault but the fault of the Philadelphia subway system. He concludes that with this realization he learned "the responsibility of a growing man." Furthermore John knows that the print code carries certain conventions for ordering and presenting discourse. His translation of the notion that "a paragraph develops a single idea" is peculiar but not illogical.

It could also be argued that John does not need to be "taught" to produce correct verb forms, or, again, at least not as such things are conventionally taught. Fifteen weeks of drill on verb endings might raise his test scores but they would not change the way he writes. He *knows* how to produce correct endings. He demonstrated that when he read, since he was reading in terms of his grammatical competence. His problem is a problem of performance, or fluency, not of competence. There is certainly no evidence that the verb errors are due to interference from his spoken language. And if the errors could be traced to some intermediate system, the system exists only in John's performance as a writer. It does not operate when he reads or, for that matter, when he speaks, if his oral reconstruction of his own text can be taken as a record of John "speaking" the idiom of academic discourse.[12]

John's case also highlights the tremendous difficulty such a student has with editing, where a failure to correct a paper is not evidence of laziness or inattention or a failure to know correct forms, but evidence of the tremendous difficulty such a student has objectifying language and seeing it as black and white marks on the page, where things can be wrong even though the meaning seems right.[13] One of the hardest errors for John to spot, after all my coaching, was the substitution of "frew" for "few," certainly not an error that calls into question John's competence as a writer. I can call this a "performance" error, but that term doesn't suggest the constraints on performance in writing. This is an important area for further study. Surely one constraint is the difficulty of moving the hand fast enough to translate meaning into print. The burden imposed on their patience and short-term memory by the slow, awkward handwriting of many inexperienced writers is a very real one. But I think the constraints extend beyond the difficulty of forming words quickly with pen or pencil.

One of the most interesting results of the comparison of the spoken and written versions of John's text is his inability to *see* the difference between "frew" and "few" or "dementic" and "demerit." What this suggests is that John reads and writes from the "top down" rather than the "bottom up," to use a distinction made by cognitive psychologists in their study of reading.[14] John is not operating through the lower level process of translating orthographic information into sounds and sounds into meaning when he reads. And conversely, he is not working from meaning to sound to word when he is writing. He is, rather, retrieving lexical items directly, through a "higher level" process that by-passes the "lower level" operation of phonetic translation. When I put *frew* and *few* on the blackboard, John read them both as "few." The lexical item "few" is represented for John by either orthographic array. He is not, then, reading or writing phonetically, which is a sign, from one perspective, of a high level of fluency, since the activity is automatic and not mediated by the more primitive operation of translating speech into print or print into speech. When John was writing, he did not produce "frew" or "dementic" by searching for sound/letter correspondences. He drew directly upon his memory for the look and shape of those words; he was working from the top down rather than the bottom up. He went to stored print forms and did not take the slower route of translating speech into writing.

John, then, has reached a stage of fluency in writing where he directly and consistently retrieves print forms, like "dementic," that are meaningful to him, even though they are idiosyncratic. I'm not sure what all the implications of this might be, but we surely must see John's problem in a new light, since his problem can, in a sense, be attributed to his skill. To ask John to slow down his writing and sound out words would be disastrous. Perhaps the most we can do is to teach John the slowed-down form of reading he will need in order to edit.

John's paper also calls into question our ability to identify accidental errors. I suspect that when John substitutes a word like "when" for "went," this is an accidental error, a slip of the pen. Since John spoke "wen*t*" when he read, I cannot conclude that he substituted "when" for "went" because he pronounces both as "wen." This, then, is not an error of dialect interference but an accidental error, the same order of error as the omission of "the" before "Principal." Both were errors John corrected while reading (even though he didn't identify them as errors).

What is surprising is that, with all the difficulty John had identifying errors, he immediately saw that he had written "chosing" rather than "choosing." While textual analysis would have led to the conclusion that he was applying a tense rule to a participial construction, or over-generalizing from a known rule, the ease with which it was identified would lead one to conclude that it was, in fact, a mistake, and not evidence of an approximative system. What would have been diagnosed as a deep error now appears to be only an accidental error, a "mistake" (or perhaps a spelling error).

In summary, this analysis of John's reading produces a healthy respect for the tremendous complexity of transcription, for the process of recording meaning in print as opposed to the process of generating meaning. It also points out the difficulty of charting a learner's "interlanguage" or "intermediate system," since we are working not only with a writer moving between a first and a second language, but a writer whose performance is subject to the interference of transcription, of producing meaning through the print code. We need, in general, to refine our understanding of performance-based errors, and we need to refine our teaching to take into account the high percentage of error in written composition that is rooted in the difficulty of performance rather than in problems of general linguistic competence.

Let me pause for a moment to put what I've said in the context of work in error analysis. Such analysis is textual analysis. It requires the reader to make assumptions about intention on the basis of information in the text. The writer's errors provide the most important information since they provide insight into the idiosyncratic systems the writer has developed. The regular but unconventional features in the writing will reveal the rules and strategies operating for the basic writer.

The basic procedure for such analysis could be outlined this way. First the reader must identify the idiosyncratic construction; he must determine what is an error. This is often difficult, as in the case of fragments, which are conventionally used for effect. Here is an example of a sentence whose syntax could clearly be said to be idiosyncratic:

> In high school you learn alot for example Kindergarten which I took in high school.[15]

The reader, then, must reconstruct that sentence based upon the most reasonable interpretation of the intention in the original, and this must be done *before* the error can be classified, since it will be classified according to its cause.[16] Here is Shaughnessy's reconstruction of the example given above: "In high school you learn a lot. For example, I took up the study of Kindergarten in high school." For any idiosyncratic sentence, however, there are often a variety of possible reconstructions, depending on the reader's sense of the larger meaning of which this individual sentence is only a part, but also depending upon the reader's ability to predict how this writer puts sentences together, that is, on an understanding of this individual style. The text is being interpreted, not described. I've had graduate students who have reconstructed the following sentence, for example, in a variety of ways:

> Why do we have womens liberation and their fighting for Equal Rights ect. to be recognized not as a lady but as an Individual.

It could be read, "Why do we have women's liberation and why are they fighting for Equal Rights? In order that women may be recognized not as ladies but as individuals." And, "Why do we have women's liberation and their fight for equal rights, to be recognized not as a lady but as an individual?" There is an extensive literature on the question of interpretation and intention in prose, too extensive for the easy assumption that all a reader has to do is identify what the writer would have written if he wanted to "get it right the first time." The great genius of Shaughnessy's study, in fact, is the remarkable wisdom and sympathy of her interpretations of student texts.

Error analysis, then, involves more than just making lists of the errors in a student essay and looking for patterns to emerge. It begins with the double perspective of text and reconstructed text and seeks to explain the difference between the two on the basis of whatever can be inferred about the meaning of the text and the process of creating it. The reader/researcher brings to bear his general knowledge of how basic writers write, but also whatever is known about the linguistic and rhetorical constraints that govern an individual act of writing. In Shaughnessy's analysis of the "kindergarten" sentence, this discussion is contained in the section on "consolidation errors" in the chapter on "Syntax."[17] The key point, however, is that any such analysis must draw upon extra-textual information as well as close, stylistic analysis.

This paper has illustrated two methods for gathering information about how a text was created. A teacher can interview the student and ask him to explain his error. John wrote this sentence in another paper for my course:

I would to write about my experience helping 1600 childrens have a happy christmas.

The missing word (I would *like* to write about . . .) he supplied when reading the sentence aloud. It is an accidental error and can be addressed by teaching editing. It is the same kind of error as his earlier substitution of "when" for "went." John used the phrase, "1600 childrens," throughout his paper, however. The conventional interpretation would have it that this is evidence of dialect interference. And yet, when John read the paper out loud, he consistently read "1600 children," even though he said he did not see any difference between the word he spoke and the word that was on the page. When I asked him to explain why he put an "s" on the end of "children," he replied, "Because there were 1600 of them." John had a rule for forming plurals that he used when he wrote but not when he spoke. Writing, as he rightly recognized, has its own peculiar rules and constraints. It is different from speech. The error is not due to interference from his spoken language but to his conception of the "code" of written discourse.

The other method for gathering information is having students read aloud their own writing, and having them provide an oral reconstruction of their written text. What I've presented in my analysis of John's essay is a method for recording the discrepancies between the written and spoken versions of a single text. The record of a writer reading provides a version of the "intended" text that can supplement the teacher's or researcher's own reconstruction and aid in the interpretation of errors, whether they be accidental, interlingual, or due to dialect interference. I had to read John's paper very differently once I had heard him read it.

More importantly, however, this method of analysis can provide access to an additional type of error. This is the error that can be attributed to the physical and conceptual demands of writing rather than speaking; it can be traced to the requirements of manipulating a pen and the requirements of manipulating the print code.[18]

In general, when writers read, and read in order to spot and correct errors, their responses will fall among the following categories:

1. overt corrections — errors a reader sees, acknowledges, and corrects;
2. spoken corrections — errors the writer does not acknowledge but corrects in reading;
3. no recognition — errors that are read as written;
4. overcorrection — correct forms made incorrect, or incorrect forms substituted for incorrect forms;
5. acknowledged error — errors a reader senses but cannot correct;
6. reader miscue — a conventional miscue, not linked to error in the text;
7. nonsense — In this case, the reader reads a non-sentence or a nonsense sentence as though it were correct and meaningful. No error or confusion is acknowledged. This applies to errors of syntax only.

Corrections, whether acknowledged or unacknowledged, would indicate performance-based errors. The other responses (with the exception of "reader miscues") would indicate deeper errors, errors that, when charted, would provide evidence of some idiosyncratic grammar or rhetoric.

John "miscues" by completing or correcting the text that he has written. When reading researchers have readers read out loud, they have them read someone else's writing, of course, and they are primarily concerned with the "quality" of the miscues.[19] All fluent readers will miscue; that is, they will not repeat verbatim the words on the page. Since fluent readers are reading for meaning, they are actively predicting what will come and processing large chunks of graphic information at a time. They do not read individual words, and they miscue because they speak what they expect to see rather than what is actually on the page. One indication of a reader's proficiency, then, is that the miscues don't destroy the "sense" of the passage. Poor readers will produce miscues that jumble the meaning of a passage, as in

> Text: Her wings were folded quietly at her sides.
> Reader: Her wings were floated quickly at her sides.

or they will correct miscues that do not affect meaning in any significant way.[20]

The situation is different when a reader reads his own text, since this reader already knows what the passage means and attention is drawn, then, to the representation of that meaning. Reading also frees a writer from the constraints of transcription, which for many basic writers is an awkward, laborious process, putting excessive demands on both patience and short-term memory. John, like any reader, read what he expected to see, but with a low percentage of meaning-related miscues, since the meaning, for him, was set, and with a high percentage of code-related miscues, where a correct form was substituted for an incorrect form.

The value of studying students' oral reconstruction of their written texts is threefold. The first is as a diagnostic tool. I've illustrated in my analysis of John's paper how such a diagnosis might take place.

It is also a means of instruction. By having John read aloud and, at the same time, look for discrepancies between what he spoke and what was on the page, I was teaching him a form of reading. The most dramatic change in John's performance over the term was in the number of errors he could spot and correct while rereading. This far exceeded the number of errors he was able to eliminate from his first drafts. I could teach John an editing procedure better than I could teach him to be correct at the point of transcription.

The third consequence of this form of analysis, or of conventional error analysis, has yet to be demonstrated, but the suggestions for research are clear. It seems evident that we can chart stages of growth in individual basic writers. The pressing question is whether we can chart a sequence of "natural" development for the class of writers we call basic writers. If all non-fluent adult writers proceed through a "natural" learning sequence, and if we can identify that sequence through some large, longitudinal study, then we will begin to understand what a basic writing course or text or syllabus might look like. There are studies of adult second language learners that suggest that there is a general, natural sequence of acquisition for adults learning a second language, one that is determined by the psychology of language production and language acquisition.[21] Before we can adapt these methods to a study of basic writers, however, we need to better understand the additional constraints of learning to transcribe and manipulate the "code" of written discourse. John's case illustrates where we might begin and what we must know.[22]

NOTES

1. Mina Shaughnessy, "Some Needed Research on Writing," *CCC,* 28 (December, 1977), 317, 388.

2. Mina Shaughnessy, *Errors and Expectations: A Guide for the Teacher of Basic Writing* (New York: Oxford University Press, 1977).

3. The term "idiosyncratic dialect" is taken from S. P. Corder, "Idiosyncratic Dialects and Error Analysis," in Jack C. Richards, ed., *Error Analysis: Perspectives on Second Language Acquisition* (London: Longman, 1974), pp. 158–71.

4. Barry M. Kroll and John C. Schafer, "Error Analysis and the Teaching of Composition," *CCC.* 29 (October, 1978), 243–48. See also my review of *Errors and Expectations* in Donald McQuade, ed., *Linguistics, Stylistics and The Teaching of Composition* (Akron, Ohio: L & S Books, 1979), pp. 209–20.

5. George Steiner, *After Babel: Aspects of Language and Translation* (New York: Oxford University Press, 1975).

6. For the term "interlanguage," see L. Selinker, "Interlanguage," in Richards, ed., *Error Analysis,* pp. 31–55. For "approximate system," see William Nemser, "Approximate Systems of Foreign Language Learners," in Richards, ed., *Error Analysis,* pp. 55–64. These are more appropriate terms than "idiosyncratic dialect" for the study of error in written composition.

7. The term "stabilized variability" is quoted in Andrew D. Cohen and Margaret Robbins, "Toward Assessing Interlanguage Performance: The Relationship Between Selected Errors, Learner's Characteristics and Learner's Explanations," *Language Learning,* 26 (June, 1976), p. 59. Selinker uses the term "fossilization" to refer to single errors that recur across time, so that the

interlanguage form is not evidence of a transitional stage. (See Selinker, "Interlanguage.") M. P. Jain distinguishes between "systematic," "asystematic" and "nonsystematic" errors. (See "Error Analysis: Source, Cause and Significance" in Richards, ed., *Error Analysis*, pp. 189–215.) Unsystematic errors are mistakes, "slips of the tongue." Systematic errors "seem to establish that in certain areas of language use the learner possesses construction rules." Asystematic errors lead one to the "inescapable conclusion" that "the learner's capacity to generalize must improve, for progress in learning a language is made by adopting generalizations and stretching them to match the facts of the language."

8. Donald C. Freeman, "Linguistics and Error Analysis: On Agency," in Donald McQuade, ed., *Linguistics, Stylistics and The Teaching of Composition* (Akron, Ohio: L & S Books, 1979), pp. 143–44.

9. Kroll and Schafer, "Error Analysis and the Teaching of Composition."

10. In the late 60's and early 70's, linguists began to study second language acquisition by systematically studying the actual performance of individual learners. What they studied, however, was the language a learner would speak. In the literature of error analysis, the reception and production of language is generally defined as the learner's ability to hear, learn, imitate, and independently produce *sounds*. Errors, then, are phonological substitutions, alterations, additions, and subtractions. Similarly, errors diagnosed as rooted in the mode of production (rather than, for example, in an idiosyncratic grammar or interference from the first language) are errors caused by the difficulty a learner has hearing or making foreign sounds. When we are studying written composition, we are studying a different mode of production, where a learner must see, remember, and produce marks on a page. There may be some similarity between the grammar-based errors in the two modes, speech and writing (it would be interesting to know to what degree this is true), but there should be marked differences in the nature and frequency of performance-based errors.

11. See Y. M. Goodman and C. L. Burke, *Reading Miscue Inventory: Procedure for Diagnosis and Evaluation* (New York: Macmillan, 1972).

12. Bruder and Hayden noticed a similar phenomenon. They assigned a group of students exercises in writing formal and informal dialogues. One student's informal dialogue contained the following:

What going on?
It been a long time . . .
I about through . . .
I be glad . . .

When the student read the dialogue aloud, however, these were spoken as

What's going on?
It's been a long time . . .
I'm about through . . .
I'll be glad . . .

See Mary Newton Bruder and Luddy Hayden, "Teaching Composition: A Report on a Bidialectal Approach," *Language Learning*, 23 (June, 1973), 1–15.

13. See Patricia Laurence, "Error's Endless Train: Why Students Don't Perceive Errors,"*Journal of Basic Writing*, 1 (Spring, 1975), 23–43, for a different explanation of this phenomenon.

14. See, for example, J. R. Frederiksen, "Component Skills in Reading" in R. R. Snow, P. A. Federico, and W. E. Montague, eds., *Aptitude, Learning, and Instruction* (Hillsdale, N.J.: Erlbaum, 1979); D. E. Rumelhart, "Toward an Interactive Model of Reading," in S. Dornic, ed., *Attention and Performance VI* (Hillsdale, N.J.: Erlbaum, 1977); and Joseph H. Denks and Gregory O. Hill, "Interactive Models of Lexical Assessment during Oral Reading," paper presented at Conference on Interactive Processes in Reading, Learning Research and Development Center, University of Pittsburgh, September 1979.

Patrick Hartwell argued that "apparent dialect interference in writing reveals partial or imperfect mastery of a neural coding system that underlies both reading and writing" in a paper, " 'Dialect Interference' in Writing: A Critical View," presented at CCCC, April 1979. This paper is available through ERIC. He predicts, in this paper, that "basic writing students, when asked to read their writing in a formal situation, . . . will make fewer errors in their reading than in their writing." I read Professor Hartwell's paper after this essay was completed, so I was unable to acknowledge his study as completely as I would have desired.

15. This example is taken from Shaughnessy, *Errors and Expectations*, p. 52.

16. Corder refers to "reconstructed sentences" in "Idiosyncratic Dialects and Error Analysis."

17. Shaughnessy, *Errors and Expectations*, pp. 51–72.

18. For a discussion of the role of the "print code" in writer's errors, see Patrick Hartwell, " 'Dialect Interference' in Writing: A Critical View."

19. See Kenneth S. Goodman, "Miscues: Windows on the Reading Process," in Kenneth S. Goodman, ed., *Miscue Analysis: Applications to Reading Instruction* (Urbana, Illinois: ERIC, 1977), pp. 3–14.

20. This example was taken from Yetta M. Goodman, "Miscue Analysis for In-Service Reading Teachers," in K. S. Goodman, ed., *Miscue Analysis*, p. 55.

21. Nathalie Bailey, Carolyn Madden, and Stephen D. Krashen, "Is There a 'Natural Sequence' in Adult Second Language Learning?" *Language Learning*, 24 (June, 1974), 235–43.

22. This paper was originally presented at CCCC, April 1979. The research for this study was funded by a research grant from the National Council of Teachers of English.

Released into Language:
Errors, Expectations, and the
Legacy of Mina Shaughnessy

At the bedrock level of my thinking about this is the sense that language is power, and that, as Simone Weil says, those who suffer from injustice most are the least able to articulate their suffering; and that the silent majority, if released into language, would not be content with a perpetuation of the conditions which have betrayed them. But this notion hangs on a special conception of what it means to be released into language: not simply learning the jargon of an elite, fitting unexceptionably into the status quo, but learning that language can be used as a means of changing reality.

— ADRIENNE RICH, "TEACHING LANGUAGE IN
OPEN ADMISSIONS (1972)" IN *ON LIES,
SECRETS AND SILENCE*

I

When Adrienne Rich reprinted her essay "Teaching Language in Open Admissions" in 1979,[1] she added in a headnote that the "profound" experiment of open admissions was, perhaps, "naively optimistic," citing a history of broken promises, disappointments, and betrayals. Basic writing teachers found themselves overworked, underpaid, and often excluded from the protection of tenure-track positions. Working-class and minority students were left to compete for resources which, she said, should have been open to all. And, in a final image, Rich added that "on the corner of Broadway near where I live, I see young people whose like I knew ten years ago as college students 'hanging out,' brown-bagging, standing in short skirts and high-heeled boots in doorways waiting for a trick, or being dragged into the car of a plumed and sequined pimp."

From *The Territory of Language,* ed. Donald McQuade (Carbondale: Southern Illinois UP 1986) 65–88.

I imagine that all of us who began teaching, or who began teaching seriously, in the late '60s and early '70s have stories to document our various disappointments, including our disappointing realization that the best teachers we knew could not or did not transform American society, the university system, or the cities we lived in. As Mina Shaughnessy convincingly and eloquently argued, however, it is teachers' expectations that justify a curriculum and enable students to imagine the radical transformation that can make learning more than a gesture of obedience to those in power or an accommodation to the status quo.

In reprinting her essay, Rich acknowledged her debt to Mina Shaughnessy, from whom, she says, "I learned — in a time and place where pedagogic romanticism and histrionics were not uncommon — a great deal about the ethics and integrity of teaching." Shaugnessy remains a figure who can teach us much about the ethics and integrity of teaching. Her work was cautious and meticulous. It made no promises about a new society, but showed us, I think, how to pay careful, sympathetic attention to the experience of students who were being released into language and, in particular, into a language that belonged to others, not to them — that belonged to us and to our universities, to our projects and agendas and our peculiar notions of power and freedom. The question remains whether entering that language, entering the privileged discourse of an academic community, can be more than either learning the jargon of an elite or fitting unexceptionably into the status .

Shaughnessy taught us to understand the problems and achievements of basic writers at a time when both were hidden to the profession, and in doing so she made possible a new kind of college English class — a class for academically unprepared students that could provide both access to college reading and writing tasks and an orientation to the goals and values of academic life. This was her charge to the profession — to teach not only skills but also an understanding of context and purpose, so that the act of writing could enable students, as she said, to begin their lives anew. I would like to review her contribution to the teaching of English and return, at the end of my essay, to the way she speaks to us still in the current debates over the literacy crisis.[2]

II

I have a vivid memory of attending the 1975 MLA Convention in San Francisco and hearing Mina Shaughnessy give a talk at the plenary session of the newly formed Division on Writing. It was a time when I was struggling to come to terms with the new direction in my professional life imposed by my first full-time appointment as a basic writing teacher and an administrator in charge of a basic writing curriculum. I had committed my career to the students she called Basic Writers and to the task of easing their precarious entry into the world of the university. At the same time, however, I was painfully aware that my ability to understand or alter their actual performance as writers was severely limited. It was a time of crisis, a crisis I found I shared with most everyone I met who was doing this kind of teaching and taking it seriously.

The crisis had partly to do with the enormity of the task presented to us, having to make writers out of young adults who, many of them, had done almost no writing at all. But the crisis was due as well to the fact that we were so profoundly unprepared and that the existing models of instruction, what there were, so often ran against both our common sense and our sense of justice.

Professor Shaughnessy's talk, entitled "Diving In: An Introduction to Basic Writing,"[3] outlined a kind of pilgrim's progress, where the pilgrim was the basic writing teacher struggling to evolve a pedagogy consistent with the needs of students and the requirements of conscience. Shaughnessy saw teachers' development in a series of stages, each stage punctuated by a crisis when the existing metaphors — metaphors for teaching and for writing — became inadequate and had to be replaced by new ones. Her talk was given a resounding reception, and the reason for this reception, I think, was that she had given labels and order to the discouraging confusion of our professional lives, and she had done so in a way that made us believe that growth was possible (and occurring). Through her own tremendous warmth and dignity, she gave the work we were doing a dignity, humanity, and complexity that made it seem the proper focus of a professional life.

In the talk, after describing the stages in which the teachers are preoccupied with their students' perceived incompetence (these stages are called, drawing upon familiar metaphors, "Guarding the Tower" and "Converting the Natives"), Shaughnessy went on to describe a point where, faced with the continual evidence that the existing notions of who these students are and how they must be taught are inadequate, teachers reconceive the problem. Rather than ask, "How is it that these students cannot learn simple lessons?" they learn to recognize the way in which these lessons are not simple at all, that, in fact, they only appear simple to those who have already learned them. And, as Shaughnessy observes.

> This insight leads our teacher to the third stage of his development, which I will name SOUNDING THE DEPTHS, for he turns now to the careful observation not only of his students and their writing, but of himself as a writer and teacher, seeking a deeper understanding of the behavior called writing and of the special difficulties his students have in mastering that skill. ("Diving In," 236)

This stage in the growth of a teacher can lead to the fourth stage, "Diving In," the point at which a teacher turns to other disciplines, such as linguistics and developmental psychology, in order to gather new data and new research methods to develop the kind of systematic inquiry that can transform the study of basic writing into a discipline.

For many teachers, the starting point for such a study is Shaugnessy's book, *Errors and Expectations.*[4] The book provides, literally, the record of her reading of four thousand student essays written by incoming freshmen at City College of the City University of New York between 1970 and 1974. The purpose of the study was to "be precise about the types of difficulties to be found in basic writing (BW) papers at the outset and, beyond that, to demonstrate how the sources of those difficulties can be explained without recourse to such pedagogically empty terms as 'handicapped' or 'disadvantaged.' " The book contains many examples of student writing, each included to "deepen one's sense of pattern and thereby [develop] the ability to make swift assessments and classifications of writing difficulties." Her study provides both a lesson in how to read this peculiar genre of student prose and a model of what it means to know one's students and, through such knowledge, become a teacher.

Shaughnessy's work, then, is an exercise in classification and interpretation, and the method is basically inductive. Rather than beginning with a set of rules — rules meant to describe "correct" writing — and letting those rules generate a pedagogy for the unruly, she begins at a more appropriate beginning, with the writing of basic writers, in order to discover categories of error, characteristic patterns of variance from the standard written idiom. Through a close reading of this staggering number of essays, she catalogues and describes errors of the following broad types (and these labels provide the chapter headings): Punctuation and Handwriting, Syntax, Common (errors of tense, inflection and agreement), Spelling, Vocabulary, and errors in performance Beyond the Sentence. By studying errors in the context of students' actual performance, Shaughnessy allows us to see basic writers as writers rather than as a group lacking skills that are somehow acquired prior to writing. This perspective acknowledges the place of error in all writing (including our own), and it provides a way of seeing error in the context of attempts at communication and understanding, where writing is an attempt to approximate a discourse and not just another way of taking a test.

Shaughnessy's study insists, then, that teachers and students see error relative to an actual writing situation, where some errors are serious and some not so serious depending on a student's project and a reader's responses. Shaughnessy goes one step further, however. The significance of various errors, she argues, must also be perceived in the context of an instructional sequence and in the context of research on language development. (I'll talk more about this research later.) If we ask students to take on a way of "talking" that is not immediately their own (and we do this when we ask any student to write), we are inviting them to make mistakes, to become confused and awkward, to err in reaching beyond their immediate skill. Some error, in other words, can be seen as a sign of growth, as a sign of students' implicit faith in writing and their willingness to take risks and experiment with a language that is not "naturally" or immediately their own. If errors — errors of syntax, errors in word choice, errors of judgment — can be seen as evidence of students' attempts to approximate the language of a more privileged group (of those who speak and write freely at the university, for example), then it may not be at all appropriate to point to an error and say, "Don't do that." To say that is to say "Don't do more than you can do," a directive that will most likely be taken for exactly what it represents by students who are excluded from the mainstream of university life. "Don't make mistakes," "Don't use jargon," "Be simple and direct" — all of these phrases quickly translate into "Don't try to be what you are not" or, more succinctly, "Go away."

The value of Shaughnessy's work extends in several directions. The method of analysis and system of classification provide the basic grammar and vocabulary for all further studies of error in writing.[5] And an understanding of the method of analysis, more than the specific exercises, enables teachers to carry the genius of the book to their own classrooms. As teachers and students learn to perceive patterns in the apparent confusion of student writing, that writing comes to represent something other than confusion. Such a process puts students in a position to objectify the strategies, rules, and ad hoc heuristics buried in their use of the language of written discourse (a language which they too easily assume uses them). Rather than sitting down to a workbook to learn the English sentence, students can begin with the study of their own sentences. And such a pedagogy frees the teacher from the faulty logic that connects a sign with a cause, the logic that has allowed teachers to conclude that a student misspells because he can't spell or writes a sentence fragment because he can't write a sentence. In place of this Shaughnessy offers both a theory of error that allows us to see error as other than random and a method for analyzing error as part of the process of articulation — where an error can be seen in relation to a student's attempt to cope simultaneously with the demands of a language, a rhetoric, and a task.

Because of this theory of error, the book can be seen as a central document in the general scholarly attempt to develop a philosophy of composition, one that can inform composition teaching and research at the broadest levels. If error can be seen, as Shaughnessy demonstrates, as something other than an accident of composing or a failure to learn — if, that is, we can discover regular, predictable patterns of error in student writing — then it will be those patterns rather than the correct features that will provide the key to learning about the development of writing ability, since those errors provide insight into the most profound contact between the learner and that which is being learned.

There are, of course, errors that are accidents, slips of the pen, but there are many errors that are not, and some of these errors are the logical products of idiosyncratic rule systems. If language learning is a process of forming and testing hypotheses about language in order to bring idiosyncratic systems into alignment with conventional ones, then the regular but unconventional features in student writing will reveal the rules and hypotheses that govern students' idiosyncratic or approximate versions of the standard idiom.

A basic writing class is the place where this conflict between idiosyncracy and convention is acted out most dramatically. A student doesn't know how to spell a word, but he invents a spelling and he invents it not out of nothing but out of his understanding of the rules that govern the way words are spelled in English. A student uses commas and periods in a manner that seems to have little to do with the structure of the sentence, but, perhaps, she is applying her version of some advice she once heard about long pauses and short pauses or about marking off "complete thoughts." The syntax of a sentence in a student paper becomes "derailed" (to use Shaughnessy's metaphor) when a student presses forward, following the various (but perhaps competing) available sentence patterns for an imagined utterance. A verb is incorrectly inflected but this can be seen to be the result of interference of spoken with written language. In each of these cases one can see a student acting systematically from within a system that challenges or misapproximates the standard system governing conventional, written English. When a student enters into the language of others, when that language is not a language of the student's own invention, he or she approximates — but only approximates — the sentence that is sanctioned or expected by the closed world the student seeks to enter.

This method of analysis can be extended, however. The moment teachers move their attention beyond the sentence, where errors are errors in taste, judgment, or understanding, this procedure for interpreting student error becomes more challenging and, in a way, more revealing. When a student fails to complete an argument or to develop a discussion or to put two sentences together, and when a student fails to do this as basic writers often fail to do it, then the hidden rules and conventions of academic discourse become suddenly visible. The errors represent the fault lines when two systems — an idiosyncratic system and a conventional system — press against each other. Shaughnessy's work suggests this as an area of research, but error beyond the sentence, particularly in the work of the basic writer, has received little direct scholarly attention.

It is here, I think, at the intersection of idiosyncracy and convention, where the skilled and unskilled adult writer have the same writing problem, where the sign of failure for one is the sign of achievement for the other. Both stand (if not for the same reason) outside the predictable range of set, prepackaged discourse. It's the average writer — the "C" student who appears with telling regularity in every class, year after year — who writes the predictable five-paragraph theme in support of a commonplace ("Sports are valuable because they teach us sportsmanship."). Both the skilled and unskilled writer are characterized by the fact that their writing locates them outside of, in opposition to, that conventional discourse with its preset contours, phrases, examples, and outcomes.

Contemporary literary criticism celebrates an image of the writer as one who no longer resides comfortably within a field of conventional learning and conventional discourse, who must, in fact, push against the force and dominance of conventional systems in order to preserve an identity (or the fiction of an identity) as an "I," a speaking subject. Here, for example, is Edward Said's account of the position of the contemporary critic. It could, in its outlines, stand as a representation of the situation and the dilemma of the basic writer:

> The problem we face today when we study Joyce, or when, untrained in classics or religion, we read Hooker, or when we deploy psychology in the study of a literary text, is a problem of irregularity, of discontinuity. That is, less background, less formal training, less prescribed and systematic information, is assumed before one begins to read, write, or work. Thus when one begins to write today one is necessarily more of an autodidact, gathering or making up the knowledge one needs in the course of creating.

Deprived of a set, "knowable" cultural tradition, and working within an ethos that is set against the commonplace, Said's modern writer is a "wanderer, going from place to place for his material, but remaining a man essentially *between* homes."[6] For an expert writer, this is a willed condition, something one achieves by writing, and not a function of one's high school education or socioeconomic status. Said's metaphor, however, also describes the basic writer, wandering between the old neighborhood and the university, belonging to neither, and left to invent academic expertise every time he sits down to write. To the degree to which the basic writer is aware of this dilemma, of the problem of convention and one's relation to convention (and I believe this is one of the first lessons a basic writer learns), he has a more mature, more complex understanding of writing than does the average student, the student who is comfortable with the five-paragraph theme. The basic writer, and I'm speaking now from my own experience in the classroom, is closer to that orientation toward language we call "critical thinking" than the mainstream freshman who decided early on that correct, orderly prose was good enough, and that the conventional five-paragraph theme was an adequate representation of a person's experience and intellect.

The image of the writer as one who stands outside a closed discourse (wandering between homes) underlies the current literature on Writing across the Curriculum, where a student on the outside works to write his way inside an academic discipline, like anthropology, by learning to write as an anthropologist, by learning to approximate the discourse that constitutes that discipline and represents its specialized, privileged way of seeing and reporting on the world.[7] The experience of the basic writer, as Shaughnessy demonstrated, allows us to resee our own experience, showing us the hidden rules, agendas, and projects that underlie a way of talking and writing that we take for granted. The study of error beyond the sentence, particularly those errors produced by students most dramatically excluded from the privileged world of academic discourse, even the generalized discourse of the freshman English class, can reveal rules that govern our "normal" ways of establishing authority, marshalling evidence, extending a discussion, and completing an argument. When we come to better understand what is involved as a student moves into a discourse, we can be better teachers of writing. We can teach more, that is, than the "jargon of an elite."

This, I think, is an honorable goal. It is a way of allowing students to enter into and participate in our academic projects, to learn them from the inside, as writers, rather than from the outside, through textbooks and tests and papers that ask students to repeat names and dates and canonical interpretations. It is honorable, I think, even if we teach students to see the world as we see it or to read primary texts as we read them, even if we do not teach students to use language to "change reality" and undo or deconstruct the systems we, as professionals, labor to preserve and extend.

III

The theory of error in *Errors and Expectations* is represented not so much by abstract discussion as by the way Shaughnessy selects and analyzes her examples from student essays. While much of the energy in the book is spent looking at student writing in order to classify types of errors, Shaughnessy offers more than just a list, since an equal amount of time is spent inferring the emotional, linguistic, rhetorical, and intellectual context within which a particular student was writing. These inferences provide the foundation for conclusions about the causes of the errors themselves. Let me try to piece together just a short example of this process of interpretation.

Shaughnessy's discussion of syntax is based upon the assumption that a reader can move inside the head of a basic writer and reconstruct both the conditions that led to the "derailment" of syntax and the meaning that was scrambled by the lack of syntactic options available to the writer while in the throes of composing. What we're offered is a narrative that fills in what would be a pause in a transcript of a writer composing orally:

> In the following sentence . . . the writer has modified the noun *job* by simple expedient of placing his adjectival elements after the noun, a "logical" strategy but not unfortunately a conventional one unless he makes use of certain forms that attach such elements to the sentence:
>
> > Now mostly every job you go to get *worthwhile* or *making a decent salary something to live off* is asking for a college degree.
>
> A similar problem arises in this sentence, where the writer's thought calls for some kind of appositional structure that will further define "intellectual period." For want of such a structure, he relies on juxtaposition alone:
>
> > I think the author tried to show, that due to the intellectual period in which we live *the need to categorize things in every respect of life* we tend to lose the natural beauty of what is happening around us. *(Errors and Expectations*, p. 66)

In the section on punctuation, and in particular after some examples of writing where commas and periods have been omitted, transposed, or interchanged, Shaughnessy draws the following conclusions:

> What one senses through such punctuation is a caution about losing control of the sentence by allowing it to become too long — too full, that is, of embedded structures, which to the unpracticed writer may well echo their deeper origins as sentences. Yet combined with this effort to simplify individual sentences grammatically by breaking them up into smaller segments is another effort to link sentences rhetorically by pressing commas into service as conjunctions, by overusing words like *and, but, that* or *because*, or by ignoring terminal punctuation altogether. *(Errors and Expectations*, p. 28)

What is remarkable here, aside from the sophistication of the analysis, is the tremendous sympathy that enables her to enter into the minds of student writers, and writers whose writing and thinking are so unlike her own.

With some notable exceptions, much of the research done on composition before the publication of *Errors and Expectations* was represented by frequency counts and computer tabulations of objective features of prose (as, for example, in the studies of syntax). It was not uncommon, in fact, to hear statistical research being praised at the expense of the anecdotal accounts that had characterized another tradition of scholarship in composition. Much of that criticism, and much of the heavy praise for "objective" research, came from people who didn't teach writing and who lacked the day-by-day contact with writers and their problems that makes the impressions and speculations of writing teachers, at least the best of them, like Shaughnessy, so valuable. Shaughnessy, like Ann Berthoff, has demonstrated how teaching and research can together be part of a professional life.[8]

Shaughnessy also helped to return a sensitivity to context to composition research. Her analysis of the work of basic writers is grounded in her reading of a writer's situation, a situation richly imagined, acknowledging the social and psychological context for an act of writing. She brings impression, speculation, and interpretation together with theory and systematic analysis to give us a more complete picture of a writer at work than any we previously had. In *Errors and Expectations,* she reconstructs the way writers work, the way they think and feel, and this provides crucial information about the composing process. Much of the most valuable research of the last few years, drawing on case study analysis and protocol analysis, has extended this view of the composing process of basic writers.[9]

IV

One could imagine Shaughnessy's study ending with the categories of errors she finds, but such a taxonomy, as she says, would misrepresent the complexity of the problems and possible responses. Any list of "Basic Writer's Errors" would only become another version of the "25 Common Errors Writers Must Avoid." The value of the taxonomy in the book is the method it defines, where one looks long and closely at a student's writing to determine what patterns emerge. Through the perception of such patterns, one can discover that errors are not random, but products of systematic decision-making — that is, evidence that there is a grammar to students' ungrammaticality — and one can begin to speculate on the causes of the specific errors, rather than begin with the buckshot approach of teaching to all possible error. What makes this book so valuable, then, is the model of interpretation it provides. As Shaughnessy says (speaking, again, of punctuation errors):

> It becomes important, then, to do more than list, prescriptively, the ways in which the student breaks with the conventional code of punctuation. Rather, the teacher must try to decipher the individual student's code, examining samples of his writing as a scientist might, searching for patterns or explanations, listening to what the student says about punctuation, and creating situations in the classroom that encourage students to talk openly about what they don't understand. (*Errors and Expectations,* p. 40)

It is important to add that the power derived from this kind of inquiry is not limited to the teacher alone: when students learn to see their writing in this way, to shift their perspective and view their writing as a reader, to see the decisions made and the options lost, they learn the key to controlling and experimenting with their language.

To say, then, that we must enable students to achieve a distance from what they do is not the same as saying that we must teach them skills they don't possess or that we must teach them something they are incapable of doing, although these are the prejudices that continue to characterize most basic writing courses. In the face of a seeming chaos of error, teachers often make the wholesale judgment that such writing is evidence that students "can't write a sentence" or "don't know how to think" and proceed to begin at what is taken as the beginning by teaching the sentence, or the grammar of the sentence, and thought or paragraph patterns. Writing and thinking are conceived, then, in terms of constituent skills, skills which could be defined, outlined on the board, and taught one by one.

Such a pedagogy meets the immediate needs of teachers frustrated by their failure to understand what could be happening in the heads of students whose writing is so radically different from their own. And it is the convenience of this pedagogy, which frees all parties, teachers and students, from ever having to talk about writing, that leads teachers to hang on to it in the face of evidence that it produces limited returns — in the face, too, of evidence not only that these students can, of course, think, but also that in their conversations and in their essays they can produce many coherent and controlled utterances. The skills curriculum is founded neither on any investigation of the language students produce nor on any systematic investigation into how writing skills are acquired.

Such negative judgments about these writers are not based on a notion of fluency but of competence, and talk about competence puts everyone on shaky ground. A teacher I once worked with came to me with a student paper that began with the following: "A decision that I had to make that didn't came easy. The time was when I had to diside if I what to play basketball in my last year of junior high school (eight grade)." This instructor said in despair that not only did this student not know how to spell or how to write a sentence, but he didn't even know the difference between "what" and "want." The words on the paper were allowed to stand for the student, and the only meaning to be found there was derived from the single perception that the language went counter to the reader's expectations. As a consequence, the teacher concluded that the student must have suffered from some species of conceptual deficit, not even knowing the difference between "what" and "want." But this is simply not adequate to explain why, for instance, although "diside" is misspelled, "decision" is not, or why the paper contained more correctly than incorrectly formed sentences. With a closer look, it is not difficult to see the syntax behind the passage above. The student began by stating his subject, "a decision that I had to make that didn't came easy," but either got lost or felt it would be appropriate to stop after the long restrictive clause and restated the subject, "the time was," and began again to complete the sentence. And, finally, assumptions about this student's incompetence don't account for the fact that, when asked to read the passage aloud, the student automatically corrected "if I what to play" and "eight grade."

This teacher was unable to read a paper like his student's, to pay the kind of attention to the text that would allow him to see the deviations from the conventions of the standard dialect, and to determine their meaning through the context of perceived intention. This failure is a peculiar one given the fact that this reader spent most of his adult life perfecting his skills as a reader of texts and could, if confronted with an e. e. cummings poem, for instance, account for the ways it deviates from conventional expectations in elaborate and sympathetic ways. He would see as much meaning, in fact, in the deviations themselves as he would in the ostensible, paraphraseable message presented in the words. Our literary training prepares us to see literature as a record of struggles with words and meaning, but to shift this habit of attention from supposedly "elevated" modes of expression to the verbal wrestlings of our students does not come easily: the nature of and the reasons for the violation of literary conventions are so much more evident to us than the nature of and the reasons for the violations of the conventions of what is taken to be a standard idiom. In our students' writing the variation is not seen as an expression of deliberate or learned behavior, but only as evidence of the absence of learning or the lack of deliberation. The individual errors are allowed to stand for Error, the proof that the poor kids can't write.

One basic principle emerges from the study of error in *Errors and Expectations*. To an inexperienced teacher, the writing of basic writers may appear to contain nothing but a chaos of error, but a close, careful analysis will reveal very little that is random or "illogical" in what they have written. The errors are not evidence that basic writers are slow or incapable of learning but, as Shaughnessy argues, that these writers are beginners and must, like all beginners, learn by making mistakes. And, in fact, the keys to their development as writers "often lie in the very features in their writing that English teachers have been trained to brush aside with a marginal code letter or a scribbled injunction to 'Proofread!' "

Shaughnessy's idea that errors may hold the "key" to basic writers' development as writers is important and needs further discussion. One aspect of this truth should be obvious by now. If we make a careful inventory of the nature and cause of the errors unique to a particular writer, our instruction can be not only efficient but more humane. Rather than conclude that a student can't write a sentence, we can conclude that he often comes unglued with embeddings signalled by "wh" words. Or rather than conclude that a student can't spell, we may find that she confuses homonyms (like "their" and "there") or has trouble because he neither speaks nor hears certain final consonants. Each case would call for a specific pedagogy. And, of course, it is comforting to both teacher and student alike to discover that in a paper containing perhaps thirteen errors, the errors fall into three basic patterns. This kind of close and systematic analysis of error provides, then, both a pedagogical and diagnostic tool.

Shaughnessy also argues that error is a key to understanding language development. This can best be explained by referring to two concepts drawn from the study of error in second language learning.[10] The first says that where a student is working with a new language and is not yet fluent, any statement deliberately intended to communicate will be meaningful. It will be systematic, rule-defined, and coherent. It will, that is, possess a grammar. And, secondly, the rules of that grammar will be derived from:

1. the rules of the first language (which, in this case, would be the mother tongue or spoken dialect — the analogy between learning to write and learning a second language is complicated by the fact that writing calls upon skills — like punctuating — that are in addition to oral skills and not learned the same way or defined by the same rules),

2. the rules of the target language (which here would be the dialect of formal, written discourse),

3. some truly idiosyncratic dialect that belongs only to this writer at this point in his development.[11]

The best evidence, then, that a speaker possesses the construction rules necessary to acquire language is the occurrence of systematic errors, or rule-governed behavior.

In the case of a writer learning to use the formal, written dialect, what we see during the learning process is either the transfer of one "language" to a situation where it is inappropriate or the creation of an "interlanguage," an "approximate system" which is evidence of the writer's transitional competence.[12] As the writer tries to approximate the vocabulary and movement of academic prose, her approximations are often only partially conceived and, at some points, she reverts to the spoken idiom, relying on its rules and strategies. Or, in the case of an approximate system, an interlangage, she relies on her knowledge that language can be made predictable and either overgeneralizes or creates a hypothesis that is "false." The interlanguage is not necessarily appropriate to an audience expecting either the first or second language, but it is coherent in itself and certainly not a sign of random behavior. In fact, it could be said to represent a particular stage of learning.

The concept of an approximate system is important for the way it modifies the notion of a spoken dialect interfering with the written dialect. The concept of interference makes the learner passive, caught between social or class roles, one of which must be overcome. Seeing those errors which reveal an interlanguage or approximate system allows us to see the ways in which basic writers are actively generating rules and strategies, and it allows us to chart and draw upon their particular learning styles.

Such an analysis allows us to distinguish three "types" of error, types that correspond to the categories in each area of Shaughnessy's study. First there are errors that are truly accidental. These may be slips of the pen, the kind that are common to all writers, where we leave out a word, or write "an" for "and," or write a word we never had in mind at all or jumble syntax as our hand rushes to keep up with our brain. Teaching to this kind of error requires that we teach students to see it in proofreading, often a surprisingly difficult task for writers unused to seeing writing as black marks on a page. Secondly, there are also errors caused when one dialect interferes with another, and this is not only a matter of idiom but also, given the unique contours of the formal written dialect and the difficulties of producing words on a page rather than sounds into the air, a whole range of other errors as well, from errors of syntax to errors caused by habits of pronunciation, as when "given" is substituted for "giving" because the two sound the same in speech. The third kind of error comes from the application of rules that belong only to the writer's approximate system, where the writer uses his own powers of analogical thinking to make an unfamiliar and irregular language predictable. There is evidence of this, for example, when a student adds inflectional endings to infinitives, as in this sentence: "There was plenty the boy had *to learned* about birds."

The conclusion that Shaughnessy draws from this third type of error is that "The student who learned to make these errors reveals through them all the linguistic sophistication he needs to correct them." The issue, then, is not a student's capacity to master formal English but "the priority this kind of problem ought to have in the larger scheme of learning to write," the formulation of a pedagogy that will enable us to assist the natural learning process, and the willingness of the student to spend the time it takes to learn. A theory of error does not carry with it any magic solutions. For both student and teacher this kind of learning means hard work with few immediate rewards. A theory of error will, however, suggest a place to begin.

The theory of error that runs through *Errors and Expectations* suggests its own pedagogy, one that is radically different from most existing strategies. The pedagogy that breaks writing up into constituent skills, as "skills" are defined by the traditional study of sentences and paragraphs, makes no sense if the source of error is the conflict caused by the interference of two existing grammars or the result of incomplete or inappropriate generalizations about language. Such courses, which rely heavily on workbook drill, deny both the student's individual competence and her own sequence for learning. And the "skills" assumed to be basic or constituent have little to do with the way writing proceeds or language is learned. The pedagogy suggested by contrastive analysis, where a teacher uses grammatical analysis to describe the points of variance between the first language and the target language in order to predict problem areas, can be criticized from the evidence that the existing interlanguage is, in fact, idiosyncratic, unique in many respects to each writer and unique to a specific stage in that writer's development. It also seems as though errors due to an idiosyncratic rule system are much more frequent than errors linked to language transfer.[13]

What we are left to conclude is that one important skill basic writers need to learn is how to read their own papers, the same skill needed by their teachers. Students need to learn how to distance themselves from and analyze the writing on the page in order to determine what information that writing holds about their performance as a writer. This is probably the most difficult skill a teacher has to teach, since a student's failure to "see" errors or to "see" the marks on the page or to "see" the information carried in his sentence — and to see what possibilities each of these reveals — is not usually due to laziness or a failure to read "carefully" but to the very real perceptual and conceptual difficulty of objectifying language and one's performance as a writer.[14] When asked to read their own writing aloud, students typically hear a voice but don't see black and white marks on the page and, in many cases, automatically read the correct form. They read in terms of their own grammatical competence.

Much of the research on error that immediately followed *Errors and Expectations* searched for the cause of error (see, for example, the essays by Ken Bruffee and Donald Freeman [cited in note 5]). The belief was that the more we knew about the causes of error, the better we could tailor instruction to head off those errors in the first place. This direction for error analysis has been complemented by recent research, much of it at the University of Pittsburgh, directed at the procedures students use to correct errors. Rather than asking what the source of an error might be, this research turns to protocols of students trying to correct errors they've identified in their own writing to see what they do next. If students have incorrectly marked sentence boundaries, this research is interested in both where, on a second pass, students put commas and periods and how they describe what they are doing when they change the punctuation in a paragraph or an essay. Students can adjust the rules they use to mark sentences, and their next approximation, which will be driven by a revision of the rule that produced the error in the first place, will give us access to the range and variation of their understanding of (in this case) the rules governing the identification of sentence boundaries. In addition students' own reports on the changes they make allow us insight into what might be called the "editing process." Glynda Hull has shown, for example, that students will follow one of three correction strategies: comprehending, intuiting, and consulting. In order to see and correct some errors students must perceive that something is wrong with the meaning of a text. Correction, here, begins with an act of comprehension. This is often the case with syntax errors. To see and correct other errors, students must consult an existing verbal representation of a rule ("Let's see, you use commas when . . ."). Or, as is often the case, students turn to their sense that something is wrong, even if the "wrongness" cannot be described, and intuit that a certain change is appropriate. While this taxonomy can be used to catalog types of errors, it has immediate pedagogical value since it provides insight into the procedures novice and expert writers use to solve the types of linguistic problems that are part of the act of editing. Students need to learn to read their own writing, then, but they also need to learn to edit.[15]

There is, of course, another problem in learning to edit, perhaps one almost as difficult, and that is motivation. How does one convince a student that it's worth the time and effort to see that a piece of writing is correct? The only answer, I suspect, is to enable students to see that correctness is in service of something other than producing a correct paper, something the student can believe in. Since it is no longer enough to appeal to correctness as a sign of godliness or gentility, this is a perplexing problem. Shaughnessy suggests that we appeal to the needs of a reader and what happens to that reader when the static of error gets in the way of the information on the page.

These are the problems teachers should be devoting themselves to, and the pedagogies that emerge must offer strategies for editing, since insisting on correctness at the moment of articulation enforces a rigor we seldom demand of ourselves. We rely on our freedom to go back and hold our writing at arm's length. And, while students need to learn how and when to worry about correctness, they also need to learn how and when to tap into the generative power of language, which requires that the editor be shut off and we be free to experiment and take risks.

If a student can learn to read his own writing as an editor, then it would appear that the most useful strategy would be something like the following. Those errors, particularly accidental errors, that are slips of the pen or result from distractions caused by the demands of making letters on a page, will disappear as a writer becomes more coordinated and more fluent. The same is true of many interference errors, since practice with the formal dialect will make this peculiar vocabulary, idiom, and syntax more readily available, and less likely to be blurred or confused. If these errors will disappear in reasonable time anyway, and research should give us fairly reliable information on what they are, then it makes no sense to waste time teaching to them. Not only is such teaching inefficient, but it is also likely to produce the kind of nervousness about making mistakes that will keep a student from experimenting with a new language in the first place.

Beyond this "level" of error would be the errors that students, with encouragement and guidance, have the resources to correct on their own as they become more proficient as readers. In a conference, a teacher can enable a student to "see" errors he has missed in his own editing. This is often best achieved by reading the paper aloud, or having the student read the paper aloud, stopping to correct mistakes and to explain what he is doing and why. When dealing with whole classes of students, teachers can assign students the task of regularly circling their own and each other's errors, and teachers can highlight an area of text, drawing a line next to three lines of prose on a student's paper and telling her that somewhere in there, there is an error. And, after students have found errors in their own writing, it should be up to them to find patterns among those errors, to give them names and find their own resources for correction. This exercise begins slowly and needs prodding, but it can become the most effective strategy in a teacher's repertoire, since it draws upon the student's own language competence. It encourages students to practice authority over their writing and responsibility for it.

Where error is the result of some idiosyncratic set of rules, this kind of self-consciousness about one's language is most important. We need to develop methods of bookkeeping to distinguish between those patterns of error that mark a stage of learning and those that indicate that learning has stopped, where the learner is no longer testing rules but relying on set patterns. Where, then, a learner has overgeneralized a rule, drill is not an appropriate strategy at all, since, if learning is going to take place, the writer must turn his attention from the perception of rules to the activity of testing rules and seeing their limits.[16]

What would remain untouched after all this is a core of error that the student cannot find or does not have the resources to correct, and this would require some formal instruction. The difficulty here is finding a way to talk about the writing, since such talk will inevitably revert to grammatical terms and concepts. Shaughnessy isolates four key grammatical concepts teachers and students will need to share for such conversations to be possible: the concept of the sentence, of inflection, of tense, and of agreement. With each key concept, Shaughnessy offers examples of how each might best be taught. The great responsibility that faces the teacher and the profession, however, is developing the ability to determine the occasion when a student's problems require this kind of instruction. Diagnosis may be more an art than a science. The problem is partly knowing *how* to make such a diagnosis, but it is also a problem of knowing when. When in the course of working with a student can we determine with authority that such instruction is necessary? And when, given the internal sequence of the student's language development, will such instruction complement rather than hinder the learning process?

Finally, it is interesting to note that in locating the resources needed to draw the sorts of inferences she does about the composing process of her students, Shaughnessy does not refer to the formal study of linguistics or rhetoric but to the information she gets, both directly and indirectly, from her students and her colleagues when they talk about specific papers or problems. And she refers to her own experience "as someone who writes and therefore understands the pressures and peculiarities of that behavior." Shaughnessy is clearly also drawing upon a thorough understanding of developments in linguistics, rhetoric, second language learning, and the range of disciplines brought together in the formal study of the composing process. For the classroom teacher without a familiarity with these disciplines, however, the point is that a key resource is our shared experience as writers. This is where a basic writing teacher's education can begin.

We are bound together by the difficulties and triumphs of expression. This is important for us to know, since it is a corrective to the notion that our students' behavior is alien or incomprehensible, and it is important for our students to know, since it can free them from the damaging belief that through some perverse fate they have been deprived of a gift granted to others. In fact, because writing is such a lonely activity, and writers are bound by the assumptions they carry with them to their desks, it is crucial for students to hear about our struggles with writing and the strategies we've evolved to overcome them. They tend to enter into writing with the belief that good writers sit down, start with an introduction and write through to a conclusion without making any mistakes along the way. Such a vision makes it rather easy to believe one can't write, and it is likely to leave the writer stuck, making his first sentence also his last.

V

Shaughnessy has convincingly demonstrated that "There are 'styles' to being wrong," and that learning to read closely to see the style of error is a crucial skill for a teacher of composition. This is one of the reasons, as I have suggested, that perhaps the best preparation for a composition teacher, including a teacher of basic writing, is a literary education.

A style, as a literary education teaches us, is more than a sign of an individual linguistic performance; a style is allusive, derivative; it refers out to a language that is a cultural legacy and that an individual writer can finally neither invent nor control. Or, as Geoffrey Hartman has recently said, "Style is not cognitive only; it is also recognitive, a signal betraying the writer's relation, or sometimes the relation of a type of discourse, to a historical and social world."[17] "Betraying" is a loaded word here, of course. Shaughnessy charts one form of betrayal when she observes the following about the work of a basic writer:

> Often, but not always, the content that is carried in such writing is short and bare, reinforcing the impression of the reader that this writer is "slow" or intellectually immature. Yet the same student might be a spirited, cogent talker in class. His problem is that he has no access to his thoughts or personal style through the medium of writing and must appear, whenever he writes, as a child. (*Errors and Expectations,* p. 192)

The writer is "betrayed" here because his writing makes him appear slow or stupid, and he is not. He has an adult mind, but he has "no access to his thoughts or his personal style" because of a problem he has with writing.

While it is undoubtedly true that this writer is neither slow nor stupid, Shaughnessy's account of the nature of his problem is sentimental and, as a consequence, not very useful as a description of the relationship between language and thought for a teacher or a researcher considering the tenuous and problematic relations between basic writers and the world of "adult thought." Clearly the student cited above has an adult mind, but it is not the "mind" represented by written, adult, academic discourse. *That* mind does not exist outside of language; it does not stand before language waiting for a language that is fluent enough to express it. That mind is, itself, a discourse.

Shaughnessy acknowledges this at other points in *Errors and Expectations,* although the contradiction is persistent. At times writing is in service of "personal thoughts and styles," and at times it is in service of the institution, an institutional way of thinking and being present in the world.[18] She is, at best, ambivalent in her role as a mediator between the world of the student (which is outside the conventional language of academic discourse) and the world of the university (which is inside).

When, for example, she talks about more advanced student writers, she talks about writers who have moved into a language they do not yet fully control:

> for all the gains in vocabulary that the writer at this stage can claim . . . the pre-packaging feature of language, the possibility of taking over phrases

and whole sentences without much thought about them, threatens the writer now as before. The writer, as we have said, inherits the language out of which he must fabricate his own messages. He is therefore in a constant tangle with language, obliged to recognize its public, communal nature and yet driven to invent out of this language his own statements. But invention is difficult at these early stages when the cliches and conventions of the formal style are fresh to the writer and before he is confident or knowledgeable enough to translate more freely into language that is closer to his thoughts. (*Errors and Expectations*, p. 208)

Clearly, knowledge and confidence are necessary goals of a basic writing course, but the key question is whether at the end of a course of instruction students are translating into a language that is closer to their thoughts or closer to ours. The question, I suppose, is whether there is a point at which students are no longer betrayed by the language that represents them on the page. This is, let me add, a pressing pedagogical issue, not just the stuff of debates at meetings of the poststructuralists, since it has to do with the final stages in a basic writing curriculum and the degree to which the work set for students should be overtly and insistently parodic and imitative. Should students, in the end, write *for* the university, or should they write against it or in spite of it?

While Shaughnessy is often ambivalent about this in *Errors and Expectations,* her tendency, I think, is to say that students should write against or in spite of the formal conventions of academic discourse. The adult writing she holds up as a model is by Orwell, Baldwin, and Hoggart, work that she says shows an "easy" merging of experience with idea. She wants to believe that the right use of language can bring together personal experience and the world of ideas while retaining the integrity of each. The movement between experience and idea in the work of Orwell, Baldwin, and Hoggart may show a stylistic ease and grace, but it is dangerous to ignore the difficult personal histories that underlie this artistic achievement. Hoggart, for example, chronicles the pain, loss, and humiliation that was a necessary part of his education away from the working-class home of his family. The ideas that came to represent his experience served also to separate him from that experience, from the past, and from his family; the transition was difficult, at times provisional. The separation was measured by the way he had learned to think and feel as well as by the neighborhood he moved into and the things he did with his time.[19]

Late in her book, where she talks about what students can gain by a course of instruction in basic writing, Shaughnessy speaks of the way that the acquisition of the "language of academia" comes only at the sacrifice of those qualities that give "life," "power," and "authenticity" to her students' writing:

Many teachers would view any such transposition as an intolerable kind of academic colonizing, discouraging the student from developing his "native" talent with language and imposing upon him a model of competence that is by comparison barren. Yet the differences we note grow out of real situations that will not dissolve simply because of our preferences for expressive over discursive, for personal over public, or spoken over written styles. (*Errors and Expectations,* p. 239)

As I understand professional writing, and by that I mean the writing that does the work of institutions, there is no easy merging of experience with idea, and yet I'll confess that I do not find the model of competence represented by academic writing (including the academic writing done by undergraduates) to be "barren," at least not if the assignments are carefully written and if students are given real work to do.[20] In fact, I think that the styles and projects of academic discourse can be exciting, creative, and liberating, even at the point at which they confine students to work that is, at least for undergraduates, ours and not theirs, and even to the degree to which that writing does not "change reality" or reshape the university and its disciplines. There are reasons, I believe, for students to learn to work within our community that are more important and more powerful than the dream of preserving their freedom.

My purpose here, however, is not to take issue with Shaughnessy's notion of "native" intelligence, but to turn again to the question of literacy and the process by which one acquires the skills of the higher literacy demanded by a university education. This process begins, I believe, when students are released into language, and not when students develop fluency with a neutral, transparent language that allows them access to their personal thoughts. It requires, that is, that students be given access to the culture, the closed culture, of the world they would enter. They must enter another's thoughts by using another's language. The question is whether they can do this and still remain themselves; it is a question of whether they can, as Shaughnessy says, use someone else's language and yet create out of this language their own statements. This is a very complicated and subtle act of appropriation. Teaching it requires a very different understanding of central concepts — "basic skills," "self-expression," "rhetorical patterns" — than that represented by most basic writing courses and most colleges and universities.

Let me turn to two recent proposals for curricula to teach general, cultural literacy. Richard Lanham in *Literacy and the Survival of Humanism* proposes a single conceptual framework — and interpretive scheme — that can unify the university curriculum by organizing and interpreting all texts, artifacts, and varieties of human performance according to a single theory of human behavior.[21] It is this scheme that allows students access to the competing voices and projects of the university community: "One thus avoids with a single step all the protracted and sterile debates about which texts are canonical and which are not, which periods and subjects and which derivative."

At the risk of turning this radical proposal into parody, let me try to summarize Lanham's argument. Human behavior, Lanham says, is governed by three motives: purpose, game, and play. Composition instruction, as Lanham argued earlier in *Style: An Anti-Text*, has tried to banish play and competition by teaching a single-minded rhetoric of purpose (where good writing is clear, brief, and sincere — known as the CBS theory of writing — and never opaque, elaborate, and self-consciously artificial). The university curriculum, in a sense, has followed suit, leaving nonpurposive behavior for literature, creative writing, and other humanities courses, and assuming that the rest of the curriculum is busy training students for a trade or a profession. This split misrepresents the work that goes on in the disciplines, including English, and, according to Lanham, it threatens our well-being.

Students can learn to observe and appreciate the range of our behavior by learning to analyze and imitate the styles of texts. They can learn, that is, to look both "at" and "through" the texts we assign them to read. A text here can be literally a text — a textbook, a literary text, a piece of scholarly writing (it makes no difference which, since any of these can be seen as either working, playing, or competing) — or it can be any variety of human performance. Lanham argues that the university curriculum must "orchestrate" these three motives and that the humanists must "harmonize" them. The starting point for such an education is the composition course:

> The writing course, when it actually works, mixes all three motives just as the curricular purposes mix in good teaching. The study of prose thus provides, once we understand it aright, a model for motive. It can, then, act as a do-it-yourself curriculum guide, can do something for students besides sharpen their verbal pencils.

The writing course is also, however, a training course. In it, students imitate and parody "all kinds of prose," not just the transparent essays (clear, brief, and sincere essays) that model purposive behavior. A composition course like this will, Lanham argues, give students a "conceptual framework that will allow them to find, and to create, some order among the humanistic disciplines," and it will make students "self-conscious about their own complex motives, their layered purposiveness."

This is, clearly, a program of instruction that celebrates the various languages of academic and public life. The chapter of the book that describes the UCLA writing program is a humbler account of what the first steps look like. The basic writing program there, as described elsewhere by Mike Rose, is currently a collection of courses, all of them, however, governed by the powerful principle that the work the students do should situate them in the context of some subject matter and some adult, academic object. Or, as Rose says, "a remedial writing curriculum must fit into the intellectual context of the university. Topics should have academic substance and, when possible, should require the student to work from text."[22] To this degree they follow Lanham's stipulation that composition courses be imitative or parodic and that they provide set interpretive schemes to analyze and connect diverse textual materials.

E. D. Hirsch, speaking in the name of Mina Shaughnessy, has offered a very different proposal, one that places a core curriculum not only at the center of a university education but as a solution to declining writing skills. Hirsch's argument is bold, compelling, and, as he acknowledged, somewhat dangerous. Hirsch argues that while it is possible to talk about generic writing "skills," skills that are independent of any given subject and any approach to and understanding of that subject, those skills alone do not produce writing. What we have ignored, he says, is the cultural aspect of writing. "No amount of training in the skills of composition, in the writing process, and in the basics will by themselves convey the additional cultural information that underlies advancement in general literacy."[23] By "cultural information" he means a general knowledge of names, book titles, key terms, famous ideas and the like. But he means more than this as well:

> I said that the craft-approach neglects the cultural dimension of writing. Alternatively, one could say that we have stressed the process and product of writing at the expense of the huge domain of tacit knowledge which is never written down at all, but which, though quite invisible, is just as operative as the visible written words. A writing task could be compared to an iceberg whose visible tip is arrangement, syntax, rhetoric, spelling, coherence and so on, but whose much bigger invisible base is tacit cultural knowledge — not just linguistic knowledge, and knowledge about the topic, but also, and most important, knowledge of what others also know and expect about the topic, about the form, about the writer, and about the world. In short, the cultural dimension is that whole system of unspoken tacit knowledge that is shared between writer and reader.

To give students the cultural literacy they will need in order to be able to write, Hirsch argues, there must be a commonly agreed upon curriculum; educators need to agree about "the *kinds* of materials we shall teach, and also about some of the particular facts and texts we shall teach." And this, he acknowledges, raises difficult and far-reaching political questions.

I think it is possible to agree that certain texts and ideas are important, even central, to a university education. In fact, it is hard to imagine the college or English department that doesn't operate under a tacit agreement to this effect. And, as I've argued, I think that to learn to write students must learn to work their way into the culture of a privileged community. We can speed this process up by providing students access to the canon. I'm not sure, however, that the sum total of the books will be equivalent to the "tacit knowledge" that is shared between similarly educated readers and writers. A student can read the *Phaedrus* and, in a sense, "have" some Plato to use in the classroom or in an essay, but I'm not sure whether that same student would have the *Phaedrus* as we have it (and I think I can generalize here), since we have learned not only the *Phaedrus* but a way of reading the *Phaedrus*; we have learned to notice some things and ignore others, to remember certain stories and forget the rest, and our students, if they have not learned this way of reading, may ignore and forget the wrong things.

For many teachers, the key response to Hirsch's proposal will be "Who gets to choose the reading list?" And Hirsch wisely recognizes that this will have to be a matter of public policy. It should not be left up to university faculty alone. The point is, however, that whether we develop and publish such a reading list, students enter into universities, departments, and classrooms where unspoken reading lists are already in operation. The lectures they hear, the texts they read are all situated within a culture that has set boundaries and predictable terrain. For me, the unanswered system in Hirsch's proposal is what students are going to be led to *do* with those books and ideas. How will the act of writing be brought to bear on the texts that make up the new canon? I see no reason to imagine that students' writing could not be critical as well as synthetic, that students could not be taught to extend or challenge or question ideas as well as report on them.[24] But developing such curricula is no simple task. I see few basic writing courses across the country that allow students any active involvement with the real work of the university, whether that work be located within the projects of individual disciplines (like a history department) or whether that work be the general intellectual project of inquiry, interpretation, and report. It is in this area that we have yet to complete what Mina Shaughnessy began.

In her essay for Gary Tate's *Teaching Composition*, she wrote:

> Still, the special conditions of the remedial situation, that is, the need to develop within a short time a style of writing and thinking and a background of cultural information that prepare the student to cope with academic work, create a distinctive tension that almost defines the profession — a constant, uneasy hovering between the imperatives of format and freedom, convention and individuality, the practical and the ideal. Just where the boundaries between these claims are to be drawn in basic writing is by no means clear. Some would argue for a gradual exposure to academic subjects and skills through the extension of the remedial concern . . . others would press for a concentrated, direct apporach to the distinctive tasks of academia, arguing that for students to lay claim to their critical and analytical powers and to cultivate the formal discursive style associated with academic work is no less 'creative' or 'personal' than the activities (poetry, stories, etc.) usually associated with those words.[25]

And, she concluded, "The debate has not yet surfaced among basic writing teachers in formal or scholarly ways. It is more an undercurrent that unsettles staff meetings and most probably confuses students who must often move between semesters from one pedagogy to another."

The distinctive tension, I think, remains. We have courses in basic writing, and yet they are courses that most often lack a subject, a context and, in a sense, a home. We have students who wander, not as Said's writer wanders, resolute in his refusal to be appropriated by outworn systems, but wander without purpose or direction, doing what they can, and using what we have taught them, only to survive. The project that can both honor and complete Shaughnessy's work is the project that will turn again to the requirements of academic writing, or any writing that moves a writer into a privileged and closed discourse, to find a subject and a context for basic writing students and to develop a course of instruction that will extend what she has taught us about the ethics and integrity of teaching.

NOTES

1. Adrienne Rich, "Teaching Language in Open Admissions (1972)," in *On Lies Secrets and Silence* (New York: Norton, 1979), pp. 51–68.

2. The preparation of this essay was supported by the Learning Research and Development Center at the University of Pittsburgh which is supported in part by the National Institute of Education. I am also grateful to Glynda Hull for her advice and assistance.

3. This talk was reprinted in *College Composition and Communication,* 27 (October 1976). 234–39. Further references to this essay will be cited in the text.

4. Mina Shaughnessy, *Errors and Expectations: A Guide for Teachers of Basic Writing* (New York: Oxford Univ. Pr., 1977). Further references to this work will be cited in the text.

5. See, for example, Barry Kroll and John Schafer, "Error Analysis and the Teaching of Composition," *College Composition and Communication,* 29 (October 1978), 243–48; Donald C. Freeman, "Linguistics and Error Analysis: On Agency," *Linguistics, Stylistics and the Teaching of Composition,* ed. Donald McQuade (Akron, OH: L & S Books, 1979), pp. 143–51 . . . ; Kenneth A. Bruffee, "Getting Started," in *Linguistics, Stylistics and the Teaching of Composition,* pp. 52–61 . . . ; Elaine Maimon and Barbara Nodine, "Words Enough and Time: Syntax and Error One Year After," in *Sentence Combining and the Teaching of Writing,* ed. Donald Daiker, Andrew Kerek, and Max Morenberg (Conway, AR: L & S Books, 1979), pp. 101–09; David Bartholomae, "The Study of Error," *College Composition and Communication,* 31 (October 1980), 253–69; D. M. Kagan, "Run-on and Fragment Sentences: An Error Analysis," *Research in the Teaching of English,* 14 (1980, 127–38; M. Harris, "Mending the Fragmented Free Modifier," *College Composition and Communication,* 32 (May 1981), 175–82; Donald C. Freeman, "Phenomenal Nominals," *College Composition and Communication,* 32 (May 1981), 183–205; Joseph Williams, "The Phenomenology of Error," *College Composition and Communication,* 32 (May 1981), 139–52; F. Kress and R. J. Bracewell, "Taught but Not Learned: Reasons for Grammatical Errors and Implications for Instruction," in *Teaching Writing,* ed. I. Pringle and A. Freedman (Ottawa: Canadian Council of Teachers of English, 1981); Elaine Lees, "An Analysis of Sentence-Boundary Errors in Novice and Expert Writers," paper presented at Composition Conference, University of Pittsburgh, 1981; M. Hystrand, "An Analysis of Errors in Written Communication," in *What Writers Know,* ed. M. Nystrand (New York: Academic Press 1982), pp. 57–74; and Elaine Lees, "Error Analysis and the Editing Behavior of Basic Writing Students," paper presented at the Conference on College Composition and Communication, 1984.

6. Edward Said, *Beginnings: Intention and Method* (Baltimore: The Johns Hopkins Univ. Pr., 1975), p. 8.

7. For articles on writing across the curriculum, see Elaine Maimon, "Talking To Strangers," *College Composition and Communication,* 30 (December 1979), 364–69; Toby Fulwiler and Art Young, *Language Connections: Writing and Reading Across the Curriculum* (Urbana, IL: NCTE, 1982); C. H. Knoblauch and Lil Brannon, "Writing as Learning Through the Curriculum," *College English,* (September 1983), 465–74; Patricia Bizzell, "College Composition: Initiation into the Academic Discourse Community," *Curriculum Inquiry,* 12 (1982), 191–207; Patricia Bizzell, "The Ethos of Academic Discourse,"*College Composition and Communication,* 29 (December 1978), 351–55. See also Patricia Bizzell's and Bruce Herzberg's annotated bibliography on writing across the curriculum in this volume.

8. See Ann Berthoff's essay, "Abstraction as a Speculative Instrument," in this volume, and also, *The Making of Meaning* (Montclair, NJ: Boynton/Cook, 1981).

9. For examples with direct bearing on basic writing, see, Sondra Perl, "The Composing Processes of Unskilled College Writers, *Research in the Teaching of English,* 13 (1979), 317–36; Sondra Perl, "A Look at Basic Writers in the Process of Composing," in *Basic Writing: Essays for Teachers, Researchers, and Administrators,* ed. Lawrence Kasden and Daniel Hoeber (Urbana, IL: NCTE, 1980), pp. 13–32; Mike Rose, "Rigid Rules, Inflexible Plans, and the Stifling of Language: A Cognitivist Analysis of Writer's Block," *College Composition and Communication,* 31 (1980), 389–401; Linda Flower, "Revising Writer-Based Prose," *Journal of Basic Writing,* 3 (Fall/Winter 1981), 62–74; C. A. Daiute, "Psycholinguistic Foundations of the Writing Process," *Research in the Teaching of English,* 15 (1981), 5–22; Patricia Bizzell, "Cognition, Convention and Certainty: What We Need to Know about Writing," *PRE/TEXT,* 3 (Fall 1982), 213–44; Susan Wall, "Revision in a Rhetorical Context: Case Studies of First Year College Writers," Diss. University of Pittsburgh, 1982; Glynda Hull, "The Editing Process in Writing: A Performance Study of Experts and Novices," Diss. University Pittsburgh, 1983; Mike Rose, *Writer's Block: The Cognitive Dimension* (Carbondale and Edwardsville: Southern Illinois Univ. Pr., 1984); Mary Epes, "Tracing Errors to Their Sources: A Study of the Encoding Processes of Adult Basic Writers," unpublished ms.

10. I am not a trained linguist, so my reading in error analysis may seem idiosyncratic to a specialist. Some essays I would recommend are: S. P. Corder, "The Significance of Learner's Errors," *IRAL* 5 (November 1967), 162–69; S. P. Corder, "Idiosyncratic Dialects and Error Analysis," *IRAL* 9 (May 1971), 148–51; and Wolfgang Zydatiss, "A 'Kiss of Life' for the Notion of Error," *IRAL* 9 (August 1974), 231–37. There is an excellent collection of essays I would recommend to composition teachers: Jack C. Richards, ed., *Error Analysis: Perspectives on Second Language Acquisition* (London: Longman, 1974). It contains the two essays by Corder listed above.

11. See S. P. Corder, "Idiosyncratic Dialects and Error Analysis," in Richards, pp. 158–71.

12. See L. Selinker, "Interlanguage," in Richards, pp. 31–54, and William Nemser, "Approximate Systems of Foreign Language Learners," in Richards, pp. 55–63.

13. See Patrick Hartwell, "Dialect Interference in Writing: A Critical View," *Research in the Teaching of English,* 14 (1980), 101–18.

14. For an excellent discussion of this problem and some suggested exercises, see Patricia Laurence, "Error's Endless Train: Why Students Don't Perceive Errors," *Journal of Basic Writing,* 1 (Spring 1975), 23–43. See also Glynda Hull, "Can Stray Dogs be Mermaids? (An Attempt to Categorize Error)," unpublished ms., and Elaine O. Lees, "Proofreading as Reading, Errors and Embarrassments," unpublished ms.

15. Glynda Hull, "The Editing Process in Writing: A Performance Study of Experts and Novices"; see also Glynda Hull, "Consulting, Intuiting, and Comprehending," paper presented at the Conference on College Composition and Communication, 1984.

16. See M. P. Jain, "Error Analysis: Source, Cause and Significance," in Richards, pp. 189–215, and Elaine Lees, "How Teachers Teach Students to Make Sentence-Boundary Errors," unpublished ms.

17. Geoffrey Hartman, "The Culture of Criticism," *PMLA,* 99 (May 1984), 371.

18. Lynn Buncher Shelly discusses this point in "The Writer and the Text: Deconstruction and Composition," Diss., University of Pittsburgh, 1984.

19. Richard Hoggart, *The Uses of Literacy* (Boston: Beacon, 1961), and *Speaking to Each Other,* vol. 1 (London: Chatto and Windus, 1970). See also Richard Rodriquez' use of Hoggart in chapter 2 of *Hunger of Memory: The Education of Richard Rodriquez* (New York: Bantam Books, 1983).

20. For examples of what I have in mind by "real work" for students, see David Bartholomae, "Teaching Basic Writing: An Alternative to Basic Skills," *Journal of Basic Writing,* 2 (Spring/Summer 1979), 85–109; and David Bartholomae, "Writing Assignments: Where Writing Begins," in *Fforum,* ed. Patricia Stock (Montclair, NJ: Boynton/Cook, 1983), pp. 300–12.

21. Richard A. Lanham, *Literacy and the Survival of Humanism* (New Haven: Yale Univ. Pr., 1983), pp. 140, 141. See, in particular, "Post-Darwinian Humanism" and "Composition, Literature and the Core Curriculum: The UCLA Writing Programs." See also Robert Di Yanni's essay on Lanham in this volume.

22. See Mike Rose, "Remedial Writing Courses: A Critique and a Proposal," *College English,* 45 (February 1983), 109–28, and Mike Rose, "The Freshman Writing Program: A Descriptive Report," an unpublished document from the UCLA Freshman Writing Program.

23. E. D. Hirsch, Jr., "Culture and Literacy," *Journal of Basic Writing* 3 (1980), 27–47. See also "Cultural Literacy," in *American Scholar,* 11 (1983), 159–69; and "Reading, Writing, and Cultural Literacy," in *Composition and Literature: Bridging the Gap,* ed. W. B. Horner (Chicago: Univ. of Chicago Pr., 1983), pp. 141–48.

24. For examples of courses, or calls for courses, that attempt to allow students to participate in adult intellectual or academic work, see David Bartholomae, "Teaching Basic Writing"; Kyle Fiore and Nan Elsasser, " 'Strangers No More': A Liberatory Literacy Curriculum," *College English,* 44 (1982), 115–28; Ira Schor, *Critical Teaching and Everyday Life* (Boston: South End Press, 1980); Mariolina Salvatori, "Reading and Writing a Text: Correlations between Reading and Writing," *College English,* 45 (1983), 657–66; and Mike Rose, "Remedial Writing Courses."

25. Mina Shaughnessy, "Basic Writing," in *Teaching Composition: Ten Bibliographic Essays,* ed. Gary Tate (Fort Worth: Texas Christian Univ. Pr., 1976), p. 152.

Inventing the University

E.ducation may well be, as of right, the instrument whereby every individual, in a society like our own, can gain access to any kind of discourse. But we well know that in its distribution, in what it permits and in what it prevents, it follows the well-trodden battle-lines of social conflict. Every educational system is a political means of maintaining or of modifying the appropriation of discourse, with the knowledge and the powers it carries with it.

— FOUCAULT, THE DISCOURSE ON LANGUAGE

. . . the text is the form of the social relationships made visible, palpable, material.

— BERNSTEIN, CODES, MODALITIES AND THE PROCESS
OF CULTURAL REPRODUCTION: A MODEL

I

Every time a student sits down to write for us, he has to invent the university for the occasion — invent the university, that is, or a branch of it, like history or anthropology or economics or English. The student has to learn to speak our language, to speak as we do, to try on the peculiar ways of knowing, selecting, evaluating, reporting, concluding, and arguing that define the discourse of our community. Or perhaps I should say the *various* discourses of our community, since it is in the nature of a liberal arts education that a student, after the first year or two, must learn to try on a variety of voices and interpretive schemes — to write, for example, as a literary critic one day and as an experimental psychologist the next; to work within fields where the rules governing the presentation of examples or the development of an argument are both distinct and, even to a professional mysterious.

From *When a Writer Can't Write: Studies in Writer's Block and Other Composing-Process Problems,* ed. Mike Rose (New York: Guilford P, 1985) 134–66.

The student has to appropriate (or be appropriated by) a specialized discourse, and he has to do this as though he were easily and comfortably one with his audience, as though he were a member of the academy or an historian or an anthropologist or an economist; he has to invent the university by assembling and mimicking its language while finding some compromise between idiosyncrasy, a personal history, on the one hand, and the requirements of convention, the history of a discipline, on the other. He must learn to speak our language. Or he must dare to speak it or to carry off the bluff, since speaking and writing will most certainly be required long before the skill is "learned." And this, understandably, causes problems.

Let me look quickly at an example. Here is an essay written by a college freshman.

> In the past time I thought that an incident was creative was when I had to make a clay model of the earth, but not of the classical or your everyday model of the earth which consists of the two cores, the mantle and the crust. I thought of these things in a dimension of which it would be unique, but easy to comprehend. Of course, your materials to work with were basic and limited at the same time, but thought help to put this limit into a right attitude or frame of mind to work with the clay.
>
> In the beginning of the clay model, I had to research and learn the different dimensions of the earth (in magnitude, quantity, state of matter, etc.). After this, I learned how to put this into the clay and come up with something different than any other person in my class at the time. In my opinion, color coordination and shape was the key to my creativity of the clay model of the earth.
>
> Creativity is the venture of the mind at work with the mechanics relay to the limbs from the cranium, which stores and triggers this action. It can be a burst of energy released at a precise time a thought is being transmitted. This can cause a frenzy of the human body, but it depends on the characteristics of the individual and how they can relay the message clearly enough through mechanics of the body to us as an observer. Then we must determine if it is creative or a learned process varied by the individuals thought process. Creativity is indeed a tool which has to exist, or our world will not succeed into the future and progress like it should.

I am continually impressed by the patience and goodwill of our students. This student was writing a placement essay during freshman orientation. (The problem set to him was: "Describe a time when you did something you felt to be creative. Then, on the basis of the incident you have described, go on to draw some general conclusions about 'creativity.'") He knew that university faculty would be reading and evaluating his essay, and so he wrote for them.

In some ways it is a remarkable performance. He is trying on the discourse even though he doesn't have the knowledge that would make the discourse more than a routine, a set of conventional rituals and gestures. And he is doing this, I think, even though he *knows* he doesn't have the knowledge that would make the discourse more than a routine. He defines himself as a researcher working systematically, and not as a kid in a high school class: "I thought of these things in a dimension of . . ."; "I had to research and learn the different dimensions of the earth (in magnitude, quantity, state of matter, etc.)." He moves quickly into a specialized language (his approximation of our jargon) and draws both a general, textbook-like conclusion — "Creativity is the venture of the mind at work . . ." — and a resounding peroration — "Creativity is indeed a tool which has to exist, or our world will not succeed into the future and progress like it should." The writer has even picked up the rhythm of our prose with that last "indeed" and with the qualifications and the parenthetical expressions of the opening paragraphs. And through it all he speaks with an impressive air of authority.

There is an elaborate but, I will argue, a necessary and enabling fiction at work here as the student dramatizes his experience in a "setting" — the setting required by the discourse — where he can speak to us as a companion, a fellow researcher. As I read the essay, there is only one moment when the fiction is broken, when we are addressed differently. The student says, "Of course, your materials to work with were basic and limited at the same time, but thought help to put this limit into a right attitude or frame of mind to work with the clay." At this point, I think, we become students and he the teacher giving us a lesson (as in, "You take your pencil in your right hand and put your paper in front of you"). This is, however, one of the most characteristic slips of basic writers. (I use the term "basic writers" to refer to university students traditionally placed in remedial composition courses.) It is very hard for them to take on the role — the voice, the persona — of an authority whose authority is rooted in scholarship, analysis, or research. They slip, then, into a more immediately available and realizable voice of authority, the voice of a teacher giving a lesson or the voice of a parent lecturing at the dinner table. They offer advice or homilies rather than "academic" conclusions. There is a similar break in the final paragraph, where the conclusion that pushes for a definition ("Creativity is the venture of the mind at work with the mechanics relay to the limbs from the cranium") is replaced by a conclusion that speaks in the voice of an elder ("Creativity is indeed a tool which has to exist, or our world will not succeed into the future and progress like it should.").

It is not uncommon, then, to find such breaks in the concluding sections of essays written by basic writers. Here is the concluding section of an essay written by a student about his work as a mechanic. He had been asked to generalize about work after reviewing an on-the-job experience or incident that "stuck in his mind" as somehow significant.

> How could two repairmen miss a leak? Lack of pride? No incentive? Lazy? I don't know.

At this point the writer is in a perfect position to speculate, to move from the problem to an analysis of the problem. Here is how the paragraph continues, however (and notice the change in pronoun reference).

> From this point on, I take *my* time, do it right, and don't let customers get under *your* skin. If they have a complaint, tell them to call your boss and he'll be more than glad to handle it. Most important, worry about

yourself, and keep a clear eye on everyone, for there's always someone trying to take advantage of you, anytime and anyplace. (Emphasis
added)

We get neither a technical discussion nor an "academic" discussion but a
Lesson on Life.[1] This is the language he uses to address the general question,
"How could two repairmen miss a leak?" The other brand of conclusion, the
more academic one, would have required him to speak of his experience in our
terms; it would, that is, have required a special vocabulary, a special system of
presentation, and an interpretive scheme (or a set of commonplaces) he could
have used to identify and talk about the mystery of human error. The writer
certainly had access to the range of acceptable commonplaces for such an
explanation: "lack of pride," "no incentive," "lazy." Each commonplace would
dictate its own set of phrases, examples, and conclusions; and we, his teachers,
would know how to write out each argument, just as we know how to write
out more specialized arguments of our own. A "commonplace," then, is a culturally or institutionally authorized concept or statement that carries with it its
own necessary elaboration. We all use commonplaces to orient ourselves in
the world; they provide points of reference and a set of "prearticulated" explanations that are readily available to organize and interpret experience. The
phrase "lack of pride" carries with it its own account of the repairman's error,
just as at another point in time a reference to "original sin" would have provided an explanation, or just as in certain university classrooms a reference to
"alienation" would enable writers to continue and complete the discussion.
While there is a way in which these terms are interchangeable, they are not all
permissible: A student in a composition class would most likely be turned
away from a discussion of original sin. Commonplaces are the "controlling
ideas" of our composition textbooks, textbooks that not only insist on a set
form for expository writing but a set view of public life.[2]

When the writer says, "I don't know," then, he is not saying that he has
nothing to say. He is saying that he is not in a position to carry on this discussion. And so we are addressed as apprentices rather than as teachers or
scholars. In order to speak as a person of status or privilege, the writer can
either speak to us in our terms — in the privileged language of university
discourse — or, in default (or in defiance) of that, he can speak to us as
though we were children, offering us the wisdom of experience.

I think it is possible to say that the language of the "Clay Model" paper
has come *through* the writer and not from the writer. The writer has located
himself (more precisely, he has located the self that is represented by the "I"
on the page) in a context that is finally beyond him, not his own and not available to his immediate procedures for inventing and arranging text. I would
not, that is, call this essay an example of "writer-based" prose. I would not say
that it is egocentric or that it represents the "interior monologue or a writer
thinking and talking to himself" (Flower, 1981, p. 63). It is, rather, the record
of a writer who has lost himself in the discourse of his readers. There is a context beyond the intended reader that is not the world but a way of talking

about the world, a way of talking that determines the use of examples, the possible conclusions, acceptable commonplaces, and key words for an essay on the construction of a clay model of the earth. This writer has entered the discourse without successfully approximating it.

Linda Flower (1981) has argued that the difficulty inexperienced writers have with writing can be understood as a difficulty in negotiating the transition between "writer-based" and "reader-based" prose. Expert writers, in other words, can better imagine how a reader will respond to a text and can transform or restructure what they have to say around a goal shared with a reader. Teaching students to revise for readers, then, will better prepare them to write initially with a reader in mind. The success of this pedagogy depends on the degree to which a writer can imagine and conform to a reader's goals. The difficulty of this act of imagination and the burden of such conformity are so much at the heart of the problem that a teacher must pause and take stock before offering revision as a solution. A student like the one who wrote the "Clay Model" paper is not so much trapped in a private language as he is shut out from one of the privileged languages of public life, a language he is aware of but cannot control.

II

Our students, I've said, have to appropriate (or be appropriated by) a specialized discourse, and they have to do this as though they were easily or comfortably one with their audience. If you look at the situation this way, suddenly the problem of audience awareness becomes enormously complicated. One of the common assumptions of both composition research and composition teaching is that at some "stage" in the process of composing an essay a writer's ideas or his motives must be tailored to the needs and expectations of his audience. Writers have to "build bridges" between their point of view and the reader's. They have to anticipate and acknowledge the reader's assumptions and biases. They must begin with "common points of departure" before introducing new or controversial arguments. Here is what one of the most popular college textbooks says to students.

> Once you have your purpose clearly in mind, your next task is to define and analyze your audience. A sure sense of your audience — knowing who it is and what assumptions you can reasonably make about it — is crucial to the success of your rhetoric. (Hairston, 1978, p. 107)

It is difficult to imagine, however, how writers can have a purpose before they are located in a discourse, since it is the discourse with its projects and agendas that determines what writers can and will do. The writer who can successfully manipulate an audience (or, to use a less pointed language, the writer who can accommodate her motives to her reader's expectations) is a writer who can both imagine and write from a position of privilege. She must, that is, see herself within a privileged discourse, one that already includes and excludes groups of readers. She must be either equal to or more powerful than those she would address. The writing, then, must somehow transform the political and social relationships between students and teachers.

If my students are going to write for me by knowing who I am — and if this means more than knowing my prejudices, psyching me out — it means knowing what I know; it means having the knowledge of a professor of English. They have, then, to know what I know and how I know what I know (the interpretive schemes that define the way I would work out the problems I set for them); they have to learn to write what I would write or to offer up some approximation of that discourse. The problem of audience awareness, then, is a problem of power and finesse. It cannot be addressed, as it is in most classroom exercises, by giving students privilege and denying the situation of the classroom — usually, that is, by having students write to an outsider, someone excluded from their privileged circle: "Write about 'To His Coy Mistress,' not for your teacher but for the students in your class"; "Describe Pittsburgh to someone who has never been there"; "Explain to a high school senior how best to prepare for college"; "Describe baseball to an Eskimo." Exercises such as these allow students to imagine the needs and goals of a reader, and they bring those needs and goals forward as a dominant constraint in the construction of an essay. And they argue, implicitly, what is generally true about writing — that it is an act of aggression disguised as an act of charity. What these assignments fail to address is the central problem of academic writing, where a student must assume the right of speaking to someone who knows more about baseball or "To His Coy Mistress" than the student does, a reader for whom the general commonplaces and the readily available utterances about a subject are inadequate.

Linda Flower and John Hayes, in an often quoted article (1981), reported on a study of a protocol of an expert writer (an English teacher) writing about his job for readers of *Seventeen* magazine. The key moment for this writer, who seems to have been having trouble getting started, came when he decided that teenage girls read *Seventeen*; that some teenage girls like English because it is tidy ("some of them will have wrong reasons in that English is good because it's tidy — can be a neat tidy little girl"); that some don't like it because it is "prim" and that, "By God, I can change that notion for them." Flower and Hayes's conclusion is that this effort of "exploration and consolidation" gave the writer "a new, relatively complex, rhetorically sophisticated working goal, one which encompasses plans for a topic, a persona, and the audience" (p. 383).[3]

Flower and Hayes give us a picture of a writer solving a problem, and the problem as they present it is a cognitive one. It is rooted in the way the writer's knowledge is represented in the writer's mind. The problem resides there, not in the nature of knowledge or in the nature of discourse but in a mental state prior to writing. It is possible, however, to see the problem as (perhaps simultaneously) a problem in the way subjects are located in a field of discourse.

Flower and Hayes divide up the composing process into three distinct activities: "planning or goal-setting," "translating," and "reviewing." The last of these, reviewing (which is further divided into two subprocesses, "evaluating" and "revising"), is particularly powerful, for as a writer continually reviews his goals, plans, and the text he is producing, and as he continually generates new goals, plans, and text, he is engaging in a process of learning and discovery. Let me quote Flower and Hayes's conclusion at length.

> If one studies the process by which a writer uses a goal to generate ideas, then consolidates those ideas and uses them to revise or regenerate new, more complex goals, one can see this learning process in action. Furthermore, one sees why the process of revising and clarifying goals has such a broad effect, since it is through setting these new goals that the fruits of discovery come back to inform the continuing process of writing. In this instance, some of our most complex and imaginative acts can depend on the elegant simplicity of a few powerful thinking processes. We feel that a cognitive process explanation of discovery, toward which this theory is only a start, will have another special strength. By placing emphasis on the inventive power of the writer, who is able to explore ideas, to develop, act on, test, and regenerate his or her own goals, we are putting an important part of creativity where it belongs — in the hands of the working, thinking writer. (1981, p. 386)

While this conclusion is inspiring, the references to invention and creativity seem to refer to something other than an act of writing — if writing is, finally, words on a page. Flower and Hayes locate the act of writing solely within the mind of the writer. The act of writing, here, has a personal, cognitive history but not a history as a text, as a text that is made possible by prior texts. When located in the perspective afforded by prior texts, writing is seen to exist separate from the writer and his intentions; it is seen in the context of other articles in *Seventeen*, of all articles written for or about women, of all articles written about English teaching, and so on. Reading research has made it possible to say that these prior texts, or a reader's experience with these prior texts, have bearing on how the text is read. Intentions, then, are part of the history of the language itself. I am arguing that these prior texts determine not only how a text like the *Seventeen* article will be read but also how it will be written. Flower and Hayes show us what happens in the writer's mind but not what happens to the writer as his motives are located within our language, a language with its own requirements and agendas, a language that limits what we might say and that makes us write and sound, finally, also like someone else. If you think of other accounts of the composing process — and I'm thinking of accounts as diverse as Richard Rodriguez's *Hunger of Memory* (1983) and Edward Said's *Beginnings* (1975) — you get a very different account of what happens when private motive enters into public discourse, when a personal history becomes a public account. These accounts place the writer in a history that is not of the writer's own invention; and they are chronicles of loss, violence, and compromise.

It is one thing to see the *Seventeen* writer making and revising his plans for a topic, a persona, and an audience; it is another thing to talk about discovery, invention, and creativity. Whatever plans the writer had must finally have been located in language and, it is possible to argue, in a language that is persistently conventional and formulaic. We do not, after all, get to see the *Seventeen* article. We see only the elaborate mental procedures that accompanied the writing of the essay. We see a writer's plans for a persona; we don't see that persona in action. If writing is a process, it is also a product; and it is the product, and not the plan for writing, that locates a writer on the page, that locates him in a text and a style and the codes or conventions that make both of them readable.

Contemporary rhetorical theory has been concerned with the "codes" that constitute discourse (or specialized forms of discourse). These codes determine not only what might be said but also who might be speaking or reading. Barthes (1974), for example, has argued that the moment of writing, where private goals and plans become subject to a public language, is the moment when the writer becomes subject to a language he can neither command nor control. A text, he says, in being written passes through the codes that govern writing and becomes "de-originated," becomes a fragment of something that has "always been *already* read, seen, done, experienced" (p. 21). Alongside a text we have always the presence of "off-stage voices," the oversound of all that has been said (e.g., about girls, about English). These voices, the presence of the "already written," stand in defiance of a writer's desire for originality and determine what might be said. A writer does not write (and this is Barthes's famous paradox) but is, himself, written by the languages available to him.

It is possible to see the writer of the *Seventeen* article solving his problem of where to begin by appropriating an available discourse. Perhaps what enabled that writer to write was the moment he located himself as a writer in a familiar field of stereotypes: Readers of *Seventeen* are teenage girls; teenage girls think of English (and English teachers) as "tidy" and "prim," and, "By God, I can change that notion for them." The moment of eureka was not simply a moment of breaking through a cognitive jumble in that individual writer's mind but a moment of breaking into a familiar and established territory — one with insiders and outsiders; one with set phrases, examples, and conclusions.

I'm not offering a criticism of the morals or manners of the teacher who wrote the *Seventeen* article. I think that all writers, in order to write, must imagine for themselves the privilege of being "insiders" — that is, the privilege both of being inside an established and powerful discourse and of being granted a special right to speak. But I think that right to speak is seldom conferred on us — on any of us, teachers or students — by virtue of that fact that we have invented or discovered an original idea. Leading students to believe that they are responsible for something new or original, unless they understand what those words mean with regard to writing, is a dangerous and counterproductive practice. We do have the right to expect students to be active and engaged, but that is a matter of continually and stylistically working against the inevitable presence of conventional language; it is not a matter of inventing a language that is new.

When a student is writing for a teacher, writing becomes more problematic than it was for the *Seventeen* writer (who was writing a version of the "Describe baseball to an Eskimo" exercise). The student, in effect, has to assume privilege without having any. And since students assumes privilege by locating themselves within the discourse of a particular community — within a set of specifically acceptable gestures and commonplaces — learning, at least as it is defined in the liberal arts curriculum, becomes more a matter of imitation or parody than a matter of invention and discovery.

To argue that writing problems are also social and political problems is not to break faith with the enterprise of cognitive science. In a recent paper reviewing the tremendous range of research directed at identifying general cognitive skills, David Perkins (in press) has argued that "the higher the level of competence concerned," as in the case of adult learning, "the fewer *general* cognitive control strategies there are." There comes a point, that is, where "field-specific" or "domain-specific" schemata (what I have called "interpretive strategies") become more important than general problem-solving processes. Thinking, learning, writing — all these become bound to the context of a particular discourse. And Perkins concludes:

> Instruction in cognitive control strategies tends to be organized around problem-solving tasks. However, the isolated problem is a creature largely of the classroom. The nonstudent, whether operating in scholarly or more everyday contexts, is likely to find himself or herself involved in what might be called "projects" — which might be anything from writing a novel to designing a shoe to starting a business.

It is interesting to note that Perkins defines the classroom as the place of artificial tasks and, as a consequence, has to place scholarly projects outside the classroom, where they are carried out by the "nonstudent." It is true, I think, that education has failed to involve students in scholarly projects, projects that allow students to act as though they were colleagues in an academic enterprise. Much of the written work that students do is test-taking, report or summary — work that places them outside the official discourse of the academic community, where they are expected to admire and report on what we do, rather than inside that discourse, where they can do its work and participate in a common enterprise.[4] This, however, is a failure of teachers and curriculum designers, who speak of writing as a mode of learning but all too often represent writing as a "tool" to be used by an (hopefully) educated mind.

It could be said, then, that there is a bastard discourse peculiar to the writing most often required of students. Carl Bereiter and Marlene Scardamalia (in press) have written about this discourse (they call it "knowledge-telling"; students who are good at it have learned to cope with academic tasks by developing a "knowledge-telling strategy"), and they have argued that insistence on knowledge-telling discourse undermines educational efforts to extend the variety of discourse schemata available to students.[5] What they actually say is this:

> When we think of knowledge stored in memory we tend these days to think of it as situated in three-dimensional space, with vertical and horizontal connections between sites. Learning is thought to add not only new elements to memory but also new connections, and it is the richness and structure of these connections that would seem . . . to spell the difference between inert and usable knowledge. On this account, the knowledge-telling strategy is educationally faulty because it specifically avoids the forming of connections between previously separated knowledge sites.

It should be clear by now that when I think of "knowledge" I think of it as situated in the discourse that constitutes "knowledge" in a particular discourse community, rather than as situated in mental "knowledge sites." One can remember a discourse, just as one can remember an essay or the movement of a professor's lecture; but this discourse, in effect, also has a memory of its own, its own rich network of structures and connections beyond the deliberate control of any individual imagination.

There is, to be sure, an important distinction to be made between learning history, say, and learning to write as an historian. A student can learn to command and reproduce a set of names, dates, places, and canonical interpretations (to "tell" somebody else's knowledge); but this is not the same thing as learning to "think" (by learning to write) as an historian. The former requires efforts of memory; the latter requires a student to compose a text out of the texts that represent the primary materials of history and in accordance with the texts that define history as an act of report and interpretation.

Let me draw on an example from my own teaching. I don't expect my students to *be* literary critics when they write about *Bleak House*. If a literary critic is a person who wins publication in a professional journal (or if he or she is one who could), the students aren't critics. I do, however, expect my students to be, themselves, invented as literary critics by approximating the language of a literary critic writing about *Bleak House*. My students, then, don't invent the language of literary criticism (they don't, that is, act on their own) but they are, themselves, invented by it. Their papers don't begin with a moment of insight, a "by God" moment that is outside of language. They begin with a moment of appropriation, a moment when they can offer up a sentence that is not theirs as though it were their own. (I can remember when, as a graduate student, I would begin papers by sitting down to write literally in the voice — with the syntax and the key words — of the strongest teacher I had met.)

What I am saying about my students' essays is that they are approximate, not that they are wrong or invalid. They are evidence of a discourse that lies between what I might call the students' primary discourse (what the students might write about *Bleak House* were they not in my class or in any class, and were they not imagining that they were in my class or in any class — if you can imagine any student doing any such thing) and standard, official literary criticism (which is imaginable but impossible to find). The students' essays are evidence of a discourse that lies between these two hypothetical poles. The writing is limited as much by a student's ability to imagine "what might be said" as it is by cognitive control strategies.[6] The act of writing takes the student away from where he is and what he knows and allows him to imagine something else. The approximate discourse, therefore, is evidence of a change, a change that, because we are teachers, we call "development." What our beginning students need to learn is to extend themselves, by successive approximations, into the commonplaces, set phrases, rituals and gestures, habits of mind, tricks of persuasion, obligatory conclusions and necessary connections that determine the "what might be said" and constitute knowledge within the various branches of our academic community.[7]

Pat Bizzell is, I think, one of the most important scholars writing now on "basic writers" (and this is the common name we use for students who are refused unrestrained access to the academic community) and on the special characteristics of academic discourse. In a recent essay, "Cognition, Convention, and Certainty: What We Need to Know about Writing" (1982a), she looks at two schools of composition research and the way they represent the problems that writing poses for writers.[8] For one group, the "inner-directed theorists," the problems are internal, cognitive, rooted in the way the mind represents knowledge to itself. These researchers are concerned with discovering the "universal, fundamental structures of thought and language" and with developing pedagogies to teach or facilitate both basic, general cognitive skills and specific cognitive strategies, or heuristics, directed to serve more specialized needs. Of the second group, the "outer-directed theorists," she says that they are "more interested in the social processes whereby language-learning and thinking capacities are shaped and used in particular communities."

> The staple activity of outer-directed writing instruction will be analysis of the conventions of particular discourse communities. For example, a main focus of writing-across-the-curriculum programs is to demystify the conventions of the academic discourse community. (1982a, pp. 218)

The essay offers a detailed analysis of the way the two theoretical camps can best serve the general enterprise of composition research and composition teaching. Its agenda, however, seems to be to counter the influence of the cognitivists and to provide bibliography and encouragement to those interested in the social dimension of language learning.

As far as basic writers are concerned, Bizzell argues that the cognitivists' failure to acknowledge the primary, shaping role of convention in the act of composing makes them "particularly insensitive to the problems of poor writers." She argues that some of those problems, like the problem of establishing and monitoring overall goals for a piece of writing, can be

> better understood in terms of their unfamiliarity with the academic discourse community, combined, perhaps, with such limited experience outside their native discourse communities that they are unaware that there is such a thing as a discourse community with conventions to be mastered. What is underdeveloped is their knowledge both of the ways experience is constituted and interpreted in the academic discourse community and of the fact that all discourse communities constitute and interpret experience. (1982a, p. 230)

One response to the problems of basic writers, then, would be to determine just what the community's conventions are, so that those conventions could be written out, "demystified" and taught in our classrooms. Teachers, as a result, could be more precise and helpful when they ask students to "think," "argue," "describe," or "define." Another response would be to examine the essays written by basic writers — their approximations of academic discourse — to determine more clearly where the problems lie. If we look at their writing, and if we look at it in the context of other student writing, we can better see the points of discord that arise when students try to write their way into the university.

The purpose of the remainder of this chapter will be to examine some of the most striking and characteristic of these problems as they are presented in the expository essays of first-year college students. I will be concerned, then, with university discourse in its most generalized form — as it is represented by introductory courses — and not with the special conventions required by advanced work in the various disciplines. And I will be concerned with the difficult, and often violent accommodations that occur when students locate themselves in a discourse that is not "naturally" or immediately theirs.

III

I have reviewed 500 essays written, as the "Clay Model" essay was, in response to a question used during one of our placement exams at the University of Pittsburgh: "Describe a time when you did something you felt to be creative. Then, on the basis of the incident you have described, go on to draw some general conclusions about 'creativity.' " Some of the essays were written by basic writers (or, more properly, those essays led readers to identify the writers as basic writers); some were written by students who "passed" (who were granted immediate access to the community of writers at the university). As I read these essays, I was looking to determine the stylistic resources that enabled writers to locate themselves within an "academic" discourse. My bias as a reader should be clear by now. I was not looking to see how a writer might represent the skills demanded by a neutral language (a language whose key features were paragraphs, topic sentences, transitions, and the like — features of a clear and orderly mind). I was looking to see what happened when a writer entered into a language to locate himself (a textual self) and his subject; and I was looking to see how, once entered, that language made or unmade the writer.

Here is one essay. Its writer was classified as a basic writer and, since the essay is relatively free of sentence level errors, that decision must have been rooted in some perceived failure of the discourse itself.

> I am very interested in music, and I try to be creative in my interpretation of music. While in highschool, I was a member of a jazz ensemble. The members of the ensemble were given chances to improvise and be creative in various songs. I feel that this was a great experience for me, as well as the other members. I was proud to know that I could use my imagination and feelings to create music other than what was written.
>
> Creativity to me, means being free to express yourself in a way that is unique to you, not having to conform to certain rules and guidelines. Music is only one of the many areas in which people are given opportunities to show their creativity. Sculpting, carving, building, art, and acting are just a few more areas where people can show their creativity.
>
> Through my music I conveyed feelings and thoughts which were important to me. Music was my means of showing creativity. In whatever

form creativity takes, whether it be music, art, or science, it is an important aspect of our lives because it enables us to be individuals.

Notice the key gesture in this essay, one that appears in all but a few of the essays I read. The student defines as his own that which is a commonplace. "Creativity, *to me*, means being free to express yourself in a way that is unique to you, not having to conform to certain rules and guidelines." This act of appropriation constitutes his authority; it constitutes his authority as a writer and not just as a musician (that is, as someone with a story to tell). There were many essays in the set that told only a story — where the writer established his presence as a musician or a skier or someone who painted designs on a van, but not as a person at a remove from that experience interpreting it, treating it as a metaphor for something else (creativity). Unless those stories were long, detailed, and very well told — unless the writer was doing more than saying, "I am a skier" or a musician or a van-painter — those writers were all given low ratings.

Notice also that the writer of the "Jazz" paper locates himself and his experience in relation to the commonplace (creativity is unique expression; it is not having to conform to rules or guidelines) regardless of whether the commonplace is true or not. Anyone who improvises "knows" that improvisation follows rules and guidelines. It is the power of the commonplace — its truth as a recognizable and, the writer believes, as a final statement — that justifies the example and completes the essay. The example, in other words, has value because it stands within the field of the commonplace.[9] It is not the occasion for what one might call an "objective" analysis or a "close" reading. It could also be said that the essay stops with the articulation of the commonplace. The following sections speak only to the power of that statement. The reference to "sculpting, carving, building, art, and acting" attest to the universality of the commonplace (and it attests the writer's nervousness with the status he has appropriated for himself — he is saying, "Now, I'm not the only one here who has done something unique"). The commonplace stands by itself. For this writer, it does not need to be elaborated. By virtue of having written it, he has completed the essay and established the contract by which we may be spoken to as equals: "In whatever form creativity takes, whether it be music, art, or science, it is an important aspect of *our* lives because it enables *us* to be individuals." (For me to break that contract, to argue that *my* life is not represented in that essay, is one way for me to begin as a teacher with that student in that essay.)

All of the papers I read were built around one of three commonplaces: (1) creativity is self-expression, (2) creativity is doing something new or unique, and (3) creativity is using old things in new ways. These are clearly, then, key phrases from the storehouse of things to say about creativity. I've listed them in the order of the students' ratings: A student with the highest rating was more likely to use number three than number one, although each commonplace ran across the range of possible ratings. One could argue that some standard assertions are more powerful than others, but I think the ranking simply represents the power of assertions within our community of readers. Every student was able to offer up an experience that was meant as an example of "creativity"; the lowest range of writers, then, was not represented by students who could not imagine themselves as creative people.[10]

I said that the writer of the "Jazz" paper offered up a commonplace regardless of whether it was true or not; and this, I said, was an instance of the power of a commonplace to determine the meaning of an example. A commonplace determines a system of interpretation that can be used to "place" an example within a standard system of belief. You can see a similar process at work in this essay.

> During the football season, the team was supposed to wear the same type of cleats and the same type socks, I figured that I would change this a little by wearing my white shoes instead of black and to cover up the team socks with a pair of my own white ones. I thought that this looked better than what we were wearing, and I told a few of the other people on the team to change too. They agreed that it did look better and they changed there combination to go along with mine. After the game people came up to us and said that it looked very good the way we wore our socks, and they wanted to know why we changed from the rest of the team.
>
> I feel that creativity comes from when a person lets his imagination come up with ideas and he is not afraid to express them. Once you create something to do it will be original and unique because it came about from your own imagination and if any one else tries to copy it, it won't be the same because you thought of it first from your own ideas.

This is not an elegant paper, but it seems seamless, tidy. If the paper on the clay model of the earth showed an ill fit between the writer and his project, here the discourse seems natural, smooth. You could reproduce this paper and hand it out to a class, and it would take a lot of prompting before the students sensed something fishy and one of the more aggressive ones said something like, "Sure he came up with the idea of wearing white shoes and white socks. Him and Billy 'White-Shoes' Johnson. Come on. He copied the very thing he said was his own idea, 'original and unique.' "

The "I" of this text — the "I" who "figured," "thought," and "felt" — is located in a conventional rhetoric of the self that turns imagination into origination (I made it), that argues an ethic of production (I made it and it is mine), and that argues a tight scheme of intention (I made it because I decided to make it). The rhetoric seems invisible because it is so common. This "I" (the maker) is also located in a version of history that dominates classrooms, the "great man" theory: History is rolling along (the English novel is dominated by a central, intrusive narrative presence; America is in the throes of a Great Depression; during football season the team was supposed to wear the same kind of cleats and socks) until a figure appears, one who can shape history (Henry James, FDR, the writer of the "White Shoes" paper), and everything is changed. In the argument of the "White Shoes" paper, the history goes

"I figured . . . I thought . . . I told . . . They agreed . . ." and, as a consequence, "I feel that creativity *comes from when* a person lets his imagination come up with ideas and he is not afraid to express them." The act of appropriation becomes a narrative of courage and conquest. The writer was able to write that story when he was able to imagine himself in that discourse. Getting him out of it will be a difficult matter indeed.

There are ways, I think, that a writer can shape history in the very act of writing it. Some students are able to enter into a discourse but, by stylistic maneuvers, to take possession of it at the same time. They don't originate a discourse, but they locate themselves within it aggressively, self-consciously. Here is another essay on jazz, which for sake of convenience I've shortened. It received a higher rating than the first essay on jazz.

> Jazz has always been thought of as a very original creative field in music. Improvisation, the spontaneous creation of original melodies in a piece of music, makes up a large part of jazz as a musical style. I had the opportunity to be a member of my high school's jazz ensemble for three years, and became an improvisation soloist this year. Throughout the years, I have seen and heard many jazz players, both proffessional and ama- teur. The solos performed by these artists were each flavored with that particular individual's style and ideas, along with some of the conven- tional premises behind improvisation. This particular type of solo work is creative because it is, done on the spur of the moment and blends the performer's ideas with basic guidelines.
> I realized my own creative potential when I began soloing. . . .
> My solos, just as all the solos generated by others, were original because I combined and shaped other's ideas with mine to create some- thing completely new. Creativity is combining the practical knowledge and guidelines of a discipline with one's original ideas to bring about a new, original end result, one that is different from everyone else's. Creativity is based on the individual. Two artists can interpret the same scene differently. Each person who creates something does so by bring- ing out something individual in himself.

The essay is different in some important ways from the first essay on jazz. The writer of the second is more easily able to place himself in the context of an "academic" discussion. The second essay contains an "I" who realized his "creative potential" by soloing; the first contained an "I" who had "a great experience." In the second essay, before the phrase, "I had the opportunity to be a member of my high school's jazz ensemble," there is an introduction that offers a general definition of improvisation and an acknowledgment that other people have thought about jazz and creativity. In fact, throughout the essay the writer offers definitions and counterdefinitions. He is placing him- self in the context of what has been said and what might be said. In the first paper, before a similar statement about being a member of a jazz ensemble, there was an introduction that locates jazz solely in the context of this indi- vidual's experience: "I am very interested in music." The writer of this first paper was authorized by who he is, a musician, rather than by what he can say about music in the context of what is generally said. The writer of the second essay uses a more specialized vocabulary; he talks about "conventional premises," "creative potential," "musical style," and "practical knowledge." And this is not just a matter of using bigger words, since these terms locate the experience in the context of a recognizable interpretive scheme — on the one hand there is tradition and, on the other, individual talent.

It could be said, then, that this essay is also framed and completed by a commonplace: "Creativity is combining the practical knowledge and guidelines of a discipline with one's original ideas to bring about a new, original end result, one that is different from everyone else's." Here, however, the argument is a more powerful one; and I mean "powerful" in the political sense, since it is an argument that complicates a "naive" assumption (it makes scholarly work possible, in other words), and it does so in terms that come close to those used in current academic debates (over the relation between convention and idiosyncracy or between rules and creativity). The assertion is almost consumed by the pleas for originality at the end of the sentence; but the point remains that the terms "original" and "different," as they are used at the end of the essay, are problematic, since they must be thought of in the context of "practical knowledge and guidelines of a discipline."

The key distinguishing gesture of this essay, that which makes it "better" than the other, is the way the writer works against a conventional point of view, one that is represented within the essay by conventional phrases that the writer must then work against. In his practice he demonstrates that a writer, and not just a musician, works within "conventional premises." The "I" who comments in this paper (not the "I" of the narrative about a time when he soloed) places himself self-consciously within the context of a conventional discourse about the subject, even as he struggles against the language of that conventional dicourse. The opening definition of improvisation, where improvisation is defined as spontaneous creation, is rejected when the writer begins talking about "the conventional premises behind improvisation." The earlier definition is part of the conventional language of those who "have always thought" of jazz as a "very original creative field in music." The paper begins with what "has been said" and then works itself out against the force and logic of what has been said, of what is not only an argument but also a collection of phrases, examples, and definitions.

I had a teacher who once told us that whenever we were stuck for something to say, we should use the following as a "machine" for producing a paper: "While most readers of _____ have said _____, a close and careful reading shows that _____." The writer of the second paper on jazz is using a standard opening gambit, even if it is not announced with flourish. The essay becomes possible when he sets himself against what must become a "naive" assumption — what "most people think." He has defined a closed circle for himself. In fact, you could say that he has laid the groundwork for a discipline with its own key terms ("practical knowledge," "disciplinary guidelines," and "original ideas"), with its own agenda and with its own investigative procedures (looking for common features in the work of individual soloists).

The history represented by this student's essay, then, is not the history of a musician and it is not the history of a thought being worked out within an individual mind; it is the history of work being done within and against conventional systems.

In general, as I reviewed the essays for this study, I found that the more successful writers set themselves in their essays against what they defined as some more naive way of talking about their subject — against "those who think that . . ." — or against earlier, more naive versions of themselves — "once I thought that. . . ." By trading in one set of commonplaces at the expense of another, they could win themselves status as members of what is taken to be some more privileged group. The ability to imagine privilege enabled writing. Here is one particularly successful essay. Notice the specialized vocabulary, but notice also the way in which the text continually refers to its own language and to the language of others.

> Throughout my life, I have been interested and intrigued by music. My mother has often told me of the times, before I went to school, when I would "conduct" the orchestra on her records. I continued to listen to music and eventually started to play the guitar and the clarinet. Finally, at about the age of twelve, I started to sit down and to try to write songs. Even though my instrumental skills were far from my own high standards, I would spend much of my spare time during the day with a guitar around my neck, trying to produce a piece of music.
>
> Each of these sessions, as I remember them, had a rather set format. I would sit in my bedroom, strumming different combinations of the five or six chords I could play, until I heard a series of which sounded particularly good to me. After this, I set the music to a suitable rhythm, (usually dependent on my mood at the time), and ran through the tune until I could play it fairly easily. Only after this section was complete did I go on to writing lyrics, which generally followed along the lines of the current popular songs on the radio.
>
> At the time of the writing, I felt that my songs were, in themselves, an original creation of my own; that is, I, alone, made them. However, I now see that, in this sense of the word, I was not creative. The songs themselves seem to be an oversimplified form of the music I listened to at the time.
>
> In a more fitting sense, however, I *was* being creative. Since I did not purposely copy my favorite songs, I was, effectively, originating my songs from my own "process of creativity." To achieve my goal, I needed what a composer would call "inspiration" for my piece. In this case the inspiration was the current hit on the radio. Perhaps, with my present point of view, I feel that I used too much "inspiration" in my songs, but, at that time, I did not.
>
> Creativity, therefore, is a process which, in my case, involved a certain series of "small creations" if you like. As well, it is something, the appreciation of which varies with one's point of view, that point of view being set by the person's experience, tastes, and his own personal view of creativity. The less experienced tend to allow for less originality, while

the more experienced demand real originality to classify something a "creation." Either way, a term as abstract as this is perfectly correct, and open to interpretation.

This writer is consistently and dramatically conscious of herself forming something to say out of what has been said *and* out of what she has been saying in the act of writing this paper. "Creativity" begins in this paper as "original creation." What she thought was "creativity," however, she now says was imitation; and, as she says, "in this sense of the word" she was not "creative." In another sense, however, she says that she *was* creative, since she didn't purposefully copy the songs but used them as "inspiration."

While the elaborate stylistic display — the pauses, qualifications, and the use of quotation marks — is in part a performance for our benefit, at a more obvious level we as readers are directly addressed in the first sentence of the last paragraph: "Creativity, therefore, is a process which, in my case, involved a certain series of 'small creations' if you like." We are addressed here as adults who can share her perspective on what she has said and who can be expected to understand her terms. If she gets into trouble after this sentence, and I think she does, it is because she doesn't have the courage to generalize from her assertion. Since she has rhetorically separated herself from her younger "self," and since she argues that she has gotten smarter, she assumes that there is some developmental sequence at work here and that, in the world of adults (which must be more complete than the world of children) there must be something like "real creativity." If her world is imperfect (if she can only talk about creation by putting the word in quotation marks), it must be because she is young. When she looks beyond herself to us, she cannot see our work as an extension of her project. She cannot assume that we too will be concerned with the problem of creativity and originality. At least she is not willing to challenge us on those grounds, to generalize her argument, and to argue that even for adults creations are really only "small creations." The sense of privilege that has allowed her to expose her own language cannot be extended to expose ours.

The writing in this piece — that is, the work of the writer within the essay — goes on in spite of, or against, the language that keeps pressing to give another name to her experience as a songwriter and to bring the discussion to closure. (In comparison, think of the quick closure of the "White Shoes" paper.) Its style is difficult, highly qualified. It relies on quotation marks and parody to set off the language and attitudes that belong to the discourse (or the discourses) that it would reject, that it would not take as its own proper location.

David Olson (1981) has argued that the key difference between oral language and written language is that written language separates both the producer and the receiver from the text. For my student writers, this means that they had to learn that what they said (the code) was more important than what they meant (the intention). A writer, in other words, loses his primacy at the moment of writing and must begin to attend to his and his words' conventional, even physical presence on the page. And, Olson says, the writer must learn that his authority is not established through his presence but through his absence — through his ability, that is, to speak as a god-like source beyond the limitations of any particular social or historical moment; to speak by means of the wisdom of convention, through the oversounds of official or authoritative utterance, as the voice of logic or the voice of the community. He concludes:

> The child's growing competence with this distinctive register of language in which both the meaning and the authority are displaced from the intentions of the speaker and lodged "in the text" may contribute to the similarly specialized and distinctive mode of thought we have come to associate with literacy and formal education. (1981, p. 110)

Olson is writing about children. His generalizations, I think I've shown, can be extended to students writing their way into the academic community. These are educated and literate individuals, to be sure, but they are individuals still outside the peculiar boundaries of the academic community. In the papers I've examined in this chapter, the writers have shown an increasing awareness of the codes (or the competing codes) that operate within a discourse. To speak with authority they have to speak not only in another's voice but through another's code; and they not only have to do this, they have to speak in the voice and through the codes of those of us with power and wisdom; and they not only have to do this, they have to do it before they know what they are doing, before they have a project to participate in, and before, at least in terms of our disciplines, they have anything to say. Our students may be able to enter into a conventional discourse and speak, not as themselves, but through the voice of the community; the university, however, is the place where "common" wisdom is only of negative values — it is something to work against. The movement toward a more specialized discourse begins (or, perhaps, best begins) both when a student can define a position of privilege, a position that sets him against a "common" discourse, and when he or she can work self-consciously, critically, against not only the "common" code but his or her own.

IV

Pat Bizzell, you will recall, argues that the problems of poor writers can be attributed both to their unfamiliarity with the conventions of academic discourse and to their ignorance that there are such things as discourse communities with conventions to be mastered. If the latter is true, I think it is true only in rare cases. All the student writers I've discussed (and, in fact, most of the student writers whose work I've seen) have shown an awareness that something special or something different is required when one writes for an academic classroom. The essays that I have presented in this chapter all, I think, give evidence of writers trying to write their way into a new community.

To some degree, however, all of them can be said to be unfamiliar with the conventions of academic discourse.

Problems of convention are both problems of finish and problems of substance. The most substantial academic tasks for students, learning history or sociology or literary criticism, are matters of many courses, much reading and writing, and several years of education. Our students, however, must have a place to begin. They cannot sit through lectures and read textbooks and, as a consequence, write as sociologists or write literary criticism. There must be steps along the way. Some of these steps will be marked by drafts and revisions. Some will be marked by courses, and in an ideal curriculum the preliminary courses would be writing courses, whether housed in an English department or not. For some students, students we call "basic writers," these courses will be in a sense the most basic introduction to the language and methods of academic writing.

Our students, as I've said, must have a place to begin. If the problem of a beginning is the problem of establishing authority, of defining rhetorically or stylistically a position from which one may speak, then the papers I have examined show characteristic student responses to that problem and show levels of approximation or stages in the development of writers who are writing their way into a position of privilege.

As I look over the papers I've discussed, I would arrange them in the following order: the "White Shoes" paper; the first "Jazz" essay; the "Clay Model" paper; the second "Jazz" essay; and, as the most successful paper, the essay on "Composing Songs." The more advanced essay for me, then, are those that are set against the "naive" codes of "everyday" life. (I put the terms "naive" and "everyday" in quotation marks because they are, of course, arbitrary terms.) In the advanced essays one can see a writer claiming an "inside" position of privilege by rejecting the language and commonplaces of a "naive" discourse, the language of "outsiders." The "I" of those essays locates itself against one discourse (what it claims to be a naive discourse) and approximates the specialized language of what is presumed to be a more powerful and more privileged community. There are two gestures present, then — one imitative and one critical. The writer continually audits and pushes against a language that would render him "like everyone else" and mimics the language and interpretive systems of the privileged community.

At a first level, then, a student might establish his authority by simply stating his own presence within the field of a subject. A student, for example, writes about creativity by telling a story about a time he went skiing. Nothing more. The "I" on the page is a skier, and skiing stands as a representation of a creative act. Neither the skier nor skiing are available for interpretation; they cannot be located in an essay that is not a narrative essay (where skiing might serve metaphorically as an example of, say, a sport where set movements also allow for a personal style). Or a student, as did the one who wrote the "White Shoes" paper, locates a narrative in an unconnected rehearsal of commonplaces about creativity. In both cases, the writers have finessed the requirement to set themselves against the available utterances of the world outside the closed world of the academy. And, again, in the first "Jazz" paper, we have the example of a writer who locates himself within an available commonplace and carries out only rudimentary procedures for elaboration, procedures driven by the commonplace itself and not set against it. Elaboration, in this latter case, is not the opening up of a system but a justification of it.

At a next level I would place student writers who establish their authority by mimicking the rhythm and texture, the "sound," of academic prose, without there being any recognizable interpretive or academic project under way. I'm thinking, here, of the "Clay Model" essay. At an advanced stage, I would place students who establish their authority as *writers*; they claim their authority, not by simply claiming that they are skiers or that they have done something creative, but by placing themselves both within and against a discourse, or within and against competing discourses, and working self-consciously to claim an interpretive project of their own, one that grants them their privilege to speak. This is true, I think, in the case of the second "Jazz" paper and, to a greater degree, in the case of the "Composing Songs" paper.

The levels of development that I've suggested are not marked by corresponding levels in the type or frequency of error, at least not by the type or frequency of sentence-level error. I am arguing, then, that a basic writer is not necessarily a writer who makes a lot of mistakes. In fact, one of the problems with curricula designed to aid basic writers is that they too often begin with the assumption that the key distinguishing feature of a basic writer is the presence of sentence-level error. Students are placed in courses because their placement essays show a high frequency of such errors, and those courses are designed with the goal of making those errors go away. This approach to the problems of the basic writer ignores the degree to which error is less often a constant feature than a marker in the development of a writer. A student who can write a reasonably correct narrative may fall to pieces when faced with a more unfamiliar assignment. More important, however, such courses fail to serve the rest of the curriculum. On every campus there is a significant number of college freshmen who require a course to introduce them to the kinds of writing that are required for a university education. Some of these students can write correct sentences and some cannot; but, as a group, they lack the facility other freshmen possess when they are faced with an academic writing task.

The "White Shoes" essay, for example, shows fewer sentence-level errors than the "Clay Model" paper. This may well be due to the fact that the writer of the "White Shoes" paper stayed well within safe, familiar territory. He kept himself out of trouble by doing what he could easily do. The tortuous syntax of the more advanced papers on my list is a syntax that represents a writer's struggle with a difficult and unfamiliar language, and it is a syntax that can quickly lead an inexperienced writer into trouble. The syntax and punctuation of the "Composing Songs" essay, for example, shows the effort that is required when a writer works against the pressure of conventional discourse. If the prose is inelegant (although I confess I admire those dense sentences) it is still correct. This writer has a command of the linguistic and stylistic resources — the highly embedded sentences, the use of parentheses and quotation marks — required to complete the act of writing. It is easy to imagine the possible pitfalls for a writer working without this facility.

There was no camera trained on the "Clay Model" writer while he was writing, and I have no protocol of what was going through his mind, but it is possible to speculate on the syntactic difficulties of sentences like these: "In the past time I thought that an incident was creative was when I had to make a clay model of the earth, but not of the classical or your everyday model of the earth which consists of the two cores, the mantle and the crust. I thought of these things in a dimension of which it would be unique, but easy to comprehend." The syntactic difficulties appear to be the result of the writer's attempt to use an unusual vocabulary and to extend his sentences beyond the boundaries of what would have been "normal" in his speech or writing. There is reason to believe, that is, that the problem was with *this* kind of sentence, in this context. If the problem of the last sentence is that of holding together the units "I thought," "dimension," "unique" and "easy to comprehend," then the linquistic problem was not a simple matter of sentence construction. I am arguing, then, that such sentences fall apart not because the writer lacked the necessary syntax to glue the pieces together but because he lacked the full statement within which these key words were already operating. While writing, and in the thrust of his need to complete the sentence, he had the key words but not the utterance. (And to recover the utterance, I suspect, he would need to do more than revise the sentence.) The invisible conventions, the prepared phrases remained too distant for the statement to be completed. The writer would have needed to get inside of a discourse that he could in fact only partially imagine. The act of constructing a sentence, then, became something like an act of transcription in which the voice on the tape unexpectedly faded away and became inaudible.

Shaughnessy (1977) speaks of the advanced writer as one who often has a more facile but still incomplete possession of this prior discourse. In the case of the advanced writer, the evidence of a problem is the presence of dissonant, redundant, or imprecise language, as in a sentence such as this: "No education can be *total*, it must be *continuous*." Such a student, Shaughnessy says, could be said to hear the "melody of formal English" while still unable to make precise or exact distinctions. And, she says,

> the pre-packaging feature of language, the possibility of taking over phrases and whole sentences without much thought about them, threatens the writer now as before. The writer, as we have said, inherits the language out of which he must fabricate his own messages. He is therefore in a constant tangle with the language, obliged to recognize its public, communal nature and yet driven to invent out of this language his own statements. (1977, pp. 207–08)

For the unskilled writer, the problem is different in degree and not in kind. The inexperienced writer is left with a more fragmentary record of the comings and goings of academic discourse. Or, as I said above, he or she often has the key words without the complete statements within which they are already operating.

Let me provide one final example of this kind of syntactic difficulty in another piece of student writing. The writer of this paper seems to be able to sustain a discussion only by continually repeating his first step, producing a litany of strong, general, authoritative assertions that trail quickly into confusion. Notice how the writer seems to stabilize his movement through the paper by returning again and again to recognizable and available commonplace utterances. When he has to move away from them, however, away from the familiar to statements that would extend those utterances, where he, too, must speak, the writing — that is, both the syntax and the structure of the discourse — falls to pieces.

> Many times the times drives a person's life depends on how he uses it. I would like to think about if time is twenty-five hours a day rather than twenty-four hours. Some people think it's the boaring or some people might say it's the pleasure to take one more hour for their life. But I think the time is passing and coming, still we are standing on same position. We should use time as best as we can use about the good way in our life. Everything we do, such as sleep, eat, study, play and doing something for ourselves. These take the time to do and we could find the individual ability and may process own. It is the important for us and our society. As time going on the world changes therefor we are changing, too. When these situation changes we should follow the suitable case of own. But many times we should decide what's the better way to do so by using time. Sometimes like this kind of situation can cause the success of our lives or ruin. I think every individual of his own thought drive how to use time. These affect are done from environmental causes. So we should work on the better way of our life recognizing the importance of time.

There is a general pattern of disintegration when the writer moves off from standard phrases. This sentence, for example, starts out coherently and then falls apart: "*We should use time as best as we can* use about the good way in our life." The difficulty seems to be one of extending those standard phrases or of connecting them to the main subject reference, "time" (or "the time," a construction that causes many of the problems in the paper). Here is an example of a sentence that shows, in miniature, this problem of connection: "*I think every individual* of his own thought drive how to use *time.*"

One of the remarkable things about this paper is that, in spite of all the syntactic confusion, there is the hint of an academic project here. The writer sets out to discuss how to creatively use one's time. The text seems to allude to examples and to stages in an argument, even if in the end it is all pretty incoherent. The gestures of academic authority, however, are clearly present, and present in a form that echoes the procedures in other, more successful papers. The writer sets himself against what "some people think"; he speaks with the air of authority: "But I think. . . . Everything we do. . . . When these situation changes. . . ." And he speaks as though there were a project underway, one where he proposes what he thinks, turns to evidence, and offers a conclusion: "These affect are done from environmental causes. So we should work. . . ." This is the case of a student with the ability to imagine the general outline and rhythm of academic prose but without the ability to carry it out, to complete the sentences. And when he gets lost in the new, in the unknown, in the responsibility of his own commitment to speak, he returns again to the familiar ground of the commonplace.

The challenge to researchers, it seems to me, is to turn their attention again to products, to student writing, since the drama in a student's essay, as he or she struggles with and against the languages of our contemporary life, is as intense and telling as the drama of an essay's mental preparation or physical production. A written text, too, can be a compelling model of the "composing process" once we conceive of a writer as at work within a text and simultaneously, then within a society, a history, and a culture.

It may very well be that some students will need to learn to crudely mimic the "distinctive register" of academic discourse before they are prepared to actually and legitimately do the work of the discourse, and before they are sophisticated enough with the refinements of tone and gesture to do it with grace or elegance. To say this, however, is to say that our students must be our students. Their initial progress will be marked by their abilities to take on the role of privilege, by their abilities to establish authority. From this point of view, the student who wrote about constructing the clay model of the earth is better prepared for his education than the student who wrote about playing football in white shoes, even though the "White Shoes" paper is relatively error-free and the "Clay Model" paper is not. It will be hard to pry loose the writer of the "White Shoes" paper from the tidy, pat discourse that allows him to dispose of the question of creativity in such a quick and efficient manner. He will have to be convinced that it is better to write sentences he might not so easily control, and he will have to be convinced that it is better to write muddier and more confusing prose (in order that it may sound like ours), and this will be harder than convincing the "Clay Model" writer to continue what he has already begun.

ACKNOWLEDGMENTS

Preparation of this chapter was supported by the Learning Research and Development Center of the University of Pittsburgh, which is supported in part by the National Institute of Education.

NOTES

1. David Olson (1981) has made a similar observation about school-related problems of language learning in younger children. Here is his conclusion: "Hence, depending upon whether children assumed language was primarily suitable for making assertions and conjectures or primarily for making direct or indirect commands, they will either find school texts easy or difficult" (p. 107).

2. For Aristotle, there were both general and specific commonplaces. A speaker, says Aristotle, has a "stock of arguments to which he may turn for a particular need."

If he knows the *topoi* (regions, places, lines or argument) — and a skilled speaker will know them — he will know where to find what he wants for a special case. The general topics, or *common*places, are regions containing arguments that are common to all branches of knowledge. . . . But there are also special topics (regions, places, *loci*) in which one looks for arguments appertaining to particular branches of knowledge, special sciences, such as ethics or politics. (1932, pp. 154–55)

And, he says, "the topics or places, then, may be indifferently thought of as in the science that is concerned, or in the mind of the speaker." But the question of location is "indifferent" *only* if the mind of the speaker is in line with set opinion, general assumption. For the speaker (or writer) who is not situated so comfortably in the privileged public realm, this is indeed not an indifferent matter at all. If he does not have the commonplace at hand, he will not, in Aristotle's terms, know where to go at all.

3. Pat Bizzell has argued that the *Seventeen* writer's process of goal-setting

can be better understood if we see it in terms of writing for a discourse community. His initial problem . . . is to find a way to include these readers in a discourse community for which he is comfortable writing. He places them in the academic discourse community by imagining the girls as students. . . . Once he has included them in a familiar discourse community, he can find a way to address them that is common in the community: he will argue with them, puttting a new interpretation on information they possess in order to correct misconceptions. (1982a, p. 228)

4. See Bartholomae (1979, 1983) and Rose (1983) for articles on curricula designed to move students into university discourse. The movement to extend writing "across the curriculum" is evidence of a general concern for locating students within the work of the university; see Bizzell (1982a) and Maimon *et al.* (1981). For longer works directed specifically at basic writing, see Ponsot and Deen (1982) and Shaughnessy (1977). For a book describing a course for more advanced students, see Coles (1978).

5. In spite of my misgivings about Bereiter and Scardamalia's interpretation of the cognitive nature of the problem of "inert knowledge," this is an essay I regularly recommend to teachers. It has much to say about the dangers of what seem to be "neutral" forms of classroom discourse and provides, in its final section, a set of recommendations on how a teacher might undo discourse conventions that have become part of the institution of teaching.

6. Stanley Fish (1980) argues that the basis for distinguishing novice from expert readings is the persuasiveness of the discourse used to present and defend a given reading. In particular, see the chapter, "Demonstration vs. Persuasion: Two Models of Critical Activity" (pp. 356–73).

7. Some students, when they come to the university, can do this better than others. When Jonathan Culler says, "the possibility of bringing someone to see that a particular interpretation is a good one assumes shared points of departure and common notions of how to read," he is acknowledging that teaching, at least in English classes, has had to assume that students, to be students, were already to some degree participating in the structures of reading and writing that constitute English studies (quoted in Fish, 1980, p. 366).

Stanley Fish tells us "not to worry" that students will violate our enterprise by offering idiosyncratic readings of standard texts:

The fear of solipsism, of the imposition by the unconstrained self of its own prejudices, is unfounded because the self does not exist apart from the communal or conventional categories of thought that enable its operations (of thinking, seeing, reading). Once we realize that the conceptions that fill consciousness, including any conception of its own status, are culturally derived, the very notion of an unconstrained self, of a consciousness wholly and dangerously free, becomes incomprehensible. (1980, p. 335)

He, too, is assuming that students, to be students (and not "dangerously free"), must be members in good standing of the community whose immediate head is the English teacher. It is interesting that his parenthetical catalogue of the "operations" of thought, "thinking, seeing, reading," excludes writing, since it is only through written records that we have any real indication of how a student thinks, sees, and reads. (Perhaps "real" is an inappropriate word to use here, since there is certainly a "real" intellectual life that goes on, independent of writing. Let me say that thinking, seeing, and reading are valued in the academic community *only* as they are represented by extended, elaborated written records.) Writing, I presume, is a given for Fish. It is the card of entry into this closed community that constrains and excludes dangerous characters. Students who are excluded from this community are students who do poorly on written placement exams or in freshman composition. They do not, that is, move easily into the privileged discourse of the community, represented by the English literature class.

8. My debt to Bizzell's work should be evident everywhere in this essay. See also Bizzell (1978, 1982b) and Bizzell and Herzberg (1980).

9. Fish says the following about the relationship between student and an object under study:

we are not to imagine a moment when my students "simply see" a physical configuration of atoms and *then* assign that configuration a significance, according to the situation they happen to be in. To be in the situation (this or any other) is to "see" with the eyes of its interests, its goals, its understood practices, values, and norms, and so to be conferring significance *by* seeing, not after it. The categories of my students' vision are the categories by which they understand themselves to be functioning as students . . . and objects will appear to them in forms related to that way of functioning rather than in some objective or preinterpretive form. (1980, p. 334)

10. I am aware that the papers given the highest rankings offer arguments about creativity and originality similar to my own. If there is a conspiracy here, that is one of the points of my chapter. I should add that my reading of the "content" of basic writers' essays is quite different from Lunsford's (1980).

REFERENCES

Aristotle. (1932). *The Rhetoric of Aristotle* (L. Cooper, Trans.). Englewood Cliffs, NJ: Prentice-Hall.

Barthes, R. (1974). *S/Z* (R. Howard, Trans.). New York: Hill & Wang.

Bartholomae, D. (1979). Teaching basic writing: An alternative to basic skills. *Journal of Basic Writing, 2,* 85–109.

———. (1983). Writing assignments: Where writing begins. In P. Stock (Ed.), *Forum* (pp. 300–12). Montclair, NJ: Boynton/Cook.

Bereiter, C., & Scardamalia, M. (1985). Cognitive coping strategies and the problem of "inert knowledge." In S. S. Chipman, J. W. Segal, & R. Glaser (Eds.), *Thinking and learning skills: Research and open questions* (Vol. 2). Hillsdale, NJ: Erlbaum.

Bizzell, P. (1978). The ethos of academic discourse. *College Composition and Communication, 29,* 351–55.

———. (1982a). Cognition, convention, and certainty: What we need to know about writing. *Pre/text, 3,* 213–44.

———. (1982b). College composition: Initiation into the academic discourse community. *Curriculum Inquiry, 12,* 191, 207.

Bizzell, P., & Herzberg, B. (1980). "Inherent" ideology, "universal" history, "empirical" evidence, and "context-free" writing: Some problems with E. D. Hirsch's *The Philosophy of Composition. Modern Language Notes, 95,* 1181–1202.

Coles, W. E., Jr. (1978). *The plural I.* New York: Holt, Rinehart & Winston.

Fish, S. (1980). *Is there a text in this class? The authority of interpretive communities.* Cambridge, MA: Harvard University Press.

Flower, L. S. (1981). Revising writer-based prose. *Journal of Basic Writing, 3,* 62–74.

Flower, L., & Hayes, J. (1981). A cognitive process theory of writing. *College Composition and Communication, 32,* 365–87.

Hairston, M. (1978). *A contemporary rhetoric.* Boston: Houghton Mifflin.

Lunsford, A. A. (1980). The content of basic writers' essays. *College Composition and Communication, 31,* 278–90.

Maimon, E. P., Belcher, G. L., Hearn, G. W., Nodine, B. F., & O'Connor, F. X. (1981). *Writing in the arts and sciences.* Cambridge, MA: Winthrop.

Olson, D. R. (1981). Writing: The divorce of the author from the text. In B. M. Kroll & R. J. Vann (Eds.), *Exploring speaking – writing relationships: Connections and contrasts.* Urbana, IL: National Council of Teachers of English.

Perkins, D. N. (1985). General cognitive skills: Why not? In S. S. Chipman, J. W. Segal, & R. Glaser (Eds.), *Thinking and learning skills: Research and open questions* (Vol. 2). Hillsdale, NJ: Erlbaum.

Ponsot, M., & Deen, R. (1982). *Beat not the poor desk.* Montclair, NJ: Boynton/Cook.

Rodriquez, R. (1983) *Hunger of Memory.* New York: Bantam.

Rose, M. (1983). Remedial writing courses: A critique and a proposal. *College English, 45,* 109–28.

Said, E. W. (1975) *Beginnings: Intention and method.* Baltimore: The Johns Hopkins University Press.

Shaughnessy, M. (1977). *Errors and expectations.* New York: Oxford University Press.

Wanderings: Misreadings, Miswritings, Misunderstandings

T o read is to play the role of a reader and to interpret is to posit an experience of reading. This is something that beginning literature students know quite well but have forgotten by the time they get to graduate school and begin teaching literature. When student papers refer to what "the reader feels here" or what "the reader then understands," teachers often take this as a spurious objectivity, a disguised form of "I feel" or "I understand," and urge their charges either to be honest or to omit such references. But students know better than their teachers here. They know it is not a matter of honesty. They have understood that to read and interpret literary works is precisely to imagine what "a reader" would feel and understand. To read is to operate with the hypothesis of a reader, and there is always a gap or division within reading.

— JONATHAN CULLER

But learning is not, of course, merely a matter of learning about, nor is it simply a process whereby a student becomes assimilated into his culture. It is primarily the action whereby a student learns who he is in relation to something outside himself.

— ROGER SALE

I

Let me begin with an anecdote, a cautionary tale. I walk into my class, an entry-level reading and writing class, and begin with what has become a standard exercise by turning to a book I have assigned, in this case Richard Rodriguez's *Hunger of Memory*. This is a very teachable book — well-suited, in its way, for a composition class. Rodriguez becomes himself a metaphor through which my

From *Only Connect: Uniting Reading and Writing*, ed. Thomas Newkirk (Montclair: Boynton/Cook, 1986) 89–119.

students can organize and think about their own experience with education, moving from one world to another, finding in the contradictions of his experience a way of talking about, of inventing even, the contradictions in their own.[1] It's a teachable book also, however, because Rodriguez's prose resists quick summation or any easy reduction to a "main idea." It requires application, extension, interpretation — not just summary. It has the grace to ask more of a reader — that is, than assent or affirmation. There is more for a reader to do than admire the author's wit and wisdom. It doesn't propose answers to all the questions it raises. It poses problems that the author has not already solved. It's a hesitant, tentative, contradictory text and, as such, it posits a role for a reader or writer that my students would not (or could not) imagine on their own.

I walk into my class, ask my students to turn to a passage I've chosen the night before, and I read it to them aloud. It's a difficult passage because it pushes against the available language of daily life — it talks about a moment when Rodriguez read Hoggart's *The Uses of Literacy*, cites a passage from that book, and talks about how that reading (Rodriguez's reading of Hoggart) gave a "shape to desire." I read the passage aloud and ask my students, "What does this say?" Not, "What does this mean?" but "What does this say?" And there is silence. I wait, as I have learned to do, since this is not a silence, I think, that a teacher should fill, not if he wants to teach composition. I wait until I pick one student from the class: "Kevin, what does this say?" And again there is silence. Although this time the student is looking at the passage, reading it over and over to himself, as if waiting for it to speak. I wait again until Kevin is forced to speak himself for the passage, and he says what he can, beginning first, however, by reading part of the passage verbatim out loud, reading back to me what I have already read to him.

I'm interested in this silence and what it can be said to represent, and I'm interested in the moment when a student breaks that silence to speak. Gadamer, in *Philosophical Hermeneutics*, said that

> The understanding of a text has not begun as long as the text remains mute. But a text can begin to speak. (We are not discussing here the conditions that must be given for this actually to occur.) When it does begin to speak, however, it does not simply speak its word, always the same, in lifeless rigidity, but gives ever new answers to the person who questions it and poses ever new questions to him who answers it. To understand a text is to come to understand oneself in a kind of dialogue. This contention is confirmed by the fact that the concrete dealing with a text yields understanding only when what is said in the text begins to find expression in the interpreter's own language. Interpretation belongs to the essential unity of understanding. One must take up into himself what is said to him in such a fashion that it speaks and finds an answer in the words of his own language.[2]

To read this passage as I would read it (and as I present it to begin a discussion of the conditions that must be given for understanding to occur), you have to take the "answer" in the last sentence — that answer a student finds in the words of his own language — as the answer in a dialogue (where someone speaks and another "answers") and not as the "answer" to a question or a problem, the answer to a question like, "What does this passage mean?" Understanding, then, is not an act of recognition but something that is initiated by a response and justified by the elaboration or extension of that response.

The textbooks say, "Find the author's main idea, look to see how he supports it, look for transitions, look up the difficult words." But this advice has little bearing on Kevin's problem. Kevin, I think, felt more like a trespasser than a trailblazer, so it isn't much use to tell him to think of reading as an organized search in difficult terrain. The "real event of understanding," to return to Gadamer's words, "goes beyond . . . methodical effort and critical self-control." It isn't really we ourselves who understand, he says, "it is always a past that allows us to say, 'I have understood.' " The real event of understanding, in other words, is the effort to justify or account for (and usually by speaking or writing) a position we have taken by speaking over or against the words of an author who gave us our beginning. Kevin's problem, in a sense, comes when he must put that passage aside and speak in turn, not when he looks at it and reviews the words on the page. At the end of his silence, Kevin says to me in class:

> It's like when Rodriguez knew that he was like a scholarship boy, like Hoggart says he was, reading all those books and doing good in school to please his teachers and not for himself. And he thinks Hoggart is wrong because it was more than that but when he thinks about himself as a scholarship boy he gets that part of himself fenced in. Hoggart is right but Rodriguez has to figure out how he's wrong.

And it is my job, then, to resist any desire I might have to say, "Yes, that's right," or "No, that's not it," and to answer only with one of the classroom versions of "So what?": "So why is this interesting?" "So what does this have to do with the 'shape of desire'?" "Why 'fenced in'?" "What can you make of the fact that you say Hoggart was both right and wrong for Rodriguez?" "So what can you say, then, about *Hunger of Memory* or about education or about teachers or about Rodriguez's relations with his parents or about Rodriguez as a reader?"

My role as a teacher, in other words, is to insist that the student re-imagine a past that will allow him to say, "I have understood." Gadamer says that this experience of reading is felt as enrichment and not as a loss of self-possession. I'm not so sure. Even if we both respect it, I think Kevin and I are aware of the violence in what we have done.

II

One must take up into himself what is said to him in such a fashion that it speaks. I want to insist in my paper that the act of interpretation begins in that first act of speaking — speaking for a text — and that the problems of interpretation can be represented by the problems represented in that initial act of aggression and translation, the moment when a student breaks the silence and gives priority to his words over the words spoken by another, in this case Richard Rodriguez, a man who speaks very well, who has written a book, a book that was assigned in a class, a book whose priority, whose right to speak, has been well established. To speak, then, my student Kevin had to do what by rights he knew he shouldn't do; he had to assume an authority that wasn't his — at least not yet.

The silence, then, could be said to be an act of respect, not a failure of understanding or an inability to comprehend, but a clear and subtle understanding of a difficult and problematic situation. For my student to speak, he would have to replace or displace the language of the text with his own language. His first response was to give the text back to me verbatim — in other words, to give me a *literal* reading (and this is the only way I can understand the concept of a literal reading, as a literal re-speaking of the words on the page — any other act of speech would be an interpretation, a recomposition of what Rodriguez had to say about Hoggart and the "shape of desire"). And if he could not give me back the words he was hesitant to displace, what could he give me? The silence, I suspect, was an attempt to find that language as well, a language that was not immediately available to him. Gadamer would say that this language was his, but I think it is more likely mine or his freshman's version of my language, or the language of the institution I represent, the sanctioned, official discourse that speaks through me, try as I might to displace it when I speak for Rodriguez. That is the language Kevin could not find ready-made, although he showed that he could appropriate a version of it, an approximation. And that was what I was insisting on when I waited and wouldn't let the class progress until he spoke. When he spoke he offered what he could — a misreading. The version of Rodriguez he offered was not what Rodriguez wrote, just as his version of my language for Rodriguez was not what I would have said.

Interpretation thus begins with an act of aggression, a displacement, an attempt to speak before one is authorized to speak, and it begins with a misreading — a recomposition of a text that can never be the text itself speaking. If you accept this scenario, then the problems for a student reader are considerable — and they are not, or at least not solely, cognitive. I am presenting reading and writing as a struggle within the languages of our contemporary life. A classroom performance represents a moment in which, by speaking or writing, a student must enter into a closed community, with its secrets, codes and rituals, and the drama of this is as intense and telling as the drama of a student's internal cognitive processes. The student has to appropriate or be appropriated by a specialized discourse, and he has to do this as though he were easily and comfortably one with his audience, as though he were a member of the academy and, of course, he is not. He has to invent himself as a reader and he has to invent an act of reading, by assembling a language to make a reader and a reading possible, finding some compromise between idiosyncracy, a personal history, and the requirements of convention, the history of an institution. George Steiner said,

> Through language, so much of which is focused inward to our private selves, we reject the empirical inevitability of the world. Through

language, we construct what I have called "alternities of being." To the extent that every individual speaker uses an idiolect, the problem of Babel is, quite simply, that of human individuation. But different tongues give to the mechanism of "alternity" a dynamic, transferable enactment. They realize a need of privacy and territoriality vital to our identity. To a greater or lesser degree, every language offers its own reading of life. To move between languages, to translate . . . is to experience the almost bewildering bias of the human spirit towards freedom.[3]

While I want Steiner to speak for me here, I would have to put freedom in brackets in that last sentence, since it could be argued, and I think in the same spirit of hope, that the experience of translation is the experience of the "bewildering bias of the human spirit" towards captivity. A translation is also a loss, a displacement of the original, a definition of oneself in terms of another or in another's terms. Or, as Culler said in the passage from *On Deconstruction* that stands at the head of this essay, "To read is to operate with the hypothesis of a reader, and there is always a gap or division within reading."[4]

I'll turn soon to some essays students have written in response to *Hunger of Memory* and Plato's *Phaedrus*. All of these will be essays from the beginning of a semester. My goal, that is, will be to look over the terrain and not to defend a curriculum or to celebrate its heroes.[5] I'll be arguing that these essays, as they represent readings, are neither right or wrong but approximate. They are, that is, evidence of a discourse that lies between what I might call the students' primary discourse (what they might write about *Hunger of Memory* were they not in my class, or any class, or were they not imagining that they were in my class, or any class — if you can imagine any student doing any such thing) and the language of the official, English class essay (which is imaginable but impossible to find). The students' essays are evidence of a discourse that lies between these two hypothetical poles. The writing is limited as much by the students' ability to imagine "what might be said" as it is by a lack of information or anything that could be identified solely as a "reading" problem. The act of writing takes students from where they are and allows them to imagine something and somewhere else. The approximate discourse, then, is evidence of change, a change that, because we are teachers, we call "development" or "growth." I wouldn't want to suggest that it is progress toward Truth or Reason or a clearer mind.

The systems we produce, teachers as well as students, are all always approximate. I never say, alas, what I would hope to say — or to put it another way, everything I write suggests its own possibilities for revision. Nor can I say at any point with precision what belongs to me and what belongs to my branch of the profession — or to put *this* another way, the use of quotation marks and the placement of footnotes is arbitrary. I know, because I know the rhetoric, what I can offer as mine and what I must attribute to someone else or place in some context other than my own sentence, but these lines of demarcation are part of the fiction of scholarship and the rules that govern these decisions are mysterious and unspoken, which is why beginning students have such a terrible problem with citation, quotation, and paraphrase. One way of describing our students' need is to say that they are people who need to learn to extend themselves, by successive approximation, into the commonplaces, set phrases, rituals and gestures, habits of mind, tricks of persuasion, obligatory conclusions and necessary connections that determine "what might be said" and constitute knowledge within the various branches of our academic community. This, at least, would make them citizens in good standing.

Some students can take their place with little pushing and shoving. When Jonathan Culler says, "the possibility of bringing someone to see that a particular interpretation is a good one assumes shared points of departure and common notions of how to read," he is acknowledging that teaching has had to assume that students, to be students, were already to some degree participating in the structures of reading and writing that constitute (here) English Studies.[6] Stanley Fish tells us "not to worry" that students will violate our enterprise by offering idiosyncratic readings of standard texts:

> The fear of solipsism, of the imposition by the unconstrained self of its own prejudices, is unfounded because the self does not exist apart from the communal or conventional categories of thought that enable its operations (of thinking, seeing, reading). Once we realize that the conceptions that fill consciousness, including any conception of its own status, are culturally derived, the very notion of an unconstrained self, or a consciousness wholly and dangerously free, becomes incomprehensible.[7]

He, too, is assuming that students, to be students (and not "dangerously free") must be members in good standing of the community whose immediate head is the English teacher. It is interesting that his parenthetical catalogue of the "operations" of thought ("thinking, seeing, reading") excludes writing, since it is only through written records that we have any real indication of how a student thinks, sees and reads. Perhaps "real" is an inappropriate word to use here, since there is certainly a "real" intellectual life that goes on independent of writing. Let me say that thinking, seeing, and reading are valued in the academic community only as they are represented by extended, elaborate written records. (Class participation, in other words, will get you little more than a plus or a minus.)

Writing, I presume, is a given for Fish. It is the card of entry into the closed community that constrains and excludes dangerous characters. The real danger, of course, is not to the English profession but to its students, those whose "communal or conventional" habits of thought threaten to keep them on the outside, somewhere in the borderland between home and school. We can improve education if we put our critical skills to the test and learn to pay attention to those acts of reading and writing that are neither here nor there.

Let me return, for the last time, to my opening anecdote. I have another way of accounting for Kevin's silence — this time to say that it represents shame. Kevin, like all of my students, equates comprehension with memory, and he is haunted, as they are haunted, by the recognition that he cannot remember all of what he has read, whether it be a passage of half a page or a book of 300 pages. And if he cannot remember it all, what he does remember, he suspects, is the very stuff he should have forgotten — material remembered arbitrarily, by chance, or perversely, because he was paying attention to the wrong things.

Frank Kermode, in *The Genesis of Secrecy*, speaks of forgetfulness, but he speaks of it as an inevitable element in a successful reading — inevitable in that we all must forget, and successful in that it puts the burden of coherence — of accounting for the appropriateness of what we remember — where it belongs, on the person who is recomposing the text. The desire to remember everything is not only obsessive, if achieved it would be madness. "A text with all its wits about it would see and hear and remember too much."[8] And a reader with "all his dull wits about him," the reader who would literally recall a text, would never be able to misread and would therefore be able to speak only the same text back to itself. The concern for getting the right meaning, for memory, a concern at the center of most reading labs and study skills centers, puts students in an impossible position.

To be a good reader is to misread. The paradox is more than an amusing puzzle. Our students are bound by the model of reading they carry to the act of reading. It's the metaphors that a teacher should pay attention to, not reading "skills" (whatever they might be). Their obsessive concern over the fact that they don't remember everything they read, their concern to dig out the right answers, their despair over passages that seem difficult or ambiguous, all of these are symptoms of a misunderstanding of the nature of texts and the nature of reading that must be overcome if students are to begin to take charge of the roles they might play in a university classroom.

The language of reading instruction, like the language of writing instruction, is loaded with images of mastery and control. A writer begins with a controlling idea. A reader finds a main idea and follows it. The practice of reading and writing, however, is nothing like this. Mastery and control, if they come at all, come late in the game. We never know what we've read until we are forced to perform as readers — as though we know what we've read — and we face all those occasions (lectures, tests, papers) with that sense of anxiety, that doubt whether we can pull it off, that is evidence of the fact that comprehension isn't something we possess but something we perform.

When I began studying the problem of student reading by looking at student writing, I was concerned with two things: with the ways students textually established their authority as readers — their right to speak — and with the ways they located, arranged and accounted for the points they were willing to call "significant" in what they read. The assigning of significance is, in a sense, an act of naming, perhaps the most basic act of naming for any reader, since it precedes any attempt to describe, categorize, elaborate or generalize. Significance may be attributed to a text ("What would you say is the central point in this chapter?" or "What point is the author making?"), to an individual reader ("What strikes you as significant in what you've read?"), or to a situation or a project ("Given the essays you've read and the essays you've written on what happens when a person becomes 'educated,' what strikes you as significant in *Hunger of Memory*?"). Each act organizes a text in a different way, causes passages that were silent to suddenly speak, or passages that spoke loudly to move into the general undersound of a chapter. It is the place where the press of the competing demands of convention and idiosyncracy are most strongly and illustratively felt.

When I talk about locating significance, then, I'm not talking about a student's ability to find a topic sentence. Nor am I talking about memory, at least not a memory for what a text said. It is more a matter of remembering what was not there, or remembering an agenda that exists functionally only after its opening stages have been revealed — an agenda that accounts for and is revealed by the check marks we put on the page, the books we pulled from the shelves while wandering around the stacks in the library, the passage that caught our eye as we leafed through the *Phaedrus*.

III

Let me look now at some written records of students' reading. As I said earlier, these essays were written in response to the *Phaedrus* and to *Hunger of Memory*. In every case these are students who would not be said to be "good readers." They don't, that is, step easily into the conventional discourse that characterizes good reading in a university class. If we look patiently and sympathetically at what they do — at their version of a reader reading — we can get a better sense of the nature of the task that is expected of them and at the problems of transition that are, at once, problems of reading, writing and teaching.

I'm interested in those moments in a text that students take to be significant and I'm interested in the ways they establish their authority to speak. A student, I've said, must act to displace the words of a text with his own. Let me put this in more immediate terms: a student must find a way of writing about the *Phaedrus* to put Socrates aside, to put him on hold, to make him silent while another speaks. (In most cases, it is Socrates they have to put aside and not Plato. They seldom read the dialogue as a text orchestrated and written by Plato, a person at a level of control beyond Socrates. Their own participation in the dialogue is at the level of dialogue. They hear Socrates speaking in the louder voice and it is to him that they respond.)

Let me look at some examples:

> In the *Phaedrus*, Socrates discusses his rules of rhetoric. On the whole, these rules are in agreement with my personal rules. For example, I agree that it is essential to know the truth about one's subject in order to make a good presentation. Also, the concept of classification is vital to see the underlying properties of the subject at hand. However, I do not agree that writing is a less noble art. I believe that writing is vital to the dissemination of information to a wide and varied audience.

The student can speak here because Socrates can speak through him, and when Socrates can't (when Socrates would say that writing is less noble) he's abandoned altogether. This is not summary, in other words, but a kind of triumphantly Emersonian appropriation of the wisdom of the ages. (Socrates has said just what I would say.) Here's the other side of this:

> There are some problems with Socrates' theories about rhetoric and dialectic, both from a practical standpoint and from within the *Phaedrus* itself. To begin with, Socrates believes that a person must know all about a subject before hand. How is this done? It is not easy to understand and use everything about a subject. For example, in the second speech Socrates states that "but about its [the soul's] form, the following must be stated: To tell what it really is would be a theme for a divine discourse . . . what it resembles, however, may be expressed more briefly in human language." He is saying that it would take a god to explain what a soul really is; therefore he must do the best he can to explain what it resembles. This conflicts with his idea of knowing everything. I think Socrates should change his statement, saying that it is necessary to know what is needed to talk or write about a subject; this simplifies things more and makes them more practical.

There is a wonderful chutzpah in both of these. Both students, clearly, are working to preserve their right to speak, but in what context? The context they imagine provides some insight into the role they can imagine a reader playing and into the model for the act of reading that enables each to write. In the first example, a reader is a person who agrees or disagrees, confers praise or blame. It is this act that establishes the reader's priority, that sets the text aside and gives him room to speak: Some of Socrates' rules agree with mine, some don't. For example, I too agree that it is essential to know the truth.

In its broad outlines, this would frame what I think we could call a successful reading. But the performance of this act of agreement, of what, for example, it might mean to know the truth — for Socrates, in the *Phaedrus*, for this student, in his experience as a reader and a writer (or, in the dialogue, through his counterpart, Phaedrus) — all of this is unspoken, taken for granted. This performance is, we are asked to believe, beyond saying. A reader is a person with opinions and his only requirement is to state what they are and how they correspond to the opinions in the text. Thus it's as easy for this student to disagree with Socrates as it is for him to agree. In fact, in the passage above, Socrates' argument is replaced by a single sentence, "I believe that writing is vital to the dissemination of information to a wide and varied audience." It's a sentence delivered in "topic sentence" language, the strongest voice the student can bring forward, but also one that is comically inappropriate. (Who cares what this kid has to say about writing? And besides, he talks like a stuffed shirt.) By silencing Socrates he acts as though he can speak in his place, appropriate his authority, and of course he can't. The student is doing his best, but he has been betrayed by his training in a situation that calls for more than topic sentence prose, one where he is asked to write as a reader.

Likewise, in the second example, the student has identified a problem that can give her a way of establishing her priority over Socrates — there is a contradiction. Socrates says that a speaker must know the truth and yet he says that there are truths that only belong to the gods. As I read the *Phaedrus,* this is, in fact, a key to finding a way to speak back to Socrates (as Phaedrus, our counterpart, does not.) And this, in fact, was the frame given to this student in the assignment — an offering which, because she is a skillful writer, she turns into her own act of invention. The problem comes when it is her turn to speak, when she can appropriate neither Socrates' words nor the assignments'. The crux comes at the moment of translation, when the student says of Socrates, "He is saying that . . ." Here she casts the original in terms she can use: Socrates cannot speak like a god, therefore he must do the best he can and speak through resemblances. The project that is announced by this translation would have a reader examining the limits of Socrates' language and his use of metaphor and myth.

At this point, however, the student fails to begin the act of writing that could enact an understanding and account for the significance of this particular passage. I'm not sure I can explain why she failed, however. It could be that she failed to attend to the agenda implicit in her own reading (or writing — the distinction no longer serves here) or that she had not yet learned to adequately monitor the process while it was unfolding. It could be that she saw what she had to do but didn't know how to begin. Or it could be that she had not learned to respect that habit of mind that takes delight in such problems and spends time on them. Whatever the case, it is at this moment that the student becomes silent again. But then not completely, since she does say that she wishes Socrates would change his mind, revise his words, and make the contradictions (and the assignment) go away, so that total silence would, in fact, be appropriate and all she would have to do is admire the *Phaedrus* and pay it a quiet respect.

She begins by identifying a problem in the text that is both practical and internal ("within the *Phaedrus* itself"). This is, in a sense, her moment of access into the conversation. But once the conversation has begun, her only move is to wish Socrates would go back and revise his speech so that Socrates could speak (without gap or division) through the student. For this student, as for the student who summarizes and re-states, a reader is a person through whom an author speaks.

For some students the pressure of hearing a strong, powerful presence speak through them (particularly in Socrates' tone of voice), combined with the scholarly requirement to displace that presence, is cause for little else but despair. Listen in the following passage to the counterpoint of summary and commentary (to the counterpoint of the text and the student speaking in turn):

> When we examine *Phaedrus* for Socrates' argument on the inferiority of written speech, we find it steeped in mythology. The written word was invented by the Egyptian god Theuth. When Theuth gave this gift to man, King Thamus criticized it as more of a bane than the first step toward civilization. He believed it would weaken men's minds and memories and cause men to become conceited know-it-alls, incapable of real judgment. As if the point weren't clear enough, Socrates bludgeons the point by saying, "Then any man who imagines that he has

bequeathed an art to posterity because he puts his views in writing, and also anyone who inherits such an 'art' in the belief that any subject will be clear or certain because it is couched in writing — such men will be utterly simple-minded." These are strong words and convictions, but for the life of me I cannot resolve them. Are we all idiots for engaging in the lowly act of writing? I guess so! Socrates had a few points which are true, but seem totally ridiculous.

The idea of a ridiculous truth, although nowhere else so succinctly stated, was common in the papers I read on the *Phaedrus*. It is a student's way of defining a conversational moment in reading, one usually represented dispassionately in a syntax like the following: "While Socrates argues . . . , it seems that . . ." In the latter, a reader has learned to see that the power of even a powerful text can be accounted for as something other than the power of truth, and he has learned to see re-reading as something other than a ridiculous act. For this learning to take place, students need a curriculum that dramatizes the politics of reading and writing.

The *Phaedrus* is an exemplary text in this regard. There is a telling moment in the dialogue, after Socrates has done his best to woo Phaedrus away from his other teacher, Lysias. Socrates offers a summary of all that has gone on in his conversation with Phaedrus. At the end, he turns to Phaedrus and says, "And now, what about the question of whether it is honorable or disgraceful to write and deliver speeches? Under what circumstances may this properly involve reproach? Wasn't this made clear a little while ago when we said . . ." And he pauses. And Phaedrus, his student, says, "What did we say?" And Socrates goes on like a freight train, without missing a stroke, to tell him what "we" said. Socrates' "we" presents a peculiar but predictable use of the pronoun. It is all too often a teacher's we, one that can never include two "I's," never include a student except as a silent partner — someone who speaks only when a teacher speaks through him.

About Socrates as a teacher, one student wrote:

> Socrates follows his rules of rhetoric, I feel, very well. He breaks things down into parts and knows the truth before he speaks. I also feel that he treats Phaedrus like a lover because Phaedrus wants to learn the truth. Socrates tries to show how important truth is when he tries to convince Phaedrus that a donkey is as good as a horse. Through the whole dialogue Phaedrus agrees, but really never learns nothing.

The opening sentences of this passage — and they are dutiful sentences, to be sure — are phrased in terms of what the student "felt" to be true about the *Phaedrus*. It is a classic example of the student reader Culler talks about.[9] The student reads and interprets by imagining what "reader" should feel and understand. This performance is broken by the last sentence where another set of "feelings" about the dialogue comes through. I don't want to romanticize the double negative. It is tempting to say that *there*, at that point, the student moves to assert his priority and speak for himself, but it is followed by silence. There is no further discussion of what Phaedrus does and doesn't learn. The point is not what the final phrase *is*, however, but what it can be made to be. By focusing on this statement for a revision of this essay, a teacher could make it part of a past that would allow a student to say that he has understood the *Phaedrus*.

If Socrates failed Phaedrus, it wasn't because he didn't let him speak, or because he listened to Phaedrus only to the degree that his words could serve his own agenda. He failed him because he was more interested in his performance than Phaedrus's. Phaedrus is never allowed to act on his own authority. The student above could best begin a revision of his paper by throwing everything away but that last sentence and addressing the question it asks: How is it that all this teaching goes on, and by a famous and intelligent teacher, and yet Phaedrus never learns nothing? The student would be helped here by being given a moment, a project, a beginning one that violates the conventional habit of mind that is dutiful and pious, one that turns the text back on itself, and one that could provide a working metaphor for the act of reading. This is a project a teacher would have to set for the student, though. He would not come to it on his own.

The students who were "better" readers at the beginning of the semester were students who were able to cast themselves into a more seamless classroom role. They could read successfully, that is, because they had learned a way of writing, a way of composing an "act of reading" that they brought with them to a book and that they used to complete their classroom requirements. Their readings were dutiful and pious — there was none of the subversion of the papers above: no suggestions that Socrates is ridiculous or that he ought to revise his ideas or that he was a failure as a teacher — but they were complete and therefore had an authority those other, marginal readings lacked. There were no obvious gaps or moments of disintegration, no places where the mask would fall away to reveal an 18-year-old kid who was puzzled, bored, lost or confused. I'm less interested in talking about them at length, partly because these papers were less interesting and partly because I have no desire to make a case for their achievement. What they do and fail to do will be immediately familiar to anyone who's spent time in an English class. I'm more interested in what they could be said to represent. I think they represent students who have learned the "topic sentence" versions of reading, school routines that are as set and conventional as their composition counterparts, even if they are not spelled out as clearly in textbooks or handbooks. (I don't think they should be belittled as monkey work, nor do I think they should be cited as examples of clear or reasonable minds at work. They are evidence of students who have learned a routine that they believe will enable them to do the work of a college classroom. The question for a college or university teacher should be, "What comes next?").

Here are two examples of more successful papers to represent two familiar tropes for the act of reading: "charting main ideas" and "discovering hidden meanings." Both these students, I would argue, give convincing, if not graceful, performances. While they write as Sheridan Baker would have students write, these are not cases where students first had ideas and then cast them into order on the page. They had a form, rather, and read accordingly. The roles they were able to imagine enabled their readings. For the first reader, reading is the celebration of what is clear, predictable, even obvious. He has found, and can speak for, the ostensible argument of the text. Whatever Socrates has "appeared" to say this writer can translate into what Socrates "clearly" said. In fact, his successful pantomime of a way of reading tends to obscure the fact that he has little to say that is not direct restatement. (I suspect that the hidden drama in this argument is the student's attempt to *not* say that Socrates has a sexual interest in Phaedrus. He is silently arguing against a subversive reading.) His style of presentation, I think we can believe, is in imitation of Socrates':

> First, it must be established what sort of man Socrates was. He claims that he is a "lover of words," but this fact is useless unless it is understood what is meant by the word "lover." Socrates appears to have defined a lover as one whose "search for love has involved the search for wisdom."
>
> Next, Socrates' reason for conducting this conversation with Phaedrus must be considered. "As for me, I'll cross the stream and go away before you put any greater compulsion on me," states Socrates, arousing Phaedrus's interest. Predictably, Phaedrus replies, "Not yet, Socrates, till the heat has gone. Don't you see that it's nearly high noon, as they call it. Let's wait and talk about what's been said." Socrates has obviously set Phaedrus up for his second speech. Clearly, Socrates was intent on trying to get a message across to Phaedrus. Socrates, a lover of words, is trying to express this sort of love to his friend Phaedrus.

Next to this, I'll place the reader who pursues the hidden, the secrets of a text, and celebrates buried rather than ostensible meanings. This is the reader set against plain wisdom, who announces that she looks beyond or more deeply — all moves in a set performance, an elaborate fiction, that enables a reader to carry out an act of reading:

> In reading the *Phaedrus* for the first time, I was struck by a certain sense of ambiguity, as if there were hidden meanings in Socrates' dealing with Phaedrus. Much of what Socrates states in his speeches is plainly his wisdom that can either be taken at face value and will still be meaningful or looked into a little more deeply for more value. In the *Phaedrus* Plato seems to be pointing out the difference between a truly wise man and a typical man. Even beyond this, he tells us about the "real" nature of man, in other words, what constitutes a man.

To other students, these two paragraphs open essays that would seem correct, exemplary, unquestionable. There is power in these performances, and it resides not so much in what the essays say, or in how they would enable another reader to go back to the *Phaedrus* with interest, but in the pat authority represented by these structures of reading. The earlier essays I've cited would be easier for students to critique because they have obvious problems in them — gaps or discontinuities between the reader and conventional classroom readings. These essays, however, seem to show a perfect fit between a reader and reading.

The last of the essays presented above makes its own argument about the politics of reading, about the way status is distributed between those who have access to secrets and those who don't. It's not really a matter of finding hidden meanings at all, however. The "secrets" she has to tell of the *Phaedrus* are stated later in her paper and they turn out not to be secrets at all but to be plain, cultural commonplaces: "man is capable of becoming wise if taught correctly by men who not only tell him certain things but show him things indirectly also." A classroom provides the occasion for an 18-year-old to speak these words, words she knows to be common, generally true, recognizable, intelligent, and yet to speak them as though they were her own discovery. Her authority as a reader is realized when she can speak the words of (what she takes to be) the adult community of readers back to that community. Within the fiction of this act of reading, however, what distinguishes the occasion is not that she has thought to say them but that she has found them "hidden" in a book, where others couldn't find them or couldn't find them quite so well. This right of privilege (to find secrets) both preceded and enabled her reading and, she believes, it establishes her position in the classroom over and against others:

> Socrates is a teacher to Phaedrus and to us, but we must be wise enough to find the value in his lessons. And everyone can find some value — some can find deeper meaning if they are capable of seeing it, but those that can't see quite so deeply will still gain something towards wisdom.

Both this student and the student who said "I believe that writing is vital to the dissemination of information to a wide and varied audience" establish their right to speak by taking as their own a general, cultural commonplace. By classroom measures, however, the first student was a failure and he was a failure because he didn't know how to act like a reader, how to frame this moment in a dramatic representation of a reader at work.

IV

I have been looking at bits and pieces — cameos — from student essays in order to highlight student approximation of the act of reading. I have been looking at student essays as metaphors for reading (or the reader), and, I believe, by unpacking those metaphors we can better imagine the work before us as teachers. This is a different view of the process of reading than that given to us by studies in the psychology of reading. The process I have been outlining is not an internal psychological process but a rhetorical act of placement, a way of writing that locates a reader and a text within an institutional setting. The key dialectic in the process as I see it is historical (what a student can understand about the contours and implications of the roles available to her as a reader, and the ways she can move within and against those roles) and not to say that beginning students cannot or can never test Socrates' argument against other possible counter-arguments or counter-examples; it is to say that, in my experience, they do not and, furthermore, they do not do it with any style or hope of gain until they've received some fairly clever teaching, which in many schools goes under the name of composition. They do not have those counter-arguments or counter-examples until they have been located, as writers, in a context that makes those arguments and examples possible.

In talking about his own teaching, Stanley Fish said that,

> we are not to imagine a moment when my students "simply see" a phys-ical configuration of atoms and *then* assign that configuration a signi-ficance, according to the situation they happen to be in. To be in the situation (this or any other) is to "see" with the eyes of its interests, its goals, its understood practices, values, and norms, and so to be confer-ring significance by seeing, not after it. The categories of my students' vision are the categories by which they understand themselves to be functioning as students (what Sacks might term "doing studenting"), and objects will appear to them in forms related to that way of function-ing rather than in some objective or preinterpretive form.[10]

I think there are finer distinctions to be made here. I think there are degrees in students' abilities to "function" as students, just as I think there are degrees to which students can be shown to *understand themselves to be* functioning as students. And I think both of the above — the ability to perform and the ability to understand the conventions governing performance — are most available when students "confer significance" textually — when they show a way of reading by writing it down; when they don't just "notice," but speak as well. And I don't think that the differences are trivial; the differences, that is, between students who are "inside" the system of classroom reading and writ-ing and those who are outside. I think the moment of transition from the out-side to the inside, where the habits of one community are privileged and the habits of another become taboo, is the key moment in undergraduate educa-tion. We are a far way, now, from "discovering new ideas" or "independent reading" or the language of any of a number of liberation pedagogies. The burden of teaching, I think, is that we can never totally free ourselves or our students from conventional ways of reading, writing, and thinking. We can, however, teach students what's at stake and what's going on.

Let me turn to my last set of examples. These will all be longer pieces — in two cases complete essays. I want to examine, in these, the larger drama of a student's reading. I'll begin with another example of silence:

> In this chapter, I see the author comparing himself to Hoggart's theory of the "scholarship boy." It seems as though the story doesn't do a thing for Rodriguez. It leaves us with mixed ideas and emotions about Rodriguez's theory. When Rodriguez says he was a "scholarship boy," a certain kind of scholarship boy, "always successful, and always portraying no confi-dence." He says he was exhilarated by his progress. Yet sad, I can't really understand why he says he's sad, even though he thinks so highly of the progress that he has made.

There is a big gap between the "I see" of the first sentence and the "it seems" (which I take as *it seems to me*) in the second. The first demonstrates the easy appropriation of the frame set up by an assignment (which asked students to look at how Rodriguez read and used Hoggart's discussion of the "scholarship boy"). The student begins to speak, in other words, by locating himself initially within the context of the assigned exercise. He "sees" a comparison but then goes on to demonstrate that there is nothing to be seen in the text at all. This is the dark version of Fish's happy student who sees what he is supposed to see because of his ability to function as a student (to "do studenting"). This student can make the opening move, but then he is abandoned by the discourse he has called up. For him, the text says nothing. Or, more properly, what it does say — that Rodriguez is both exhilarated and saddened by what happened to him — allows only for silence. "I can't really understand why he's sad, even though he thinks so highly of the progress that he has made."

The paradox — it seems to say something but it doesn't say anything — is repeated in the second paragraph of the essay:

> Rodriguez seems to charish or idolize Hoggart and his theory about the scholarship boy. I believe this theory does help him, it seems like a type of incentive for him. He often relates himself with this scholarship boy that Hoggart so often speaks of. I feel that it is a sign of both a loss and a gain. I say this because he often refers back to the days when he was not as educated, they seemed like happy memories for him. But when he talks about how much he's learned he is very proud.

In the first paragraph, the student wrote that Hoggart's "story doesn't do a thing for" Rodriguez. Now for this he substitutes, "I believe this theory does help him" and tries to find a set of terms that will allow him to talk about the role the Hoggart passage played for Rodriguez. It's a "help" and "incentive." He can "relate himself" to what Hoggart said. Hoggart can speak to Rodriguez in this student's account only as a boy's father might speak to his son as he heads off for school. (Rodriguez could be seen to be much more feisty in this exchange. I think he could also be seen to be saying that Hoggart has got the experience of the "scholarship boy" wrong in significant ways.)

The strong statement, "I feel that it is a sign of both a loss and a gain" is appropriated from the assignment ("what did he lose? what did he gain?") and isn't so much a strong statement as it is a way out of the contradictions the student (rightly) finds in Rodriguez's attitudes toward his education. These terms, even as they are taken as a statement of what I (he) felt, cannot operate to organize the reading. The "but" of the last sentence — "they seemed like happy memories for him, but when he talks about how much he's learned he is very proud" — stands for an opposition he still cannot resolve. He has worked himself back into the language of the project that he imagines the assignment has called for, but he cannot make the language work for him. And the reason is evident from the ending of the paper.

> When looking at the aspects of education, I would say in the situation that Rodriguez faces that it was good for a wide variety of different things. He truely needed to be educated, his parents knew it and he

eventually realized it. Education in my opinion is good for everything, no one should be denied an education. It is a lot of long hours and hard work along with frustration, but in the end, when your education is completed, it all pays off.

What this student "would say" about *Hunger of Memory* makes a good part of the book disappear. The argument of the book is that education is also violation and loss, that the pay-off is equivocal, that it is not good for all things — that, in fact, for some things it is death. The student who is writing this paper, a student who is also a scholarship boy, translates Rodriguez's story into terms consistent with the necessary belief that the long hours and hard work *will* all pay off, that education *is* good for everything. The question of Rodriguez's "sadness" had to be put aside for this reading to complete itself.

This is not, I would argue, a case of ego-centrism or of a student who could not read beyond his own identity themes. I don't think this student believes that education is good for everything. I don't think this is a student who had so much invested in his own hard work that he could not look at or "see" Rodriguez's sadness. I do, however, think that this is the fiction that the student wrote through; its part of the communal fantasy, a way of talking that enables this reading, with its concerns, perplexities, moments of significance and conclusions. This essay presents the case of a student who, when he imagines himself as a reader, comes to imagine a reader who must turn away from perplexity (from questions that don't begin to speak their own answers: "I can't really understand why he's sad") to speak with authority, and the voice of authority that is most readily available to him is the voice of conventional wisdom, the voice that speaks the commonplace, "Hard work pays off in the end." And in our community that way of speaking is taboo: clichéd, trite, predictable (as predictable, in fact, as our responses would be, but here predicting the wrong sort of habit of mind).

You see a similar process at work in the following excerpts from other student papers. Notice in the following paragraph how the student begins with quotation or paraphrase, an example of Rodriguez's "significant" words, and translates them into available commonplaces:

Mr. Rodriguez writes that education is not an inevitable or natural step in growing up and that one chooses to become a student (p. 48). This is very important and something we tend to forget in the era of mandatory education. If someone does not want to learn and invariably tunes himself out it is almost impossible to teach this individual. In another passage (p. 55), Mr. Rodriguez points out how he "wanted to be like his teachers, to possess their knowledge, assume their authority, their confidence and persona." This is an example of how the student imitates the teacher in hopes of acquiring the teacher's traits. In yet another passage (p. 64), he writes, "I vacuumed books for epigrams, scraps of information, ideas, themes — anything to fill the hollow within me and make me feel educated." Here Mr. Rodriguez seems to be wondering if feeling educated is the same as being educated. "He read to acquire a point of view." Mr. Rodriguez seems to say that education in the sense that he acquired it is a collection of facts and ideas of other men."

The problem here is not, at least not immediately, that the student fails to connect up these various statements and observations, but with the essential act of translation itself. The counterpoint here — quotation and commentary — shows the student translating statements that break the pattern of conventional wisdom back into conventional wisdom. The gap between saying that education isn't natural and saying that students who tune out are impossible to teach is a way of showing that Rodriguez is a better writer than my student. It is also, however, a way of showing how each understands the situation of the writer — one trying to push against the ready-made language for describing education (to whom education is an unnatural act, a loss of something as well as a benefit); the other trying to find a place of authority, a place to enable an utterance that can stand next to Rodriguez, by putting himself within the language that speaks the received wisdom of the community. To speak, one must imagine or write one's way into a privileged discourse and for students — outside the closed discourse of the university — the privileged discourse they can immediately imagine is the wisdom of the community and its elders. Students work to locate themselves within a commonplace where, as Aristotle says, they can find a stock of arguments to which they may turn for a particular need. The difficulty for such students is that the university is a place where common wisdom is only of negative value — or, perhaps, more properly, where students go to have one set of commonplaces replaced with another.

The writer of the passage above concluded his essay by turning to the commonplace that sets originality against imitation (we, of course, would have him use those terms oxymoronically — original imitation, imitative originality — to talk about the role books played early on in Rodriguez's education):

I suppose this type of education has its merits but it is not original though and therefore this type of education has limited uses. Many supposedly educated people can sit around and quote other's works, but the true test of an education comes when one is asked to sit down and compose an original symphony, design a new form of architecture, or write a novel that is truly novel.

This is one of those passages that, if you present them to a class, appears seamless, perfectly complete and self-contained, unassailable. The power of a commonplace has little to do, in other words, with whether it rings true to experience or not. It provides a set of terms within which one can control difficult or problematic information and its power to do so determines its merit. Students, at least my students, will be quick to admire the way that conclusion speaks with power and authority — even with art ("novels that are truly novel"). And they will continue to speak of its power even after I puncture it and make them laugh by asking how many of them would pass an exit exam that required them to compose an original symphony, design a new form of architecture, or write a novel that is truly novel. A passage like this is more powerful than a teacher. A teacher can displace it, to be sure, but only by the most overt act of aggression. It is a passage beyond laughter or parody, which is one of the things that makes teaching such a funny business.

The student above was trying to locate himself within a discourse that would work, that would enable the work of a reader in my course. In the paper that follows you'll see a student who does this more gracefully, but who gets stuck trying to figure out whose turn it is to speak: the text's or the reader's. I'll divide this essay into three sections. The first introduces the essentials: a reader, a book and a project or agenda.

> Throughout the book the author is frequently alluding to his true feel-ings for his family. This is best represented by the last chapter entitled Mr. Secrets. It is here that Rodriguez talks specifically about his family. He deals with the fact that his parents have always and continue to sep-arate themselves from a public identity. Rodriguez explains that his par-ents see only the family as their private society. He also mentions the fact that no matter how well they act in public, there is always the ever pre-sent distinction between public and private. This distinction between public and private is shown by the high-pitched voice his mother uses with those who are not relatives. Rodriguez's mother also used this voice with his own friends. It always made Rodriguez feel badly that she could never adjust herself to be as friendly as his friend's parents were to him.

I am trusting that this passage will have a familiar ring to it. This student's performance does not seem unusual the way the earlier student's did (that is, the student who confessed he could not figure out why Rodriguez would be sad). The student here steps more easily into the role of a reader. I'd like to look at what this reader is (or does).

The reader in this first paragraph is a person who sets the stage ("Throughout the book the author is frequently alluding to his true feelings for his family."), warms up the audience ("This is best represented by the last chapter entitled Mr. Secrets."), and then points to passages in the text so that they may speak for themselves ("He deals . . . ," "Rodriguez explains . . . ," "He also mentions . . ." "This distinction is shown by . . ."). In fact, the metaphor of "showing" is dominant here. The reader makes certain decisions about where to look or where to point, but the text then shows or displays what it says. It speaks through the reader, who has decided that she had best remain silent, organizing Rodriguez's words into thesis and example but without speaking herself. She has nothing to add after the presentation of the example. What the example says, how it might be read, all of this goes with-out saying. It is the structure that speaks here and not the words or bits and pieces from the text — or, for that matter, the historical drama reenacted in this presentation, a drama that plays itself out in the present by telling this girl to keep quiet. It plays itself out in my classroom by telling students there to keep quiet too. It is the rare student who would see anything troubling in this reading — troubling in either what it says about the act of reading and the role of the reader, or troubling in the way it talks about *Hunger of Memory*. (For example, you could read the book to argue that Rodriguez's distinction between public and private is challenged, not "shown," through the example of his mother speaking to his friends as though they were strangers.) The reading may not be graceful but it seems complete.

The second paragraph reproduces the drama of the first until here, after the presentation of the "best" example (to best "show" what the the the text says), the reader speaks in turn:

> This feeling of separation also blocked family unity and is shown by their holiday dinners. Everyone would be gathered around the table eating and talking but there was something missing. Rodriguez easily talks to his family but he leaves the reader with the feeling that his family members are just saying meaningless words. Examples of this are shown in the types of conversations the family engage. Rodriguez sits next to his youngest sister and they gossip and talk about mutual friends. The reader never gets the impression that the family talks intimately. It is Rodriguez who states that he is the one who does most of the talking. The best example of this is seen when he says, "I talk having learned from hundreds of cocktail parties and dinner parties how to talk with great animation about nothing especially." (pp. 191–92) This is a rather odd comment about one's own family. Although the reader does sense that they could all be close. If they did not care about one another and their parents, they would never come to the family gatherings anyway. I felt that they all had very different lives. Their education and their parents' feeling of isolation kept distance between family unity. The family's public identify was carried over into their private lives.

The single channel of this discussion is broken, or interrupted, at the point at which she introduces the example of Rodriguez saying, "I talk having learned from hundreds of cocktail parties and dinner parties how to talk with great animation about nothing especially." It's not that the example has nothing to do with the discussion it is meant to serve; it's that it is too good or too big for the kind of discussion we've been hearing. It's a bit like saying, "King Lear is an example of a man with a bad temper." I don't, in other words, think that the writer pulled out this example to serve her discussion. I think this was one of the moments in a text that stuck with her, or stuck out as she was paging through the book looking for an example and, even though it was generally appropriate, it would not fit into the performance she had underway. It is, then, an "odd comment" because it belongs to a way of talking about (of reading) the relationships between public life and private life that stands outside of the project or agenda begun in this essay.

I want to resist the notion that this is a moment where the student's feelings broke in and therefore she was compelled to speak. The feeling that families get together because they care about one another is no more *her* feeling than it is the Hallmark Card Corporation's or the producers of *The Waltons*. I think the oddness of the moment she recalled and then let speak in her essay created a problem she felt interested in solving and that she turned to even though she did not have ready access to the words that would make the problem manageable. She moves from the language of family sentiment to the strange syntax of the final two sentences, where she tries to put together the key words of her discussion: public, private, distance, unity, education, and identity.

The next paragraph in the paper draws out more examples of the "emptiness" of the family Christmas dinner. And at one point the student writes, "It is here that I felt a loneliness for Rodriguez." It's an interesting sentence. It still does more pointing than talking, but it places her in a new relation to Rodriguez — not so much feeling his loneliness, letting him speak through her, but feeling it for him, casting an interpretation on a text that does not announce, "Rodriguez felt lonely."

And this is the final section of the final paragraph:

> The parents who were the force behind the family gatherings were unable to bring the family together. In their alienation from a public society they alienated themselves from their children. There were family gatherings but not familial ties. This produced in each a longing for unity that could not be attained, resulting in a search for this comfort in other areas. For Rodriguez, it seems to be achieved in the writing of *Hunger of Memory* and for his brothers and sisters in their childrens' acceptance into the public society. It is for the parents that there seems to be no relief, only yearning.

I have no interest in offering this as a right reading or a good reading of *Hunger of Memory*. I think it is an interesting answer to the question, "What's wrong with this family?" It's a good question to ask of this book, since it is a question with many rich examples and no set answers. And I think it is the question this writer set for herself once she shook herself free from an earlier agenda and its way of reading. Perhaps the most noticeable difference in this final paragraph is its air of authority. The writer plays against the "naive" language of family life ("There were family gatherings but not familial ties"), she appropriates key terms ("alienation," "public society") and makes them counters in sentences where it is the reader, rather than the text or its author, who is speaking. What the reader has to say is clearly more important than what Rodriguez has to say. She provides a commentary that he could not provide — or so the fiction behind this reading would require us to believe. I could imagine, in fact, that a later step in this reader's education would have her considering this way of reading (now felt, I imagine, as achievement) as a way of unnecessarily limiting what Rodriguez can be shown to know and understand and, therefore, of unnecessarily limiting her own performance in an act of understanding.

This is a mid-term issue, however. For the moment I suspect that the key pedagogical question for this paper is how it might be revised. I think, and I think I have shown, that it would be a mistake to try to work on the "writing" in this paper — to work on its unity, to add or subtract examples, or to "re-see" its ideas. I think it would be a mistake unless the writing of the paper can be represented to the student as the same thing as a reading, for I think that the first thing she must do is to consider what she is doing in this assignment as a reader and why.

Recent literary criticism has celebrated misreading as an achievement, as an occasion for the individual reader to break free from the tyranny of a text or the prison house of institutionally sanctioned procedures for reading, representing and thereby understanding texts. The reader is cast, then, neither as an empty vessel to be filled with the authoritative readings of his teachers or the ostensible wisdom of the text, nor is he cast as a good citizen, carrying on the work of his elders and his community. He is cast, rather, in an agonistic role, struggling against teachers and canonical interpretations — or, in my account of student readers, struggling to find teachers and interpretive procedures that will enable the work of the classroom.

In *Beginnings*, Edward Said gives an account of the problems facing the modern writer that reminds me of the problems facing my students. He says that while there may have been a time when readers and writers saw a text as a "system of boundaries and inner constraints held intact by successive generations (a heritage passed on through time)," for the modern writer a text is "an invitation to unforeseen estrangements from the habitual." He says

> The problem we face today when we study Joyce, or when, untrained in classics or religion, we read Hooker, or when we deploy psychology in the study of a literary text, is a problem of irregularity, or discontinuity. That is, less background, less formal training, less prescribed and systematic information, is assumed before one begins to read, write, or work. Thus when one begins to write today one is necessarily more of an autodidact, gathering or making up knowledge one needs in the course of creating.[11]

Said is not making an appeal to tired notions of creativity — where, on the boundaries of culture, the scholar makes up new ideas. He is talking about the academic version of street knowledge, about a willed, brash toughness of mind that enables a writer to bluff his way into a high stakes struggle for turf, for priority, without knowing all the rules or what moves will work, and without knowing beforehand whether he can carry it off should he win in the end.

The power of this metaphor is the way it enables us to frame the work of a student writer. For me it is poised against the metaphor of the student with a purpose or with a controlling idea. It is important to know, as a teacher, that when a student is making it up as he goes along he may very well be carrying out the essential work of the imagination, the very work that will enable him to move from one end of the block to the other, from the outside in. For this writer, Said also offers the metaphor of the wanderer.

> It is less permissible today to imagine oneself as writing within a tradition when one writes literary criticism. This is not to say, however, that every critic is now a revolutionist destroying the canon in order to replace it with his own. A better image is that of a wanderer, going from place to place for his material, but remaining a man essentially *between* homes. In the process, what is taken from a place ultimately violates its habitual way of being: there is a constant transposition. . . .[12]

For an expert writer, this wandering is a willed condition, something one achieves by writing and not a function of one's high school education or socio-economic status. Said's metaphor, however, also describes the students I teach, wandering between the old neighborhood and the university, belonging to neither, and left to invent academic expertise everytime they sit down to write. Misreading, for my students, is no easy route to academic status, and not even in my classroom (and even though I think the students who have trouble with college reading and writing are often in a better position to be students than those who are confident that they know how to "do English"). The misreadings we honor push against conventional systems, our conventional systems, and these readings are different from the misreadings that push against the habits of home or neighborhood or that seek to approximate the imagined requirements of the classroom. Education in the midst of this is push and tug, it is a scramble for power and for violation; it is not the transfer of reading or writing "skills" in a reading or writing laboratory.

At least that's how it has always felt to me — now, as a teacher, and before, as a student. Harold Bloom speaks eloquently of the violent dynamics of the classroom, with its struggle for authority, its necessary appeasements and its shocking violations of identity, when he talks about the dialectics of tradition and influence.

> Influence, as I conceive it, means that there are *no* texts, but only relationships *between* texts. These relationships depend upon a critical act, a misreading or misprision, that one poet performs upon another, and that does not differ in kind from the necessary critical acts performed by every strong reader upon every text he encounters. The influence-relation governs reading as it governs writing, and reading is therefore a miswriting just as writing is a misreading.[13]

The force of Bloom's argument for me is the way he places influence functionally in the imagined presence of a single person, a teacher or an author whose presence cannot be ignored or easily categorized, whose writing a student cannot help but imitate and whose presence, then, becomes both an inspiration and a burden. It is through such encounters that we place ourselves in and thereby invent a cultural, intellectual history. Bloom says, in *A Map of Misreading*, "You cannot write or teach or think or even read without imitation, and what you imitate is what another person has done, that person's writing or teaching or thinking or reading."[14]

This is no simple matter, however, since the young poet/student (like Bloom's Shelley) faced with the older poet/teacher (like his Milton) struggles to assert his own presence or priority in the very text that the older figure made possible. Or, as Bloom says, "A poet . . . is not so much a man speaking to men as a man rebelling against being spoken to by a dead man (the precursor) outrageously more alive than himself."[15]

My own experience as a student tells me that I have learned more, or perhaps learned more deeply through these encounters than through a regular exposure to books and ideas and classes. The most dramatic educational experience I had was my contact with Richard Poirier in my first year of graduate school. The first three years of my graduate training were driven by a desire to be able to do what he did — to be able to read and speak and write like him. I would, for example, copy out difficult or impressive sentences he had written in order to get the feel of them. I can feel them now in many sentences I write. It is a mixed feeling. I state it simply, but it wasn't simple at all. I tried for a whole semester to write a paper using the word "language" as he used it in talking about how the language "worked" in "Upon Appleton House." It took me a whole semester to use the word in a sentence that actually made sense to me, in a sentence I felt I could control. I felt that I had gained access to a profession by exercises like these. At the time it didn't feel like surrender. It was inspiring to feel that I could use his language and mimic, as I could, his way of reading and writing.

And I remember very well how shocked I was when one of my other professors, after admiring a paper I had written, commented in passing to me in the hall, "Don't you ever get tired of that Poirier routine?" It was not then, nor could it ever be for me now, simply a "routine," largely because what Poirier taught and how he taught and how he wrote were and remain central to my own beliefs and my professional identity. I felt ashamed, however, and began in my dissertation to try to write myself free from his influence, to find a project and a way of talking that I could claim for my own. This was a difficult and unsettling thing to attempt. I felt that I had found a place for myself, a way of thinking and talking that located me in the world of professionals, and now I had to push against it, misread it, in Bloom's terms. This is not a battle that a student wins, but for me it marked a stage in my education.

This is why I have little patience for Stanley Fish and the apparent pleasure he takes in revealing the gamesmanship of the classroom. In *Is There a Text in This Class?* he tells the following story:

> Thus, while there is no core of agreement *in* the text, there is a core of agreement (although one subject to change) concerning ways of *producing* the text. Nowhere is this set of acceptable ways written down, but it is a part of everyone's knowledge of what it means to be operating within the literary institution as it is now constituted. A student of mine recently demonstrated this knowledge when, with an air of giving away a trade secret, she confided that she could go into any classroom, no matter what the subject of the course, and win approval for running one of a number of well-defined interpretive routines: she could view the assigned text as the instance of the tension between nature and culture; she could look in the text for evidence of large mythological oppositions; she could argue that the true subject of the text was its own composition, or that in the guise of fashioning a narrative the speaker was fragmenting and displacing his own anxieties and fears.[16]

I find myself arguing both with and against Fish. I'd like to call his student's bluff, give her a copy of (say) *Hunger of Memory* and ask her to write an essay. If she could do what she says she can do, and if she could do it well, write a paper that is not mechanical and deadly, then she could not speak of what she has learned in such a flip way, for she would have learned the power as well as the emptiness of those routines, she would have felt the achievement as well as the betrayal. If these routines do not grant wisdom, they grant position, an enabling power, not just title; they grant not only a teacher's approval, but a place within a discourse that makes intellectual work possible.

I would agree, however, that what we must finally concern ourselves with is not what is in the text but in ways of producing the text. And for this reason, a reading course is necessarily a writing course and a writing course must be a course in reading.

NOTES

1. My work on this paper was supported by the Learning Research and Development Center at the University of Pittsburgh. LRDC, in turn, is supported by grants from NIE. I'm grateful. I'm grateful also to Steve Carr who helped me gather papers on the *Phaedrus*, who taught me how to read it, and who showed me how a fine and serious teacher might go about teaching such an elusive and difficult book. Portions of this essay are drawn from other pieces of mine: "Inventing the University" in *When a Writer Can't Write*, ed. Mike Rose (New York: Guilford P, 1985); "Facts, Artifacts and Counterfacts" (with Anthony R. Petrosky) in *Facts, Artifacts and Counterfacts*, eds. Bartholomae and Petrosky (Upper Montclair, NJ: Boynton/Cook, 1986) and "Against the Grain" in *Writers on Writing*, ed. Thomas Waldrep (New York: Random House, 1985).

2. Hans-Georg Gadamer, *Philosophical Hermeneutics*, ed. and trans. David E. Linge (Berkeley: University of California Press, 1977), 57. This quotation and the passages that follow all come from the chapter "On the Problem of Self-Understanding." Mariolina Salvatori introduced me to Gadamer in her essay, "The Dialogical Nature of Reading and Writing," in *Facts, Artifacts, and Counterfacts*. I owe a debt also to Salvatori's essays "Reading and Writing a Text," *College English* 459L983) 657–67; and "*If on a Winter's Night a Traveler*: Writer's Authority, Reader's Autonomy" in *Modern Literature*, forthcoming.

3. George Steiner, *After Babel* (New York: Oxford University Press, 1975) 473.

4. Jonathan Culler, *On Deconstruction: Theory and Criticism After Structuralism* (Ithaca, NY: Cornell University Press, 1982) 67.

5. This paper is not meant to be in defense of any particular curriculum. I've got one to defend, however, and I would be willing to send a sequence of assignments to anyone who writes. See also Bartholomae and Petrosky, *Facts, Artifacts and Counterfacts*.

6. Jonathan Culler, *Structuralist Poetics* (Ithaca, NY: Cornell University Press, 1975) 28. Cited in Fish, *Is There a Text in This Class?* (see below).

7. Stanley Fish, *Is There a Text in This Class? The Authority of Interpretive Communities* (Cambridge, MA: Harvard University Press, 1980) 335.

8. Frank Kermode, *The Genesis of Secrecy: On the Interpretation of Narrative* (Cambridge, MA: Harvard University Press, 1979) 45.

9. Culler, *On Deconstruction* 67.

10. Fish, 334.

11. Edward Said, *Beginnings: Intention and Method* (Baltimore: Johns Hopkins University Press, 1975) 8.

12. Said 8.

13. Harold Bloom, *A Map of Misreading* (New York: Oxford University Press, 1975) 3.

14. Bloom 32.

15. Bloom 19.

16. Fish 343.

Writing on the Margins: The Concept of Literacy in Higher Education

T he term BW *student* is an abstraction that can easily get in the way of teaching. Not all BW students have the same problems; not all students with the same problems have them for the same reasons. There are styles to being wrong. This is, perversely, where the individuality of inexperienced writers tends to show up, rather than in the genuine semantic, syntactic and conceptual options that are available to the experienced writer.

— Mina Shaughnessy
(*Errors and Expectations* 40)

For those who approach literary studies with literary sensitivity, an immediate problem arises. They cannot overlook *style,* their own or that of others. Through their concern with literature they have become aware that understanding is a mediated activity and that style is an index of how the writer deals with the consciousness of mediation. Style is not cognitive only; it is also recognitive, a signal betraying the writer's relation, or sometimes the relation of a type of discourse, to a historical and social world.

— Geoffrey H. Hartman
(*"The Culture of Criticism"* 371)

I

There are obvious dangers in talking about problems of literacy on college campuses. Perhaps the greatest danger is that we think we are making a precise distinction when we say that some students have it and others don't. It seems obvious to us that students come with diverse skills as readers and writers and that this diversity can be segmented and arranged — usually, or

From *A Sourcebook for Basic Writing Teachers*, ed. Theresa Enos. (New York: Random, 1987) 66–83.

at least initially, in a binary opposition: marginal or mainstream, remedial or regular, noncredit or credit, English 101 or Basic Writing.[1] I don't question that students bring diverse skills to our classrooms, nor do I question either the pedagogical value of grouping students according to levels of ability or (and this is a more difficult admission) distinctions that place some students on the margins of the university while placing others in the center. It is in the nature of intellectual work to force distinctions between the center and the margins. Most of us would say that our lives as students were marked initially by a struggle to enter into those habits of mind (those ways of reading and writing) that define the center of English Studies, just as many of us would say that the later stages were marked by a desire to push against that center — to debate, redefine the terrain, and establish a niche that somehow seemed to be our own. (In fact, in my ideal curriculum, the most advanced students would be pushed toward the margins and not into the center of the work represented by university study.[2]) I do, however, think there is reason to examine the assumptions about the nature of literate skills represented by the decisions we make in placement exams or tracking procedures.

As a profession, we have defined basic writing (as a form or style of writing) by looking at the writing that emerges in basic writing courses. We begin, that is, with what we have been given, and our definition is predetermined by a prior distinction, by a reflex action to sort students into two groups (groups that look "natural" or "right"). It is not driven by conscious theory or by any prior analysis of the nature and development of that species of advanced literacy represented by textual studies in the academy. We know who basic writers are, in other words, because they are the students in classes we label "Basic Writing." As Shaughnessy says, this abstraction can easily get in the way of teaching. It is based on the assumption that basic writers are defined by what they don't do (rather than by what they do), by the absence of whatever is present in literate discourse: cognitive maturity, reason, orderliness, conscious strategy, correctness.

Our curricula take for granted that some students lack the required literate skills for college study. These students are required to take special "developmental" courses to prepare them to work within the mainstream, yet the very presence of these students in our courses testifies to their ability to use language to achieve privileged status in our society. They are *in* college (or somewhere on the margins of the university); they are not out there, doing some other kind of work. These marginal students (and I will call them basic writers, but out of default, since I argue that this is a slippery label) are where they are because of the ways in which they read and write. We act as though we can be fairly confident in marking the boundary lines between those students who can read and write with fluency yet the question of what this facility actually is, like the institutional processes that determine who is included and who is excluded, remains largely unexamined. It is not the case, for example, that basic writers represent writers for whom writing is absent, since they write essays and the essays can be read as approximations of the work of their mainstream counterparts. (They do not represent a species of language use, that is, that lies totally outside our conventional expectations.) It would be convenient to say that basic writers write just like their mainstream counterparts but that they happen to make more grammatical mistakes along the way. Many curricula are organized along these lines. Students who make a lot of sentence-level mistakes are put into one pile and students who don't are put into another. There are few basic writing programs, then, that include students who don't make the kind or number of sentence-level errors that are taken as the primary indicator of a basic writer. It is not, however, the case that sentence-level errors are the only indicator of students who cannot do the work of the university. The style of error extends beyond the sentence to the ways of organizing texts, of producing them, or of imagining their possible uses. These distinctions are harder to make, since they demand a closer reading than a quick or impressionistic error count, but it seems telling that we don't look for styles of presentation (even in relatively error-free placement essays) that demonstrate a student working radically outside the conventional modes of presentation of academic discourse.

In the last decade, much of the scholarly work on problems of basic writing (which is not necessarily the same as the work on teaching methods) has prepared us to call into question "obvious" statements about basic writers.[3] It is no longer possible to say (at least with the same innocence) that these are the students who "can't think" or who "can't write a sentence." It is not possible to say, that is, that these are students for whom language is absent. They often think and write sentences in conventional ways (so that the interesting question is not whether they "possess" thought or the sentence but when and where they do and do not produce conventional textual forms), and the unconventional structures they produce on the page show evidence of their own logic or systematicity (so that the key pedagogical problem is not how to "give" students the sentence or how to "give" them thought, but to learn what those actual systems represent and how they can be transformed or translated to bring them more into line with conventional expectations).

As Shaughnessy argued, what a basic writer writes can be said to make sense if it is seen as a style, a way of using language, or as one of the many styles of being wrong. And basic writers are not the only ones who are wrong when they write. They are not the only ones who make mistakes and who present their work in ways that are inappropriate for a university. Mainstream freshmen, senior English majors, graduate students, our colleagues may all produce work that is naive, wrong, or off the track. The issue, then, is not who misses the mark but whose misses matter and why. To say this is to return attention to institutional processes of selection and exclusion. The errors that count in the work of basic writers have no clear and absolute value but gain value only in the ways that they put pressure on what we take to be correct, in the ways that these errors are different from acceptable errors. The work that remains for the profession is to determine the place of those unacceptable styles within an institutional setting, within an institution with its own style or styles of being right, its own habitual ways of thinking and writing. The work of basic writers calls into question our assumptions about orderly presentation, standards of copy editing, and the stability of conventional habits of thinking. This is not to say that order, correctness, and convention should not be goals of a literate education. It is to say, however, that the borderlines between our work and theirs are not as clear as we like to assume.

In order to place the work of basic writers, we have looked at the shapes and styles of an abstract correct form (at an ideal representation of what they don't have), looking for the shape of reason, of the correct sentence, or of an argument. We have not looked at the borderlands, comparing the actual work of students who are newly in the mainstream with those who are caught on the margins.[4] This is where we are stuck, and we are stuck because we have begun to imagine the problem as an abstract problem and because we have chosen to define the problem — this relationship of one style to another — within the language and methods of developmental psychology. Basic writers, we are asked to imagine, work with a style that is preacademic. They are caught at some earlier step in cognitive development (at the level of concrete rather than formal operations, for example), or they belong to a culture that is pretextual (an oral culture, like those that preceded the development of alphabetic writing) and that hinders the cognitive development required for literate participation in a textual culture.[5] It is not incidental that both of these theoretical formulations of the problem of the basic writer seem to work within the metaphorical frame of earlier "naive" accounts of the problem. Basic writers, in other words, are seen as childlike or as uncultured natives. There is an imperial frame to this understanding of the situation of those who are not like us. We define them in terms of their separateness. We do not see ourselves in what they do.

In both cases, the distinguishing mark of the basic writer is that he works outside the conceptual structures that his more literate counterparts work within. (I would question whether anyone works so happily or so completely within or outside a language system.) I hope to demonstrate that the boundaries are not so rigidly defined in practice (in the actual work of basic writers when seen in the context of more successful student writers) and that the problems of basic writers can be seen more immediately (and more generally) as a writing problem — as a problem, that is, that all writers face. In particular, this is the problem of moving into and appropriating the specialized discourse of a privileged community. A student, to be a student (and not someone caught on the outside of the academy), must write his way into the university by speaking through (or approximating) a discourse that is not his own —one that is necessarily on the outside, part of the habitual ways of thinking and writing of the community he would enter, a community with its peculiar gestures of authority, its key terms and figures, its interpretive schemes. I take this as a textual problem, something that can be achieved only in and through an act of writing (it is not something one has prior to writing) and something that can be observed only in the writing on the page, where the style, as Hartman says, betrays the writer's relations, or sometimes the relation of a type of discourse, to an historical and social world. The writing problems I imagine, that is, are not internal or cognitive. They are manifest in the competing styles within the text and in the competition between the text and those other texts that surround it (in whose name it is accepted or rejected). This competition is evidence of a social or historical struggle as an individual writer seeks to locate himself and his work (an "I" empowered to speak and a discourse to make that textual "I" possible) within the privileged discourse of a closed community. A "style," then, is a sign of this struggle for appropriation. As Foucault says in "The Discourse on Language":

> Education may well be, as of right, the instrument whereby every individual, in a society like our own, can gain access to any kind of discourse. But we well know that in its distribution, in what it permits and in what it prevents, it follows the well-trodden battle-lines of social conflict. Every educational system is a political means of maintaining or of modifying the appropriation of discourse, with the knowledge and the powers it carries with it. (227)

If the university officially places some students on the margins (in remedial writing courses), that position is a representation (perhaps in its most dramatic and telling form) of the position of every writer.

I realize that "appropriating a specialized discourse" may sound like the same thing as "achieving a level of cognitive development" or "learning the distinctive modes of thought in a literate culture." The difference comes in the distinctions this definition enables. The "modes of thought" represented by the actual uses of language in the academy, for example, are less stable and more varied if seen as a variety of specialized and competing discourses (including the approximate versions of those discourses offered by successful, mainstream undergraduates). It is more difficult to assume, therefore, that the structure of texts can be represented by an abstract logical structure — by the syllogism, for example, or by five possible paragraph patterns. The structure of a text, rather, is the dramatic, dialectical pattern of relinquishment and possession. If we take the problem of writing to be the problem of appropriating the power and authority of a particular way of speaking, then the relationship of the writer to the institutions within which he writes becomes central (the key feature in the stylistic struggle on the page) rather than peripheral (a social or political problem external to writing and therefore something to be politely ignored). Finally, if we see writing problems in these terms, then we cannot assume that we can teach the sentence or the paragraph as though they were context-free (as we do in workbook exercises or in courses that offer a version of writing that has little to do with writing in the academic disciplines). We must put marginal students immediately within representative academic projects (in courses like the seminars we offer to advanced students) so that we can see (and they can see) the position of their writing within the context of those varieties of writing that enable the work of the academy.[6]

Perhaps the best way to highlight the position of the basic writer is to return to the passage from *Errors and Expectations* that begins this essay. Shaughnessy says that "there are styles to being wrong," and her book remains our most powerful demonstration of how to read the distinctive styles of basic writers. It is an exercise in close reading, and in it she shows how a teacher might get inside the language of basic writers to see what they are doing and how they are working. It was with this book, in fact, that the easy distinctions between mainstream and marginal students first became problematic.

Her reading of sample sentences, passages, and essays gave the profession a way of seeing basic writing as a particular and systematic use of language — not as random production or as the evidence of "mechanical" problems. The errors, she demonstrated, could not only be understood as evidence of strategy or intent — as signs of attempts to make the language workable — but the errors, or at least some of them, were rule-governed. Certain patterns of error represented an idiosyncratic rule system, but not purely idiosyncratic, since the "rules" weren't invented from nothing but came from a student's "sense" of the rules governing conventional form. The language on the page, then, was approximate, a student's approximation of a conventional form. Seen as such, the errors that had been seen as signs of incompetence could be seen as signs of the very competence necessary to a writer. And the errors could be seen to mark stages in the development of a writer as the writer moved, through successive approximation, to the achievement of a conventional written utterance. There was, then, a pattern of development that could be charted in the work of a single student that was not so much an internally cued pattern of development as the record of a process of accommodation.

There is not a style to error, in other words, but "styles." And, she said, "This is, perversely, where the individuality of inexperienced writers tends to show up, rather than in the genuine semantic, syntactic and conceptual options that are available to the experienced writer."

It is difficult to know how to read these references to a perverse and a genuine style. The distinction is both contradicted and reaffirmed at later points in the book. The root of the problem, I believe, is Shaughnessy's ambivalence about the goals of a literate education, an ambivalence that can be taken as representative of the professions' ambivalence.[7] To phrase this ambivalence in its broadest terms, the question is whether the goal of such an education is to develop a natural competence (in service of a natural or genuine mode of expression, where written language speaks for one's experience or where expression and intention are congruous) or whether it is to acquire an unnatural, artificial discourse for purposes of assimilation (where intention and experience are displaced or translated by a language that is not one's own).

To speak of the "genuine" style of mainstream students is to suggest that for some there are genuine options, whereas for others these options are postponed or withheld. For some, in other words, the language of the university is authentic and natural; for some (for "experienced writers," like those granted immediate access to the mainstream) there is no tension between the available language for experience and experience itself, no gap between the academy's habitual ways of thinking and writing and an individual's way of thinking and writing. These are students who are "at home" in our language. (I'm assuming that the notion of being "at home" in the academy is a difficult thought — both tempting and frightening — even for those of us who are more accurately "at home" in it.) If this is a happy occasion, when there is no gap between a discourse and a person, it is so within the belief that the language of the academy is single and that it is the language of reason or intelligence itself. The academy, that is, is not the place of competing, arbitrary ways of thinking and writing. If we think of the academy as a peaceful place, where reasonable people speak with the voice of reason, then "experienced" writers are already on the inside and, by virtue of that position, empowered to do its work.

Shaughnessy is too generous a reader for me to say that the "perversity" of the perverse style is the perversity of students who could be similarly at home if only they would choose to be. The perversity lies, rather, in the situations we are forced to create when we acknowledge the failures of some (of marginal students) and demonstrate that they are outside the charmed circle. Let me be clear about the direction of my own argument here. Shaughnessy is correct in saying that some students are displaced by the language of the university. I share her sense of dismay over what we do to basic writers when we do our best in our classrooms. However, I do not think that any writer resides so easily in the academy. In fact, the most perverse thing we do is to allow some (including ourselves) to believe that the language of the university is genuine.

The implication of the distinction between perverse and genuine styles is that as teachers we must either give students genuine options or transform the university system so that all styles are equally genuine. This is a utopian construction that is used to serve several ends: to argue that all students and teachers must learn to use a pure, reasonable common tongue (in which case the distinction between a professional and a lay person, an expert and a novice, or school and home would disappear at the level of language) or to argue that the university must be omnivocal, where everyone is free to speak as he or she chooses. Both speak to an equality that language does not allow, since the act of writing (except, perhaps, in rare cases) defines a center that puts some on the margins. It is impossible to speak like an expert without pushing against ways of speaking that are taken to be naive.

For Hartman, in my other headnote, style is both cognitive and recognitive. It is the evidence of mediation and, at times, of a writer's consciousness of that mediation. It is language that mediates, that stands before a writer and determines what he will say. When a student, for example, is asked to write an essay about "How I Learned a Lesson," that essay, in a sense, is already there in the institution, with its understanding of what a lesson is or what learning is, with its available introductions, transitions, and conclusions, with its language appropriate for such a narrative. A student moves into that discourse; he does not invent it for the occasion. Understanding, then, is not "genuine" but is acquired through an act of appropriation. Perhaps what an experienced writer has that an inexperienced writer lacks is a consciousness of that appropriation, particularly as that consciousness is manifested in the style on the page — in its record of push and shove — and not just in a writer's felt sense of loss, his sense that whatever he has written is not quite right, that the very act of writing has pushed him somehow onto the margins. Let me look at some examples.

II

Because I have been working on a yearbook for the National Society for the Study of Education, I had the occasion to read the last yearbook devoted to composition: *English Composition: Its Aims, Methods, and Measurement*, written by Earl Hudelson in 1923. Hudelson's book actually is more about measurement than about aims and methods in English composition. He was conducting a study of high school instruction, and in the course of this project he sent out sample student essays for teachers to rank and to comment on. To his horror he found out that there was little agreement on the ranking of essays. He had assumed that the distinctions would be obvious and that good, experienced teachers from around the country would have no trouble agreeing. He found, however, not only that his teachers failed to agree, but that a single essay received both the highest and the lowest ranking.

In response to this, he set out to construct a scale that could be used nationally to systematically rank the work of students at a single grade level (twelfth grade). He constructed two sets of writing assignments: one that would reliably elicit themes "typical" of student writing at a particular grade level and one that would reveal students' "maximal" abilities in composition. With these he constructed a rating scale (from 0–9) represented by sample student essays at each level taken from a file of essays written in response to the standard topics. By studying the samples, he argued, teachers could give a national standard to essays written by local students. The "typical" scale would be used to place students at the beginning of a semester, the "maximal" scale to evaluate their progress at the end of the year.

Hudelson's is an early attempt, then, to distinguish between students who could and could not do the writing required by the schools. His sample papers are interesting, both because they come from an era well before essay testing and holistic scoring became a standard practice (and represent, therefore, a more innocent judgment) and because the essays themselves come from a past whose literary values were different enough from our own to help me make my point. The styles taken for granted in 1923 are less transparently "natural" or "genuine" to a reader in the 1980s.

The essays I will include below were written in response to the following prompt. Teachers were to say to their students, "I want you to write me a composition today. When I give you the title, you are to write it on your papers. Then you will have fifteen minutes in which to write the best composition you can on that subject" (126). The title was, "How I Learned a Lesson." Here are four essays from the bottom, middle, and top of Hudelson's scale:

Sample 1

> When I chewed tobacco and they found it owt they whipped me for about fifteen minnutes with popo bush. they broke ten switches out on me. but i kept on chewing. They found it out and my papa and Mamma whipped me for abowt twenty minnutes and learn me a lesson. (83)

Sample 2

It is said that experience is a dear teacher and *that* is one of the lessons I learned along with the real lesson.

One day I came home from school (as I have been in the habit of doing for the past eleven years) to find the house locked. When our house is locked up and the family go out there are just two ways I know of to get in. The first and by far the easiest is to get the particular key that belongs to the lock in the front door and after inserting it in the lock, turn it, push forward and the door will come open. If a key cannot be obtained there is just one way left, as I know of (and I have had years of experience) and that is to get a good heavy brick and heave it thru the window. Not that I have ever tried this method but its the only sure remidy left as I *Have* tried all the others my brain could conjur up. (84)

Sample 3

Two years ago I worked for a meat shop. Every day I spent a good deal of money on such things as soft drinks, ice cream, and other good things. I did this all summer. My mother warned me against it, but I kept indulging in these things.

By the time school sommenced I began to have stomach trouble. Mother made me quit eating anything I wanted, and kept me on a diet. Finally I was cured of the trouble. Since then I do not "eat drink and be merry" as much as then. (85)

Sample 4

When I sat down to think over the experiences of my life that have been profitable to me my memory wandered back to one of the big lessons I learned when I was yet a little child.

I was in the sixth grade in a little country school. Here I mingled with children from all stations in life and made friends with them all. There was, however, something insincere about my friendship for the poorer children. It was due, I now believe, to a feeling of superiority over them. I resented the ravenous manner in which they ate their lunches I divided with them; I detested their furtive glances when we talked; and I could not tolerate their tendency to lie. In all, they had an uncouth bearing that I could neither understand nor forgive.

That spring our teacher invited me to go with her while she took the enumeration. After visiting a number of homes we came to a place called Grub Hollow where several of our school patrons lived. In one little shack we found the family huddled around a little stove, the walls and floors bare, and everything most squalid and depressing. In another, a dirty, miserable hovel, we found a blind father, an indolent, flabby mother, and three mangy children. Finally we found a family of fourteen living in one room amid unspeakable conditions.

On our way home Miss Marxson was strangely silent, and, child that I was, tears stood in my eyes. I had heard "the still sad music of humanity," and it had given me a new understanding. Never again did I feel haughtily toward those children; and all through life that experience has modified my judgment of human conduct. (89–90)

I'm offering these essays as a mirror within which we can see our own similar judgments when we rank students by levels of ability. I think the rank order of these essays would be maintained today in university testing programs throughout the country, and I suspect that the key break would come between the second and third sample papers (the exact middle on Hudelson's scale); on one side you would have the mainstream students and on the other the basic writers.

You could say that these papers can be distinguished by the rate and level of error (meaning sentence-level error). The spelling mistake in Sample 3 ("sommenced") could be taken as accidental, a slip of the pen, while the spelling mistakes in Sample 1 ("owt," "abowt," "minnutes") seem to be of a different order. The syntax of Sample 2 seems less controlled than the syntax of Sample 3. The writer of Sample 3 doesn't get into the same kind of trouble as the writer of Sample 2 (with his parentheses). Perhaps that is a sign of his skill and perhaps it is a sign that he is cautious. Grammatical mistakes, however, seem like the least interesting or telling features dividing these papers. If you read through the errors, the difference between the top and bottom rank is marked by the ease with which a student (in 15 minutes) could place himself within a conventional discourse (a way of speaking about life and lessons).

While none of these papers could be said to lack form, there is certainly a difference in the strategies of elaboration. Sample 4 tells its story within a general frame that balances a prior understanding against a new understanding. Sample 1 tells a simpler narrative of action and consequence. While all of the papers shape a narrative in service of an abstraction ("How I Learned a Lesson"), in some the lesson is restated in general language that is a step above the language of the narrative ("Never again did I feel haughtily toward those children; and all through life that experience has modified my judgment of human conduct"). The presentation in some is more detailed than in others (particularly in the presentation of "telling" detail — Sample 2 gives a detailed account of putting a key in the door and *those* details, I suspect, are of negative value in a rating). The detail, in other words, is predetermined by a way of seeing that belongs to an available statement about "How I Learned a Lesson." None of the essays, however, could be said to show evidence of a student at a retarded stage of cognitive development (where he is unable to think abstractly or to conceptualize), nor (except perhaps metaphorically) could any be said to represent speech written down. The question, rather, is the type of form that is represented or the appropriateness of the language or of the detail. The value of a sentence like the one cited above ("Never again did I feel haughtily toward those children; and all through life that experience has modified my judgment of human conduct") could be said to have little to do with the conceptual power represented by the generalization (did he "invent" that sentiment or "figure it out" for himself?) and much to do with a twelfth grader's ability to talk like he was 50 ("all through life that experience has modified my judgment of human conduct"). And I think I can safely argue that the "new understanding" he claims as his own in this paper (the conceptual leap the essay dramatizes in its structure) is not an idea he invented but a posture, with its attending language, that stood before this paper (or its writing) and that the twelfth grader successfully brought forward to enable his narrative, "his" story of "his" experience. It was the sort of thing a decent, educated person ought to say about the poor.

The key differences, in other words, are the ways the styles of these pieces constitute (or in Hartman's terms, "betray") the relation of a writer to a discourse or to a social or historical world. In part, to say this is to say that the "world" of the English class (a world represented by its acceptable ways of talking about experience or "lessons") values lessons learned from sympathetic participation in the lives of others (like the poor) more than it does lessons learned from experiences of overeating or of being beaten. To write this essay, in other words, a student has to know what is represented by "How I Learned a Lesson," as that title represents an invitation to bring forward certain kinds of experience and to let others remain silent.

There is also, however, a way of talking about experience that belongs "naturally" to classroom accounts of experience. Perhaps the most telling sign of this is the enabling gesture in Samples 2, 3, and 4. In each, the writer locates his experience (in order to authorize it) within a phrase whose authority is derived from its position in a prior text. For each of these more experienced writers, the primary value of the experience he brings forward is its context within that which has already been said, within the available language to characterize a lesson: "It has been said that experience is a dear teacher and *that* is one of the lessons I learned along with the real lesson." In fact, the range of allusions exhibits another rank ordering. They move from "it has been said that experience is a dear teacher" to "eat, drink, and be merry" to "the still sad music of humanity," beginning with a general commonplace drawn from the common culture to increasingly more remote literary sources. Each, however, speaks finally (and initially) and with the greatest authority as he speaks through the language of his culture.

Part of the telling drama of Sample 2, in fact, is that writer's difficulty getting his experience to fit the frame, since repeated experience seems to have actually taught him only what he already knew — that if he forgets his key he has to stand out in the cold. The only other lesson (that he could get a "good heavy brick and heave it thru the window") takes him again outside the range of the acceptable. It's tempting to say that the "real" lesson he alludes to in the opening sentence is that the language the discourse gives him for his essay is something of a stupid language after all. You can hear *that* version of the writer in the parenthetical asides ("as I have been in the habit of doing for the past eleven years") that seem simultaneously to be an attempt at scholarly precision and a funny demonstration that he is, in fact, "experienced" even if his experience was not much of a teacher.

If this is a writer who has trouble fitting comfortably within the story he knows he is to tell, then Samples 3 and 4 give evidence of writers who can find a seamless fit. Sample 3 seems to me to be the kind of tight, correct essay that could easily be taken as a sign of the writer's problem rather than his achievement. I said earlier that I thought this was a cautious essay, and I think it is, but its size and structure can be accounted for also as evidence of a writer experienced enough to believe that writing doesn't matter. The lesson of indulgence is so obvious and so right, the fit between this writer and the story he knows he is to tell is so tight, that the essay is beyond writing. What he has to say goes without saying. All it takes is a few telling details, the assurance that the lesson has been learned, and the job is done. There is no struggle here because the writer has been completely prefigured in the discourse.

I'd like to look briefly at a similar essay drawn from my own files. This one comes from a placement exam in which students were asked to write about a time they did something they took to be "creative." They were to tell the story but also to draw some conclusions about "creativity."

> During the football season, the team was supposed to wear the same type of cleats and the same type socks, I figured that I would change this a little by wearing my white shoes instead of black and to cover up the team socks with a pair of my own white ones. I thought that this looked better than what we were wearing, and I told a few of the other people on the team to change too. They agreed that it did look better and they changed there combination to go along with mine. After the game people came up to us and said that it looked very good the way we wore our socks, and they wanted to know why we changed from the rest of the team.
>
> I feel that creativity comes from when a person lets his imagination come up with ideas and he is not afraid to express them. Once you create something to do it will be original and unique because it came about from your own imagination and if any one else tries to copy it, it won't be the same because you thought of it first from your own ideas.

This is another seamless paper, where the fit between a writer and a set way of talking about creativity enables the "details" of the event (an event on a football field that stands also before writing) to be read willfully and arbitrarily (as though the reading were "natural"). The power of the commonplace in this essay (creativity as original invention) overcomes any gap between the story it has to tell and the story the writer has to tell (which for football players is also a story of imitation, since professional football players have been wearing white shoes for some time).

The difference between this paper (or Sample 3) and Sample 4, I would argue, lies in the language but not in the writing. The writer who, he says, "learned" to feel sympathy for the poor shows that he has learned to work himself into a powerful way of speaking ("I resented the ravenous manner in which they ate their lunches I divided with them; I detested their furtive glances when we talked; and I could not tolerate their tendency to lie.") which has a particular resonance for readers of nineteenth-century fiction, where it is used to represent a character type quickly. He also knows the stance to take against this attitude: "In all, they had an uncouth bearing that I could neither understand nor forgive" (where understanding leads to forgiveness and then to grace). There is here an appropriate display of character and judgment, one that we have trouble calling anything but "mature." The power of those sentences, and their counterparts in the description of the event that enabled the new understanding ("In one little shack we found the family huddled around a little stove, the walls and floors bare, and everything most squalid and depressing. In another, a dirty, miserable hovel, we found a blind father, an indolent flabby mother, and three mangy children."), speak against the argument of the paper (that he was moved to a new understanding of these scenes), but they in no way jeopardize the "truth" of the final sentiment (with the child's tears and the reference to "the still, sad music of humanity"). To overcome that language would require something very different from this writer — either a different language to talk about the poor (one that was not available to him) or a way, stylistically, of disowning or pushing against the very language that was given to him. I'm not suggesting that this writer should be expected to solve the problem of how to talk about the poor with sympathy. It is an enduring problem. I am suggesting that the next step in the development of this writer is to make him aware of the problems inherent in the language he takes as genuine (a language that takes privilege for granted, that even justifies it by providing appropriate gestures of sympathy). This writer, like many writers, is at work within a discourse that he cannot undo. It precedes the writing and establishes the authority and the forms of understanding that define this writer. An appropriate goal for a literate education is to enable this writer (but also the writer of Sample 1) to work against the habitual ways of thinking that are represented in ways of writing, those that make his position in society (and his form of understanding) inevitable. You could say, then, that this writer's skill does not include the "consciousness of mediation," the awareness that understanding is a mediated activity, that I suggested might be a quality of that advanced literacy represented by the university curriculum. While I do not have the room to demonstrate this here, I think that this awareness, or at least the stylistic evidence of this awareness, is often found in the writing of students whose essays (because they are incorrect) identify them as basic writers. Similarly, the lack of this awareness — or the lack of stylistic evidence of this awareness — can be found in students who are placed easily in the mainstream.[8]

Literacy, as I've been defining it, requires the ability to work within and against the languages of a closed, privileged discourse. This definition is similar to Robert Pattison's in *On Literacy: The Politics of the Word from Homer to the Age of Rock*. For Pattison, literacy involves more than the basic abilities to read and to write. It requires, as well, a consciousness of "the questions posed by language" (5). "Consciousness of the uses and problems of language is the foundation of literacy, but the literate person must also be able to express this consciousness in the ways evolved and sanctioned by the culture in which he lives" (6).

Pattison defines culture broadly and argues that the critical power of this conscious, disciplined use of language can be put to work within the various forms of contemporary American culture — from classical literary studies to freshman English to rock music to the movies and television. Pattison's "new literacy" would eliminate the very distinctions between popular and academic culture that I have taken for granted, since it would take everyone — in school or out — from the margins and put them in the center of a single but multiple cultural life. "I am suggesting a world," he says, "where ordinary students learn Greek and Latin, read Shakespeare in his own words, and still keep their own new literacy" (211). I find it hard to imagine a four-year course of study that would give students this range of reference, although I see no reason to question his assertion that a literate person can and should turn his critical powers to the various forms of his culture. I am not convinced that the result of this, however, can or should be an equal appreciation or acceptance of all forms of thought or expression. I remain convinced that the problems of language require wary as well as generous attention.

I have argued that the exemplary culture within which our students live — in our classrooms, that is — is academic culture, with its powerful ways of representing the world. This is where our students find themselves, as readers and writers, and it is in this specific context that they can best begin to develop an understanding of the problems and uses of language. It is not enough to imagine a world in which readers and writers are equals, particularly when the classroom is the place where this is not so, where there are people empowered by their knowledge and people who are excluded from that power. The classroom can seem like a pleasant enough place when students are willing (or able) to write as we would have them write and be satisfied that this is a natural or genuine mode of expression, an expression of their own rather than a discursive performance that locates them within a system of thought. It appears differently when we look at the basic writing classroom, a classroom where the dialectic of struggle and appropriation is not so easily ignored.

III

I will end where I might have begun, with the question of sentence-level error. We are closer to agreeing on the boundary lines between mainstream and marginal sentences than we are on mainstream and marginal uses of language, but the greatest advances in pedagogy came when we learned to look at nonstandard sentences as though the lines were not so clearly drawn. This method for analyzing sentences is often referred to as error analysis.

As a procedure, error analysis is a method for reading nonstandard sentences by seeing the actual sentence within the context of what we imagine to be its "intended" form. Each written sentence has its counterpart. This shadow sentence, however, is drawn not from the student's language but from our own, from our own repertoire of sentences. It is not enough, then, simply to notice that the student's sentence is strange, unusual, or incorrect. When we read like this, we are performing an act of interpretation, but a generous one, since it requires us to begin by getting inside the style of error and to imagine the written statement as an approximation of a conventional form, as a sentence we might have written. (In my own and my colleagues' work, this has been supplemented by student interviews, so that we could hear students explain the decisions they made while writing.) By reading as though we were seeing two systems at once, we could spot the key moments of variance between the idiosyncratic and the conventional statement and deduce the "rule" that governed a student's actions while he was at work inside our language. Error analysis once may have seemed like a key to the grammar of error — to the general idiosyncratic rule systems that underlie the development of writing ability — but its real power has proved to be its exemplary method: the way it has taught teachers to read students' writing. It has not given us access to a developmental sequence but to a way of imagining the forces at work within a single discursive event.

Let me give an example. The following are four fragment errors; three are pulled from my files (the students were writing about a passage by Rebecca West concerning a lesson she learned from her contact with a young upholsterer); one comes from *Errors and Expectations* (62):

- For Example, the upholsterer scanned the room. Picking out items that defined Rebecca's personality.

- The upholsterer proved there is versatility within generations. That one generation can relate to another without always showing negative feelings and defying the others morals.

- I would say that Rebecca's faith comes in knowing that as long as there is one person in this world who is not nasty, who does not judge a person on material objects or on what she sees on the outside, and who does have a mind with which she can bring these points across to others. In other words, as long as there is one good person left in this world there is a chance that it may survive.

- In my opinion I believe that you there is no field that cannot be effected some sort of advancement that one maybe need a college education to make it.

If we see the style of each as evidence of a student's struggle to work within a set pattern, we could argue that this one type of error has four different causes — that we have, in fact, four different writing problems. In the first case, the student might explain (or show consistently in her writing) that the final fragment was put there for emphasis, a construction not uncommon in print advertising. We could say, then, that this error is only an error within the set expectations of classroom writing. The error in the second example may be evidence of a student who does not consistently recognize sentence boundaries (the first student could; it was the recognition that enabled her decision to write a fragment). This may be a student who, when embedding additional information, fails to punctuate it within the frame of the base clause. The third case may be evidence of a student who just got lost in the middle of a long sentence, didn't know what else to do, and so put a period on the page and started over again. This would be, then, a production or performance error (rooted in the demands of writing a sentence rather than speaking one or thinking of one). Experienced writers also get lost occasionally but know to read back, get their bearings, and put matters under control again. The final error — and I would say that this piece is also a fragment — seems to indicate a more radical kind of confusion. If you take the "finished" sentence to be, "In my opinion, I believe that one maybe needs a college education to make it," then you could say that what you have here is evidence of a student writing down all the possible versions of the sentence that occurred to him while he was composing it.[9] The production is all manifest. There is no silent, unrecorded editing as possible sentence completions are tried out and then rejected. The student, in other words, has not run through that internal monologue where a writer tries and then puts on hold possible next clauses or phrases.

A sentence without both a subject and a predicate can, in other words, be read in a variety of ways. And, I would insist, the value of the procedure is not determined by whether these readings are "true" or not (whether it is or is not, in fact, the case that the third student got lost in her sentence) but by the ways in which the readings (and the method they represent) give us a better understanding of the drama represented by the styles of error. I would like to believe that we can extend this method of analysis to other forms of error as well: to misreadings of assigned texts or miswritings of standard assignments, to failed arguments, unacceptable conclusions, or inappropriate uses of examples, all of which could be said to represent a style enacting a writer's relation to a type of discourse, to a social and historical world. Should we undertake to do this work, it will lead us to examine not only the distinctions we make between mainstream and marginal students but the very structures and uses of language we assume to be central to literate performance.[10]

NOTES

1. I have not listed speaking as a literate skill. I think speech is valued in a university setting only to the degree that it is a version of writing. It is writing spoken (as writing is sometimes, and I think wrongly, said to be speech written). I am comfortable, then, defining language use at the university as basically and essentially textual. For my purposes, we have no "oral" culture. I'll return to the oral/textual distinction below.

2. In accepting the basic binary distinction we force by labeling some students marginal students and others mainstream students, I do not accept all the uses of this distinction. I think it is unjust, for example, to use this distinction to justify the practice of making some students pay for worthless courses — courses, for example, that carry no credit. There are theoretical and pedagogical reasons for separating students into insiders and outsiders. This is not to say that some are not real students or that they are not participating in university study.

3. This work began with teachers in New York City. They brought a humane and scholarly tradition to the situation of students who came to the university through the open admissions programs of the late 1960s. This work is represented most often by Mina Shaughnessy's *Errors and Expectations*.

4. This has been my own project for the last three years. I have begun with students who are said to be acceptable or unacceptable readers and writers according to teachers' judgments or placement decisions. I wanted to define the literate skills of a college student by looking at features of successful and unsuccessful performance in the work of actual students. The richest examples, then, are often those that fall right at the fault line. I've found it useful to try to define differences where the differences are not so obvious. For examples of these studies see "Inventing the University" and "Wanderings: Misreadings, Miswritings, Misunderstandings."

5. I am broadly sketching the outlines of a scholarly debate with a much richer texture. See, for example, Frank D'Angelo, "Literacy and Cognition: A Developmental Perspective"; Andrea A. Lunsford, "Cognitive Development and the Basic Writer"; Thomas J. Farrell, "IQ and Standard English"; the replies to Farrell by Greenberg, Hartwell, Himley, and Stratton in *College Composition and Communication* 35 (1984), 455–78; David Olson, "The Languages of Instruction: The Literate Bias of Schooling" and "From Utterance to Text: The Bias of Language in Speech and Writing"; and David Olson and Nancy Torrance, "Writing and Criticizing Texts." For arguments that have enabled my own, see also, Patrick Hartwell, "Dialect Interference in Writing: A Critical View" and Patricia Bizzell, "Cognition, Convention, and Certainty: What We Need to Know About Writing."

6. Mike Rose makes a similar argument in "Remedial Writing Courses: A Critique and a Proposal" and in "The Language of Exclusion: Writing Instruction at the University." See also David Bartholomae and Anthony Petrosky, *Facts, Artifacts, and Counterfacts*.

7. I have more to say about Shaughnessy's ambivalence in my review essay, "Released Into Language: Errors, Expectations and the Legacy of Mina Shaughnessy." For the profession's ambivalence, see Patricia Bizzell, "Composing Processes: An Overview."

8. I say more about the stylistic evidence of this awareness in "Inventing the University." In that essay, I also discuss the "football shoes" paper cited earlier.

9. Shaughnessy translates this sentence as, "A person with a college degree has a better chance for advancement in any field," and argues that this is an example of the kind of trouble an inexperienced writer gets into when he begins sentences with phrases like "I think that" or "It is my opinion that." Let me be clear that I would not say that she is wrong. The measure of an interpretation is not whether it is right or wrong but whether it is pedagogically useful. I've seen students write both kinds of sentences.

10. Preparation of this manuscript was supported by the Learning Research and Development Center of the University of Pittsburgh, which, in turn, is supported by the National Institute of Education.

WORKS CITED

Bartholomae, David. "Inventing the University." In *When a Writer Can't Write: Studies in Writer's Block and Other Composing Process Problems*. Ed. Mike Rose. New York: Guilford P, 1985.

——. "Wanderings: Misreadings, Miswritings, Misunderstandings." In *Only Connect: Uniting Reading and Writing*. Ed. Thomas Newkirk. Upper Montclair, NJ: Boynton/Cook, 1986.

——. "Errors, Expectations, and the Legacy of Mina Shaughnessy." In *The Territory of Language: Linguistics, Stylistics, and the Teaching of Composition*. Ed. Donald McQuade. Carbondale: U of Southern Illinois P, 1986.

Bartholomae, David, and Anthony R. Petrosky. *Facts, Artifacts and Counterfacts: Theory and Method for a Reading and Writing Course*. Upper Montclair, NJ: Boynton/Cook, 1986.

Bizzell, Patricia. "Cognition, Convention and Certainty: What We Need to Know About Writing." *PRE/TEXT* 3 (1982): 213–44.

——. "Composing Processes: An Overview." In *The Teaching of Writing*. Eds. David Bartholomae and Anthony R. Petrosky. Chicago: U of Chicago P, 1986.

D'Angelo, Frank. "Literacy and Cognition: A Developmental Perspective." In *Literacy for Life: The Demand for Reading and Writing*. Eds. Richard W. Bailey and Robin Melanie Fosheim. New York: MLA, 1983, 97–115.

Farrell, Thomas J. "IQ and Standard English." *College Composition and Communication* 34 (1983): 470–85.

Foucault, Michel. *The Archaeology of Knowledge and The Discourse on Language*. New York: Harper & Row, 1972.

Hartman, Geoffrey H. "The Culture of Criticism." *PMLA* 99 (1984): 371–97.

Hartwell, Patrick. "Dialect Interference In Writing: A Critical View." *Research in the Teaching of English* 14 (1980): 101–18.

Hudelson, Earl. *The Twenty-Second Yearbook of the National Society for the Study of Education*. Part 1. *English Composition: Its Aims, Methods, and Measurement*. Bloomington: Public School Publishing Company, 1923.

Lunsford, Andrea. "Cognitive Development and the Basic Writer." *College English* 41 (1979): 38–46.

Olson, David. "The Languages of Instruction: The Literate Bias of Schooling." In *Schooling and the Acquisition of Knowledge*. Eds. Richard C. Anderson and William E. Montague. Hillsdale, NJ: Lawrence Erlbaum, 1977, 65–89.

——. "From Utterance to Text: The Bias of Language in Speech and Writing." *Harvard Educational Review* 47 (1977): 257–81.

Olson, David, and Nancy Torrance. "Writing and Criticizing Texts." In *Explorations in the Development of Writing*. Eds. Barry M. Kroll and Gordon Wells. New York: Wiley, 1983, 31–42.

Pattison, Robert. *On Literacy: The Politics of the Word from Homer to the Age of Rock*. New York: Oxford UP, 1982.

Rose, Mike. "Remedial Writing Courses: A Critique and a Proposal." *College English* 45 (1983): 109–28.

——. "The Language of Exclusion: Writing Instruction at the University." *College English* 47 (1985): 341–60.

Shaughnessy, Mina P. *Errors and Expectations: A Guide for the Teacher of Basic Writing*. New York: Oxford UP, 1977.

Telling Secrets: Student Readers and Disciplinary Authorities

WITH

CAROLYN C. BALL AND
LAURA DICE

SOCRATES: What do you think, Meno? Has he answered with any opinions that were not his own?

MENO: No, they were all his.

SOCRATES: Yet he did not know, as agreed, a few minutes ago.

MENO: True.

SOCRATES: But these opinions were somewhere in him, were they not? So a man who does not know has in himself true opinions on a subject without having knowledge. . . . if the same questions are put to him on many occasions and in different ways, you can see that in the end he will have a knowledge on the subject as accurate as anybody's. . . . This knowledge will not come from teaching but from questioning. He will recover it for himself.

— PLATO, THE MENO

"Fellowships of discourse". . . function to preserve or to reproduce discourse, but in order that it should circulate within a closed community, according to strict regulations, without those in possession being dispossessed by this very distribution. An archaic model of this would be those groups of Rhapsodists, possessing knowledge of poems to recite or, even, upon which to work variations and transformations. But though the ultimate object of this knowledge was ritual recitation, it was protected and preserved within a determinate group, by the, often extremely complex, exercises of memory implied by such a process. Apprenticeship gained access both to a group and to a secret which recitation made manifest, but did not divulge. The roles of speaking and listening were not interchangeable.

— MICHEL FOUCAULT, THE DISCOURSE ON LANGUAGE

From *Developing Discourse Practices in Adolescence and Adulthood,* ed. Richard Beach and Susan Hynds. (Norwood: Ablex, 1990) 337–58.

INTERROGATING A PEDAGOGY OF RECOLLECTION

Meno, the straight man to Socrates' wit, asks one of the fundamental questions of education: "Can you tell me Socrates — is virtue something that can be taught? Or does it come by practice? Or is it neither teaching nor practice that gives it to a man but natural aptitude or something else?"

Despite the clichéd nature of the question (and it is a cliché the moment Meno voices it), the answer one imagines radically determines the activities of the classroom — not only what the characters do (teachers and students) but how they stand in relation to each other and to knowledge of their subject. If we assume that language produces truth — that both the person knowing and what the person knows are constructions, and that language, culture, history, ideology, institutions, and not only the individual alone are doing the constructing — then the class hour will be organized differently than if we assume that language originates in and expresses a transcendent Truth. If teachers needed only to tell the truth, and students to listen, then the important problems of education would be limited to problems of delivery, getting the goods to the consumer. If, with Foucault (1972), the classroom is where certain ways of speaking (each expressions of the "will to truth") are organized and controlled, produced and protected, distributed and appropriated, then the problems of education have a more complex economics, one that involves the necessarily unequal distribution of power, authority, and value.

Socrates has played a powerful role for modern teachers, if only through the general evocation of a "Socratic method," where teachers question rather than lecture, and knowledge is represented by a method as well as by a set of received (and paradoxically also "discovered") truths. Teachers have used Socrates to name their desire for a scene of instruction where the positions of speaker and listener (if not their roles) could become interchangeable, erasing any inequalities that could be attributed to class, culture, gender, or history. In the course of his dialogue with Meno, Socrates argues that knowledge is not "taught" but recollected by making one of Meno's slaves, who is completely uneducated, reason out geometrical truths "by himself." Socrates uses the slave boy's experience to argue that the soul "remembers" truths from before birth and that these truths can be recollected with the help of questioning, his version of dialectic. Thus, a pedagogy of recollection is one in which the teacher questions the student, who may be as uneducated as the slave boy or as naive as Meno, in order to elicit truths which would otherwise remain hidden, unremembered in the depths of the soul.

Such talk of souls and the transmigration of knowledge is enough to set most educators today laughing, bearing more resemblance to the psychobabble of crystals and Shirley MacLaine than educational theory. Nevertheless, much of what we do as teachers bears startling resemblance to a pedagogy of recollection, and to some degree it must, for it is in the nature of teaching that we must always begin, in some sense, with what our students know. It was the revolution of process-centered pedagogies to acknowledge this fact. Since Mina Shaughnessy (1977), Basic Writing teachers have seen the grammatical errors in a student's paper as evidence of knowledge, as attempts, however mistaken, to approximate the conventions of correctly written prose. Such a pedagogy begins with the student's text, with the "knowledge" she has, and works from there. A similar pedagogy is in operation when students are asked to use their personal experience as the subject of their essays and comments in class. More subtly, but nevertheless a product of the pedagogy of recollection, is the advice to "Remember your audience," followed by a series of questions designed to elicit information about that particular group, whether it be the readership of *Seventeen Magazine* or the editor of a local newspaper or the president of the university. In each of these scenarios, students are asked to draw on what they know in order to do the work of writing, whether it be constructing a sentence or composing an autobiography or imagining an audience.

In this essay we wish to honor the motive to credit the knowledge students already possess, a motive underlying most of the progressive pedagogies deservedly receiving attention in efforts to reform the teaching of reading and writing, including reading and writing in the subject areas. Our primary concern, however, is to raise questions about the knowledge that is said to reside "in" students, the knowledge that could be said to reside "in" the academic disciplines (the knowledge that stands as currency in the academy), and the possible relationships between the two, at least as these relationships are acted out in the classroom and in the students' work.

Students' "common" understanding of things places them outside the specialized ways of knowing in the academic disciplines; education is the process of bringing students into the circle of disciplinary understanding by a combination of practice, recitation, and ritualized initiation.[1] While this opposition between "inside" and "outside" ultimately breaks down, it nevertheless grounds cultural attitudes and academic theorizing. The very rootedness of the distinction we make between communities of discourse marks it as both a necessary and fruitful place to begin thinking about how knowledge is imagined to relate to the self and the institution.[2]

When we started work on this chapter, we began by collecting a set of student essays written for various courses at our school, the University of Pittsburgh, and by reviewing both what the students wrote and what their professors said about what they wrote (usually in marginal comments). In particular, we asked the faculty to give us examples of students who, in their minds, could and couldn't do what the discipline expected them to do with texts, who could and couldn't do the reading and writing necessary for work in their course and, by extension, in their discipline. We have used these documents as the material for our study of how students are positioned, and how they position themselves, in relation to disciplinary authority — to their professors and to the texts that they are asked to read, to understand, and to use as material in their own writing.

It is our contention that the positions which students take in relation to authority — the ways in which they insert themselves into the discourse of the discipline — determine in crucial ways their academic success or failure.

Yet, knowledge of the status relations surrounding discourse production is kept out of the classroom and away from students, who are left to "remember" it for themselves. Such a pedagogy pretends that this crucial knowledge is located "inside," in a student's native intelligence or powers of logic or intuition. In actuality, however, this knowledge is socially constructed; it is itself cultural coinage, simultaneously minted and won through elaborate and ongoing culture wars in which various groups struggle for the power to define knowledge and set standards of language and behavior.[3] Michael Apple (1986) identifies the connection between cultural warfare and education in his introduction to Ira Shor's (1986) *Culture Wars:*

> We should always ask a series of questions about the knowledge that schools teach and the ways they go about teaching it. "Whose culture?" "What social group's knowledge?" "In whose interest is certain knowledge being taught in our educational institutions?"
>
> In this perspective, our educational system provides an arena in which different groups with different conceptions of what is important to know, and often different power, fight it out, so to speak. The culture that ultimately finds its way into the school is the result of these battles, compromises, and what has been called "accords." (p. ix)

The wealth of legitimated knowledge must be acquired; it can never, we would argue, be produced by acts of remembrance: monetary standards are always cultural constructs, arbitrary assessments of worth rather than measurements of innate or essential value. When we fail to recognize in our teaching that some knowledge can never come from inside, from the self, we implicate ourselves in an educational practice which locates "error" in the student rather than as an effect of discursive systems which marginalize some students and reward others.[4]

In this chapter we argue for a pedagogy which makes apparent the status relations surrounding discourse as well as the systems of discourse production which operate in the academic disciplines and the university at large. We want to examine how knowledge becomes legitimated as school knowledge and how such knowledge, riddled with gaps and silences, helps to position students in relation to texts, institutions, and their own lives.

SYSTEMS OF DISCOURSE AND DISCURSIVE CONVENTIONS

Meno's slave boy was able to bring forward knowledge about geometry which consisted of facts about squares and triangles. Being a mathematician, however, consists of more than possessing factual truths about numbers; it involves knowing what kinds of questions to ask, what objects are appropriate for study, what methods are acceptable to a mathematician — not a person good with numbers but a member of the profession of academic mathematicians. These questions and methods are routine, habitual. They seem natural. Sociology claims a field different from, but related to, anthropology, and these institutional divisions, too, seem obvious and natural, an inevitable part of the landscape of reasonable inquiry. Foucault's (1972) definition of an academic discipline is a useful one, for it highlights the artificial nature of divisions which seem commonsensical to us:

> Disciplines are defined by groups of objects, methods, their corpus of propositions considered to be true, the interplay of rules and definitions, of techniques and tools: all constitute a sort of anonymous system, freely available to whoever wishes, or whoever is able to make use of them. (p. 222)

The student who is asked to write like a sociologist must find a way to insert himself into a discourse defined by this complex and diffuse conjunction of objects, methods, rules, definitions, techniques, and tools. He must master, to be successful, the conventions of written discourse, rules of grammar and syntax, rules of style and diction, rules of structure and organization, all varying with purpose and audience. In addition, he must be in control of specific field conventions, a set of rules and methods which marks the discourse as belonging to a certain discipline. These vary even within disciplines; a reader response critic will emphasize one set of textual elements, a literary historian another, and the essays produced will contain these differences. To perform successfully as a practitioner, one must be more than reasonable: One must have more than information about a subject.

A third set of conventions to be accounted for are institutional, rules which mark the discourse as belonging to a specific institutional setting. An essay on literacy written within the English department will differ from one written under the auspices of United Nations development work. And even within the academic setting, the rules vary; an anthropologist writing about literacy produces an essay markedly different from a composition researcher's. *College English* and *Research in the Teaching of English*, both journals located within an academic setting, provide forums for related yet discontinuous disciplinary activity. The texts appearing in these journals differ markedly as to style, diction, format, rules for citation, acceptable subject material, and methods. Moreover, the journals themselves constitute institutions, complete with ruling boards and financial resources. This example only begins to suggest the ways in which these sets of conventions, complex in themselves, interact in elaborate and intricate ways to form discourses which, to complicate matters further, are continuously changing. Thus, the student who is set the task of writing a history paper must be aware not only of written discourse conventions, field conventions, and institutional conventions, but she must possess at least an inchoate sense of how these sets of conventions interact in multidirectional relationships. Students must be able to produce the appropriate intersection of conventions at the appropriate time (although they need not be able to say what this intersection is).

It is no wonder that Foucault corrects himself when he writes that the anonymous system of discourse is "freely available to whoever wishes," adding the crucial qualification: "or whoever is able to make use of them." This qualification of "whoever wishes" to "whoever is able to make use of them," precisely defines the position of the sociology student who may very much wish to make use of that anonymous system but either doesn't know it exists or is only conversant with a portion of it.

But familiarity is not the only issue here. It is not as though a student could freely choose or freely reject (or freely manipulate) those ways of speaking that are quickly at hand, that constitute her cultural heritage and enable her to speak. It is not as though, in reaction to the difficulties of academic writing (writing sociology, for example), the student could turn freely to personal experience (an exercise that is often offered as a starting point or an alternative for the student having trouble with "academic" discourse). This discourse of personal experience carries little value in the academy. Students may write in journals in the sociology class, but these are private, ungraded. And at the moment at which experience is cast into language, it becomes language. Correctly written prose is produced by an elaborate and arbitrary set of rules which dictate not only the order of words in the sentence, but the movement from the beginning of writing to the end, a movement we fondly call the movement of mind but which is more appropriately the disciplining of language, a determined program to insure that students will produce predictable and recognizable discourse. School is the place where this discipline is ritualized by department and degree; schools are institutional sites organized to produce reading and writing, readers and writers. The students' knowledge — or experience, of sociology, of language — is never freely transcribed but instead is shaped and mediated by an "anonymous system" which produces knowledge and text. When asked to write about a moment in her own life, a student becomes instantly enmeshed in the activities of choice and selection, where she cannot ever freely choose or know the experience as it happened. To this degree, writing for school, in whatever form, will always be writing for school, even though school sanctions a multitude of types of writing — the sociology paper, the journal, the lab report, literary criticism, the essay exam.

In each of these situations, a student is asked "naturally" and "freely" to produce a text which is in actuality highly mediated and artificial. In the movie *Educating Rita*, the English professor gives Rita, a minimally educated working-class woman, an essay exam which asks how she would work with the staging problems of a well-known play. She writes the single sentence response, "Do it on the radio." Despite the fact that a radio production would adequately solve the production problems, that the response is in its own way quite brilliant, the professor points out that it is nevertheless in error, for it lacks the elaborate set of field conventions which surrounds the activity of writing literary criticism. Few students are as blissfully unaware (or as consciously resistant?) as Rita, and the story of her education is of her journey away from this naive but happy ignorance. Most students are painfully aware that these anonymous systems of knowledge production exist, but they are equally aware that the workings of these systems are just that, anonymous, a ubiquitous disciplinary secret attributable to and recoverable from no person or source. It is no wonder students fall silent when asked to account in some way for a text they've read; they are being asked to act as if they possess what they very well know they lack, and to take on a role they have not mastered in front of the powerful figures who help to determine how their lives might proceed.

The Situation of the Novice and the Authority of the Institution

Perhaps the quickest index to both the possibilities and problems students face when they situate themselves in relationship to the disciplines can be seen in the way students make use of the words and ideas of experts in their own writing. In quotation and paraphrase students are literally as well as figuratively creating a relationship with the past, with tradition, and with the authority of that discourse privileged by their teachers and the institution.

Here, for example, is a selection from a student paper in an entry-level composition course. The student has read a chapter from Paulo Freire's *The Pedagogy of the Oppressed* (1970), a chapter in which he develops the metaphor of education as "banking" (that is, where teachers make deposits in students), and the student has been asked to use Freire as a way of reading a moment in his own education.[5]

> As a high school senior, I took a sociology class that was a perfect example of the "banking" concept of education, as described by Freire. There were approximately thirty students enrolled in the class. Unless each of our brains was computerized for long memorization, I don't understand how we were expected to get anything out of the class.
>
> Each class began with the copying of four to five pages of notes, which were already written on the blackboards when we entered the classroom. Fifteen to twenty minutes later, the teacher proceeded to pass out a worksheet, which was to be filled out using only the notes we previously copied as our reference. If a question was raised, her reply was, "It's in the notes."
>
> . . . In order to pass the class, each piece of information printed on her handouts needed to be memorized. On one occasion, a fellow classmate summed up her technique of teaching perfectly by stating, "This is nothing but education by memorization!"
>
> Anyone who cared at all about his grade in the class did quite well, according to his report card. Not much intelligence is required to memorize vocabulary terms. Needless to say, not too many of us learned much from this class, except that "education by memorization" and the "banking" concept of education, as Freire puts it, are definately not an interesting nor effective system of education.

The figure of the reader here, we would argue, is typical of students whose strategies in the face of texts are limited to that form of agreement that is functionally equivalent to submission, to silence. In the face of what Freire says, the student says "me too," his words are mine. It is a grand, if empty gesture, appropriating Freire's authority wholesale. It is, in a sense, a student's somewhat desperate attempt to make the roles of speaker and listener interchangeable.

The story he tells is designed to show his professor that he has read Freire, understood him "perfectly," and can now reunderstand his experience "perfectly" in Freire's terms: "Needless to say, not too many of us learned much from the class, except that 'education by memorization' and the 'banking' concept of education, as Freire puts it, are definately not an interesting nor effective system of education." He agrees with Freire's evaluation of traditional education "totally," we can almost hear him say, because it coincides with his own experience. He demonstrates his agreement with, and intellectual debt to, Freire by telling a story which is "covered" by Freire's terminology of banking education. What he fails to acknowledge, probably fails to realize, is the degree to which the story is a representation made to fit, and fit perfectly, Freire's framework. This perfect fit, what we see as caricature, constitutes his bid for authority. He establishes his right to speak by deferring to Freire and speaking through him, a move designed to both establish his textual expertise and free him from the responsibility of entering the discourse in his own name as a speaker, as someone who can have a conversation with Freire.

From this position, everything does become "Needless to say," for the essay is predicted from the start; the writer will restate Freire's main points and provide a story which "fits" his argument. Anyone who has read Freire and attended school can spin out this essay or one very like it, making the whole exercise "Needless to say," except for the student's felt need to establish simultaneously his authority and apprenticeship, a seemingly contradictory position which the student believes cannot be achieved by asking questions.[6]

This oddly aggressive and deferential stance, arising in part from contradictory needs, locates the student in a passive relation to the text he is reading and writing about. This passivity is inscribed in the final sentence of the text in which the student attempts to critique his high school experience as an example of banking education. The (mis)construction of this sentence suggests instead that he learned about Freire and banking education in the very class he was critiquing for its reliance on a pedagogy of memorization. This (mis)construction is particularly apt because it represents the writer's position in relation to Freire's text as the same as that required by the high school teacher he critiques: In both cases the student has taken a passive, banking approach to learning. This passivity is so pervasive among today's students that educators have diagnosed a crisis in literacy and begun designing curricula to teach critical thinking skills.

In a provocative essay "Writing and Criticizing Texts," Olson and Torrance (1983) argue that students' "uncritical attitude . . . results not simply from a logical incapacity but rather from a lack of social authority. The reader does not believe that he or she is in a position to criticize authoritative persons or texts (except perhaps with groans and marginalia)" (p. 39). Olson steps out of the framework of cognitive science to posit in institutional terms what is often described as a reading problem when he acknowledges that all acts of reading occur within a social context and therefore are fraught with the "managing of status relations." Such a view begins to recognize the anonymous system of methods, truths, and rules which constitutes the discipline.

Olson suggests by way of solution that both readers and writers need to recover "a sense of authority, not necessarily of superiority to an audience, but of an equality to the readers who make up the writer's peer group. . . . As a reader, one must come to see the writer of a text as basically equal to one-self, and as a writer, one must come to see the audience, including the teacher as reader, as basically equal to oneself" (p. 40). Such a vision is an attractive view of the academy and of the discipline, positing teachers and students as dedicated equals in the ongoing search for truth where the roles of speaker and listener are interchangeable, where there is an exchange of value and yet nothing is lost. It is, in its own way, as lovely a vision as the classroom which empowers students by acknowledging their knowledge and experience as solely or primarily valid in the learning process. Both visions fail to ade-quately recognize the status relations within the classroom, the discipline, and the university. The sociology student's problem, when writing a sociology paper, will not be solved because she manages to talk herself into believing she is the equal of her professor as well as of Émile Durkheim and Karl Marx. Nor will it be solved by relying on her own experience to stand in as or mag-ically become sociological knowledge, a kind of educational pulling one's self up by one's own bootstraps. Either stance would more than likely lead her astray, one leading to the bluster and arrogant caricature of the previous essay, the other to credulity and provincial blundering. The status relations the sociology student must manage are exceedingly tenuous and tricky: She is asked to speak as a professional sociologist would speak, aware at every moment that she lacks the knowledge she needs to do so, but simultaneously she must speak as a student speaks, acknowledging that she lacks the knowl-edge she is supposed to pretend she has. Our refusal to recognize these parameters, to uncover the anonymous systems of our disciplines, only fur-ther invites students to produce discourses which remain on the edges of knowledge, unrecognized and unrewarded.

SELF-EFFACEMENT AND ERROR

We can begin to uncover disciplinary systems (and secrets) by examining the ways in which the institution, through its representatives, rewards or cen-sures the positions students assume in relation to disciplinary authorities. The excerpt which follows is taken from a research prospectus written for an upper-level course in Anthropology.

Prospectus

The Mulligan Company has been contracted by John Forni Con-

struction, Inc., to perform market research on the feasibility of a miniature

golf course facility within the Oakland area. The proposed project has

many commercial and structural aspects, that the Mulligan Company will   ∧

not attempt to analyze. Rather, examine a single feasibility consideration, i.e., the consumer perception of the proposed miniature golf complex. The Mulligan Company performed a detailed study of the public's attitude and its acceptance-denial ratio. John Forni Construction has placed an additional emphasis for this report to reflect any probability that the black minority of the population using the miniature golf facility would have an adverse effect on the white majority's usage of the facility. This is a sensitive racial issue but one that must be explored for a comprehensive analysis of the proposed plan and for an informed decision to be reached.

~~With the~~ *In* consultation *with* of John Forni Construction, the Mulligan Company has developed a list of variables which ~~shall~~ provide pertinent and necessary data for this study. These variables are placed in question- *B* naire form and cover particular aspects concerning such items as age, sex, and academic status, and personal views concerning the proposed miniature golf course complex (Appendix B). ~~Observed~~ *were* data ~~from these variables was~~ analyzed through statistical means. Statistical analysis provided basic concepts, including mean, midrange, and graphic representation of *C* these variables.

Use double spacing. It is difficult to edit a typescript otherwise.

p. 1A This research has only a single feasibility consideration, which is the attractiveness of such a facility as determined by consumer perception.

p. 1B Variables do not provide data, they give guidance for seeking data. Variables are not placed in questionnaire form. Questionnaires are designed to elicit data addressing specified variables.

p. 1C You should say that data obtained using these variables were subjected to statistical analyses of mean and midrange. (You should also justify using particular statistical analyses.)

You have problems of clear communication. The writing is far from lucid.

This paper received a D. Let us be quick to say that we are not concerned with this grade as a teacher's judgment. For our purposes, we want to take this moment as evidence of the discipline, acting through a representative, encouraging the production of certain forms of knowledge and discouraging others. To that end, it is useful to recall the discourse the student is attempting to reproduce. In "Fieldwork in Common Places," Mary Louise Pratt (1986) discusses the practice of ethnographic writing within the discipline of anthropology. She describes the difference between ethnographic fieldwork which "produces a kind of authority that is anchored to a large extent in subjective, sensuous experience" and "the text which the ethnographer must produce to describe the experience" (p. 32):

> But the professional text to result from such an encounter is supposed to conform to the norms of a scientific discourse whose authority resides in the absolute effacement of the speaking and experiencing subject.

The student who hopes to perform as an anthropologist must understand this difference in forms of authority and produce a text which represses all references to an experiencing self and which pretends the objectivity of science. Yet, as the commentary on this student's performance demonstrates, an understanding of this difference is not enough to insure success. Here we have a student who is obviously aware that he must produce a self-effaced, "scientific," discourse. At no point in this excerpt does he refer to himself either as student or as writer; the facade of "The Mulligan Company" is never directly broken. And even within the fiction of the Mulligan Company, the student never directly reveals the presence of a human researcher at work behind the scenes (except perhaps with the sentence about sensitive racial issues). Moreover, he knows that in order to achieve this pretense he must use certain syntactic forms, like the passive voice, and the specialized language of his discipline. It is in his attempts to deploy the specialized language and syntax of his discipline, however, that he fails: His grammatical error and misappropriation of terms betray his subjectivity, his position as a student. He attempts to take on the master's role, but in the end his position as apprentice betrays him.

Much of the institutional commentary on this paper is aimed at what are often characterized as the "fundamentals" of writing and seen as rooted in an abstract English free from the specific historical or cultural context of its user. The marks on and through the text of the essay are designed to point out and in some cases correct grammar and punctuation errors, violations of written discourse conventions. These grammatical lapses are analogous to the student's inability to master the discourse of statistical analysis which is so valued by the discipline. By the third comment [1c] on this (the first) page, the professor has moved from explaining the proper use of terms like "feasibility" and "variables" to offering a general comment about the student's project: "You have problems of clear communication. The writing is far from lucid."

Versions of this comment appear throughout the paper and become the dominant and overriding explanation of the student's failure. For example, in marginal comment 12A the professor again points out the student's misuse of statistical terminology: "Analysis does not commence (begin) a study. The writing style strains to be formal but slips easily into being pretentious. Greater clarity comes with simplicity and directness."

These comments, which imply that anthropological discourse is simple and direct, locate the origin of the student's problem in the domain of writing (*qua* writing). They suggest that the methods of anthropology, the forms of argumentation and proof, the conclusions such methods produce, are inevitable and obvious. Thus, in this representation of disciplinary work, the student's difficulty lies not in construing anthropological knowledge but in the later stages of the project, the stages of writing, when predetermined knowledge is cast into language.

This separation of disciplinary knowledge and language allows for scientific discourse to derive its authority from claims to transsubjectivity (experienced by all observers rather than a single observer) and therefore objectivity. When the writer removes herself from the process of writing (not just the product), the whole enterprise proceeds properly and smoothly as the right words attach to their objects without the idiosyncratic interference of the writer, or so these comments imply. This student fails because he overcomplicates and obfuscates what would otherwise, naturally, be "clear" and "lucid" — if he didn't get in the way. There is no room for the writer in the almost mathematical formulation, "Greater clarity comes with simplicity and directness," nor is there space in anthropological discourse for any language which calls attention to itself, either by error or misappropriation (or irony or metaphor or any of the other textual elements off limits in anthropological discourse).[7] It may seem odd to include what we see as obvious errors in the same category with the most valued of literary devices. This juxtaposition allows us to understand, however, why misuse of terminology is so severely censured: Such textual excesses, identified here as "pretension," call attention to the text as a constructed rather than a natural object and thereby undermine the discursive claim to objective rather than constructed (and self-interested) truth. A failure to be clear is in practice a failure to cloak the many acts of construction and representation which constitute the process of writing, and which, when apparent, direct the reader's gaze to the asserted rather than effaced subject. Ironically, then, it is an act of cloaking which is required to produce the illusion of transparency and complete self-effacement which authorizes scientific discourse. And it is in these terms that the professor summarizes the problem of the paper as a whole:

> It is cloaked in a writing style that pretends to be objective, factual, and analytical, but which fails to mask the absence of organized data supporting conclusions that meet the objectives of the research problem.

The professor's comment, with its negations and inversions of presence and absence, is no more clear, meaning easy to read, than the student's "misspoken" sentences. It begins to suggest, however, the complexity of disciplinary activity which requires a student to negotiate between clarity and cloaking, between simplicity and pretense, between directness and masking (comment 10A: "The pretense of being a professional marketing survey is carried too far"). This student will move no closer to a correct approximation of anthropological discourse by working on his writing, by trying, for example, to be "simpler" or "more direct," because a discourse only appears simple and direct to those who already know the lay of the land — the terms, rules, conventions, objects, and methods which define a disciplinary field. It is this subtle complex of injunctions and limitations which the student must begin to master. In practice, a discourse is "clear" when all members sharing disciplinary space can understand each other, when they all draw the same lines marking textual excess, when they all understand, for example, how far to carry the pretense and what is carrying it too far. A student cannot enter this circle of understanding by willing himself into it, by willing himself equal to those in the know, for he simply cannot will the knowledge he needs to establish his equality. Against Olson's assertion that students need to see themselves as equal to their teachers and the writers of the texts they read, we place Foucault's reminder that the roles of speaker and listener, in an apprenticeship, are not interchangeable.

Within this context, we can reunderstand the often short comments which mark student success. "Very nice introduction." "This is excellent." "These are brilliant insights." Comments like these mark the students' conformity to disciplinary lines. The professor is saying, "You are doing what we do, and you know what that is because you're doing it." What is masked, however, are the terms within which the authority of niceness or excellence or brilliance has been granted. "This is clear" in practice means, "You have shown me a self which pretends not to be a self but which we both know is really and truly a self; let us be happy in sharing this secret." Both professor and student continue, however, to talk about "clarity" as a characteristic of writing rather than as disciplinary performance. This deflection serves a purpose. The comments pretend that the successful student's authority resides *in* his text, in the style or structure or ideas, a deception which reinforces the belief that this textual brilliance originates in the student. In actuality, the student succeeds because he matches the lines drawn by his discipline; the crucial element lies not so much in the lines themselves, in the specific styles or structures or ideas, but in the act of conforming, of controlling excess. Because the comments themselves cloak the ways in which the discourse operates, the ubiquitous secrets of disciplinary activity and discursive success have been passed on without ever having been revealed. The professor is not dispossesed of his knowledge, and the closed space of the discipline (and the power of its practitioners) has not been threatened by the revelation and circulation of knowledge about how the discipline protects, defends, and preserves itself.

The deflection of a student's gaze away from the discipline and onto writing serves yet another function. Positioned thus, they cannot question, or revise, the discipline: only their papers. When disciplinary operations are uncovered, we can posit that the critical reading problem is produced in part by an anonymous system of discourse which to some degree expects and rewards a passive relation to disciplinary authority.

SELF-ASSERTION AND ERROR

The contradictory and deceptive messages given to students about the practice of self-effacement also surround the practice of self-assertion. One of the most common and powerful pieces of advice offered to student writers is that they develop their "own" ideas and write in their "own" words. The complexity of assuming a position of self-assertion, of "owning" the words one writes, is exemplified by the institutional response to an essay written for a survey course in Sociological Theories. The professor describes the problem of the paper as he explains the grade of D–:

> This paper suffers from a major problem that makes it very unsatisfactory: it draws too much of its sentences directly from the text with minor changes. When you do not do this, you directly quote very often, filling up the space with lines from the textbook. There is no way such a paper can convince me you understand the theories. When you do write your own sentences from your own ideas, you are caught in another basic problem: your choice of Coser and Simmel is a poor one. Coser was working very closely with Simmel's ideas. As a result, you have to strain to find some difference which is barely there. If you revise this paper, I would suggest starting over fresh. Use the Coser theory in some application context or compare Coser with a different theorist. Use some examples of your own and discuss them in order to develop the ideas in your own words.

This writer has engaged in many of the activities of academic writing: paraphrase, quotation, comparison. She has, nevertheless, failed because she hasn't achieved the proper balance. How many words must one change in order to paraphrase rather than plagiarize and at the same time stay close enough to the text that one isn't charged with idiosyncratic interpretation? How many lines must one quote in order to provide textual support without quoting *too* many? How different must two theorists be before differences can be located "without strain"? These questions point to the complexity and artificiality of textual activities which teachers often assume are simple and straightforward. The primary advice offered to this student directs her back to herself, however, rather than outward into the discipline: "Use some examples of your own and discuss them in order to develop the ideas in your own words." This final directive suggests that the student's problem will begin to be solved if she relies on her own experience and her own language instead of that of the text, that is, if she asserts rather than effaces her "self." A sociology text, however, is not primarily a medium for authentic self-expression, as such advice would indicate, but is instead, like anthropology, a form of scientific discourse requiring some degree of self-effacement. An examination of a successful sociology paper will reveal the hidden principles behind the directive to write "in your own words."

An A paper from the same sociology class begins with a two-page story, unintroduced, about a group of five students who worked together on a class project. At the top of page three, the writer explains the intention of her paper: "In this paper I am going to analyze this group based on three theorists and their ideas." The next two pages are given over to explanations of the theories. For example, the writer defines Parsons' AGIL Model: "AGIL stands for how a system adapts to its environment, how it defines and attains goals, how it integrates its parts, and how it goes about latent pattern maintenance. The AGIL Model is a structural-functional model of society analysis." The remaining four pages are devoted to a discussion of the class group in terms of the three theories.

This paper is successful in part because it offers as a subject for analysis an extended example drawn from the writer's personal experience. This narrative no doubt contributes to the impression that the writer has indeed managed to write "in her own words." However, the story itself offers no surprises. The group was formed on the basis of "common interests" and "people who could work well together," and it did work well together because each of the members could contribute to the group in a unique but necessary way: "The psychology and sociology majors could do most of the research, the writing major could write the paper, the communications major could type the paper, and the computer science major could do most of the work on a video. . . ." In the formation of the narrative, we can already see the sociological perspective providing a representational framework; the group is already being represented in terms of function, a sociological concept which has so saturated our cultural consciousness that the story itself is highly conventional and stereotypical, hardly an original idea of the writer's.

Nor does the writer explain the theories "in her own words," as the section quoted earlier on the AGIL Model demonstrates. These lines are not taken word for word from the textbook, as infelicities such as "society analysis" suggest, but the language is very close. This particular writer, however, is not chided for drawing the sentences from the text with only minor changes. She realizes, and is rewarded for knowing, that in order to claim authority as a sociologist she must produce the self-effaced discourse of science. She knows when it is appropriate, and indeed necessary, to sound like the textbook, to efface herself, and when it is better that she assert herself.

The "original" sections of the paper are those where she offers her view of the theories and her application of them to the extended example from personal experience. These are moments in the text when she locates herself in relation to the textual authorities she has read. She offers this translation of the theories she has described:

> Durkheim, Goffman, and Parsons all share a common view. Each of these theorists see people as being motivated, but the source of motivation differs. For Durkheim the motivation is the sacred object. Goffman sees the individual as being the motivation, and to Parsons there is a specific goal that is doing the motivating. The actions performed in regards to these motivations are what promote group stability and solidarity.

This is the moment in a paper when we expect the writer to produce an insightful and interesting translation of the theories. What we get in this case is a statement of the obvious: These theorists see people as being motivated, but the source of motivation differs. One need hardly have read these theorists to produce such a bald generalization. While the D– writer failed to convince the teacher that she had read the text because she quoted extensively from it, this particular writer succeeds, even though she could easily have written these lines without ever having read Durkheim, Goffman, or Parsons.

While the institution does censure this paragraph, it remains clear that the lapse falls within the realm of acceptable error, while the D– writer has erred in ways that the discipline simply will not excuse. The marginal comment alongside this paragraph reads: "This is neither clear nor convincing." As was the case with the anthropology paper discussed earlier, the problem of this paragraph is represented as a writing problem, a matter of "clarity." We would argue, however, that the problem is not that the writing lacks clarity, but that what it presents is so obvious. Rather than addressing the complex issue of what constitutes an acceptable translation or reading of sociological theories, an issue which threatens to raise disciplinary questions, the institutional voice has displaced the problem as a writing problem. As a result, the anonymous machine of the discipline is kept anonymous and what is in actuality a very complex and difficult problem is made to seem clear-cut and trivial, a problem of "clarity," which could be solved by choosing more accurate words, or of persuasion (being "convincing"), which could be solved by offering more explanation or support. None of these strategies, however, can rescue this paragraph from its shallow "sociological" commentary.

The other moments of textual translation occur when she applies the theories to her own experience. At these points she often relies on such clichés as "it was the good aspects of deference and demeanor and the realization that people don't have to like each other to work well together that kept this group together," or "Each of the members tried hard to work with all of the other members, and they tried not to let personal feelings get in the way of what had to be done." Again, the writer fails to provide powerful translations in the moments we expect them, offering instead cultural commonplaces we all recognize.

Nevertheless, this writer succeeds, despite the commonness of her observations (and perhaps because of them; it may be an aspect of the role of student to speak in clichés, as Plato understood when he gave Meno his voice). She succeeds because she knows how to sound like a student of sociology: She knows how to use the languages of sociology and of the commonplace in such a way that she sounds "like herself," a sociologist and a student. This particular example foregrounds the ways in which the "self" is composed of multiple languages drawn from different settings and different cultures: advertising, textbooks, cultural commonplaces, church, the neighborhood, and on and on.[8] In institutional settings, some languages are designated appropriate in some situations (and these situations can vary, as we have seen, from paragraph to paragraph); some languages are almost never appropriate. Thus, speaking "in your own words" means speaking the words that are acceptable in a particular context, not words which are familiar from personal settings, as any student from a background of nonstandard dialect well knows.

This institutional wisdom, "be yourself," "use your own words," is obviously curious advice, since what is being asked for is often some repetition of knowledge and language which originates elsewhere, in the discipline and the culture at large. Such directives function in much the same way as the comments discussed in the previous section: to occlude the discovery that knowledge is constituted rather than natural. Students are therefore placed in a position of relative powerlessness in relation to the discipline and disciplinary knowledge; prevented from working on the discipline, they are left to work on themselves as learners — to memorize faster, study longer hours, read more books — but these activities cannot guarantee the learning of disciplinary knowledge necessary for success in school.

Positioning Students as Workers in a Discipline

When a student positions herself in relation to disciplinary authorities, she must in every case grapple with determining what "self" to present. In some cases, she must "efface herself" and show forth the anonymous face of scientific discourse (an elaborate deception which involves cloaking the interpretive self-interest of all acts of writing). In these rhetorical and classroom settings, to err is to let one's self appear. In other cases, she must "assert herself" and produce an organization and language "of her own" (an elaborate deception which involves pretending one creates language and organization which have already received authorization in other institutional contexts). In these settings, to err is to choose the wrong language or balance of languages, to let the "non-self" appear, to copy or to be inauthentic. Whether self-effacement or self-assertion, the position the student assumes is in actuality a textual construct composed of complex and elaborate sets of conventions. An authentic self is as much a textual construct as an effaced self; neither is a direct transcription of the individual who is doing the writing. Thus, knowledge of which "self" to show forth in a particular rhetorical context can never be gotten simply by looking inside as if searching one's closet for the appropriate outfit: Outfits must be made. One must know what materials and designs are appropriate to the social event in question; one must know how to make or acquire the materials and how to design the designs; one must know what's been worn before, which variations would be fresh and which outrageous. It is this kind of knowledge, however, the constitutive knowledge of the discipline, which is naturalized and kept hidden by institutional representations of disciplinary work.

We can pull at two of many threads in this complex problem of educational success and failure. On the one hand, we must reassert that knowledge must be taught and learned in order to balance pedagogies of recollection which may, with all good intentions, overemphasize the role of the student's own language and experience in learning. In doing so, we must remember the spirit of those good intentions: a desire to see students — all students — as whole and powerful figures in their own learning and living.

The other thread of the problem pulls less easily. We must recall the culture wars which surround the educational enterprise and determine which knowledge gets taught and which languages and behaviors become standard. It is not enough to reassert the necessity of teaching certain kinds of knowledge to disadvantaged students. We must also contend with disadvantage; that is, we must examine the ways in which cultural warfare legitimates the knowledge, language, and behavior of one group and marginalizes or exiles that of others. Many "back to basics" programs reassert that knowledge, "the basics" or "fundamentals," must be taught and learned. They fail, however, to address the issues of cultural contention, legitimation, and domination which run through any pedagogical practice. We question whether it is enough to provide suitable wardrobes, "cultural literacy," for the disadvantaged without asking in a persistant and hard-minded way who sets the standards of "suitability," who benefits, and who loses.[9]

We have only begun in this essay to show how the positions available to students for entering disciplinary discourse require and reinforce a passive relation to discursive and institutional authority. Certainly the process of disciplinary and cultural reproduction is more complicated than what we have outlined in these brief sketches of disciplinary activity. The simple and bold strokes of these scenes can only suggest in a crude way patterns which must be more fully, more minutely investigated. Even such incomplete sketches as these, however, argue against an idealized scene of instruction in which teacher and student are equal, their roles interchangeable. Students will not be empowered as disciplinary practitioners by relying on their own experience and language to stand in as disciplinary knowledge; nor will their passive positions be made active by teaching them one segment of disciplinary knowledge, the "basics" or "content," while keeping secret knowledge of how the discipline operates. If students are to see themselves as something other than "inspired" or "shooting the bull" or "guessing" — representations of disciplinary activity which posit them as essentially passive in relation to the work at hand — we must begin to make visible and available the machinery which produces the university's disciplines and its multiple discourses.

NOTES

1. For other discussions of the ways in which students' acts of reading and writing are constituted by disciplinary conventions and institutional power relations, especially for students who enter the university speaking a language different from the language expected in the classroom, see Bartholomae (1985, 1986, 1987).

2. The opposition of "inside" and "outside" ultimately breaks down insofar as subjectivity — what we commonsensically think of as "inside" — is structured by linguistic, psychoanalytic, and institutional factors. How this structuring occurs is the subject of current theoretical debate. A useful introduction to this debate can be found in Wolff (1984). For a specific treatment of how education structures subjectivity, see Althusser (1971).

3. Carr (1988) examines the set of student positions constructed and made available through the McGuffey Readers. She discusses how the Readers represent and constitute literacy as cultural coinage, and how students from multiple cultures are positioned by such a practice.

4. We have to some degree oversimplified the process of educational reproduction since some students, those with access to traditional elite education, seem able to produce knowledge by acts of remembrance. For these students, however, there was still a time when this knowledge was not

already known, although it does seem to become "natural" for them earlier and more easily than for most students without access to this form of education.

The process by which this knowledge becomes naturalized for some students (and not others) needs further research, at both the institutional and individual levels. Such research is underway in studies of education and the reproduction of class structure. See Apple (1982), Aronowitz and Giroux (1985), Bowles and Gintis (1976). These authors examine how educational institutions, through specific practices such as labeling and tracking, reproduce existing hierarchies of social class. A useful introduction to this perspective on education can be found in Ferguson (1988).

5. This assignment appears in "The Aims of Education" sequence in Bartholomae and Petrosky (1987).

6. The extent to which it is acceptable practice for students to question and critique an authoritative essay varies from program to program. The teacher for whom this essay was written expected more than a summary of Freire's text; most high schools, however, discourage the kind of questioning which would lead to a more sophisticated reading of Freire and of the student's own experience. This is another example of how discourse practices vary with institutional setting.

7. Chamberlain (1989) examines how composition textbooks and handbooks on writing discourage students from the use of irony (as they might use it to excess) and thereby deny them access to one language of power. Such advice reproduces a structure of relations in which the practitioners of a discipline have and are able to deploy knowledge which is kept from those who are supposed to be learning what the practitioners know.

8. The concept of the author as a unified and originary source of meaning, and as a figure of "genius," is critiqued in Barthes (1977) and Foucault (1977). The implications of this critique for the composition classroom are explored by Berlin (1988).

9. E. D. Hirsch's (1988) educational program (argued for in *Cultural Literacy*) is an example of a "back to basics" curriculum which fails to address in a serious way the ideological question. His list of items with which every "culturally literate" person must be familiar imposes a set of legitimated knowledge on all who would be educated. The construction of the list, however, is not a neutral activity, and it remains to be asked who sets the list and whose interests are represented? The list itself becomes a powerful weapon of cultural warfare.

REFERENCES

Althusser, L. (1971). Ideology and the ideological state apparatuses (notes toward an investigation). In B. Brewster (Trans.), *Lenin and philosophy and other essays* (pp. 127–86). London: Monthly Review Press.

Apple, M. W. (Ed.). (1982). *Cultural and economic reproduction in education: Essays on class, ideology and the state.* London: Routledge & Kegan Paul.

Apple, M. W. (1986). Series editor's introduction. In I. Shor (Ed.), *Culture wars: School and society in the conservative restoration 1969–1984* (pp. ix–xiii). New York: Routledge & Kegan Paul.

Aronowitz, S., & Giroux, H. (1985). *Education under siege: The conservative, liberal and radical debate over schooling.* South Hadley, MA: Bergin & Garvey.

Barthes, R. (1977). The death of the author. In S. Heath (Ed. and Trans.), *Imagemusic-Text* (pp. 142–48). Glasgow: Fontana/Collins.

Bartholomae, D. (1985). Inventing the university. In M. Rose (Ed.), *When a writer can't write: Studies in writer's block and other composing-process problems* (pp. 134–65). New York: Guilford P.

——. (1986). Wanderings: Misreadings, Miswritings, Misunderstandings. In T. Newkirk (Ed.), *Only connect: Uniting reading and writing* (pp. 89–118). Upper Montclair, NJ: Boynton/ Cook Publishers, Inc.

——. (1987). Writing on the margins: The concept of literacy in higher education. In T. Enos (Ed.), *A sourcebook for basic writing teachers* (pp. 66–83). New York: Random House.

Bartholomae, D., & Petrosky, T. (1987). *Ways of reading: An anthology for writers.* New York: St. Martin's Press.

Berlin, J. (1988). Rhetoric and ideology in the writing class. *College English, 50,* 477–94.

Bowles, S., & Gintis, H. (1976). *Schooling in capitalist America.* New York: Basic Books.

Carr, J. F. (1988). *McGuffey Readers and the construction of American literacy.* Unpublished essay. University of Pittsburgh, PA.

Chamberlain, L. (1989). Bombs and other exciting devices, or the problem of irony. *College English, 51,* 29–40.

Ferguson, M. (1988). Teaching and/as reproduction. *The Yale Journal of Criticism, 1,* 213–22.

Foucault, M. (1972). The discourse on language. In A. M. S. Smith (Trans.), *The archaeology of knowledge & the discourse on language* (pp. 215–38). New York: Harper & Row.

Foucault, M. (1977). What is an author? In D. F. Bouchard (Ed.), *Language, counter-memory, practice: Selected essays and interviews* (pp. 113–38). Ithaca, NY: Cornell University Press.

Freire, P. (1970). *Pedagogy of the oppressed.* New York: The Seabury Press.

Hirsch, E. D., Jr. (1988). *Cultural literacy: What every American needs to know.* New York: Vintage Books.

Olson, D. R., & Torrance, N. (1983). Writing and criticizing texts. In B. Kroll & G. Wells (Eds.), *Explorations in the development of writing* (pp. 31–42). New York: John Wiley.

Plato. (1961). Meno. In E. Hamilton & H. Cairns (Eds.), *The collected dialogues of Plato* (pp. 353–84). Princeton, NJ: Princeton University Press.

Pratt, M. L. (1986). Fieldwork in common places. In J. Clifford & G. E. Marcus (Eds.), *Writing culture: The poetics and politics of ethnography* (pp. 27–50). Berkeley: University of California Press.

Shaughnessy, M. (1977). *Errors and expectations: A guide for the teacher of basic writing.* New York: Oxford University Press.

Shor, I. (1986). *Culture wars: School and society in the conservative restoration 1969–1984.* New York: Routledge & Kegan Paul.

Wolff, J. (1984). *The social production of art.* New York: New York University Press.

Postscript: The Study of Error

This first cluster of essays stages out a study of error that has occupied much of my career, one initiated (at least in print) by the CCC essay that carries the name. Why error? The quick answer is that at the end of my graduate career, I was interested in how "everyday" and "ordinary" language (and "everyday and ordinary people") could serve the projects of serious, critical thought. I was reading Raymond Williams and Victorian novels, and I was reading and teaching Robert Frost and Richard Poirier on Frost. I was interested in how ordinary language could serve complex and revisionary intellectual projects, and Freshman English seemed like just about the most interesting place a person could be with interests like that.

I never thought that these forms of thinking belonged solely to the academy. I knew about the esoteric languages and methods of the disciplines, including my own. But I thought (perhaps naively) that the academy could or should also be a place where students learned to work, as writers and readers, with the texts and ideas that were valued by a broad national (or international) intellectual audience. I was not interested in what would later be called "writing across the curriculum" and then even later, "writing in the disciplines." I was interested in what students might be able to *do* with Emerson or Freud or Rich or Woolf, serious writers with a broad circulation both inside the academy and out.

And I was interested in where and how the work of writers, including student writers, failed or fell short of institutional expectation — as it inevitably and rightly would. This was a left, liberal motive — I wanted to characterize, explain, and value student writing in such a way that their work could be taken seriously. And I wanted the work to be read carefully and taken seriously so that we (as faculty) could better understand the processes by which students could best approximate and enter the discourses of intellectual exchange. With such grand ambitions, I arrived at the University of Pittsburgh in 1975 to help to direct a newly redesigned composition program, with the specific charge to develop the writing center and courses in basic writing. In the first few years I was writing course materials and articles on curriculum and pedagogy, as these forms seemed natural to the work I was doing as a teacher and an administrator. But I felt pressure to define a "research" project, and in 1975 there wasn't much to turn to for models.

At Pitt, I had become acquainted with Bob Glaser and Lauren Resnick, the directors of Pitt's well-known Learning Research and Development Center (LRDC). Bob appointed me as a Center Associate, which means I had a separate office for writing, away from the English department, and it meant that I could participate with and present work to the other "researchers" at the center. Bob was a cognitive psychologist; he used to joke that he would turn me into an "experimentalist."

And, in a sense, he did. These were the days of residual structuralism, when it seemed possible to imagine that there were systems underlying the patterns of culture. I wanted to do something systematic, something that could be replicated in thinking about basic writers, and in particular, in thinking about error in written language. Glaser introduced me to research on math errors, research showing the patterns in errors children made doing problems in addition and subtraction. David Brumble, a colleague in English, introduced me to research on error in second-language learning.

And by this point I had met and begun to work with Tony Petrosky, who had come to Pitt's School of Education as a Composition Specialist. These were the days when a credentialed composition specialist in a School of Education had taught little, if any, composition, and Tony, to his great credit, asked if he could teach courses in our program, which he did. Soon after this we were working closely together on a number of projects — and almost 30 years later we continue to work together as friends and collaborators. As part of my training in the study of error, Tony introduced me to miscue analysis. A group of us, including graduate students, were reading Labov and (later) Smitherman on Black English. And, finally, we were inspired by Mina Shaughnessy's *Errors and Expectations*, a manuscript copy of which a friend (Susan Miller) sent to me before its publication. In Shaughnessy, we saw careful, systematic efforts to name and categorize error, and we saw the application of the very compelling arguments of error analysis, that errors were not random but (often) patterned and regular, that they were not evidence of ignorance but applications of alternative systems, that they had their own logic and style.

We began an attempt to gather together large numbers of placement and classroom essays, all written by students identified on our campus as "basic writers," with the idea that we would see where and how we could group and cluster what we saw, using Shaughnessy's terms and categories or, where they would not serve or fit, inventing our own. As the essay "The Study of Error" recounts, the most interesting moments for me came when I began to interview students and, finally, to tape their reading aloud of a paper, this in advance of an interview in which I would ask them to find and identify errors and to explain what they were doing or intending at that moment in writing.

As I suggested above, this was part of a very productive and exciting period on our campus, when many of us were working together teaching and designing basic writing courses. The literature on basic writing contains much of that work, work by Nick Coles, Bruce Horner, Glynda Hull, Elaine Lees, Min-zhan Lu, Tony Petrosky, Mariolina Salvatori, Bill Smith, and Susan Wall. And the work of that period is represented in the book Tony and I wrote with our colleagues, *Facts, Artifacts and Counterfacts: Theory and Method for a Reading and Writing Course* (1986) a book that, I'm pleased to say, is still in print, still in circulation, and still serving to help shape courses on campuses across the country.

In the period following "The Study of Error," I was committed to the idea that we could determine a grammar of error, a predictable pattern true for all learners and keyed to stages of development. I still have copies of the "error taxonomy" we developed for a large, computer-based project funded through LRDC. This was, of course, a vain hope, although the methods we developed for understanding and responding to sentence-level error have had considerable application in basic writing programs generally. With colleagues in my department, I was also reading Barthes, Derrida, and Foucault. (In the early 1980s I gave my first MLA paper, titled "Derrida: Writing, Underwriting and Unwriting," with *Of Grammatology* and M. H. Abrams's "The Deconstructive Angel" as its key points of reference.) And I was also reading the very fine work of Joseph Williams, including "The Phenomenology of Error." As the work we were doing on error and the sentence reached its limits, it made greater and greater sense to begin to think about error as a social and institutional rather than a psycholinguistic phenomenon, as something produced by the university rather than as something residing in student writers or in their prose. Instead of looking in the student essays, we began looking at the systems that pronounced them wrong.

I began a set of projects to study the academy and the logic (and the systems) behind the regular and inevitable decisions that identified certain students as "unable" to read and write, who did so, ironically, on the basis of work they had produced as readers and writers, work that had its own sense and style and even eloquence. And I began to look beyond the sentence, to look at the larger discursive features of the written work of students who were said to be unable to read or to argue or to have ideas. I wrote a series of papers to think this through — " 'Released into Language': Errors, Expectations and the Legacy of Mina Shaughnessy"; "Wanderings: Misreadings, Miswritings, Misunderstandings"; "Writing on the Margins: The Concept of Literacy in Higher Education"; "Telling Secrets: Student Readers and Disciplinary Authorities" (coauthored with Carolyn Ball and Laura Dice, two fine graduate students and colleagues); and "Inventing the University."

Mike Rose commissioned "Inventing the University" for his volume, *When a Writer Can't Write: Studies in Writer's Block and Other Composing-Process Problems.*" I wrote the essay during my first sabbatical leave (1982–83), while I was teaching in Spain at the Universidad de Deusto (and teaching a composition course in a lecture hall to 350 students — I remember this as one of the most successful writing courses I ever taught, but that is another story). Mike asked for the essay on the basis of "The Study of Error," which had begun to be anthologized and used as part of the literature on the "composing process." I was no longer trying to script what could be known about the mind and/or behavior of the writer; I was interested in thinking about the educational system as "a political means of maintaining or of modifying the appropriation of discourse, with the knowledge and the powers it carries with it." This was from my epigraph to that essay, drawn from Foucault's "The Discourse on Language."

I think Mike was more than a little surprised by what he received. We wrote back and forth for several weeks as I made the case for both a different way of thinking about student error and for a different kind of essay. Mike was, as he always is, open and generous and willing to add a kind of odd rejoinder to his collection. In his preface he said, "David Bartholomae, Director of Composition at the University of Pittsburgh, relies on textual analysis informed by recent Continental literary theory to argue that any piece of writing is produced within a particular linguistic-rhetorical context, a context that places profound constraints on a writer's composing process" (xi).

Frankly, it has been thrilling to see this essay used, anthologized, and cited so often and in so many places — including freshman writing courses. I know it is reproduced and used in freshman courses because I often receive e-mails from students asking me about this or that, or sending me copies of what they have written. It has also been discouraging to see how often the essay is misread — or how often my name is used to identify positions I have never taken, in this essay or elsewhere, on the proper relations between a student and the academy. This has not gone unnoticed. In his essay "Genre as Social Institution," Jim Slevin notes:

> While Bartholomae, in this article and elsewhere, has problematized this notion of privilege and sought ways of reconceiving power relations within the academy, that nuance has not always been noticed by those who have derived their own analyses, curricula, and pedagogies from him. (150)

He continues:

> But the more basic problem, as I see it, is that students, if they are to understand their positions as writers within the complex generic system (not the single genre) we call "academic discourse," need not to imitate its surface form or receive instruction in its conventions, but rather to engage in the kind of analysis in which Bartholomae himself is engaged. That is the point Bartholomae himself makes, his most important point, really, and unfortunately the one that has often gotten lost. (150)

Jonathan Monroe makes a similar point: in "Poetry, the University, and the Culture of Distraction":

> Though Bartholomae's essay may be reductively misread as advocating something like an indoctrination into the discursive practices of the various disciplines . . . , I take his argument to be rather that these discursive practices function as a kind of reality principle which those writing in an

academic environment have little choice but to negotiate, whether to conform to them or challenge them, in order to write effectively. (n. 12)

My concern in "Inventing the University" was to locate student writing within the structures of power and knowledge in the academy. I was describing the position of the student writer; I wasn't advocating this position or encouraging it or using it as the occasion to feel smug. I have often been asked why I didn't follow up on "Inventing the University." It is clear to me that I did. The concerns and the energy were directed toward the textbook projects, best represented by *Ways of Reading*.

Ways of Reading was derived from a course at the University of Pittsburgh that we designed to give students productive access to figures (to individuals and to ways of thinking) that were valued in the academy. In most composition courses, we argued, students were given trivial materials and then reviled for trivial thinking, for having little interesting to say. Our primary concern in our courses was to teach the writers what the academy valued but that were generally withheld from students (Emerson, Freud, Geertz, Griffin, Pratt, Rich, Foucault, for example) and withheld because students were unprepared to read them. The freshman writing course, we argued, should be the arena of such preparation. Students should be given work beyond their immediate reach, work that was *not* written for them, thus they (and their instructors) could take seriously their positions as students. They could, for openers, understand difficulty as a necessary and positive condition for a student reader or writer. And a writing course, we believed, should give students assignments and exercises that could allow them to use writing to find a way in, to establish points of purchase, places from which they, too, can have something to say and to have something to say in the presence of others, figures of power, precedence, and authority. This required a classroom where students were allowed the right to speak about matters that they had not yet mastered, to write from a limited experience and a limited perspective and yet to write with conviction and authority. The goal of the writing assignments was to move students beyond paraphrase and summary so that they could materially, on the page, find themselves speaking alongside and in the manner of some of the major thinkers and writers of our time. Thus, the textbook presented "re-reading" as a standard practice, and the writing assignments were divided between those that asked students to work with and through the essays in the anthology and those that asked students to work inside the experimental or alternative or challenging forms of the essay represented in the readings. I think of *Ways of Reading* as offering an alternative pedagogy; I also think of it as an alternative to the usual anthologies of contemporary nonfiction. (For some specific classroom practices, see the "Questions We Are Often Asked" section of the *Ways of Reading*, Instructor's Manual.)

The textbook projects have occupied a very large part of my writing time from 1985 to the present. I think the textbook is an interesting and challenging genre. I think some textbooks, although not all, make profound interventions in the field. It sounds overstated and grandiloquent, but in the mid-1980s I wanted to shape the work and the values of thousands, even hundreds of thousands, as they taught and wrote. I could not do this by writing for the journals alone. Actually, from the time I entered the profession I knew I wanted to write textbooks, although I waited until I was tenured to make the textbook central to my professional writing. It is a very special and rare reader who reads a textbook without having to, and who reads a textbook as scholarship, as a way of writing theory or as a serious engagement with the field. I would like my readers to see "Inventing the University" and *Ways of Reading* as coherent elements in a single career.

WORKS CITED

Monroe, Jonathan. "Poetry, the University, and the Culture of Distraction." *Diacritics* 26, 3 & 4 (Fall/Winter 1996) 3–30.

Rose, Mike ed. *When a Writer Can't Write: Studies in Writer's Block and Other Composing-Process Problems.* New York: Guilford P, 1985.

Slevin, James F. "Genre as Social Institution." *Introducing English: Essays in the Intellectual Work of Composition.* Pittsburgh: U of Pittsburgh P, 2001.

PART TWO

Teaching Composition

Teaching Basic Writing:
An Alternative to Basic Skills

At the University of Pittsburgh, we teach Basic Writing to around 1,200 students each year. The instruction is offered through two different courses — Basic Writing (3 hours, 3 credits) and Basic Reading and Writing (6 hours, 6 credits). We also have a Writing Workshop, and basic writers frequently attend, but their attendance is voluntary, and the workshop is not specifically for writers with basic problems.

The courses are not conventional remedial courses: they carry full graduation credit and there is little in the activity the courses prescribe to distinguish them from any general or advanced composition course. In fact, because of the nature of the assignments, the courses would be appropriate for students at any level. This is certainly not to say that there is no difference between a basic writer and any other student writer. There are significant points of difference. But it is a way of saying that writing should be offered as writing — not as sentence practice or paragraph practice — if the goal of a program is to produce writers. The assignments, about 20 in a 15-week term, typically ask students to consider and, from various perspectives, reconsider a single issue, like "Identity and Change" or "Work and Play."[1] In the most general terms, the sequence of assignments presents writing as a process of systematic inquiry, where the movement from week to week defines stages of understanding as, week by week, students gather new information, attempt new perspectives, re-formulate, re-see, and, in general, develop a command of a subject.

The instruction in writing, which is basically achieved through discussion of mimeographed copies of student papers, directs students in a systematic investigation of how they as individuals write, and of what they and their fellow students have written. The assumption behind such a pedagogy is that growth in writing ability is individual; that is, it will follow its own developmental logic, one that derives from a syllabus "built into" the learner, and such growth takes place not through the acquisition of general rules but through the writer's learning to see his language in relation to the languages

From *Journal of Basic Writing* Spring/Summer 1979: 85–91.

around him, and through such perception, to test and experiment with that language. Such a process begins not with the study of Writing in the abstract, but only when a student develops a way of seeing his own writing, and a way of seeing that his writing has meaning beyond its paraphrasable context, that it is evidence of a language and a style.

We set out, then, to construct a pedagogy to develop that analytical reflex that would enable students to see their writing as not only "what they said," but as real and symbolic action: real, as deliberate, strategic, and systematic behavior, not random or outside the realm of choice and decision; and symbolic, as dramatically represented through such terms as "voice" or "writer," "audience," "approach," and "world view."[2] For the basic writer, this might mean the recognition that the errors in his writing fall into patterns, that those patterns have meaning in the context of his own individual struggle with composing, and that they are not, therefore, evidence of confusion or a general lack of competence.[3] This perspective might mean the recognition that one's writing defines a stance in relation to an imagined audience or an imagined subject and that any general improvement would include improved control over that kind of imagining. Or this perspective might bring about the recognition that writing is deliberate and strategic, not random, not something that just happens to a writer. When students are able to see that they have been making decisions and exercising options, other decisions and other options become possible.

The nominal subject of the course, then, is defined by an issue like "Work and Play," but the real subject is writing, as writing is defined by students in their own terms through a systematic inquiry into their behavior as writers. Behind this pedagogy is the assumption that students must be actively writing and simultaneously engaged in a study of their own writing as evidence of a language and a style, as evidence of real and symbolic action.

Most basic writing programs I observe, and most basic writing texts, are developed as though this were not possible. They begin with the assumption that the writing of basic writers is a "simpler" version of a universal writing process, or that it is evidence of unformed or partially developed language behavior, that the performance of basic writers is random, incoherent, as if basic writers were not deliberately composing utterances but responding, as the dominant metaphor would have it, mechanically and doing so with unreliable machinery. The end product of this reasoning is that basic writers need, finally, to learn basic or constituent skills, skills that somehow come prior to writing itself. Before students can be let loose to write, the argument goes, they need a semester to "work on" sentences or paragraphs, as if writing a sentence in a workbook or paragraph in isolation were somehow equivalent to producing those units in the midst of some extended act of writing, or as if the difficulties of writing sentences or paragraphs are concepts rather than intrinsic to the writer and his struggle to juggle the demands of a language, a rhetoric, and a task. These basic skills are defined in terms of sequences — "words, sentences, paragraphs, essays" or "description, narration, exposition, persuasion" — that, in turn, stand for a pedagogy.

Such a pedagogy meets the immediate needs of teachers who are frustrated by an almost complete inability to understand what could be happening in the heads of students whose writing seems to be so radically different from their own, or from the writing they've learned to read. And it is the convenience of this pedagogy, which frees all parties, teachers and students, from ever having to talk about writing, that leads teachers to hang on to it in the face of evidence that it produces limited returns. The skills curriculum is not founded on any investigation of the language that students produce, nor any systematic investigation into how writing skills are acquired. If there is a syllabus common to such skills courses, it derives its logic and its sequence from the traditional study of the sentence and the paragraph, units the learner is seen as incompetent to produce, rather than from any attempt to imagine a sequence of instruction drawing on the syllabus built into the learner, corresponding to his particular competence and the stage of his development in the acquisition of the formal, written dialect.

The distinction that needs to be made, I think, is the distinction between competence and fluency.[4] Mina Shaughnessy's brilliant study of the writing of basic writers in *Errors and Expectations* shows the fallacy behind the thinking that equates signs with causes, that necessarily assumes a student misspells because he can't spell, leaves endings off verbs because he doesn't know how tenses are formed, or writes a sentence fragment because he doesn't understand the concept of a sentence. Her work defines both the theory and the method of analysis that can enable us to see student error as other than an accident of composing or a failure to learn. In fact, she argues that the predictable patterns of error are, themselves, evidence of students' basic competence, since they show evidence that these writers are generating rules and forming hypotheses in order to make language predictable and manageable.[5] Errors, then, can often be seen as evidence of competence, since they are evidence of deliberate, coherent action. Error can best be understood as marking a stage of growth or as evidence of a lack of fluency with the immensely complicated process of writing, where fluency can be as much a matter of manipulating a pen as it can be of manipulating constituents of syntax.

A pedagogy built upon the concept of fluency allows distinctions analogous to those Frank Smith makes in his analysis of the reading process. A fluent reader, according to Smith, is one who can immediately process large chunks of information, as compared to the reader for whom the process is mediated by mental operations that are inefficient, inappropriate or a stage in some necessary developmental sequence.[6] Basic skills, then, are basic to the individual's ability to process information and can be developed only through practice. The natural process of development can be assisted by pedagogies that complement an individual developmental sequence, and by those that remove barriers, false assumptions, like the assumption that readers read each word, or read sounds, or understand everything at every moment.

BASIC WRITING

Our program begins, then, with the recognition that students, with the exception of a few who are learning disabled or who have literally never been taught to form words, possess the skills that are truly basic to writing. They have the ability to transcribe speech into writing, and the writing they produce is evidence of the ability to act deliberately in the production of units of discourse to some degree beyond the single sentence. We separate out, as secondary, what can justifiably be called mechanical skills, skills that can be taught as opposed to those that can only be developed.[7] D'Angelo has defined these skills as handwriting, capitalization, punctuation, and spelling.[8] Since a knowledge about these is of a different order than linguistic or rhetorical knowledge, they are not the immediate subject of a course in composition. Since, however, errors of capitalization, punctuation, or spelling are not necessarily due to a simple lack of information about capitalization, punctuation, or spelling but must be seen in the context of an individual's confrontation with the process of composing through written language, this is not to say that a concern for those errors is secondary.

A responsible pedagogy, I've been arguing, begins by making the soundest possible speculation about the syllabus built into the learner, rather than imposing upon a learner a sequence serving the convenience of teachers or administrators. We have decided that the key to such a sequence lies in what we might call a characteristic failure of rhetorical imagining, a failure, on the part of basic writers, to imagine themselves as writers writing. Or, to phrase it another way, the key to an effective pedagogy is a sequence of instruction that allows students to experience the possibilities for contextualizing a given writing situation in their own terms, terms that would allow them to initiate and participate in the process by which they and their subject are transformed. This, I take it, is the goal of Friere's pedagogy for non-literate Brazilians, a "problem-posing" education that enables the individual to turn his experience into subject matter and himself into the one who names and, thereby, possesses that subject.[9]

The goal of instruction in basic writing at the University of Pittsburgh is to enable students to locate ways of perceiving and describing themselves as writers. We've chosen to do this by involving them, through class discussion of student papers, in the regular, systematic analysis of what they have written and how they went about writing it. The only text for the course, then, is the students' own writing and if there is a theory of instruction, it is embodied in the kinds of conversations we have in class about that writing. The classes are designed to enable students to develop, for themselves and in their own terms, a vocabulary that will allow them to name and manipulate their own idiosyncratic behavior as writers. The conversations in class, as the class evolves over the term, approach writing in four ways. The approaches, of course, overlap and at times seem identical rather than different, but for convenience's sake let me describe four perspectives we want students to develop on their performance as writers.

The first of these "approaches" asks students to consider writing as an experience by asking them to analyze and describe their experience with our assignments over the course of the semester. If they do nothing else, discussions about how an assignment was done, what it was like, and how it felt can enable students to see the ways in which writing is a human activity, one that can be defined in personal terms. For students who see writing as a mystery, or as a privilege of caste, it is liberating to hear others, including instructors, talk about how sloppy the process is, or about ways others have dealt with the anxiety and chaos that so often accompany writing. It's liberating to hear of the habits and rituals of other writers. It's liberating to find out that ideas often start out as intuitions, as a sense of a connection it would be nice to make, and that the ideas only become reasoned and reasonable after repeated acts of writing. It's helpful to discover that other writers get stuck or have trouble starting at all, just as it is helpful to hear about ways others have found of getting past such blocks. And finally, it is always liberating for students to hear that successful and experienced writers produce good sentences and paragraphs only after writing and throwing away a number of lousy sentences and paragraphs. This is not how writing is described in our textbooks, and students, even if they know how to talk about "topic sentences," "development," or "transitions," don't know how to talk about writing in ways that make sense given their own felt experience with the process.

Writing is a solitary activity and writers are limited by the assumptions they carry with them to the act of writing. They are limited, that is, by the limits of their ability to imagine what writing is and how writers behave. The basic writers we see characteristically begin with the assumption that good writers sit down, decide what they want to say and then write straight through from an Introduction to a Conclusion without making any mistakes along the way. So if it is liberating to hear about the struggles and rituals of other writers, the power of such liberation extends beyond the comfort that one is not alone, since the process of identifying a style of composing, and seeing that style in relation to other styles, is the necessary prelude to any testing and experimenting with the process of writing.

In addition, the activity of collecting information from the reports of other students, generalizing from that information, and defining a position in relation to that general statement recapitulates the basic intellectual activity of the course. It is exactly what students are doing as they write papers on "Work and Play."

One way of approaching student writing, then, is to have students, once they have finished an assignment, gather specific information on what was easy and what was hard, what was frustrating and what was satisfying, where they got stuck, what they did to get going again, and so on.

Another way of approaching writing is to have students analyze their performance as a task or a problem-solving procedure.[10] Since writing is, by its nature, a strategic activity, any discussion of strategy in general ought to begin with students' analyses and descriptions of the strategies underlying and perhaps inhibiting their own performance as writers. The point of such discussion is not to give students rules and procedures to follow, recipes for putting a paper together, but to put them in a position to see their own writing as a deliberate, strategic activity and to put them in a position to find labels for that phenomenon.

There are any number of ways of initiating such an inquiry. We ask students, once they've finished a series of papers, to go back and find what they see to be their best piece of writing in order to draw some conclusions about where those ideas or where that writing came from. We also ask students to conduct a general survey of how people write. Each student is asked to describe the preparation of a specific assignment as evidence of distinct "stages" in the writing process, and each class develops its own model of the composing process by pulling together the information from the individual accounts and defining categories, or general definitions of stages. This model, and the labels students invent to define it, serves as a point of reference throughout the term. Students may return at a later date to consider their activity in a single stage, like revision or pre-writing, through the same process of analysis. Again, students are gathering information, generalizing and locating themselves in relation to general truths.

Clearly one of the lessons that emerges from this inquiry is that there is no one way of describing writing, since individual composing styles will define points that can't be brought together by a generalization. So if it is true that a writer's performance is limited by his ability to imagine how writers behave, then the process of objectifying a composing style and measuring it against the styles of other writers, and against models for the composing process offered by the instructor, is one way of improving that performance.

There are two occasions when the instructors step in and impose terms on the general inquiry. Early on, if students' own responses don't lead us to it, we make a distinction between generating and editing, since we are anxious to involve students with two different "modes" of writing — one self centered or subject centered and the other audience centered. Writing in the first mode, which can be tentative, exploratory and risk-free, a way of talking to oneself, doesn't ever emerge without extensive prompting.

We also direct students, after the first few weeks, to both write and re-write. And re-writing is defined as separate from editing, which is presented as clean-up work. Rewriting is defined as the opportunity for the discovery of new information and new connections, where the first draft serves as a kind of heuristic. It is also the occasion for consolidating and reshaping the information in the first draft, where the first draft is a rough draft. Every assignment, in fact, falls into a sequence in which papers are rewritten at least once. The rewriting is done with very specific directions and the resulting papers are reproduced and considered in the next class discussion. The emphasis on rewriting reflects our own bias about how successful writers write, and about the importance of enabling non-fluent writers to separate the various demands, like generating and editing, that writing makes upon them in order to postpone concentrating on some while focusing on others. In conjunction with this, there is an assignment that asks students to consider successive drafts, both their own and others', in order to draw conclusions about what they see happening, and to come up with advice they could offer to other writers.

The third focus for conversation is the students' writing as evidence of intellectual activity, as a way of knowing. Each focus could be represented by a basic question. The questions for the first two might be something like, "What was writing like?" and "How did you do it?" The question representing this third area of focus would demand a much higher degree of reflexiveness, since it asks students now to see their writing as symbolic action. The appropriate question would be something like, "Who do you become by writing that?" or "What sort of person notices such things and talks about them in just such a way?" Or perhaps the question would be, "Who do I have to become to take this seriously, to see reading this as the occasion for learning and discovery?" The aim of such questions is to enable students to imagine a rhetorical context, another way of seeing "meaning" in their language beyond its paraphrasable content. If writing is a way of knowing, each act of knowing can be represented by dramatizing the relation between writer, subject, and audience. A student's uncertainty about how one establishes authority in a paper, or about what constitutes intelligent observation, can be represented for that student in dramatic terms when, for example, the discussion in class leads to a description of the writer as a parent pounding on the dinner table and giving Lessons on Life to a wayward child.

It's been noted in several contexts that when basic writers move from report to generalization they characteristically turn to formulary expressions, Lessons on Life.[11] In response to students' difficulty in producing meaningful generalizations, much attention is being paid to research in cognitive psychology, presumably in hopes of finding a key to the mechanism that triggers generalization. A response more in keeping with our own training, however, is to acknowledge the motive in such an utterance and to redirect the writer by asking him to reimagine both his audience and his reason for writing. While it is initially funny for students to realize the role they have cast for me and for themselves in such writing, discovering an alternative is a problem they will wrestle with all semester, since it requires more than just getting things "right" the next time. It means finding a new way of talking that is, at the same time, a new way of representing themselves and the world.

This approach to the relation between the student's language and the conventions of academic discourse is more likely to engage a student's own sense of his knowledge, of the ways in which he can become an intelligent observer and recorder, than any set of lessons on the structure of academic prose, since it is based in a student's own writing and represents that writing as a dramatic act of verbal placement rather than as the mechanical yoking of something called "ideas," on the one hand, and "form," on the other.

There are also more specific ways to account for the difficulty these students have participating in the world of ideas. Surely part of the problem can be seen as external to a student's innate competence as a concept maker, since one universal of basic writing is the students' conviction that while other people's lives provide the stuff out of which concepts are made, this is certainly not true of their own. Basic writers' relations to the world of verbal culture are often defined in such a way as to lead them to conclude that no relation is possible. To use a metaphor offered by one student of mine, ideas may be "stolen" from books or from teachers. It is foolish, then, to assume that they can be "offered" or "shared."

The responsibility of a pedagogy is to enable students to imagine the kind of relation between themselves and their world that allows them to turn their experience into "subject matter" and to define a relationship with that subject that makes creative thinking possible. This is not just a matter of a lesson in class or a pep talk, since whatever we say in class will be understood only in relation to our actual assignments, where we are, in effect, establishing the conditions of such a relationship. Let me describe one response to this problem by describing a sequence of assignments taken from our Basic Reading and Writing course.

The students write a series of papers that describe a change that has occurred in their lives in the last two or three years in order to draw conclusions about how change occurs in adolescence. These papers lead up to a longer autobiographical essay that asks them to draw some conclusions about change in general. At the same time, they are reading autobiographical accounts of children and young adults caught up in change — Margaret Mead in *Blackberry Winter*, Maya Angelou in *I Know Why the Caged Bird Sings*, Holden Caulfield in *The Catcher in the Rye* and Huck in *The Adventures of Huckleberry Finn*.[12] The autobiographical essays are reproduced, bound together, and offered to the class as the next text in the series of assigned readings. Students read the autobiographies in order to report, in writing, on what they see to be the significant patterns — common themes and experiences or contradictory themes and experiences — and to provide names or labels for those patterns. They do this in order to go on to speculate, in general, on the ways adolescents change and the kinds of changes that occur. The next set of assignments directs them to the first half of Gail Sheehy's *Passages*, where they see her involved in an identical process of inquiry, report, labeling and speculation. As writers, they are asked to go back to reconsider the autobiographies, this time using Sheehy's labels as well as their own. The last two books for the course are Edgar Friedenberg's *The Vanishing Adolescent* and Margaret Mead's *Coming of Age in Samoa*.

The point of the sequence is to allow students to reconsider the positions they have achieved in their own study of adolescence by defining new positions in relation to the more formal representations of psychologists and anthropologists. But their own attempts to categorize and label provides the source of their understanding of Sheehy, Friedenberg, and Mead. The labels and categories of academic culture are not given prior to the students' attempts to make sense out of the subject in their own terms. As a consequence, the students are allowed not only an aggressive stance in relation to these ideas, but also, and this is the most important point, in relation to the intellectual activity which these ideas represent. Theories, in other words, are seen as things real people make in order to try and make sense out of the world, not as gifts from heaven. These assignments also provide occasion for students to consider the methods they used for going back to a book and rereading in preparation for writing, and to confront, through a consideration of their own papers, the question of presenting information through quotation and paraphrase.

Earlier in this paper I argued that basic writers are limited by the ways they imagine writers behave. It is also true, however, that they are limited by their assumptions about how thinkers behave. When we chart in class, whether through a student paper or some problem-solving exercise, the *ad hoc* heuristics that underlie a student's thinking, the most common heuristic is the heuristic of simplification. Basic writers, because they equate thought with order, profundity with maxims, often look for the means of reducing a subject to its simplest or most obvious terms. Ambiguity, contradiction, uncertainty — those qualities that are most attractive to academics — are simply "wrong" in the minds of students whose primary goal is to produce controlled and safe essays.

As long as writing teachers' instruction represents thinking in terms of structures, and not process, the attitude that courts uncertainty or contradiction is unlikely to develop. Consider, for example, what one formula for paragraphing invites students to do. We tell them to begin by stating an idea, which means they will put down the first thing to come to mind, which, for any of us, is most likely to be a commonplace. Then we tell them to "restrict" that idea and to "support" it with some examples, so that writing "about" the idea precludes any chance to test or probe that idea. If a piece of contradictory evidence worms its way in, or if a student changes his mind half way through, he has, as my students never fail to remind each other, made a "mistake," since the contradictory movement — the one place where something might be said to happen — destroys the "unity" and "coherence" of the paragraph. This image of coherence invites students to be stupid, and that invitation is confirmed whenever we praise an empty paragraph for being well developed.

At the University of Pittsburgh, courses are designed, then, to enable students to see their own writing from various perspectives: as an experience, as a task, as a way of knowing. The last perspective we need to provide for basic writers is a way of analyzing their writing for error. Since our courses are designed to invite students to take risks, to try to do and say things they cannot immediately do and say, we are inviting them to make mistakes. To cover their papers with red circles would be a betrayal of this trust, and yet it would be irresponsible to act as though error didn't matter. Since each set of assignments makes a distinction between first drafts, revisions, and editing, we have the opportunity to provide a context where focus on error can be meaningful, where it can be seen in relation to other ways of talking about writing.

We make no reference to error or to editing at all for the first third of the term. We've found that certain errors will disappear and others will become less frequent as students simply practice writing and become more limber and fluent. In addition, we want to establish firmly a way of talking about and valuing writing as something other than the production of correct sentences, since a recognition of what writing can be and the ways one can be serious about writing can provide the incentive to spend the time it takes to make writing correct.

We introduce editing by tacking a third stage onto writing and rewriting, a time set aside to re-read final drafts in order to circle mistakes and then, if possible, make corrections. We have found, from this, that one of the most difficult tasks we face is teaching students to spot errors in their writing, and this difficulty is not necessarily due to an inability to distinguish between "correct" and "incorrect" forms.[13] Consider, for example, the student who wrote the following:

> This insight explain why adulthood mean that much as it dose to me because I think it alway influence me to change and my outlook on certain thing like my point-of-view I have one day and it might change the next week on the same issue. My exprience took place in my high school and the reason was out side of the school but I will show you the connection. Let me tell you about the situation first of all what happen was that I got suspense from school. For thing that I fell was out of my control sometime but it taught me alot about respondability of a growing man. The school suspense me for being late ten time. I had accumate ten dementic and had to bring my mother to school to talk to a conselor.

When this student read the passage out loud, he automatically filled in the missing words, corrected *every* incorrect verb by speaking the correct form, and added S's where they were missing from plurals. He also gave the correct phonetic representation of "accumate" (accumulate) and "dementic" (demerit). And he made all these corrections as a reader even though in most cases he could not, at least without a great deal of coaching, see the discrepancy between the words he read and the actual black and white marks on the page. The issue with this student is not so much one of competence but of fluency with the extremely complicated process of transcription.

The fact, then, that students overlook errors while editing is not necessarily due to carelessness or a lack of understanding of standard forms. In most cases, we've found the difficulty lies in the trouble basic writers have objectifying their language and seeing it as marks on a page rather than perceiving it as the sound of a voice or a train of ideas. Students "see" correct forms when they proofread because they read in terms of their own grammatical competence. Clearly there is a class of error, most often errors of syntax, that some students cannot see because they lack some basic conceptual understanding, such as an understanding of the boundaries of the sentence. But there is another class of error that students have great trouble spotting which makes it impossible to generalize that basic writers fail to see errors because the errors represent ignorance in the first place.

We teach editing by having students edit their own papers and those of their colleagues. We also do sentence-by-sentence editing of papers as a group, where the students are directed to both look for patterns of error, in order to draw conclusions about the kinds of errors and sources of errors, and to speculate in general on editing as a strategy. This allows instructors the occasion to offer the standard advice about reading out loud and reading from bottom to top. Students do all their editing in red, with errors both circled and corrected on a separate sheet, so that the instructors can work with individual students to chart and document the patterns that emerge. This allows the instructors to identify the students who can manage editing on their own, or with only a minimum of coaching, and those who will require close individual supervision in order to cope with both the errors that they have the resources to correct but cannot find, and those errors that they cannot find and cannot correct. We have found that no matter how similar the kinds of errors students make, a diagnosis of those errors leads us to sources so bound to individual problems and individual styles as to make general instruction virtually impossible, with the exception of instruction in a generally unknown piece of punctuation like the semicolon.

By giving students typed copies of their papers to work with, by highlighting groups of three lines and indicating the number of errors these lines contain, by reading passages out loud and having students read their writing out loud, we can determine which errors lie beyond a student's immediate competence, and we have found that we can both increase a student's ability to spot errors and develop those reflexes that allow him to make decisions about correct forms. It has become commonplace to note that such decisions can be made independently of "knowledge about" language, without, that is, knowledge of schoolbook grammar. Once students learn to spot errors on the page, which is a matter of learning to see their language as a language, a significant percentage of students we work with have the resources to correct a significant percentage of the errors themselves.[14] We encourage students to trust their own "sense" of correctness and to test that "sense" against the editing we do as a group. We want to assist, then, the natural process of testing and rule formation. In individual sessions with students, we remain as silent as possible, serving primarily to focus their attention on the page. Students chart their own errors looking for patterns and speculating on what the patterns mean in terms of their own specific activity as writers. We insist, however, that students provide their own names for the errors they observe, since it makes no pedagogical sense for them to work from our labels through to the phenomena they observe in their own writing, particularly if the goal of the instruction is to allow students to develop their own resources for correcting.

Finally, however, we are left with a core of students who make a set of errors that they cannot find and do not have the resources to correct. The difficulty here is finding a way to talk with students about their writing, since such talk will inevitably need to revert to grammatical terms and concepts. Here we have reached the point where there is information, "knowing about," students must have. Shaughnessy isolates four key grammatical concepts that teachers and students will need to share for such conversations to be possible: the concept of the sentence, of inflection, of tense, and of agreement.[15] In our

Basic Reading and Writing course, the course where problems are such that this kind of instruction is often required, we use a series of sentence-combining exercises that run throughout the semester, so that we have an additional resource for talking to students about constitutents of syntax. Our instruction at this level, however, is based almost entirely on the sample exercises in *Errors and Expectations.*

BASIC READING AND WRITING

This 6-hour course was developed in response to a need to provide another mode of instruction for students with skills equivalent to the third, or bottom level of proficiency described by Shaughnessy in *Errors and Expectations.*[16] Students are identified for the course on the basis of a writing sample and the Nelson-Denny Reading test. Of the group identified for the course, approximately the bottom 5% of the freshman class, the mean vocabulary score on the Nelson-Denny Reading test was 24.1 (the 8th percentile for grade 13) and the mean comprehension score was 18 (the 35th percentile), with the mean total score falling at the 29th percentile. No one scored above 40 on the vocabulary test or 27 on the test of comprehension, and scores went as low as 10 in vocabulary (with 10% at or below 15 and 24% at or below 20) and as low as 9 in comprehension (with 24% at or below 15).

These are students whom we found could read through an essay like those found in freshman readers but who seemed powerless to make any response to the reading. When they were done reading, they literally had nothing to say, and we came to define comprehension for our own purposes as the ability to follow an act of reading with a written response that was pertinent and coherent. We learned from a survey that they were also students, who had, by and large, never read a book. They had crammed for tests from textbooks, and had learned to strip-mine books for term papers, but most of them had never had the experience of working from cover to cover through books of their own choosing, of deciding what to read and paying consistent deliberate attention to a text.

In designing a course, we were seeking, then, to provide for students who were not being served by the existing Basic Writing courses. We decided that these needs would not be best served by an additional semester of writing instruction, since the additional time for writing offered by an extra 15 weeks is really no time at all given the extremely slow growth of writing abilities and the diminishing returns of back-to-back writing courses, where students are actually denied the opportunity to test new behavior against "real" writing situations or to allow these newly found skills to follow their own developmental sequence. We decided, rather, to argue for more concentrated instruction at the outset, where we could double the amount of writing and the time spent analyzing the activity of writing, and where we could include experience with, and analysis of, acts of reading.

The design of the course, in part, was motivated by my frustration with the existing reading instruction on campus. I had done some work with reading specialists and had grave reservations about the model of reading presented through instruction in reading skills. Such instruction relies primarily on exercises that take the paragraph as the basic unit of a reader's comprehension. In a reading "lab," students read paragraphs in order to answer questions on main ideas, vocabulary, and inferences. Whether or not the paragraph is the key unit in reading comprehension, and I doubt it is, comprehending a paragraph isolated in a workbook is so very different from comprehending a paragraph embedded in a whole text, and so very different from comprehending a whole text, as to make it virtually impossible for one to stand for the other. With the workbook approach, students can take a semester of reading instruction without, in effect, ever doing any reading, at least as reading means reading whole texts. And the overriding problem with the concept of a single, identifiable "main idea" that all readers will agree upon is that it denies readers their own transaction with a text, and it denies them the perception that reading is such a transaction, not a series of attempts to guess at meanings that belong to someone else. It does not involve a student in an active process of meaning-making, where meaning is determined by the individual reader, his purpose for reading, and prior understanding of the subject. In fact, the exercises used in reading skills instruction are set up as if these variables didn't exist, or as if they were just static, mere annoyances.

We also decided not to model our curriculum on the study skills approach to reading, which is, more or less, instruction in how to read a textbook, and which becomes, given the ethos of such survival courses, instruction in how to avoid reading by learning to read only topic sentences or tables of contents. Our goal was to offer reading as a basic intellectual activity, a way of collecting and shaping information. As such, we were offering reading as an activity similar, if not identical, to writing. The skills we were seeking to develop were not skills intrinsic to "encoding" or "decoding"; that is, they were not basic or constituent skills, like word attack skills, vocabulary skills or the ability to recognize paragraph patterns.

We wanted to design a pedagogy to replace those that define reading as the accurate reception of information fixed in a text, and fixed at the level of the sentence or the paragraph, since that representation of reading reflects our students' mistaken sense of what it means to read. They see the inevitable confusion that comes with working through a whole text, at least one worth reading, as evidence that they have "gotten lost" or "missed something." They are primarily concerned that they can't remember everything they read. This, they feel, is what separates them from "good" readers. In place of this misrepresentation, this inability to imagine themselves as readers reading (for what reader doesn't forget?), we wanted to offer a model that allowed them to postpone their immediate need for certainty in order to read for the larger context that makes individual bits of information meaningful, or worth remembering. We wanted to offer a model of comprehension that allowed students to work with whole texts and to see the ways in which reading requires that they re-assemble a text in their own terms by discovering patterns of significance that are as much statements about themselves as readers as they are statements about a text. This interaction between reader and text is the source of those meanings that transform the paraphrasable content of the text into some other form of meaning.

We were not concerned, then, with decoding, with questions about what a text said, but with what one could say about a text and with what could be said about any individual act of saying. Extended written responses were the only way of representing the kind of comprehension we were interested in teaching, and such written records were the only source of inquiry into the acts of comprehension our students could, at any moment, perform.

We reviewed the recent work in psycholinguistics and reading, work which defines comprehension in terms of the processing of syntax, where general fluency and comprehension can be developed through activities like sentence-combining. Some of the work in this area, like the work by Stotsky[17] and Sternglass,[18] is quite compelling and may be appropriate for students with problems different in kind from those we confronted in our students. We felt, in designing the course, that our concern should be with acts of comprehension beyond the sentence or the paragraph, and our bias towards larger units of discourse was justified by later findings from the research we did on the course. We administered a series of Cloze tests, which are tests of literal comprehension, of the ability to process syntax and predict meaning, and we found that all of our students, even with the tests at the beginning of the term, scored above the level that indicates adequate literal comprehension of texts whose readability was scaled at grade 13. We concluded that students' low reading speeds, their general failure to comprehend or give adequate response and the general difficulty they had with academic reading tasks must be attributed to something other than difficulty processing syntax.

The writing assignments in the course were developed on the same principles as those for the Basic Writing course described earlier. There were two types of reading assignments, each defining a different context for reading. Students read regularly in class from books of their own choosing.[19] If, as is certainly the case, students learn to read complete texts by reading complete texts, and if our students have little or no experience with this, then a reading class ought to be a place where people read. And ours was — twice a week, for 30 and then 45 minutes we all, students and teachers, sat and read. Our primary goal was to help students develop the discipline and attention it takes to sit down and pay consistent, careful attention to a book. Many of the students in the classes I taught confessed that this experience was entirely new to them. By the amount of reading in these books that went on outside of class, and on the basis of conversations I've had with students since the course, there is reason to believe that some students discovered the habit of reading.

For this in-class reading, students declared an area to read in, something they had always wanted to have the time to pursue, and they went to the library or bookstore and prepared a list of books to read. After each reading session, students wrote in a journal they kept as a record of their reading. At first these entries were open. Students were asked to record whatever struck them as important in what they read. As the course developed, we asked for more formal representations of what they had read — summaries, comparisons with earlier reading, or speculation about where the book was going, and so on. We reviewed the journals each week and used them as the basis for conferences on individual problems.

There was also a core of seven assigned texts, all relating to the theme of "Identity and Change" which provided the subject for the course. The books represented a variety of modes — fiction, autobiography, and analytical works written for a general academic audience.

We approached the reading in three ways. Initially we asked students to talk about their experience with a particular text and, in response to these discussions, to look for patterns in the experience that their colleagues reported. The primary goal was to define reading as a human activity, one that can be understood in intimate, personal terms rather than in terms of mystery or maxims. By talking about where people got stuck and what they did, about the anxiety and frustration they felt, about what one can expect to remember and what any reader is sure to forget, we could also make specific points about successful reading — about dealing with unfamiliar words, for example, or dealing with the confusion that always comes with the beginning of a book. We were allowing students a way of imagining what reading is like in order to imagine themselves as readers.

We also asked students to analyze reading as a task, as something necessarily embodying a strategy, in order to have them draw conclusions about the strategies underlying and perhaps inhibiting their own behavior as readers, behavior they are quick to believe lies totally outside their control. We approach the analysis of reading strategy in two ways. Strategy is seen as the deliberate approach to a specific text and purpose for reading, so that a student could be prepared to talk, for example, about the best strategy for reading a textbook. But students' reading is also analyzed to reveal those predictable individual responses, strategic but not at the level of deliberate strategy, that characterize an individual's reading style. By enabling students to perceive the decisions they make while reading, we make other decisions possible. This kind of discussion of reading also provides the occasion for instructors to make specific points about pre-reading, re-reading, underlining and so on.

The bulk of the instruction in reading, however, comes with the writing that is assigned in response to the reading, and with the work students do during class in groups to prepare reports on what they've read. With few exceptions, the assignments require students to write about the books before there is any discussion in class. The students use writing, then, to locate a stance in relation to a book and to locate something to say. The discussion in class begins with these individual positions and considers them in relation to the text, to each other, and to the specific task set by the assignment.

The assignments, and they are all variations on a single assignment, define a heuristic for the reading process, a model of how a thoughtful reader responds to a book. We assume that a text becomes meaningful and acquires a structure, or a set of intentions, through a reader's own immediate needs (which includes his imagined purpose for reading) and prior experience with the subject (or what he defines as a "subject"), both of which determine patterns of significance in a text. The process of assigning significance is central to the version of reading we were teaching in our classes, since it is a way of demonstrating how one connects with a book, how a book becomes meaningful through a personal rather than formulaic transaction.

If, after locating patterns of significance, students were to record what they "know" about a book, they would record summaries of sections that stand out for them as somehow important. They would, to use the jargon of tagmemics, have segmented the phenomena into manageable units (and, in analyzing their responses, we found that our students tended to see "particles" and "waves" rather than "fields"), but the representation would still be at the level of narrative. Our goal was to move students from narrative to some position from which they could conceptualize, from which they could see the information or patterns of information they have located as representative, as having meaning beyond any summary or report. In teaching reading, then, we are finally teaching that process of naming, of locating conceptual analogs, of discovering a language that can move the information in the book to the level of dialectic. Teaching reading, then, is teaching invention, that skill we defined as most "basic" to the development of these students as writers.

Because I did research on this part of the curriculum, I have evidence that it was successful, beyond my own and my students' enthusiasm for a course that allows people to read and write rather than be condemned to the drudgery of workbooks or textbooks. The pre- and post-tests of reading comprehension (the Nelson-Denny Reading Test) showed little change. This, however, ran counter to the instructor's impression of what happened to these students as readers. The reason for the lack of statistical evidence of change, we feel, is due to the nature of the available reading tests, tests that ask students to read paragraphs and identify main ideas. It can be argued that tests like these monitor students' ability to take such tests, not their ability as readers, since they don't pose real reading situations and since they are based on such a limited notion of comprehension itself.[20]

The pre- and post-tests of writing ability, however, showed very different results. Students taking the six hour course showed significant improvement on a standardized test of writing ability (STEP), a holistic assessment, and the Daly-Miller measure of writing anxiety. In every case, the Basic Reading and Writing students began the semester well behind students in the regular Basic Writing course, and in every case they ended the 15 weeks on almost an exact par with those students at the end of their 15-week course. So if the purpose of the concentrated course was to bring this special group to the level of the general population in a single term, that purpose was achieved.

DIAGNOSIS AND EVALUATION

It's hard to know how to describe the students who take our basic writing courses beyond saying that they are the students who take our courses. Students are screened for basic writing during summer orientation. They write an essay which is holistically scored and take the Nelson-Denny Reading Test (Forms C and D). The mean SAT verbal score for those taking Basic Writing last fall was 429, with scores ranging from 240 to 580. The mean SAT verbal score for those taking Basic Reading and Writing was 362, with scores ranging from 200 to 480.

Those of us working with basic writing programs ought to be concerned about our general inability to talk about basic writing beyond our own institutions, at least as basic writing is a phenomenon rather than a source. We know that we give tests and teach courses and we know that this is done at other schools, but we know little else since there is no generally accepted index for identifying basic writing. Perhaps the only way to compare one's students with those elsewhere, since there is a good reason to be suspicious of SAT scores or error counts or objective tests, is by sharing something like the essays that are used as models to prepare readers for holistic readings. I can briefly describe the writing that characterizes our "range-finders" by pointing to three features we have isolated in a study of orientation essays written by students whose instructors felt they were correctly advised into Basic Writing. The first feature is the type and frequency of error. Since our analysis was based on Mina Shaughnessy's taxonomy of error in *Errors and Expectations,* there is no need to provide any explanation of "type" except to say that it is possible to distinguish between "deep" errors and those that are characteristic of the writing of more fluent students.

The second feature we identified was coherence, coherence as evidence of relatedness between sentences and larger units of discourse, but coherence also as evidence of the ability to define a subject as a problem that can be addressed systematically. While reading the essays, we look for evidence that the writer imagines the act of writing as doing something, no matter how conventional that "something" might be. We identify those students whose papers lack either type of coherence as basic writers.

The third characteristic feature presents the biggest problem to our readers since, at one remove, it seems to be a universal characteristic of student writing. We found, in our analysis of the writing of basic writers, that even when presented with an assignment that specifically called for it, these students were unable to draw general conclusions. If asked to describe a time when they made a decision and to draw some conclusions about decision-making, most writers could report an experience, but few could offer more in the way of a generalization than a single sentence ("Therefore decision making is difficult.") or a collection of maxims ("Experience is the best teacher." "Follow your conscience.").

When we contrasted these essays with those written by writers with higher holistic ratings, we found the successful writers were, in fact, often able to represent themselves as decision-makers as well as someone making a simple decision. They were able to see their experience as representative experience, and to extend the general discussion dialectically, so that they began to manipulate the terms they had used to re-name their experience (terms like "peer pressure," "responsibility," "deduction") in order to represent that experience as something other than what it was for them when they began writing. Where their papers never went beyond narrative, the narrative was shaped so that, in itself, it was clearly making some point that remained unarticulated. The basic writers, on the other hand, produced undifferentiated accounts of experience, in which the representation of the experience could be described as a random recollection of what happened ordered, at best, by chronology. We have many students taking Basic Writing, then, who are not "bound by error," as that phrase is illustrated by the writing of the students Shaughnessy studied.

One of the most difficult questions a program director faces is the question of what, exactly, a passing grade in a writing course represents. The university operates with an Algebra I/Algebra II paradigm — 15 weeks of Algebra I and a test determine who goes on to Algebra II. Given the very real difficulty of measuring, or even defining, proficiency in writing, and given the irregular pace and nature of growth in writing for any group of students, there is no such thing as knowing exactly what any grade "means" in terms of actual writing ability. At the same time, however, because enrollment in basic writing represents an institution's judgment that the student lacks skills necessary for full participation in the college curriculum, a passing grade in basic writing is expected to stand as certification that such skills have been acquired. The question we faced was how to reasonably determine that a passing grade in Basic Writing did indicate a specified level of proficiency without misrepresenting the limits of our ability to make judgments about writing ability. We finally settled on an end-of-term review for all Basic Writing students.

At the end of each semester, students in all Basic Writing sections are given two hours to write an in-class essay. The two hours are meant to provide ample time for preparing, revising, and editing. Each essay is then evaluated by members of the complete composition staff who make only a pass/fail distinction. A "pass" on the exam means that a student has demonstrated the proficiency assumed of students in the opening weeks of our general composition courses. The models, or "range-finders," we use to prepare readers for the reading were chosen by the staff after considering hundreds of student papers written during a trial examination program.

We also provide both students and instructors, however, with a general set of criteria that are the result of our attempt to summarize features that have distinguished passing from failing essays. In order to pass, students must be able to write a paper that

- is reasonably error-free — "reasonableness" makes allowances for commonly misspelled words, errors with fine points of punctuation or unobtrusive errors of punctuation, errors with "who" and "whom"; "reasonableness," that is, makes allowances for the kinds of errors most of us make and those instructors are generally willing to tolerate in freshman writing,

- is coherent — which means that what is said can be understood and understood as an attempt to address the assigned problem systematically,

- shows the ability to state general principles on the basis of specific evidence, and to develop a general discussion beyond a single sentence.

A failing score on the essay does *not* mean that a student fails the course. Holistic scoring, particularly of essays written under such artificial conditions, is simply not reliable enough to allow us to make that kind of decision. When a student fails the essay review, a folder containing all his work for the term is reviewed by a committee of three staff members. If the work done in the last quarter of the term confirms the judgment made by the readers, the student is not given credit for the course. At the end of a semester of Basic Reading and Writing, on the other hand, students are either passed on to Basic Writing or passed into the general curriculum without restriction.

NOTES

1. For an example of such a sequence of assignments, and for discussion of sequence as a concept, see: William E. Coles, Jr., *Teaching Composing* (Rochelle Park, New Jersey: Hayden Book Company, 1974) and William E. Coles, Jr., *The Plural I* (New York: Holt, Rinehart and Winston, 1978). My debt to Bill Coles will be evident everywhere in this paper.

2. I am making a distinction here very similar to that in Richard Ohmann, "In Lieu of a New Rhetoric," College English, 26 (October, 1964), 17–22.

3. I am, of course, summarizing one of the key findings of Mina Shaughnessy, *Errors and Expectations* (New York: Oxford University Press, 1977). This paper draws heavily on Shaughnessy's work.

4. For a discussion of this distinction between fluency and competence see David Bartholomae, "The Study of Error," *Linguistics, Stylistics and the Teaching of Composition,* Donald McQuade, ed. (Akron, Ohio: Akron University Press, scheduled for publication in November, 1978).

5. Shaughnessy, *Errors and Expectations,* 104–05, 117–18.

6. Frank Smith, *Understanding Reading* (New York: Holt, Rinehart and Winston, Inc., 1971).

7. John Warnock, "New Rhetoric and the Grammar of Pedagogy," *Freshman English News,* 5 (Fall, 1976), 12.

8. Frank J. D'Angelo, "The Search for Intelligible Stucture in the Teaching of Composition," *College Composition and Communication,* 27 (May, 1976), 142–47.

9. Paulo Freire, *Pedagogy of the Oppressed* (New York: The Seabury Press, 1968). See chapter two.

10. For a "task analysis" approach to writing see: Susan Miller, *Writing: Process and Product* (Cambridge, Massachusetts: Winthrop Publishers, Inc., 1976). For writing as problem-solving see: Linda Flower and John R. Hayes, "Problem-Solving Strategies and the Writing Process," *College English,* 39 (December, 1977), 449–62.

11. See, for example: Thomas J. Farrell, "Literacy, the Basics, and all that Jazz," *College English,* 38 (January, 1977) 446–47, and Shaughnessy, *Errors and Expectations,* 230–33.

12. Our sequence of reading and writing assignments grew out of our reading of James Moffett, *Teaching the Universe of Discourse* (Boston: Houghton Mifflin Company, 1968), especially chapter four.

13. For a full discussion of this problem and some suggested exercises see: Patricia Laurence, "Error's Endless Train: Why Students Don't Perceive Errors," *Journal of Basic Writing,* 1 (Spring, 1975), 23–43.

14. This is an impression. I have no data on this at this time although we have begun research in this area.

15. Shaughnessy, *Errors and Expectations,* 128–59. Shaughnessy also makes a basic distinction between grammatically based errors and performance based errors.

16. Shaughnessy, *Errors and Expectations,* 2. This course was designed with the assistance of Professor Anthony Petrosky, University of Pittsburgh School of Education, and tested in a pilot study in fall term, 1977.

17. Sandra L. Stotsky, "Sentence-Combining as a Curricular Activity: Its Effect on Written Language Development and Reading Comprehension," *Research in the Teaching of English,* 9 (Spring, 1975), 30–71.

18. Marilyn S. Sternglass, "Composition Teacher as Reading Teacher," *College Composition and Communication,* 27 (December, 1976). See also, Marilyn S. Sternglass, "Developing Syntactic Fluency in the Reading Process," ERIC.

19. For a description of "sustained silent reading" see: Charles Cooper and Tony Petrosky, "A Psycholinguistic View of the Fluent Reading Process," *Journal of Reading,* (December, 1976).

20. James Moffett and Betty Jane Wagner, *Student-Centered Language Arts and Reading, K-13* (Boston: Houghton Mifflin, 1976), 123–24.

Writing Assignments:
Where Writing Begins

To begin to write is to "know" what at the outset cannot be known except by inventing it, exactly, intentionally, autodidactically.
— EDWARD SAID, BEGINNINGS

I want to use this occasion[1] to work on the paradox at the center of this passage from *Beginnings:* to begin to write is to "know" what cannot be known. It has become commonplace for English teachers to talk of writing as a "mode of learning," or of writing as "discovery." And it has become common to represent the writer's struggle as a struggle for realization: "How can I know what I mean until I see what I've said?" This representation of writing is conventionally in service of a pedagogy whose primary aim is to enable students to work *out* something that is inside them: insight, vision, ideas, connections, wisdom.

If, however, we take knowledge to be something that is outside the writer, something inscribed in a discourse — the commonplaces, the texts, the gestures and jargon, the interpretive schemes — of a group from which the writer is excluded, then the paradox must be read differently. To discover or to learn, the student must, by writing, become like us — English teachers, adults, intellectuals, academics. He must become someone he is not. He must know what we know, talk like we talk; he must locate himself convincingly in a language that is not his own. He must invent the university when he sits down to write.

This is what I take Burke to be talking about when he talks about persuasion as "identification":

The individual person, striving to form himself in accordance with the communicative norms that match the cooperative ways of his society, is then, concerned with the rhetoric of identification. To act upon himself persuasively, he must variously resort to images and ideas that are formative. Education ("indoctrination") exerts such pressure upon him from without; he completes the process from within. (1969, p. 39)

From *Fforum* Fall 1982: 35–46.

The struggle of the student writer is not the struggle to bring out that which is within; it is the struggle to carry out those ritual activities that grant one entrance into a closed society. Or, as Foucault would have it, "The discourse of struggle does not oppose what is unconscious, it opposes what is secret."

Teachers as priests of mystery, teaching as indoctrination, writing as identification — these are not popular definitions. They do, however, provide a way of talking about the business of assigning writing to students. For me it is a necessary way of talking. Let me work this out by telling some stories.

When I was first a Director of Composition, and before I was tenured (this is to add spice to the story), at about the tenth week of classes, a bunch of students came into my office to register a complaint about one of their teachers, a senior colleague of mine, a full professor and a distinguished scholar. It seemed that he had assigned one paper in the first week of the term but hadn't assigned any writing since. His students, rather, had been listening to lectures on the paragraph and the sentence, on style and organization, and they had, as well, been given the task of copying out longhand essays by Lamb, Macaulay, Ruskin and Carlyle. The students were wondering how in the world he was ever going to grade them, since he seemed to be collecting such unusual artifacts to judge.

I mustered up my courage and went to visit this professor, told him of the complaints, and mentioned as gently as I could that the rest of us were assigning one — and in some cases two — papers a week. Here is his response: "I assigned a paper early in the term and they wrote miserably. If I assign more writing, they'll only make more mistakes." When I asked whether this meant, then, that the best writing course is the one in which students never wrote, where potential never had to be compromised by execution, he said, "No. When they are ready to write, I'll set them to writing again."

Let me call this the Big Bang theory of writing instruction. Students are given instruction in writing as a subject — sometimes through lectures, sometimes through textbooks, sometimes through classroom analyses of prose models — and then, when they are ready, they write. The assignment, then, serves as a test. It is the students' opportunity to show that they have mastered the subject. There are Little Bang versions of this available everywhere: in most textbooks, for example, where writing is broken up into sub-skills — description, narration, exposition, argumentation.

Now if writing is conceived of as *technique* — as a means for communicating what is known and not as a way of knowing itself — and if the techniques being taught are simple enough — the 5-sentence paragraph, ABAB comparisons — then it is not unreasonable to suppose that students can pass the weekly test. If, however, the students are also to learn to write like Lamb or Macaulay, to represent themselves within those peculiar gestures and patterns — and I am not willing to quickly condemn the copying out of essays in that course — then that copying will have to be accompanied by assigned writing of quite another kind. The ability to write like Macaulay, in other words, will not come in a big bang. The indoctrination will have to be "completed," in Burke's terms, by acts of writing that complete the shaping of a writer. "If he does not somehow *act* to tell himself (as his own audience) what the various brands of rhetoricians have told him, his persuasion is not complete." (1969, p. 39)

Perhaps this leads to our first principle of assignment making. If assignments invite students to enter into a discourse which is not their own, and if their representations will only approximate that discourse (if they don't come in a big bang), then assignments must lead students through successive approximations. The movement through successive approximations is a cycle of expectation and disappointment. There is no clear-cut developmental sequence here; students do not move easily from one level of mastery to the next. This is what it means to be going after secrets. As Kermode says,

> Hot for secrets, our only conversation may be with guardians who know less and see less than we can; and our sole hope and pleasure is in the perception of a momentary radiance, before the door of disappointment is finally shut on us. (1979, p. 145)

Here is my second story. A teacher at a school I recently visited gave what I thought was a wonderful assignment — and she gave it knowing that her students, at least most of them, would have to write their papers over again, perhaps several times, since in many ways it was an impossible assignment. She asked students to read through the journals they had been keeping over the semester and to write about what they had learned about themselves from *reading* the journal. What I admired in this assignment, and what makes it such a difficult assignment, is that students were asked to write about what they had learned by reading the journal and not what they learned by writing in the journal. This is a nice stroke, since it defines the journal as a text and not an experience, and it defines the person writing as a composite of several people and not as a moment of feeling or thought. The assignment defines the student as, simultaneously, a textual presence — the "I" in a passage dated September 3rd and the "I" in a passage dated October 5th — and as an interpreter of texts, someone who defines patterns and imposes order, form, on previous acts of ordering. Who is to say quickly what *that* person might learn? The subject of this assignment, then, is language and language using. Students are not invited to believe that a subject can be something else — experience, truth, data — something that exists outside language, something language can record. This is often the trap of journal writing; students are led to believe that the journal is a true record of true feelings — a rare occasion for self-expression. As Bruner says (and I've taken this passage from a fine article by Ken Dowst describing the kind of composition course that depends most heavily on carefully crafted and carefully conceived assignments):

> A student does not respond to a world that exists for direct touching. Nor is he locked in a prison of subjectivity. Rather, he *represents* the world to himself and acts in behalf of or in reaction to his representations. . . . A change in one's conception of the world involves not simply a change in what one encounters but also in how one translates it. (Dowst, 1980, p. 68)

A change in one's conception of the world by means of a change in how one translates it — perhaps here we have the beginnings of a second principle for assignment-making. We shouldn't provide a subject only; we should provide the occasion for translation. To put it more simply, the journal assignment undercuts students' impulses to write about journal writing without writing about the writing in the journal. It allows them to translate (or to "read") those moments of "feeling" as moments of artifice or representation, as evidence of the roles defined as a writer shaped experience, history, the "stuff" of his or her life.

My next story comes again from my own school. A group of us were asked to put together an experimental course, not just a reading course or a writing course, but a course to, as we later said, introduce students to the language and methods of university study. We decided that this should be a course in which students didn't learn a subject — something already prepared by one of the traditional academic disciplines — but it should be a course in which students invented a subject by inventing a discipline, one with its own specialized vocabulary and its own peculiar interpretive schemes.

Now this course would need a nominal subject — a subject that would provide the occasion for a discourse. And the subject we chose was "Growth and Change in Adolescence." It seemed to provide, in Freire's terms, a "generative" theme, one that students could write on with care and energy. The first assignment, then, had to be an impossible one. Students could write about adolescence, but not as we would write about it. They would use the language, and the commonplaces, immediately available to them, but these would not be the language or commonplaces of a small, professional, closed, interpretive community. The sequence of assignments would have them writing about the same subject over and over again, with each act of writing complicating and qualifying the previous act of writing, each paper drawing on the language developed by the group. The papers were regularly duplicated and used as the basis of class discussion. The instructors would outline, highlight and push on class discussion; they would not provide theories or terms of their own. The last assignment in the course, then, would be a record of this new discipline — the study of the process of change in adolescence developed by the group.

The assignments went something like this. There was a group of assignments that asked students to develop a theory on the basis of their own experience.

- Think of a time in the last 2 or 3 years when something significant happened to you, something that caused you to change or to change your mind. Then do what you can to help the rest of us understand the process of change.

- Think of another time. . . . What now can you say to help us understand the process of change?

- Think of a time when, by all popular expectation, you went through an experience that should have caused you to change, but it didn't. What now . . . ?

- Think of a time when you decided to make a change in yourself. What happened? What now . . . ?

Students began to develop a process of interpretation, one that dealt more with the dynamics of change (family, school, friends, enemies, goals, self-images) than with the mechanism of change. And they developed a shared set of terms: the Jones dilemma (competition with an older, successful brother); the Smith syndrome (anger directed at a parent who had left home); the Kowalski problem (wanting to be good but wanting, as well, to be cool).

These papers served as the basis for a longer paper, one we called, "A Section of Your Autobiography," dealing with the sorts of changes the students went through in the last three years. We took the class's autobiographies to central printing, had them bound, and sold them back to the class as a text. They became, then, "case studies." And we led students through a series of papers that asked them to read the autobiographies, locate patterns of themes and experiences, invent names for those patterns and develop theories to account for them.

The final set of assignments directed the students to rework those papers in the context of three standard, academic accounts of adolescence — one by a psychologist, one by a sociologist, and one by an anthropologist.

This became an enormously popular and successful course. In fact, when my college began its own version of "writing across the curriculum," it was offered as a model for courses in departments other than the English department. One psychologist was quite interested until he realized, as he said,

> You know, the problem is, that at the end of the course they're likely to get it all wrong. After all — what about Piaget and Erikson? They're not going to get that stuff on their own.

Of course not, that's the point. They can only approximate the conventional methods of academic psychologists, only pretend to be psychologists or sociologists or anthropologists, and they will not *get* the canonical interpretations preserved by the disciplines. But they will learn something about what it means to study a subject, to carry out a project. And they will begin to learn what a subject is — how it is constituted, how it is defended, how it finds its examples and champions, how it changes and preserves itself. There is, then, a way of studying psychology by learning to report on textbook accounts or classroom lectures on the works of psychologists. But there is also a way of learning psychology by learning to write and, thereby, learning to compose the world *as* a psychologist. In his four years of college education, a student gets plenty of the former but precious little of the latter. He writes many reports but carries out few projects. And this leads me to my next principle of assignment making. Individual assignments should be part of a larger, group project. I'll have more to say in defense of this.

My last story comes from Tolstoy; although to be honest, it came to me from Ann Berthoff and is available in her wise and eloquent book, *The Making of Meaning* (1981, pp. 61–94; pp. 140–47). Tolstoy set out to teach the children of his newly emancipated serfs to read and write. He began, he said, by asking his students to write about what seemed easiest — the most simple and general subject.

In the first class we tried compositions on given themes. The first themes that must have naturally occurred to us were descriptions of simple objects, such as grain, the house, the wood, and so forth; but, to our great surprise, these demands on our students almost made them weep, and, in spite of the aid afforded them by the teacher, who divided the description of its growth, its change into bread, its use, they emphatically refused to write upon such themes, or, if they did write, they made the most incomprehensible and senseless mistakes in orthography, in the language and in the meaning.

Now Tolstoy was not a Big Banger. He tried again; in fact, he tried, as he says, different assignments. "I gave them, according to their inclinations, exact, artistic, touching, funny, epic themes — and nothing worked."

By chance, however, he hit upon a method (and "method" is his term) that did. He happened one day to be reading proverbs ("a favorite occupation") and carried the book with him to school. "Well," he said to his students, "write something on a proverb." The best students pricked up their ears. "What do you mean by on a proverb? What is it? Tell us!" the questions ran. Tolstoy goes on:

I happened to open to the proverb: "He feeds with the spoon, and pricks the eye with the handle." "Now imagine," I said, "that a peasant has taken a beggar to his house, and then begins to rebuke him for the good he has done him, and you will get that 'He feeds with the spoon, and pricks the eye with the handle.' "

"But how are you going to write it up?" said Fedka and all the rest who had pricked up their ears. They retreated, having convinced themselves that this matter was above their strength, and betook themselves to the work which they had begun. "Write it yourself," one of them said to me. Everyone was busy with his work; I took a pen and inkstand, and began to write. "Well," said I, "who will write it best? I am with you."

Tolstoy began to write the story to accompany the proverb and wrote a page. He says, and you'll now begin to see the point this story, the story of this, assignment, makes for Tolstoy:

Every unbiased man, who has artistic sense and feels with the people, will, upon reading the first page, written by me, and the following pages of the story, written by the pupils themselves, separate this page from the rest as he will take a fly out of the milk: it is so false, so artificial and written in such bad language. I must remark that in the original form it was even more monstrous, since much has been corrected, thanks to the indications of the pupils.

The sight of the teacher writing caused a flurry in the classroom. One student said, "Write, write or I'll give it to you!" Others crowded around his chair and read over his shoulder. The commotion was such that Tolstoy stopped and read his first page to them. They did not like it. Nobody praised it. In defense of himself, Tolstoy began to explain the "plan" of what was to follow. They

butted in, "No, no, that won't do," he made corrections, and they began helping him out. All, Tolstoy says,

> were exceedingly interested. It was evidently new and absorbing to be in
> on the process of creation, to take part in it. Their judgments were all, for
> the most part, of the same kind, and they were just, both as to the struc-
> ture of the story and to the details and characterizations of the persons.
> Nearly all of them took part in the composition: . . .

Two, however, stayed on and worked late into the night, annoyed when
Tolstoy wanted a break. One of those who remained asked, "Are we going to
print it?" When Tolstoy said yes, he replied, "Then we shall have to print it:
Work by Mákarov, Morózov, and Tolstoy."

There are many ways of reading this story. It could be said that Tolstoy
was lucky enough to find the right assignment: a theme on a proverb. It's as
though you could go to the exercise exchange and find the assignment whose
subject is just right for your students — sports for the athletes, drugs for the
heads, movies for the rest, proverbs for the children of Russian peasants. I
don't choose to read the story this way. While I believe it is important for
teachers to consider carefully the subjects they present to students, and while
I believe students write best about subjects that interest them — subjects they
believe in, subjects they know something about, subjects they believe there is
reason to write about and for which they can imagine an occasion for writing
(witness Booth's story about his frustrated graduate student in "The Rhetorical Stance") — the very notion of motive is misunderstood if a motive is taken
to reside in a subject. The question, rather, is one of how students can be
taught to imagine a subject as a subject, not as a thing they like or don't like,
but as a discourse, as a set of conventional, available utterances within which
they can locate utterances of their own. The question is not one of which subject will work, but of how students can learn to work on a subject and of why
such work is worth the effort.

Tolstoy's students didn't leap to the proverb assignment; they told *him* to
write the theme, convinced the subject was "beyond their strength," and went
back to their own work. Their first question, you remember, to Tolstoy's
assignment, "write something on a proverb," was, "What do you mean '*on* a
proverb'? What is it? Tell us!" Tolstoy read them a proverb, but they never
started writing until he answered the *first* question and showed them what it
meant to write *on* a proverb. He did this by writing with them, by showing
them not a subject, but the subject as a potential discourse, a story about a
beggar and a peasant who abuses him while offering charity. It was at that
point that the students had a subject, and the subject was not the story and
not the proverb, but the act of amplification. A subject is not a thing but
an action — thinking, describing, analyzing, elaborating, naming. All subjects, and this is what I take to be the burden of the post-structuralists, are as
Richards says, "characteristic uses of language." Tolstoy, then, gave his students not just a language but a discourse, a conventional procedure for elaborating a subject.

How else might we read the story of Tolstoy and the proverb? It could be read as support of the notion that teachers should write papers along with their students. I'm not very keen on this, either as a reading or a practice. Writing teachers should be writers, this I believe deeply. But they should be too busy with their own projects, and with the exacting task of writing assignments and writing to students about their writing, to have time for weekly papers in concert with a class. Besides, the presence of Tolstoy writing in the classroom had only shock value. The students became writers only when they participated in his writing. They began to learn when they began assisting him in a project he had begun, and a project can be begun by the text of a well-crafted and self-conscious assignment, one that presents not just a subject but a way of imagining a subject *as* a subject, a discourse one can enter, and not as a thing that carries with it experiences or ideas that can be communicated.

One could read the story as evidence that students should begin with narrative, with storytelling, since this draws upon patterns of organization closest to the pattern of experience. I don't believe that this is a true statement about narrative, and the evidence Tolstoy provides shows the children choosing detail and projecting narrative as an interpretation of a concept (another interpretation) coded in the proverb.

Tolstoy does argue, however, for a form of "natural" expression that is only impeded or thwarted by education. Here is his interpretation of the event:

> It is impossible and absurd to teach and educate a child, for the simple reason that the child stands nearer than I do, than any grown man does, to that ideal of harmony, truth, beauty, and goodness, to which I, in my pride, wish to raise him. The consciousness of this ideal is more powerful in him than in me. All he needs of one is the material [and we have to wonder what "material" means in this sentence], in order to develop harmoniously. The moment I gave him full liberty and stopped teaching him, he wrote a poetical production, the like of which cannot be found in Russian literature. Therefore, it is my conviction that we cannot teach children in general, and peasant children in particular, to write and compose. All that we can do is to teach them how to go about writing.

We cannot teach children to compose; all we can do is to teach them how to go about writing. This is another paradox, and I'd like to try to make sense out of it.

Now in working on the Tolstoy Paradox, I do not choose to read these passages as celebrations of natural innocence, where a good assignment replaces "teacher-sponsored writing" with "student-sponsored" writing, freeing a student from the fetters of an oppressive culture.

Tolstoy's own accounts of his "method" show him getting in his students' way more than his narrative would lead one to believe. The prime consideration, he says, in designing a sequence of "themes" should not be length or content but "the working out of the matter." And this, the working out of the matter, was the occasion for teaching.

At first I chose from the ideas and images that presented themselves to them such as I considered best, and retained them, and pointed out the place, and consulted with what had already been written, keeping them from repetitions, and myself wrote, leaving to them only the clothing of the images and ideas in words; then I allowed them to make their own choice, and later to consult that which had been written down, until, at last, . . . they took the whole matter into their own hands. (Tolstoy, 1967, p. 224)

When Tolstoy talks about choosing, selecting, preserving, and remembering, he is not talking about "natural" acts but a system that is imposed. He, and the text he has in mind, *allow* for certain choices. The procedure must be learned.

Derrida has taught us that the Rousseauesque notions of a "natural" language are all symptoms of a longing for a perfect relation between the word and the thing it is meant to signify for a language that gives us direct access to the truth, without the mediation of the stuff and baggage of a culture, for a form of understanding that represents data raw and not cooked, for a mode of composition in which thinking and writing do not interfere with each other. What comes before speech, he argues, is writing, that conventional system, discourse, that inscribes us as we inscribe it. There is, then, no natural or pure language because the language we use always precedes us, belongs to others, and it, and not the writer, determines what is written. The writer does not write but is rather, written, composed by systems he did not invent and he cannot escape. Our language is derived, "stolen," never original. The celebration of innocence, Derrida argues, is not a denial of teaching but a denial of writing.

But Tolstoy, in his rejection of education, does not reject writing, even though he feels the burden of the role of the teacher. In fact, in a telling passage, he says that after the episode with the proverb he felt not just joy, but dread —

Dread, because this art made new demands, a whole new world of desires, which stood in no relation to the surroundings of these pupils, as I thought first.

This is the Tolstoy that gives his student "material." All they need of me, he says, is material — not pencils and paper, not subjects, but the material (as in fabric) that is woven with the habits, discriminations, preconceptions — the "stuff" of his material, that is, textual, culture. It is exclusive. It privileges some statements at the expense of others. It is driven by a law of exclusion — this then fits, that, "the world of his pupils," does not. At one point, one child in a "fatigued, calmly serious and habitual" voice comments on his text. Tolstoy says, "The chief quality of any art, the feeling of limit, was developed in him to an extraordinary degree. He writhed at the suggestion of any superfluous feature, made by some one of the boys."

Let me put my cards on the table, and explain why I want to read Tolstoy this way. I think a good assignment teaches by interfering. It interferes with a student and his writing.

Tolstoy's "method" — the method that does not teach composing, but how to go about writing — could be seen to be in service of what we now comfortably call the "Process" approach to composition instruction. If the act of composing is beyond a teacher's art, if it is a natural or mysterious facility, then a teacher can at least attend to the behavior of composing — to the business of prewriting, revising and editing. This is how I take the pedagogies of the "new rhetoric." The tagmemics, the pentads, the class-room heuristics — all these are devices that precede writing. They are not part of a project. The nine-fold grid may give a new perspective on, say, a tree (and the metaphor of vision is telling) but it does not give a language. What happens to the student when he begins to write, when he locates himself in a discourse, is that he is caught up in all those available phrases about nature, and ecology and the pastoral world that turn his "vision" into an occasion for cliché.

Don't get me wrong. Writing is a behavior and a good set of assignments teaches a student to understand this — to experiment with varieties of planning activities, to take time with his writing, to (often for the first time) revise by reworking and not just re-copying a text, and to edit, to make corrections. I'll confess, however, that I think most of the attention to pre-writing is a waste of time, unless pre-writing is, in fact, the first act of writing — in Tolstoy's terms — the first "working out of the matter." Most pre-writing activities, however, treat "ideas" as though they existed independently of language, of the sentences that enact them. And, in my experience, students treat these exercises the way they used to treat outlining; they either do them after they have written the paper, or they do them and then go about writing the paper the same damn way they have always written — starting at the top, working to the bottom and then handing it in for a grade.

Let me go back to Ann Berthoff. Here is what she says about Tolstoy and his teaching:

> Nothing is needed more urgently in the current reassessment of what we think we have been doing in teaching composition than a critical inquiry into this concept of the simultaneity of thinking and writing, of the role of consciousness in composing, Tolstoy's description here is a useful point of departure for that inquiry because it reminds us that composing is both creative and critical and that it is an act of mind; it doesn't just happen; it is conscious. (1981, p. 89)

This consciousness is critical consciousness, not consciousness as it is represented by classroom heuristics. It is rooted in an act of reading. She says, elsewhere in her book, that "writing can't teach writing unless it is understood as a nonlinear, dialectical process in which the writer continually circles back, reviewing and rewriting: certainly the way to learn to do that is to practice *doing* just that." (1981, p. 3). The key words here are "reviewing" and "dialectical," and they are difficult words to understand. Let me try to put them into the context of assignment making.

I'm concerned now with that version of "thinking" which is textual, not mental, since it involves reading and interpretation ("reviewing") and a use of language in service of dialectic. Here's an assignment: It was given to me by a teacher at a school I visited as a consultant.

> Pick a poem that you like. Discuss why you like it by analyzing its features rather than defending your response. Think before you write so that you produce a coherent and well-organized essay.

This is the sort of assignment that most likely will prove the law of reciprocity — what you ask for is what you'll get. It's poorly written and demonstrates, more than anything else, a teacher's boredom and inattention, and it would be the exceptional student who would make anything of it other than the occasion for poor writing and inattention. There is no indication of how or why the fact that one likes a poem is dependent on an "analysis of its features." Nor is there any clue as to what it means to "discuss" while at the same time not "defending a response." The final sentence, "Think before you write so that you produce a coherent and well-organized essay," is a not-quite-so-polite way of saying, "Please do a decent job of this" and it finesses the whole question of how "thinking before writing" (making an outline? getting one's thoughts together?) leads to a "coherent, well-organized essay." There is, however, a rhetoric at work here — the rhetoric of the controlling idea in service of what seems to be an act of new criticism — but the demonstration that Tolstoy provided, the way he assisted students in a project he had begun — and it was *his* project, belonging to his culture — this assistance is missing. The word "analyze," for instance, exists as an invocation, a magic word calling up powers to possess the student. It does not belong to the vocabulary shared between teachers and students; it does not, in fact, belong to the vocabulary shared between teachers in different academic departments. It presumes to tell students to do what they cannot know how to do — and that is to carry out an act of analysis as it is represented by the conventions of the discourse of a certain form of literary criticism.

Our assignments are often studded with such words — think, analyze, define, describe, argue. These words, however, are located in a very specialized discourse. Analysis, for example, is a very different activity — its textual forms, that is, vary greatly — in an English course, a history course, a sociology course, or a chemistry course. When we use such words, we are asking students to invent our disciplines, to take on the burden of the mindset of our peculiar pocket of the academic community. This is not a bad thing to do, even though it is cause for dread as well as joy. It is why, for me, a good set of assignments leads a class to invent a discipline, a set of specialized terms (a jargon) and a subject with its own privileged materials and interpretative scheme.

Because writing — or writing that is not report or debate — is the invention of such a project, writing is also, as we are fond of saying, a mode of learning, where learning is a matter of learning to use the specialized vocabulary and interpretative schemes of the various disciplines. To learn sociology — and to learn it as an activity, as something other than a set of names and canonical interpretations — is to learn to write like a sociologist, for better or for worse. Students cannot do this, however, without assistance, since the conventions that govern a rhetoric do not "naturally" belong to the mind, the heart, reason, or the soul. Reason, in fact, is not an operative term if one begins with a conception of rhetoric. It is a metaphor, a way of authorizing one discourse over another, but it is not a descriptive term.

Here is a sequence of assignments that offers more by way of assistance in the "working out of the matter." It comes from a source in nineteenth-century fiction.

BLEAK HOUSE

I. In order to prepare a paper on the narrative in *Bleak House,* I'd like you to do the following:
   1. Locate two passages that, as you read them, best characterize the voice and perspective of Esther Summerson as she tells the story. Write them out.
   2. Locate two passages that, as you read them, best characterize the voice and perspective of the other, the unnamed narrator. Write them out. Working primarily from one passage for each narrator, write a paper that compares the way they see the world of *Bleak House* and the way they tell a story. Be sure to look at sentences as well as sentiments; that is, pay attention to language each uses to locate a perspective and a world.

   Then, when you've done this, go on to speculate about how the presence of two narrators controls your reading of the story.

II. I'd like you to look, now, at the first and last chapters. Who gets the first word and who gets the last word and the difference it makes. What difference does it make, that is, to you and your attempt to make sense out of the novel?

III. Here is a passage from an essay by J. Hillis Miller. In it, he offers one account for the effect on a reader of the presence of the two narrators. I'd like you to write a paper that talks about the way his reading is different from yours, and about what difference the difference makes to you. Be sure, again, to talk about sentences as well as sentiments. What, for example, does Miller notice that you didn't? And what did you notice that he leaves out? What special terms does he use that you don't. What difference do they make?

IV. On the basis of these 3 papers, write an essay to help us better understand narrative technique in *Bleak House.* Don't feel you have to settle the question once and for all. Remember, that is, that the rest of us are working on this problem too, and that we're looking for your help. We're not beginners and we have a lot invested in our own projects.

Often any such assistance is at odds with the peculiar rhetoric of the composition class, with its obsessive concern for the thesis, the controlling idea.

When, for example, we ask students to write about texts, the tyranny of the thesis often invalidates the very act of analysis we hope to invoke. Hence, in assignment after assignment, we find students asked to reduce a novel, a poem or their own experience into a single sentence, and then to use the act of writing in order to defend or "support" that single sentence. Writing is used to close a subject down rather than to open it up, to put an end to discourse rather than to open up a project. This, I think, is the rhetoric that is "natural" to our students. If English teachers can have any effect on students' writing, it should be to counter this tendency. To interfere with it.

The term "interference" comes to me from Kenneth Burke, whose writing I admire for the way it enacts a constant dissatisfaction with the thesis. Burke's rhetoric is in service of a form of knowledge that is not equated with certainty. His sense of a dialectical use of language is a use of language that allows the writer not only to translate "reality" — the subject that is only a *thing* to be written about — but also to transcend the conventional and often oppressive gestures built into the history of our language, to transcend, then, the inevitable reduction caused by writing. Burke says

> We would only say that, over and above all, there is implicit in language itself the act of persuasion [that domination or closing down of a subject]; and implicit in the perpetuating of persuasion, there is the need for interference. For persuasion that succeeds, dies.

Burke, then, brings me to my last principle of assignment making. A good set of assignments assists students toward a subject by interfering with their immediate procedures for dominating a subject by reducing it to a closed set. Edward Said, whose words stood at the beginning of this essay, said that writing requires the writer to maintain an "obligation" to "practical reality" and a "sympathetic imagination" in equally strong parts. By obligation, he means

> the precision with which the concrete circumstances of any undertaking oblige the mind to take them into account — the obligation not just passively to continue, but the obligation to begin by learning, first, that there is no schematic method that makes all things simple, then second, whatever with reference to one's circumstances is necessary in order to begin, given one's field of study.

And by "sympathetic imagination," he means

> that to begin to write is to "know" what at the outset cannot be known except by inventing it, exactly, intentionally, autodidactically. (1978, p. 349)

I have been offering a defense of a sequence of related and redundant assignments, assignments that define both a project and a way of working on a project, assignments that are designed to enact for students that there is no schematic method to make all things simple. And I have been arguing that an intellectual project requires indoctrination, assistance, interference, and trust.

Let me conclude with a passage from the poet, William Stafford.

> A writer is not so much someone who has something to say as he is someone who has found a process that will bring about new things he would not have thought of if he had not started to say them. That is, he does not draw upon a reservoir; instead he engages in an activity that brings to him a whole succession of unforeseen stories, poems, essays, plays, laws, philosophies, religions, or — but wait!
>
> Back in school, from the first when I began to try to write things, I felt this richness. One thing would lead to another; the world would give and give. Now, after twenty years or so of trying, I live by that certain richness, an idea hard to pin, difficult to say, and perhaps offensive to some.

A sequence of assignments is repetitive. It asks students to write, again, about something they wrote about before. But such a project allows for richness; it allows for the imagination that one thing can lead to another, that the world can give and give. This is an idea hard to pin, difficult to say, and, perhaps, offensive to some.

Our students have come to us, however, to learn. It is not enough to say to them that knowledge is whatever comes to mind. If we have them write one week on Democracy, and the next on Pollution and the week later on My Most Memorable Character, that is what we are saying to them. Tell me what comes to mind. The writing that I value, that demands something of me as a reader, that turns back on whatever comes quickly to mind, requires repeated and on-going effort. Students need to work at finding something to say. They have to spend time with a subject. That, to me, is what it means to be a writer at a university.

NOTE

1. This paper was presented as the keynote address at the Delaware Valley Writing Council Conference, March 1982.

BIBLIOGRAPHY

Berthoff, Ann E. *Forming/Thinking/Writing: The Composing Imagination.* Montclair, NJ: Boynton/Cook, 1981.
——. *The Making of Meaning: Metaphors, Models, and Maxims for Writing Teachers.* Montclair, NJ: Boynton/Cook, 1981.
Presents the philosophical argument for the centrality of interpretation in the processes of writing.
——. *Reclaiming the Imagination.* Montclair, NJ: Boynton/Cook, 1984.
Essays by artists, philosophers, and scientists concerning the processes involved in making sense of experience.
Booth, Wayne C. *Modern Dogma and the Rhetoric of Assent.* Chicago: University of Chicago Press, 1974.
——. "The Rhetorical Stance," *College Composition and Communication,* 14 (October, 1963), pp. 139–45.
Bruner, Jerome S. *The Process of Education.* Cambridge, MA: Harvard University Press, 1965.
——. *Toward a Theory of Instruction.* Cambridge, MA: Harvard University Press, 1966.
Bruner, Jerome S., R. Oliver, and P. Greenfield. *Studies in Cognitive Growth.* NY: John Wiley, 1966.
Burke, Kenneth. *A Grammar of Motives,* NY: Prentice-Hall, 1952.
——. *A Rhetoric of Motives.* Berkeley: University of California Press, 1969.
Dowst, Kenneth. "The Epistemic Approach: Writing, Knowing, and Learning," *Eight Approaches to Teaching Composition.* (Eds.) Timothy R. Donovan and Ben W. McClelland, Urbana, IL: NCTE, 1980.

Foucault, Michel. "Language to Infinity," *Language, Counter-memory Practice.* (Ed.) Donald F. Bouchard. Ithaca: Cornell University Press, 1977, pp. 53–67.

Kermode, Frank. *The Genesis of Secrecy: On the Interpretation of Narrative.* Cambridge: Harvard University Press, 1979.

Richards, I.A. *Interpretation in Teaching.* London: Routledge and Kegan Paul, 1938.

———. *Practical Criticism: A Study of Literary Judgment.* NY: Harcourt, Brace, 1929.

———. *The Philosophy of Rhetoric.* London: Oxford University Press, 1936.

Said, Edward. *Beginnings: Intention and Method.* Baltimore: Johns Hopkins University Press, 1978.

Against the Grain

D o we choose a tradition or does it choose us, and why is it
necessary that a choosing take place, or a being chosen? What happens if one tries to write, or to teach, or to think, or even to read
without the sense of a tradition?

Why nothing at all happens, just nothing. You cannot write or
teach or think or even read without imitation, and what you imitate
is what another person has done, that person's writing or teaching
or thinking or reading. Your relation to what informs that person is
tradition, for tradition is influence that extends past one generation,
a carrying-over of influence. Tradition, the Latin *traditio*, is etymo-
logically a handing-over or a giving-over, a delivery, a giving-up
and so even a surrender or a betrayal.

— Harold Bloom, *A Map of Misreading*

I

How I write is against the grain. I think this has always been the case,
although now that I've been doing it for several years — doing it to the point,
now, where I think of myself as a professional writer — the terms and conditions of interference have changed. There are things that get in the way of my
writing and things that I put in the path of my writing that are different now
than they were when I was younger, but the essential resistance — both mine
and writing's — remains.

Writing gets in my way and makes my life difficult, difficult enough that
I sometimes wonder why I went into this business in the first place. There is
work that comes easier to me. Writing gets in my way, but when I write, I
almost always put up barriers — barriers to show my sense of duty — to stand
(like parentheses) in the way of writing. I feel, as a matter of principle, that
writing should not go smoothly and that when it does, unless I'm writing a

---

From *Writers on Writing*, ed. Tom Waldrep (New York: Random, 1985) 19–29.

memo (but even there I try to plant buried jokes or unofficial countervoices), when it does go smoothly, it's not doing the work of a professional or showing proper respect for what Thoreau referred to as the "extra-vagrance" of things.

I think of writing primarily as a matter of resistance. At the same time, however, I will quickly admit that I have developed habits and changed habits to make writing more efficient. I've learned to revise, I've learned to use a word processor, I've learned to develop a schedule and to find a place that can make regular writing possible. Writing still, often, makes me unhappy, makes me sick, makes me do things — like smoke, for instance — that disgust me. I have my habits and quirks and behaviors, like other writers, and I've learned that thinking about them has helped me to put them to use, and I've learned that talking about them can help me speak with greater authority to my students. I can remember, in fact, the day when, as a graduate student, I was talking to my freshman composition class about topic sentences and came to the troubling realization that while I knew what they were I did not know if there were any in anything that I wrote. What I did know was that I never thought about topic sentences while I was writing, and I vowed that I would try never again to say words to a class that made no sense to me as a writer.

What are my habits and quirks? I revise a lot and, as a consequence, I push my students to do the same. I spend a lot of time letting a paper bounce around in my head before I start writing. I begin my papers always with *things*, never with ideas or theses. I begin, that is, with a folder full of examples, or two books on my desk that I want to work into an essay, or a paragraph that I cut from an earlier essay of my own, or some long quotations that puzzle me and that I want to talk about and figure out (like the Bloom passage above).[1] I like green pens, I never outline, I work with two yellow pads (one to write on; one for making plans, storing sentences, and taking notes). I've learned to do all these things and they are a part of who I am and what I do as I write, but they strike me as unimportant when weighed on the scales of the Western tradition.

I'm not just being snide here. I feel a sense of historic moment when I write — not that I'm making history, but that I am intruding upon or taking my turn in a conversation others have begun before me. I feel a sense of the priority of others. Some of them, I think, are great writers, some of them are my colleagues and contemporaries, some of them are my teachers, some of them are strangers or students. I feel a sense of historic moment when I write that I'll confess I never felt at marches and rallies and that I never feel at university committee meetings or other public occasions.

What interests me most, then, and what I think about when I think about the composing process is another kind of drama altogether. There is another form of struggle, resistance, and achievement that I experience more profoundly when I write, and I will call it, drawing a phrase from Harold Bloom, the "dialectics of influence."

Bloom, in the passage at the top of this essay, says that "nothing happens" without imitation and, therefore, tradition. I take this very literally.

For me, nothing happens, or could happen, until I imagine myself within a discourse — a kind of textual conversation/confrontation with people whose work matters to me and whose work, then, makes my own possible. But I experience another kind of personal confrontation as well, one with a figure — or sometimes figures — not immediately addressing the subject or argument of the paper I'm working on (a person not likely to appear in the footnotes, for example). This is the most powerful influence and it is the influence of another writer, a person represented by a verbal, textual presence — a set of terms, a sound and a rhythm, a sensibility — that I cannot push out of my mind or erase from my own writing. When I write I find I am appropriating authority from others while trying to assert my own. This is the dialectic that I feel when I write and that shapes what I do when I put words on a page.

When I talk about the pressure of another writer's work on my own, I am talking about a particular person — not Writer in the abstract, but someone I know or someone that I am reading. There have been several who have functioned this way for me, but two most powerfully. These were not my composition teachers — actually I never took a composition course — but my writing teachers nevertheless, people whose writing would not leave me alone but stood, and stands still, as a challenge, an echo, a model, a burden. If I think of my own experience as a writer, the most powerful terms I can use to discuss the composing process are not prewriting, writing, and revision, but tradition and imitation and interference and resistance.

II

When I was an undergraduate, my career as an English major was more distinguished by my enthusiasm and my love of abstraction and glossy generalization than by my skill as a writer. I hated to write, partly because it was such an uncomfortable thing to do but also because I think I believed that it wasn't important — not as important as my ideas and my energy and my enthusiasm — and with the lingering sense that writing gave the lie to my expertise as a student of literature and language.

I figured that I could attend to writing later and learn to take my ideas and report them more efficiently or elegantly. I was playing football at the time (not as successfully as I was doing English) and learning that what distinguished the really good player was not that he was bigger or stronger or had more skills than I had, but that he understood the game and movement and fitness in ways that I did not. I learned early on that I was not yet in the league with those players and I learned what it would take for me to get there. I don't know that I learned the same lessons about writing. Roger Sale says that the first real lesson he learned about his writing came when he was out of graduate school and in his first teaching job. He was carrying on, he says, about something when a colleague asked, "Why do you talk in that boring way?" It was said in a way and at a time in his life when it could make sense. For Sale, the message was, "Quite simply, I did not know what I meant most of the time I spoke or wrote." And, he says, after that writing got harder and harder.[2]

Maybe these lessons are impossible for undergraduates. I could learn what made a serious football player but not what made a serious student of English. No one asked me why I talked and wrote the way I did, and I was comfortable believing that my performance on the page didn't matter, was essentially irrelevant to the work I was undertaking. When I think of what it was like to write then, how I did it, I think of my nine-year-old son, who has so many things he wants to do on a Saturday afternoon, and such strong feelings about it all, that he sits and morosely stares at the wall, or flits from comic book to TV set to the refrigerator. My teachers characteristically said that my papers were full of interesting ideas but poorly written — turgid, difficult, disorganized. I received mostly As and became determined to make a career out of English because one of my teachers, David Osborne, insisted not that I write well but that I at least know something. He taught the Victorian period and made us learn names and dates and read documents that were neither novels nor poems.

I don't think I really learned to write until graduate school, and there learning came through two deeply — I think I would say profoundly — felt experiences. My dissertation adviser rejected my dissertation because it was poorly written, and I came into contact with the first strong teacher of my academic life, Richard Poirier.

The dissertation story is an easier one to tell. I wrote the whole thing, about 350 pages or so, while I was away for a year in England, and when I gave it to my adviser he wouldn't read past page 100, saying that it was all just too poorly done. I think I knew that writers reworked or revised what they were writing — in fact, I think I told my students that this was true — but I had never done it, and so, for the first time in my career, I began to revise. I knew how writers acted, but I did not act and, as far as revision is concerned, had never acted like a writer. It all seems so matter-of-fact in the telling, but I still remember it with all the force and resonance of those experiences where we first learn the deep, troubling significance of something we thought we had known all along. I reworked the whole dissertation, and the final draft bore little resemblance to the first manuscript I sent from England. It was better than the first draft, and I learned a lot about my subject (Thomas Hardy) from doing the work.

When I went back to the first draft, after returning to this country and after a year of teaching, I saw two problems. The manuscript was sometimes incomplete, sometimes overdone, and often disorganized. And so I learned to add, subtract, and rearrange — the kind of revision that comes when you can step back, look again, and rework a piece you have begun. I find this kind of work to be fundamentally different from the kind of work that is involved in putting words on the page for the first time. I am, frankly, grateful to be able to do this kind of revision, since it allows me a certain grace or forgiveness when I pound out a draft. I don't think that it is hard to learn to do this, and I don't think it is difficult to teach.

The other problem I saw with the first draft was harder to solve. It remains for me one of the problems central to my writing. I was less troubled by the disorganization in the first draft than I was by its glibness. The writing seemed to me a sign of someone who knew how to do a dissertation (or do English or do school) but who would never be taken seriously by teachers or readers who paid attention. The problem here was not so much what I had to say about Thomas Hardy but what I did with what I had to say and how, in fact, I went about saying it. It's hard to learn how to deal with this — with the pressure of language to be pat, complete, official, single-minded; with the pressure of language against complexity, uncertainty, idiosyncracy, multiple-mindedness — and it's very hard to teach students to work against fluency, the "natural" flow of language as it comes to a writer who has a grasp of a subject.

I still feel a combination of bitterness and gratitude when I sit down to rework a paper. I find adding, subtracting, and reorganizing to be comfortably routine — not easy, that is, but manageable and predictable. I do this at least until I get to the parts where I am confused or clearly wrong, and then I try to see if I can save what I've said by making it reasonable or convincing. What I still find hard is pushing against my own language, resisting its smooth finish or apparent direction, trying often to complicate rather than simplify, or to disturb rather than quiet the rhythm of my sentences. The work I do here — resisting, interfering — goes on also when I am writing for the first time.

In practice, however, revision for me has never been a line-by-line matter. My revisions still bear little resemblance to my first drafts. I will, for example, begin pushing at the first sentence and find myself writing ten pages, following a line of thought that was repressed in the first writing. This business of stopping and reworking a passage until it grows and grows and takes over the paper occurs also when I am working on a first draft. In fact, I often work with two or three yellow pads at a time, each containing a level or a layer of the piece I am writing.

I often think of writing as multilayered, although not in the sense that there is a center, like the center of an onion, that can be revealed or discovered once the layers are peeled away or sloughed off. I think, rather, that I revise to add a layer, often discordant, over a layer that will also remain — so that there is a kind of antiphony. One layer speaks the words that are authorized. It speaks departmentally, professionally, carrying out the work that is charged by the institution. The other layers speak the words of my teachers, of the books I read; and they speak of my need to locate myself in all of this as a person who has read, and who can do respectable work, but who has the need to assert his own presence as well.

I revise to figure out better what I can say and to say it in such a way that it seems eloquent, in an Emersonian sense — so that it seems to assert the presence of someone who speaks as more than the representative of an institution or a brand of research or a discipline. I try very hard to interfere with the conventional force of writing, with the pressure toward set conclusions, set connections, set turns of phrase. The lesson I learned when I revised my dissertation radically changed the way I write. When I write I dump and revise, and then I continue to revise until I feel finished or until I can no longer ignore a deadline. What I learned first as a behavior (working on a paper for a second or third or fourth time), I've come to think of as a matter of belief or principle (working against the "natural" — that is, the conventional — flow of words on the page).

III

I find I cannot talk about how I write without talking about matters of belief and principle. I did not invent the principles that guide my writing. I suppose I could say that I inherited them. There is certainly a long Western tradition of writers, writing styles, and theories of writing, which is set against the belief that writing should be clear, brief, and sincere, or against the belief that good writing is efficient writing, or against the belief that writers shape and express their own meanings. I have learned to be able to make allusions to ancient and modern texts to borrow authority for my beliefs. At the level of belief, however, or at the level of deeply felt experience, the tradition exists for me through my contact with strong teachers, the teachers who influenced my writing.

I use the word "strong" to echo the way Bloom uses the word when he refers to strong poets or strong poetry and to the anxiety of influence. I think if we are lucky we come up against strong teachers, teachers whose presence, whose sensibility, whose manner of speaking and writing define almost completely our own historical moment, the context within which we might think, speak, read, or write. Bloom, in the passage I've put at the head of this essay, says, "You cannot write or teach or think or even read without imitation, and what you imitate is what another person has done, that person's writing or teaching or thinking or reading." This is no simple matter, however, since the young poet/student (like Shelley) faced with the older poet/teacher (like Milton) struggles to assert his own presence or priority in the very poetry that the older poet made possible. Or, as Bloom says, "A poet . . . is not so much a man speaking to men as a man rebelling against being spoken to by a dead man (the precursor) outrageously more alive than himself."

The force of this argument for me is the way Bloom argues that tradition exists functionally for us through the presence of a single person, a person who cannot be ignored, whose speech we cannot help but imitate and whose presence becomes both an inspiration and a burden. Through this encounter we place ourselves in and thereby invent a cultural, intellectual history. My own experience tells me that I have learned more, or perhaps learned more deeply, through these encounters than through a regular exposure to books and ideas and classes and so forth. The most dramatic educational experience I had was my contact with Richard Poirier in my first year of graduate school. The first three years of my graduate career were driven by a desire to be able to do what he did — to be able to read and speak and write like him. I would, for example, copy out difficult or impressive sentences he had written in order to get the feel of them. I can feel them now in many sentences I write. It is a mixed feeling. I state it simply, but it was not simple at all. I tried for a whole semester to write a paper using the word "language" as he used it in talking about how language "worked" in "Upon Appleton House." It took me a whole semester to use the word in a sentence that actually made sense to me. I felt that I had gained access to a profession by exercises such as these. At the time it did not feel like surrender. It was inspiring to feel that I could use his language and mimic, as I could, his way of reading and writing.

I remember very well how shocked I was when one of my other professors, after admiring a paper I had written, commented, "Don't you ever get tired of that Poirier routine?" It was not then, nor could it ever be for me now, simply a "routine," largely because what Poirier taught and how he taught and how he wrote were and remain central to my own beliefs and my professional identity. I felt ashamed, however, and began in my dissertation to try to write myself free from his influence, to find a project and a way of talking that I could claim for my own. This was a difficult and unsettling thing to try and do. I felt that I had found a place for myself, a way of thinking and talking that located me in the world of professionals, and now I had to push against it. This is not a battle that a writer wins, but for me it marked the next dramatic stage of my education.

As I think of the key experiences in my intellectual life, they all follow a similar pattern. My academic life has been marked by people, not by ideas or theories alone or in the abstract, and my development as a writer has been marked by my attempts to take on and then struggle free from the presence of others. The experiences, obviously, have not all been so intense; and not all, particularly the most recent, have been through teachers I actually see and talk to. I have recently been reading and rereading two essays by Emerson, for example, and I can't seem to get them out of my head.

The other equally key moment for me was meeting and working with Bill Coles. I knew about composition and work in composition before I met him, but I never really entered the field until I met him, felt the force of his presence as a teacher, and read his prose. I could never have imagined his eloquence or his wisdom on my own. I can leave it at that. He gave me a place to begin as a teacher and student of composition. There is nothing that I have written that I could have written without that starting point. As my teacher, I believe, he made eloquence and wisdom possible and defined for me how and why I would work in the field. In what Bloom calls the "dialectics of influence," this has been a matter of working with him and a matter of working against him, a matter, in its way, of interference and resistance, of giving over and giving up, of surrender and betrayal. This is how I think a writer learns, by learning to write within and against the powerful writing that precedes him, that haunts him, and that threatens to engulf him.

IV

I have learned one more important lesson about writing. It is the last important lesson I think I have learned, so perhaps it marks a later stage of development. When I was thirty-two, I wrote on my own for the first time in my life.

Now I have been arguing that no writer ever writes on his own but always in the presence of others. Learning to write means learning this and learning to handle it. So I don't mean that I wrote something fresh and original, or that

I wrote something I made up completely all by myself. What I mean is that I wrote something without having to. Actually, even this has to be qualified, since I was still untenured, but as I felt it and as I think back on it, I wrote an essay, actually two of them, both fairly long, just because I had to write them. I know that teachers talk about self-sponsored writing and expressive writing, but these terms never made much sense to me, except perhaps as metaphors.

There are, I think, things that writers are compelled to write about — subjects or themes that try as they might they cannot evade. I know this is true of my own writing. These themes may be said to "express" something basic to the makeup of a writer. The point I want to make, however, is that the presence of such themes doesn't naturally or necessarily give a person the motive or the ability to write about them. What does, or what did for me, was the moment in my career when I had a project — when I found myself in the midst of work that had gone on long enough, that had, in a sense, developed its own force of tradition so that the next step became visible, necessary, and inevitable. Because of what I had done, and the coherence of what I had done, there was a next step rather than a "starting all over again." For years I had felt that every paper I wrote meant that I had to figure things out for the first time. I am not sure what happened — whether I learned to see or insist on the coherence, or whether I had built up a critical mass of work to make the next step possible. I do know that I suddenly felt that there was work that I had to do. Bits and pieces of things that I would read, for example, would jump forward as if magnetized because of the way they could serve the project I was working on. I have heard people say that artists have a special vision, that they don't see the world the way the rest of us do. This never made much sense to me until I thought of it in my own terms. If artists have something, it is a project, a body of work that is ongoing, that defines their professional lives, and that makes them notice things that seem invisible or unimportant to others.

There is, perhaps, a point at which a writer has written so many sentences, read so many books, had so many arguments about a subject, that his work, and the progression of his work become inevitable. It's not so much the preoccupation with a theme that counts as the storehouse of words, the available sentences, the anticipated arguments, the general sense of having a place and a role in a discourse. In my mid-thirties, in the middle of my first job, I had the feeling I had in graduate school and early in my career — the feeling that I had found a place for myself. Now I worry a lot about this routine I've established, about the problems of self-parody, and about the debts I owe to others.

V

As I think about how I write, I know that my work will always begin with other people. I work with other people's words, even as I do my own work; other writers make my work possible, even as I begin to shape projects of my own. I don't put much stock in what I hear about invention and originality. I think it is a myth teachers foist on students in order to make teaching easier or less risky.

I think of Whitman as a strong and risky teacher. For me, he represents the paradox of teaching and learning:

> I am the teacher of athletes,
> He that by me spreads a wider breast than my own proves the width of
> my own,
> He most honors my style who learns under it to destroy the teacher.

He knows, however, that teachers don't die so easily, "I teach straying from me, yet who can stray from me?" And he concludes this section of "Song of Myself" with these lines:

> My face rubs to the hunter's face when he lies down alone in his blanket,
> The driver thinking of me does not mind the jolt of his wagon,
> The young mother and the old mother comprehend me,
> The girl and the wife rest the needle a moment and forget where they are,
> They and all would resume what I have told them.

As for my teachers, I resume what they have told me when I move to speak in turn. But never willingly and only sometimes with a most difficult grace.

NOTES

1. Harold Bloom, *A Map of Misreading* (New York: Oxford University Press, 1975), pp. 31–32.
2. Roger Sale, *On Writing* (New York: Random House, 1970), pp. 52–55.

Wistful and Admiring: The Rhetoric of Combination

T he first in time and the first in importance of the influences upon the mind is that of nature. Every day, the sun; and, after sunset, night and her stars. Ever the winds blow; ever the grass grows. Every day, men and women, conversing, beholding and beholden. The scholar must needs stand wistful and admiring before this great spectacle. He must settle its value in his mind.

— EMERSON, "THE AMERICAN SCHOLAR"

In the opening sentence of the preface to the second edition of *The Writer's Options*, Daiker, Kerek, and Morenberg refer to the "composing process,"[1] and there is, I think, a useful distinction to be made here. If the composing process refers to the quirks and behaviors, the observable drama of a writer's work on a text, the combining process refers to an intellectual activity, perhaps an activity of the imagination, that is sometimes linguistic and sometimes rhetorical. The purpose of this paper is to examine the outlines and the potential of a combinatory rhetoric, a rhetoric of combinations. While *The Writer's Options* allows for such a rhetoric (and I want to suggest that it is, at least potentially, a radical rhetoric), I am not sure that it teaches it overtly. But, as Emerson reminded the American scholar, "One must be an inventor to read well" and, by reading well, to free a lesson from its educational package.

The appendix (pp. 213–15) gives two consecutive exercises from the "Building Paragraphs" section of *The Writer's Options*. In the textbook, the purpose of these exercises is to show how a list of apparently random or contradictory statements can be controlled by a controlling idea. Students are to select items from the list to support the controlling idea and to organize those items into a paragraph that can be unified by the controlling idea. In the case of the first exercise, "Physical Fitness," the list is to be controlled by this sentence: "Catering to physical fitness has become a multimillion-dollar business." The rhetoric at work here is not a rhetoric of combination, but a rhetoric of selection

---

From *Sentence Combining: Toward a Rhetorical Perspective*, eds. Donald Daiker, Andrew Kerek, and Max Morenberg (Carbondale: Southern Illinois UP, 1995) 303–21.

and exclusion, a rhetoric that governs most of the traditional instruction in paragraphing to be found in composition textbooks and classrooms.

The reference to business creates an interpretive frame that determines how the list of statements might be read. Some statements become immediately appropriate (like the statement about the dollar value of the tennis clothes purchased each year), some statements remain neutral (like the statement that sex and age are no barrier to physical training), and some statements are excluded — in a sense, they become meaningless (like the statement about middle-aged joggers suffering heart attacks). A hypothetically neutral list of statements, in other words, is charged with positive and negative values by an interpretive screen, one signaled by the appeal to business. The job of the student is to read through the list, perhaps to annotate the entries with a code (in "Physical Fitness," a *B* is placed next to items that refer to business or economic value), and then to arrange the statements according to conventional patterns of statement and illustration, generalization and detail. The most basic essay, then, would read something like this:

Physical Fitness

A recent Gallup poll indicates that 47 percent of Americans take part in some form of physical fitness daily. Sex and age are no barrier to physical training. Catering to physical fitness has become a multimillion-dollar business. More than $200 million worth of tennis clothes are sold annually. There are more than 1300 books on fitness in print now. *Runner's World* magazine increased from 35,000 circulation in 1975 to over 200,000 circulation by 1978. The United States now has over 500 racquetball clubs. There are over 8 million joggers in the country, over 29 million tennis players. There are now over 3000 health clubs and spas around the nation with millions of total members. YMCA membership has increased by 16 percent in the past decade. Adidas alone sells over 200 styles of athletic shoes. Over $2 billion worth of sports equipment is sold every year. Some people jog in $100 jogging suits — with stripes down the sides — and $50 shoes.

Some transitions and embeddings could make this a more elegant paragraph, to be sure, and by rearranging sentences — perhaps beginning the essay with the last sentence, the most colorful one, and following it with the sentence about a multimillion-dollar business — a student could change the patterns of focus and emphasis within the paragraph. These are allowable options within the technology of sentence combining. But, in either case, the rhetoric would be the same. A controlling idea, which is always commonplace, has determined what counts and what has meaning in a writer's world. The statement about business has determined how a writer will see and interpret the list of possible statements about physical fitness. The list has been controlled by making it common, familiar, recognizable.

As Kenneth Burke has said over and over again, however, a way of seeing is also a way of not seeing.[2] An interpretive screen allows us to see one way, but always at the expense of seeing other ways. In the case of the "Physical Fitness" exercise, three types of statements are excluded: statements about enthusiasm, statements about changing tastes in sports, and statements about fitness, health, and medicine. Now, as the directions to the second exercise ("Game Shows") suggests, these, too, could be included in an essay with the general title, "Physical Fitness," by being grouped into additional paragraphs with additional controlling ideas or topic sentences. There could be a paragraph about fitness and business, one about fitness and health, and one about fitness and the growing boom in participants. The same rhetoric is at work, however, a rhetoric of selection and exclusion rather than a rhetoric of combination. A combinatory rhetoric would require that a writer account for all the statements as being equally about the same thing. It would interpret them all within a frame that would make them all, equally, examples of a single principle or idea. For Burke, in fact, the job of the rhetorician was to carry out the job of combining items — examples, concepts, phrases — under new terms, dialectical terms, and to do this rather than to select and arrange according to standard and, he would argue, less useful frames of reference. Burke's primary motive was to find similarities, not differences.

The rhetoric of selection, of the controlling idea, is a rhetoric in service of order and, in fact, in service of conventional principles of order. This, I imagine, is why it dominates classroom texts. It begins with the statement of a commonplace and reduces the world to a storehouse of examples to prove or support that commonplace. The interpretive process behind this is, in my experience, the natural or ad hoc heuristic students bring to most writing tasks — where their primary motive is to make the world manageable and not to make it dense and distracting, rich with contradiction and clutter. They are not prone to stand wistful and admiring before a great spectacle.

A student, for example, begins with a commonplace, "Sports are valuable because they teach us sportsmanship." He or she searches for examples to support that commonplace: children playing in the backyard, boys on the playing fields of high school, the inspirational value of having a team like the Steelers in Pittsburgh. If and when writing does its devilish work and brings in material to break the frame — children squabbling in the back yard, the pressure on high school athletes, the problem of defections to the USFL that haunt the Steelers — the writer stumbles into a contradiction, and contradictions, as any student writer knows, must be cut out, removed in a later draft to keep them from destroying the unity of the essay in support of the commonplace, "Sports are valuable because they teach us sportsmanship." There is a circle of belief here that can complete an essay and define a view of the world, but the space that it encloses is very small and, to use the language of the sentence combiners, not very mature.

What would happen in the Fitness essay if the writer were required to account for every item in the list as belonging equally to an elaboration of the statement that the fitness boom is an example of the business world putting pressure on private life? (I am not, now, suggesting an exercise where a student is left to state a generalization that can accommodate the twenty sentences on physical fitness.) I am trying to imagine an exercise where the student has to work with the given frame ("Catering to physical fitness has become a multimillion-dollar business.") to more completely carry out an interpretive project. What this exercise would require is the dogged refusal to ignore any statement as meaningless or trivial or contradictory. The requirement is not, then, unlike the requirement placed upon any writer working within or through an interpretive system that is believed to have the power to open what appears to be a closed system. Like a Marxist set upon demystifying a neutral account of history, or a Freudian critic accounting for the meaning of the most apparently insignificant images in a Brontë novel, the job of our student is to insistently work on every detail in the list in order to demonstrate his or her authority by the ability to make the most trivial or insignificant statement significant. The student's power lies in this, and not in the ability to present us with the obvious — that Adidas is catering to the market by presenting over 200 styles of athletic shoes.

If we define the project this way, the writer will have to account for the items missing from the original paragraph, the paragraph written by the "naive" writer who could only follow the clear choices in the list. The writer will have to account for the enthusiasm of the fitness buffs, for the changes in taste over the last decade, and, perhaps the most difficult, for the references to health and medicine — where jogging both causes and prevents heart attacks. And he or she will have to do all of this by demonstrating business's intent to "cater" to consumers. The resulting paragraph might look like the following:

Physical Fitness

A recent Gallup poll indicates that 47 percent of Americans take part in some form of physical fitness daily. The United States now has over 500 racquetball clubs and 3000 health clubs and spas. The YMCA has increased its membership by 16 percent in the past decade. There are over 8 million joggers in the country, over 29 million tennis players. Since exercise is good for our physical and mental health, this makes good sense. Exercise also makes good business, however, and this is a fact that has not been lost on the American business community, which is now selling over $2 billion worth of sports equipment every year. Sex and age are no barrier to physical training, so the available market is greater than the market for most consumer items. *Runner's World* magazine increased from 35,000 circulation in 1975 to over 200,000 circulation by 1978, and a magazine that once functioned like a bulletin board, featuring races, tips and winning times, now serves as a fashion magazine, featuring glossy ads for $50 shoes and $100 jogging suits — with stripes down the sides. Some joggers report a feeling of euphoria — not unlike a drug-induced high — from runs of more than 3 miles. Who would not pay top dollar for a good high or a fashion image, for the promise of a renewed sense of vitality, of goals conquered, of a confidence in coping with life? Exercise, as the marketing specialists have found, can become an addiction, and those who exercise become evangelists, recruiting others. The sports industry, and the magazines that serve it, have created a large market where once there was nothing but Keds and gym suits. Adidas alone now sells over 200 styles of athletic shoes. The push for new markets has, effectively, created not only new gear but new sports. In response to advertising and the general marketing of fitness, Americans are rejecting sports like golf and bowling for jogging, bicycling, tennis, swimming, and racquetball. They are buying into the "healthy" sports — jogging, for example, helps protect against two causes of heart attacks: inactivity and tension — but they are also buying new equipment and joining new clubs. With all the concentration on health, naturally the health industry has been careful to get its share of the market. Centers for Sports Medicine are popping up and treating everything from tennis elbow, the inflammation of the tendon that joins the forearm muscles to the elbow, to heart problems, the failure of the heart when a middle-aged jogger in poor condition sets off without proper advice. Catering to physical fitness has become a multimillion-dollar business.

I certainly don't want to claim that something dramatic or original has happened here. The second "Physical Fitness" paragraph has an equally predictable outcome. And this, I've argued, is always the case when a writer works with a controlling idea. The exercise remains an exercise. At best, it is illustrative. It is not an example of what many teachers would want to call "writing." I do, however, want to argue that the act of combining, and thereby not selecting and excluding, has provided a very different task for the writer. The combining process makes different demands than the job of finding a paragraph hidden in the list of sentences. That job, the job of selecting and excluding, makes the first exercise a version of the word search games you find in the newspapers, where you have to find whole words hidden in jumbles of letters. The second exercise makes the writer responsible for combining things that don't fit together easily. And that, I suggest, is a way of representing what real writers do.

Let's imagine, now, that a kind of combinatory Puck, or an antic and goat-footed sentence combiner, snuck into *The Writer's Options*, took away the titles and the instructions, and presented students with the thirty-four items from these two exercises — "Physical Fitness" and "Game Shows" — all shuffled together. What would a combinatory rhetoric make possible — or what might be the outcome of the combining process?

Once they are held together, items on each list lend themselves to such a cross-over.[3] Which is the more appropriate referent, jogging or game shows, for each of the following?

- forces people to dress up in ridiculous costumes
- when contestants win prizes, they often become hysterical and cry
- encourages contestants to go for the most expensive item displayed
- enthusiasts gain a renewed sense of vitality, of a goal conquered, and of confidence in coping with life

It is possible to imagine the sentences from these two exercises combined, then, into an essay called, "Physical Fitness: The New American Game Show."

The beginning of the essay might look something like this:

Physical Fitness: The New American Game Show

A young, attractive man, wearing the latest fashions — a $100 jogging suit, with stripes down the sides, and $50 Adidas Waffle-Trainers — hops on to the set. He's surrounded by flashing lights, driving music, and sexy women right off the cover of *Runner's World* — handsome, energetic, long-legged, dressed in silk shorts and runners' tops. "Come on down," he says. Come on down and put on these silk shorts and this runner's top and show the folks out there what you can do. Act like a child again. Run three miles. Feel the euphoria. Say goodbye to inactivity and tension.

He is like an evangelist, recruiting others. Contestants on his show are encouraged to use cut-throat tactics to eliminate their competition. Prizes are displayed in the flashiest way possible to make them appear more exciting. What he has to offer is a renewed sense of vitality, the promise of goals conquered, and a confidence in coping with life. What a participant gets, however, is often something else, something that by comparison seems to be defective, the wrong model, and color.

The game show can be made to stand for physical fitness and physical fitness can be made to stand for the game show. Both, I think, become something different when they are hooked together. The sentences of one list become different sentences when they are put in contact with the sentences of the other. The ability to solve such a problem or to carry out such a process involves the ability to work metaphorically — to verbally yoke together two seemingly dissimilar entities, to let one thing stand for another, and to see through the metaphor to understand each side of the combination in a new way. The metaphor serves, then, not for the purpose of illustration (as Aristotle would define the use of metaphor) but for purposes of invention or interpretation (as Richards or Ricoeur would define its uses).

I have tried to demonstrate that it is possible to combine sentences that aren't already precombined according to rules of selection and exclusion. The rhetoric of the controlling idea can be undone or transformed by the rhetoric of combination and an exercise that appears to be a closed game (find the paragraph the exercise-maker had in mind) can become a game of another kind altogether. In fact, I think it is safe to say that in a combinatory rhetoric anything can be combined with anything else. It just happened that "Game Show" and "Physical Fitness" were together in the book. I might have sat down to "Shacking Up" and "Rent Control." Such conjoinings are possible because the grammar of discourse is not as fixed as the grammar of the sentence. It is a conceptual grammar or a semiotic grammar. It allows for possibilities of combination that the paragraph exercises in the sentence-combining textbooks don't begin to explore. In the preface to *The Writer's Options*, Daiker, Kerek, and Morenberg say to students, "If you do the exercises carefully and creatively and then consciously use in your own writing the same structures, patterns and strategies, you can expect to become better writers." I am uncertain about the degree to which formal exercises can be exercises in creativity, and I am uncertain that a request for creativity can ever be sufficient. But I do believe that there are structures, patterns, and strategies for understanding that are available to student writers and that are not represented by exercises in selection and exclusion.

I have demonstrated one way in which the paragraph exercises can be expanded or, perhaps more correctly, one way in which they can be undone. When I read this paper at the Miami Conference, I was asked what exercises, in fact, I used in my own classes — I could only answer indirectly. I am not writing here about my composition classes. The purpose of this essay is to demonstrate how a textbook might be read and how set exercises might be presented to a class, and, through this demonstration, to make an argument for a kind of writing that is often ignored or devalued by composition teachers. I think that all textbooks, including the best of them, are rigid and that the job of a teacher is to teach students to work against the rigidity of their assigned texts. This, too, is a lesson in writing.

Walker Percy argues that formal education makes learning impossible when it places a powerful and compelling educational package between students and the "thing" it is meant to teach them to see and understand. The package, in a sense, becomes more immediately present than the subject or point of the lesson. Or, as Percy puts it,

> the educator whose business it is to teach students biology or poetry is unaware of a whole ensemble of relations which exist between the students and the dogfish and between the students and the Shakespeare sonnet. To put it bluntly: A student who has the desire to get at a dogfish or a Shakespeare sonnet may have the greatest difficulty in salvaging the creature itself from the educational package in which it is presented.[4]

And so, Percy proposes, in order for the students to recover the dogfish or the sonnet on their own, they will have to have a strategy for avoiding or overcoming the insistent argument of the textbook or the prepared classroom. "I propose," says Percy, "that English poetry and biology should be taught as usual, but that at irregular intervals, poetry students should find dogfishes on their desks and biology students should find Shakespeare sonnets on their dissecting boards."[5]

Percy is concerned that "sovereignty" be returned to students — that they be located in relation to objects of study as students rather than as consumers. If, then, a student might learn something about the power of combining things by combining things beyond their official margins, by using the act of combination to defy or transcend (Percy would say, "dialectically transcend") given forms, then perhaps the point of my exercise with the paragraph building exercises is not that new exercises should be written for *The Writer's Options* but that they should seem, sometimes, as surprising as a dogfish in a Shakespeare class.

Writers have the ability to make everything count, to render nothing that they can refer to superfluous. To say this is not to say that writers use language this way. The style of a combinatory rhetoric is not a dominant style in our culture or in our classrooms. It is a significant and powerful style nonetheless, and it is a particularly American style — democratic and transcendental at once — since it carries with it a bias toward a multiple world of things and concepts, each with an equal potential to be meaningful. It is the style, I think, of Thoreau's *A Week on the Concord and Merrimack Rivers*; it is the style of Emerson's essays, of Burke's *Rhetoric of Motives,* and of Edward Said's *Beginnings.*

Emerson, in "The American Scholar," outlines a principle of education for the ideal American scholar, a scholar who is bound to neither the authority of established ideas nor to the authority of texts and teachers. The rhetoric required by such a program of education would not be an Aristotelian rhetoric, as it would be set against the commonplaces of a communal discourse and not, as in Aristotle's rhetoric, in service of them. Emerson's scholar is situated before nature. The scholar, he says,

> must needs stand wistful and admiring before this great spectacle. He must settle its value in his mind. What is nature to him? There is never a beginning, there is never an end to the inexplicable continuity of this web of God, but always circular power returning into itself. Therein it resembles his own spirit, whose beginning, whose ending he never can find — so entire, so boundless. Far, too, as her splendors shine, system on system shooting like rays, upward, downward, without centre, without circumference, — in the mass and in the particle nature hastens to render account of herself to the mind.[6]

In the face of this multiplicity, where there is no single controlling idea to provide a center, the student who would speak, act, or write — who would, that is, move from wistful admiration to action — must articulate a system, in service of rather than at odds with nature. The student must, as Emerson would have it, proceed by "tying things together, diminishing anomalies, discovering roots running under ground, whereby contrary and remote things cohere, and flower out from one stem." And Emerson sees this achievement as evidence of a kind of intellectual maturity, something that is learned rather than given. To the "young mind," he says, everything is individual and stands by itself. Later, the mind learns how to "join two things, and see in them one nature; then three, then three thousand."[7]

The scholar must discover roots running underground, tie things together, demonstrate how contrary and remote things cohere. Whitman's grand catalogs, Emerson's essays and Thoreau's prose, it is common to observe, enact this very process. Thoreau, for example, in *A Week on the Concord and Merrimack Rivers* presents a leisurely trip down a river that is also a leisurely accumulation of observations of natural and civilized life, close observations of immediate scenes alongside the river but also observations of scenes recollected or imagined, interlarded with quotations and paraphrases from his reading, all bound together by the active presence of a writer whose primary motive is to find and celebrate connections. The transitions from scene to scene are not the transitions of argument or dialectic. They are associative but not, at the same time, either random or senseless. Here is an example from the journal record of "Friday." I include it to give some sense of the texture of the whole.

Already the cattle were heard to low wildly in the pastures and along the highways, restlessly running to and fro, as if in apprehension of the withering of the grass and of the approach of winter. Our thoughts, too, began to rustle.

As I pass along the streets of our village of Concord on the day of our annual Cattle Show, when it usually happens that the leaves of the elms and the buttonwoods begin first to strew the ground under the breath of the October wind, the lively spirits in their sap seem to mount as high as any plough-boy's let loose that day; and they lead my thoughts away to the rustling woods, where the trees are preparing for their winter campaign. This autumnal festival, when men are gathered in crowds in the street as regularly and by as natural a law as the leaves cluster and rustle by the wayside, is naturally associated in my mind with the fall of the year.[8]

This leads his thoughts to rustle on past farm workers and farm life, Greek festivals, the nature of poetic genius, floods, Aristotle, and so on. The problem Thoreau presents to readers, or academic readers, is the problem of whether such an accumulation of scenes and thoughts can be said to be "artistic." For Matthiessen, Thoreau's prose works when it can, in fact be shown to have a subtle and effective arrangement, an arrangement driven by what he calls the "organic principle."[9] I think I am a more forgiving reader. For me the prose is justified by the presence on the page of the "Thoreau" whose mental rustlings I find pleasant and interesting.

As I think of characteristically American writers, I think also of Kenneth Burke, whose *Rhetoric of Motives* is a journey through an incredible catalog of authors and texts — from Milton to Marx to Empson — and where the writer's motive, again, is to demonstrate that all these authors are talking about the same thing, where the primary goal is to find similarities and not differences, to include rather than exclude, to speak of everything in the same breath.

The opening chapter of *A Rhetoric of Motives* asks us to consider Milton's "Samson Agonistes" and Arnold's "Empedocles on Etna" and "Sohrab and Rustrum" as poems that must, for critical reasons, be thought of together — "we are trying to bring these poems together as instances of the *same* motivation." (Burke's italics.) And he wants to do this because he wants us to imagine suicide and warlike death as the same thing. And he wants us to do this because he wants us to be able to connect these poems with Coleridge's "Religious Musings," with the "estheticism of Pater, and thence to father-problems as transformed perversely in the estheticism of Oscar Wilde." And all of this is to enable us to see how the principles of "transformation" can bring together things that appear contrary and remote. The process is a process of combination — "by adding one more confusion, we may add the element that can bring clarity" — and it is in service of what Burke calls "dialectic": "ironically making motives interchangeable which might usually be considered mutually exclusive," so that things may (at least verbally) cohere and we may see roots running underground.[10]

Edward Said, in *Beginnings: Intention and Method,* one of the most important recent American critical works, speaks of his own method in writing his book. A critic, he says, is not a "revolutionist destroying the canon in order to replace it with his own." He does not, in other words, pose an idea to be the center for everyone else's argument. He is rather, "a wanderer, going from place to place for his material, but remaining a man essentially *between* homes." (Here, and in all that follows, the emphasis in the quoted passages is Said's.) Work of this sort requires its own method, one that can allow a writer to be set against traditional patterns of exclusion and to be set against "controlling" ideas, but that will still enable the writer to speak about this novel and not that one, or to speak about this critic and not the other, and that will still enable the writer to speak of ideas, whether they be reigning commonplaces or radical concepts. Work of this sort requires the presence of a writer who is not a "writer" as we traditionally think of him. Said says this about the method of this book:

> Learning what I could from Valery, I embarked on what I called a medi-
> tation on beginnings. Because the *Topos* is neither a traditional nor a usual
> one, I could not geometrically define it beforehand. I undertook, however,
> to let it make possible a system of relationships, a field or constellation of
> significance in which my writing moved in order to gather in both the
> grosser and the more rarefied thoughts, images, and instances that crowd
> around beginnings. The logic of exposition I follow is not precursive; that
> is, my exposition follows no course determined in advance by convention,
> imitation, consecution, or thematics. The form of writing I chose was the
> meditative essay — first, because I believe myself to be trying to form a
> unity as I write; and second, because I want to let beginnings generate in
> my mind the type of relationships and figures most suitable to them.[11]

And he says,

> Since every beginning is different, and since there is no hope of dealing
> with everyone, I arrange examples in *series* whose internal rule of coher-
> ence is neither a logic of simple consecutiveness nor random analogy.
> Rather, I adopt a principle of *association* that works, in a sense, *against*
> simple consecution and chance.[12]

Beginnings is a difficult book. It argues for a method of writing that is also a method of interpretation. The problem that Said sets for himself, however, is I think an Emersonian problem, and it is a problem that exists for the writer at the level of method or technique. The key, for Said, is to make consecution nei-ther simple nor arbitrary and to make the act of association a critical act, a way of seeing this text through that one, where neither a text nor an idea functions in a primary way as a control. In a way, Said proposes a writer who is absent rather than present, yet, at the same time, the greatest pressure on this writer is a moral obligation, the obligation to *make* something of what he is doing.

Let me add one final voice to my list of American writers. The transition here is a difficult one, since my only reason for adding William Stafford after Said is my desire for one more, although I can imagine how I might go on to talk about both if I wanted to do something other than cap off a list.

In his essay, "A Way of Writing," Stafford talks about his own experience and preparation as a writer:

A writer is not so much someone who has something to say as he is someone who has found a process that will bring about new things he would not have thought of if he had not started to say them. That is, he does not draw on a reservoir, instead he engages in an activity that brings to him a whole succession of unforeseen stories, poems, essays, plays, laws, philosophies, religions, or — but wait!

Back in school, from the first when I began to try to write things, I felt this richness. One thing would lead to another; the world would give and give. Now, after twenty years or so of trying, I live by that certain richness, an idea hard to pin, difficult to say, and perhaps offensive to some. For there are strange implications in it.[13]

This passage is often taken as an argument for diving in, for beginning to write in order to see what will happen. And it is such an argument. Stafford is talking about the process of composing. He is also, however, talking about a way of writing — one that is potentially difficult and offensive, since it defines a writer as a person committed to the demonstration that anything can lead to anything else. To argue this is not just to make the process of composing a disorderly process; it is to acknowledge that the purpose of writing, in the best Emersonian sense, is to celebrate and not deny "richness" — system on system shooting like rays, upward, downward, without center, without circumference — unified only by a writer's ability to unify everything.

A writer who would combine is led in three directions: toward the sequence, toward dialectic, and toward metaphor. The sequence represents the potential for all things to be combined and held in series. Winston Weathers[14] argues that the length of a series has a rhetorical force of its own. By his calculus, a two-part series creates the aura of certainty and confidence, of didacticism and dogmatism. A three-part series impresses upon us that the divisions are normal, reasonable, and logical. The material is assembled, that is, according to a standard form. The series of four or more, however, suggests, according to Weathers, that we are in the presence of the human, the emotional, the diffuse, the abundant, the inexplicable. It is here that the rhetoric of combination insists on an Emersonian coherence, where the multiple or boundless is joined together by a presence that is at once wistful and admiring, more interested in expansion than control. An extended series tied to a central interpretive frame, by the same logic, identifies a process of interpretation that is rigorous, dogged, inexhaustible, in which all the various stuff of the world can be made meaningful.

Burke defines dialectic as the process of joining together disparate material under general terms that allow for "transcendence," a next higher level of understanding and discussion. Here is the definition he gives in an essay, appropriately, on Emerson:

The machinery of language is so made that things are necessarily placed in terms of a range broader than the terms for those things themselves. And thereby, in even the toughest or tiniest of terminologies — terminologies that, on their face, are far from the starry-eyed transcendentalism of Emerson's essay — we stretch forth our hands through love of a farther shore; we consider things in terms of a broader scope than the terms for those particular things themselves.[15]

This is one way of working against a "consecutiveness" that is driven only by chance, and it is a way of writing about ideas without beginning with controlling ideas. Said, I think, is writing about something other than dialectic. He is, to be sure, combining things under some broad general concepts — the concept of a beginning that is not an origin, for example — but Said would not claim the evolutionary or apocalyptic force for his discourse than Burke would claim for his. The movement for Said is circular; it does not head toward the stars.

The combination of items may also be a procedure for the making of metaphor. And, it could be argued, the most productive metaphors are those that begin as mistakes — like the yoking of physical fitness and game shows — where the act of combining defies conventional combinations and asserts and values unconventional ones.

Walker Percy, in the essay "Metaphor as Mistake," argues that such metaphors as these allow one to regain his sovereignty over the world of experience; they allow the apprehension of a thing that defies efforts of naming, that appears before us without prior classification. The feeling of "wrongness" that certain metaphors provide, he argues, is a feeling of mystery which is, itself, the very condition of knowing, actually knowing anything at all. The mistake in the metaphor is "itself the instrument of knowing and is an error only if we do not appreciate its intentional character."[16]

Lakoff and Johnson, in their recent book, *Metaphors We Live By*,[17] tell the story of an Iranian student at Berkeley who heard the phrase "the solution of my problems" as a beautifully sane expression of the situation of any person who is perplexed and troubled. The meaning the phrase had for this student, however, was not the meaning carried by the phrase as we commonly use it. By "solution" he imagined a chemical solution, a bubbling, smoking solution containing all of his problems, some of them dissolving away and some of them forming into solids. According to Lakoff and Johnson, the student was terribly disappointed to discover that the students at Berkeley had no such chemical metaphor in mind at all. His mistake, however, gave him both a new view of the idea of a problem and a version of Percy's happy experience of suddenly knowing something for the first time. (The story they narrate, however, carries also the reminder that such knowledge is generally "wrong.") For a metaphor to be a tool for interpretation, it must provide a frame that frees us from conventional systems of understanding (or the writer must work at a second remove and see it, the metaphor as an argument for a conventional system of understanding). As such, a metaphor is not just a way of decorating a paper but is, itself, a way of understanding.

Combinations, then, can produce a style in service of a view of the world as diffuse, multiple and yet unified by the presence of a writer and by the power of language. And a writer, then, can begin with the motive to combine rather than to select and exclude. There is a history to this style and a theoretical justification for this style — and both the history and the theory are, I think, part of a desire for both democracy, or a democratic discourse, and transcendence. And, I've argued, the pedagogy of combination requires the careful cultivation of chance, surprise, and mistake as well as a willing acceptance of the desire to look wistfully this way and that.

I would also argue, finally, that the combining process can be seen as a version of the composing process — as evidence of a certain kind of behavior that can make writing possible. Ann Berthoff says that when she sees a writer sitting alone with a pencil and a blank page, she is tempted to say, "But wait a minute! Where are your notes to yourself? Where are your lists? Where is your lexicon? Where are your quoted passages? Where is your chaos?"[18]

I'll confess that I often begin writing with the kind of chaos Berthoff has in mind — a couple of books that I can't get off my desk, three or four long passages that I know I want to work into whatever I write, the text of a paper I worked on long ago but never published. This paper, in fact, began with just such an assortment of items. Don Daiker wrote me about the conference when I was in the middle of teaching Emerson's "The American Scholar" and selections of *A Week on the Concord and Merrimack Rivers* to Spanish students at a Spanish university. I knew then, and I warned him, that Emerson and Thoreau would somehow work their way into what I could say about sentence combining. I am, in addition, always trying to find ways of working Walker Percy and Edward Said into my papers, since I admire their work enormously and feel that they have much to say about what we call the composing process, and yet their names are seldom heard at conferences on composition. I had used the Stafford passage in an assignment for my composition course early in September. I saw that Ken Dowst was going to be on the program for the conference and I remembered him telling me that he admired Winston Weathers' essay in the Graves anthology.

These are the books, papers, and quotations that cluttered my desk when I sat down to write. As I began writing, my job as I saw it was to find a way to talk about them all, to make one a context for the others, to figure out how to make contrary and remote things cohere. This is a motive, I believe, that can define a project for a writer.

APPENDIX

Physical Fitness

Select from the list below all the notes that support the controlling idea that "catering to physical fitness has become a multimillion-dollar business." Then organize those notes into an explanatory paragraph unified by the controlling idea.

B1. More than $200 million worth of tennis clothes are sold annually.

2. Fitness enthusiasts gain a renewed sense of vitality, of a goal conquered, and of confidence in coping with life.

3. Sex and age are no barrier to physical training.

4. Tennis players and racquetball enthusiasts suffer tennis elbow, the inflammation of the tendon that joins the forearm muscles to the elbow.

B5. There are more than 1300 books on fitness in print now.

B6. *Runner's World* magazine increased from 35,000 circulation in 1975 to over 200,000 circulation by 1978.

7. Middle-aged joggers in poor condition may be setting off heart attacks if they begin without proper advice.

B8. A recent Gallup poll indicates that 47 percent of Americans take part in some form of physical fitness daily.

9. Jogging is one of the best cures for depression, report many psychologists.

10. Exercise can become an addiction, and those who exercise become evangelists, recruiting others.

B11. The United States now has over 500 racquetball clubs.

12. Some joggers report a feeling of euphoria — not unlike a drug-induced high — from runs of more than 3 miles.

13. Fitness buffs are rejecting sports like golf and bowling for jogging, bicycling, tennis, swimming, and racquetball.

B14. Some people jog in $100 jogging suits — with stripes down the sides — and $50 shoes.

15. Jogging helps protect against two causes of heart attacks — inactivity and tension.

B16. There are over 8 million joggers in the country, over 29 million tennis players.

B17. There are now over 3000 health clubs and spas around the nation with millions of total members.

B18. YMCA membership has increased by 16 percent in the past decade.

B19. Adidas alone sells over 200 styles of athletic shoes.

B20. Over $2 billion worth of sports equipment is sold every year.

Game Shows

Construct a unified and ordered paragraph by picking one of the three statements below to serve as a controlling idea and then choosing appropriate supporting details from the notes.

A. Game show prizes aren't always as good a deal as they seem to be.

B. Game shows use gaudy sets, sex, and gimmicks to create excitement.

C. Game shows thrive on placing contestants in humiliating situations.

1. Game show hosts are usually young and attractive.
2. They dress in the latest fashions.
3. Game show sets are alive with flashing lights and gaudy colors.
4. Women assistants on shows like "The Price Is Right," "Let's Make a Deal," and "Treasure Hunt" are dressed in sexy outfits.
5. On "The Price Is Right" contestants called down from the audience are told to run from their seats to the stage.
6. They often exhibit no regard for others sitting in their area.
7. Contestants on all the shows are encouraged to use cut-throat tactics to eliminate their competition.
8. Prizes like cars, boats, and furs are displayed in the flashiest way possible to make them appear more exciting.
9. Contestants display their greed when they consider the value of their prizes or decide which door to choose.
10. Most shows don't allow winners to substitute cash value for the prizes.
11. When prizes do arrive, they are often defective, the wrong model, or the wrong color.
12. People from certain areas of the country have no use for sailboats, scuba gear, or snowmobiles — common game show prizes.
13. Since taxes on prizes are high, many winners are forced to sell their prizes for money to pay the taxes.
14. Winners frequently report having to wait for months before getting their prizes.
15. Some people have strong moral objections to fur coats — common prizes.
16. Certain prizes require expensive upkeep.
17. Many of the game shows are gimmicky.
18. They are geared to creating a false sense of suspense.
19. Contestants often act like children in order to amuse the host or audience.
20. When contestants win prizes, they often become hysterical and cry.
21. Hosts take advantage of contestants' peculiarities to make them look ridiculous.
22. The "Newlywed Game" exposes intimate personal information about couples and encourages family arguments on stage.
23. "Let's Make a Deal" forces people to dress up in ridiculous costumes.
24. All the shows encourage contestants to go for the most expensive items displayed.

NOTES

1. Donald A. Daiker, Andrew Kerek, and Max Morenberg, *The Writer's Options: Combining to Composing,* 2nd ed. (New York: Harper & Row, 1982), p. x.

2. Kenneth Burke, *Permanence and Change: An Anatomy of Purpose* (Indianapolis: Bobbs-Merrill, 1965), p. 49. I will argue later that Burke is an example of a writer whose primary motive is to combine rather than to select. The act of combining, in fact, is a route to his version of dialectic. In the section of *Permanence and Change* that includes the passage on seeing and not seeing, for example, Burke combines a concept from Dewey with a concept from Veblen to demonstrate how he (Burke) can argue that two seemingly disparate sets of phrases can be considered "interchangeable." This is a characteristic maneuver in Burke's writing.

3. Just, I suppose it is appropriate to add, as Veblen and Dewey could be seen to be saying the same thing when shuffled together by Burke.

4. Walker Percy, *The Message in the Bottle* (New York: Farrar, 1954), p. 57. I am quoting from chap. 2, "The Loss of the Creature."

5. Percy, p. 61.

6. Ralph Waldo Emerson, *The Collected Works,* I (Cambridge, MA: Harvard Univ. Pr., 1971), pp. 54–55.

7. Emerson, p. 54.

8. *The Portable Thoreau,* ed. Carl Bode (New York: Viking, 1964), pp. 204–5.

9. F. O. Matthiessen, *The American Renaissance* (New York: Oxford Univ. Pr., 1968), pp. 166–75.

10. Kenneth Burke, *A Rhetoric of Motives* (Berkeley: Univ. of California Pr., 1969), pp. 1–13. I am forcing the connection with Emerson by using Emerson's terms to refer to Burke. I will later, however, include Burke on Emerson.

11. Edward Said, *Beginnings: Intention and Method* (Baltimore: Johns Hopkins Univ. Pr., 1975), pp. 15–16.

12. Said, p. 16.

13. William Stafford, "A Way of Writing," in *A Writer's Reader,* ed. Donald Hall and D. C. Emblen (Boston: Little, Brown, 1979), p. 371.

14. Winston Weathers, "The Rhetoric of the Series," in *Rhetoric and Composition: A Sourcebook for Teachers,* ed. Richard L. Graves (Rochelle Park, NJ: Hayden, 1976), pp. 95–102.

15. Kenneth Burke, "I, Eye, Ay — Emerson's Early Essay 'Nature': Thoughts in the Machinery of Transcendence," in *Transcendentalism and Its Legacy,* ed. Myron Simon and Thornton H. Parsons (Ann Arbor: Univ. of Michigan Pr., 1966), p. 23.

16. Percy, *Message in the Bottle,* p. 81.

17. George Lakoff and Mark Johnson, *Metaphors We Live By* (Chicago: Univ. of Chicago Pr., 1980), pp. 143–45.

18. Ann E. Berthoff, "Recognition, Representation, and Revision," *Basic Writing,* 3 (1981), 20.

The Reading of Reading:

I. A. RICHARDS AND M. J. ADLER

After that first year of teaching, I had few illusions left about my literacy. Since then, I have been teaching students how to read books, six years at Columbia with Mark Van Doren and for the last ten years at the University of Chicago with President Robert M. Hutchins. In the course of years, I think I have gradually learned to read a little better.

— MORTIMER ADLER, *HOW TO READ A BOOK*

[*How to Read a Page*] went down . . . perhaps where the ground was prepared . . . with the teachers who at that time were feeling, as I was — many of us were — feeling really swamped by the Chicago sort of thing. And all of our effort had been, you know, in the opposite direction. There were so many badly conceived courses that just grabbed Great Authors right and left, and threw them in.

— REUBEN BROWER,
IN AN INTERVIEW WITH I. A. RICHARDS,
I. A. RICHARDS: ESSAYS IN HIS HONOR

Since many of us are once again feeling swamped by the Chicago sort of thing, it is instructive to consider its 1940 manifestation, Mortimer Adler's *How to Read a Book* and I. A. Richards' peculiar response, *How to Read a Page*.

Adler tells his story this way: "I did not discover I could not read until after I had left college" (6). He looked — and I think it is fair to say he looked bravely and acutely — at what he *didn't* know about the books he had read as a student, saw in his ignorance a sign of a general failure in our educational system — one confirmed by his recent experience as a teacher of undergraduates, by professional studies (including Richards' *Practical Criticism*), by academic conferences, and by a recent Carnegie Report — and set about to devise a pedagogy for teaching young adults to read great books with understanding.

From *Audits of Meaning*, ed. Louise Z. Smith (Portsmouth: Boynton/Cook, 1988) 55–71.

Richards had already established his concern for the problems of reading and education, most recently in *The Philosophy of Rhetoric* (1936) and *Interpretation in Teaching* (1938). Of his next book, he said:

> I had admired Mortimer Adler immensely but I somehow got irritated by *How to Read a Book*. So I wrote a counter-blast: *How to Read a Page*. Instead of a hundred *books*, chosen regardless of what translation, version or anything, I wanted to take just a hundred *words* and then I revolted again and made it a hundred and three. And it so happens that the Great Books are now a hundred and three. It was partly a bit of fun. But it was a very serious book, unusable, I know now, for the populations I hoped I was addressing. . . . It didn't go down where it was hoped it would go down. One has to be used to that. (Brower, Vendler, and Hollander 36)

Adler's book was at the top of the best-seller list for over a year; Richards' is long out of print and seldom read.

I would like to talk about *How to Read a Book* and *How to Read a Page* as blast and counterblast, the "Chicago thing" in one corner and poised against it something else altogether. As I reproduce passages from these books, you will find yourself in familiar territory. Almost fifty years later, teachers are fighting the same battles, in the same terms, while standing on the same turf.

I

I need to begin, then, by establishing a place called "Chicago," a place where they have powerful and distinct ways of speaking about reading, writing, and teaching. (Mortimer Adler is there, but also Alan Bloom, Wayne Booth, and — at least in my Chicago — E.D. Hirsch.) None of these people in Chicago quite agrees with the others, but this Chicago I'm talking about is big enough to contain competing voices and still remain the same place. There are disagreements about this exercise or that text, but the talk all issues from the same source. Here, for example, is someone from Chicago talking to students about reading and writing. It is not Adler speaking, but in its tone and language it sounds remarkably familiar to anyone who has recently read *How to Read a Book*. It is, in other words, a fine example of the Chicago sort of thing:

> Just as exercise, study, and discipline can improve our health, they can also improve our "verbal health" — our power to use and respond to language. People often act as if being able to read a newspaper or ask for directions proves that they are fluent in their native tongue. But in fact most of us perform even these basic language tasks less well than we could. People who think they "know how to read" often misread even the simplest news accounts, as all newspaper editors and reporters learn to their sorrow. And we all have had the experience of finding ourselves on the wrong side of town because we either asked for directions unclearly or received unclear directions from someone else. The number of our confusions, misunderstandings, and misspeakings can be decreased if we only know how, but not without work, not without

the exercise, study, and discipline that strengthened our performance. The main objective of this course is to provide such systematic exercise in reading and writing. (Booth and Gregory 3–4)

This is an introduction to a textbook, Wayne Booth and Marshall Gregory's *The Harper and Row Reader*. It sets up the terms through which students, and their teachers, can begin to imagine the work of the course — reading and writing. My guess is that the course description will read as a familiar document to any English teacher: its language seems inevitable, seamless, natural, right. And depending on where you stand, of course, it is. Reading and writing are good for you; they make you healthy (or healthier); they require discipline and exercise; the goal is to reduce misunderstanding and improve communication.

Perhaps the best way to get a purchase on this excerpt is to imagine what it excludes, to imagine what can't be said (or asked) in Chicago, not necessarily because of taboo but because, to this way of speaking, such statements or questions simply aren't there.

We have all, it is true, phrased questions poorly or received unclear directions. There are other ways, however, of imagining the difficulty of language use, particularly in a class where, as I look at the table of contents in Booth's reader, students are going to read essays by Freud, Marx, and Adrienne Rich. There are, that is, problems of understanding that are rooted in problems of interpretation, problems that require critical methods (ways of asking questions that don't come naturally, for example), problems that follow when competing ideologies or irreconcilable ways of thinking are brought into the scene, and these problems are of a different order than problems of mis-speaking on the street or misunderstanding directions. If you look in on this from the outside, it is possible to imagine problems with Freud or Rich that require a method, and not just discipline and exercise.

It is possible to imagine a course in reading and writing that is a course in method ("method," that is, as Berthoff defines it: the critical tool enabling us to interpret our interpretations, to think about thinking, to understand not only what our ideas are but "how they are working for us — or against us"), but it is impossible to imagine such a course in a setting where Booth's words are the inevitable language of instruction (Berthoff 4).

The trivial example (bad directions) and the obvious evasion (the absence of any reference to the essays that make up this "reader") are not, as I am reading the passage, a slip or a strategic mistake but the inevitable result of a way of speaking about reading and writing that cannot refer to certain kinds of reading and writing — where a student, for example, tries to make sense out of or do something with Adrienne Rich.

And, in fact, if you turn to the writing assignments in the Booth reader, you will see the presence of this absence in classroom practice. The Rich essay in the textbook is "The Kingdom of the Fathers" (from *Of Woman Born*), a selection that asks students to think about the situation of women by thinking about patriarchal structures of oppression. The writing assignment that follows the selection asks students to describe a member of the opposite sex, "the kind of person you would consider marrying" and "the kind of relationship that you think would form a satisfying and stable union." Students are told to organize their essays according to three levels of expectations:

> first, the features (or traits) of character and behavior you think are essential in a mate; second, the features that you think are highly desirable but which might be negotiable; and, third, the features you would like to find in a partner, but which, like ice cream on your cake, are dispensable.
>
> Take care as you go to correct any mistaken notions you think members of the opposite sex hold about the needs and expectations of your sex. The point of your essay is to lay out the basis of a healthy relationship. (450)

One of the methods Richards developed for writers was a series of "specialized quotation marks" to indicate how a word should be taken. One of these was a superscript exclamation point, to indicate "Good Heavens! What a way to talk!" Such marks seem entirely appropriate to Booth's use of "opposite sex" or "healthy" or "marriage" as innocent or unproblematic terms for a discussion of Rich's essay.

Booth's writing assignment makes Rich's essay, and the reading of it, disappear; in a sense, it says put away (as in erase) what you have, now that you have read this essay, and write as though there were nothing inappropriate in using Rich as an occasion to talk about marriage and choice in your usual way of speaking (where it is simply a matter of taste or desire: "I've always loved a great pair of legs"), or in speaking about choosing a mate as necessarily a matter of choosing from the opposite sex, or in assuming that the issue is simply one of "mistaken notions" about sex roles (as though we just don't speak clearly when we talk to each other on the street), or in implying that this conflict between men and women (the unhealthiness in our relations) could be resolved if students would just "take care" in a weekly essay.

II

The point of the preceding exercise was to highlight a way of speaking and to characterize the scene it creates, where students (writers/readers) are situated in a necessary relationship to books and teachers, reading and writing (as activities), and to the values of a culture and an institution. Whatever the instruments of education (great books, pre-reading exercises, question-asking procedures), those instruments are used, particularly by novices, only as they can be imagined to be used. You give a student a book, particularly one that she has reason to believe she *cannot* read, and she will imagine a way of beginning with that book according to the available terms to define reading — terms, that is, that define what a person might do with such a book.

This, anyway, is the guiding assumption of both Richards' and Adler's pedagogies. Both assume that they are addressing an audience who knows how to read — an audience, that is, who knows how to read sentences, who feels confident with common material, like the newspaper. Both assume that these readers have a problem reading, and that the first step in addressing that problem is to re-imagine what reading is and what a reader does — for both, the first step is to "read" or "re-read" reading. One sign of this is that Adler writes 116 pages of introduction, playing at length with the implications of a statement like "reading is learning," before he gets down to the "rules" for how to read a book. And, although Richards subtitles his book, "A Course in Efficient Reading," those looking for a self-help manual may well complain that he never gets around to talking about how to read a page at all.

For Adler, the "problem" of reading resides in certain kinds of books, books that are "great" and (the equation goes) hard and, therefore, resist the "average" reader. And, he says, the problem resides in the average reader's ignorance of (or misapplication of) techniques for handling a book as a medium of presentation. In the second case at least, problems of understanding are procedural. Adler tells the story of students who could not, at Mr. Hutchins' request, summarize the argument of Lucretius' *The Nature of Things*:

> I repeat, we did not have to teach them logic or explain in detail what the argument was. . . . But they could not find arguments in a book because they had not yet learned to read *actively*, to disengage the important sentences from all the rest, and to observe the connections the author made. Reading Lucretius as they read the newspaper, they naturally did not make such discriminations. (222)

When Adler begins to offer lessons in how to read, he offers procedures for "finding arguments in books," and they include disengaging key terms and sentences and charting the connections between them (characteristically referred to in Adler's pedagogy as the connections "an author made").

Adler has a three-part system (which I will not summarize) for dealing with the difficulties of a long and complex text and for countering the unproductive habits of "novice" readers. Here are some of the guidelines: you need to preview a book before you read it, begin with a sense of the subject area and the problems the writer wants to solve; you need to make connections between what you are reading and other books you have read, other courses you have taken or with your own experience; you need to look for the key terms in a discussion and distinguish between an author's use of them and common usage; readers should withhold judgment, ask questions while they are reading and not later, and put complex passages in their own words; readers should learn to write in the margins and develop the ability to talk back to a writer.

I have spent a good bit of time in my career reviewing the kind of research on reading that is conducted by reading "specialists," and I have read much on reading instruction. I can't recall a book that offers more good advice on how to handle a long and complex text than Adler's, and I would say that fifty years of reading research has offered no improvement on the suggestions he makes to adult readers. Adler certainly has more good advice to offer than

Richards, who actually offers little that could be called advice at all. In all of this, however, Adler is not talking about reading, as reading involves interpretation or decisions about meaning. He is talking, rather, about how to handle or manage a book — how to work with this strange form of verbal communication. The problems generally come down to problems in "finding" things in a book or managing the complicated flow of information. The meaning is taken to be fixed, something inside the book if one only has the proper techniques for getting to it or getting it out.

Books, then, represent an unusual system for communication whose buried logic and strategies need to be unearthed for students. Once they know how the system works, the argument goes, they'll know how to move around in it.

This is one problem of reading. The other is represented by the gap between a "great" book and an "average" reader. And this problem is represented in familiar terms of precedence and authority:

> The writer must be superior to the reader, and his book must convey in readable form the insights he possesses and his potential readers lack. . . . The reader must be able to overcome this inequality in some degree, seldom perhaps fully, but always approaching equality with the writer. To the extent that equality is approached, the communication is perfectly consummated.
>
> In short, we can learn only from our betters. We must know who they are and how to learn from them. The man who has this sort of knowledge possesses the art of reading in the sense with which I am especially concerned. (32)

And, as one might suspect in Chicago, the triumph of this knowledge (which is both a knowledge of what one might do and where one stands) is "democracy" (also called "freedom," "the good life," and "happiness").[1] The fruit of this knowledge is "the good life," and the good life is defined as a place of constant intelligent conversation, which comes to mean, as Adler extends the scene, the occupation of a space totally free from the language of daily life (or, perhaps more practically, the periodic withdrawal to a place free from the language of daily life):

> Reading . . . is a basic tool. Those who can use it to learn from books, as well as be amused by them, have access to stores of knowledge. They can furnish their minds so that the prospect of hours spent alone is less bleak. Nor, in the hours they spend with others, need they fear that hollow sound of empty conversation. (vii)

It is also a place of peaceful conversation, free from competing voices or naysayers.

The crude representation of Adler's argument goes something like this: if you have the right technique, you can get what an author said ("Your success in reading is determined by the extent to which you get all that the writer intended to communicate" [26]), and if you get what an author says, you can have a conversation with him. (Readers, Adler says, can ask questions and "talk back.") The goal of reading is the achievement of a community bound together by a shared language — which means a common set of key terms and examples, a common background, a common set of values, and so on. (Or, perhaps more properly, the goal of instruction is to define a use of language to celebrate the values of such a commonality.) I see no reason to dwell on the dark secrets of this community (the identity and status of those who would be excluded — those, in the rubric, who lack "normal" intelligence), except to point out how Adler's argument provides a gloss to more recent, similar arguments about literacy and community.

This democracy must be a place where disagreements are impossible — "real" disagreements, that is, between "reasonable" men, since reasonable men agree that an "argument is both empty and vicious unless it is undertaken on the supposition that there is attainable truth which, when attained by reason in the light of all the relevant evidence, resolves the original issues" (248). It is a world, then, in which there is no interpretation, and differences are signs only of error, ignorance, or viciousness. "Yet to the extent that men are rational, these obstacles to their understanding one another can be overcome. The sort of disagreement which is only apparent, resulting from misunderstanding, is certainly curable" (247).

If this democracy comes to sound like an idealized college seminar, perhaps it is because that was its founding vision. The Great Books program began with John Erskine's memories of Columbia where "good conversation had flourished and, more than that, there had been friendships with respect to ideas as well as on the playing field or in the fraternities" (356–57). In such a community, Erskine said, "democracy would be safe."

For Adler, similarly, the power of reading is that books "form a community of friends who share a common world of ideas." If all of this sounds a bit like fraternity rush, the echo apparently was not completely lost to Adler, who confronts, at least momentarily, the exclusionary agenda of this vision:

> Good conversation requires all those who engage in it to speak within the same frame of reference. Communication not only results in something common; it usually needs a common background to begin with. (356)

This is one way of explaining why it is impossible, in Chicago, to ask students to read, that is, enter into serious conversation with, Adrienne Rich. There is no way of establishing common ground:

> What I am saying may sound as if it had drastic implications. Not only do I want you to learn to read, but now I am asking you to change your friends! I fear there is some truth in that. Either you yourself will not change very much, or you must change your friends. I am only saying what everyone knows. . . . (356)

Change your friends (that is, remake them) or change your friends (that is, leave them); there is no possibility for community on other grounds: such terms define the either/or of a community bound together by this version of cultural literacy.

III

There is little to summarize or paraphrase in Richards' *How to Read a Page*, since the book provides more demonstration than exposition. It offers demonstrations of how one (but most often I.A. Richards) might read a page from Aristotle's *Posterior Analytics*, Collingwood's *Metaphysics*, Whitehead's *Modes of Thought*, Locke's *Of Human Understanding*, and Plato's *Republic*, and demonstrations of how one might "read" (that is, imagine the possible uses of) certain key words ("the words we should study most if through them we are to understand the others"): make, get, give, love, hate, seem, be, do, see, mind, thought, idea, knowledge, reason, purpose, and work.

The purpose of Richards' demonstrations is to reflect on the process by which words come to be meaningful. If Adler is concerned with how books work (or how people might work on books), Richards is concerned with language, with how words work (or how people might work with words). Most chapters, then, establish a counterpoint between text and paraphrase, where Richards takes a line from his source (Aristotle, for example) and considers not only ways of reading the line but also the consequences of choosing one reading over another. (He is demonstrating, then, both the making of meaning and the audit of meaning.) For Richards, reading is not a conversation with great teachers from the past (Adler's metaphor) but that "internal drama in which what a word is to mean in a place is decided" (237). Words, phrases, sentences, pages — these things can be read in many ways

> because they touch us at points at which each one of us is himself many-minded. Understanding them is very much more than picking a possible reasonable interpretation, clarifying that, and sticking to it. Understanding them is seeing how the varied possible meanings hang together, which of them depend upon what else, how and why the meanings which matter most to us form a part of our worlds — seeing thereby more clearly what our world is and what we are who are building it to live in. (13)

Richards enacts the drama of reading for us, but the sources and passages he chooses also provide the occasion for reflection on what he calls the "archproblem" in the study of reading: "What should guide the reader's mind?" (240). If reading is a matter of choice and negotiation, who decides when decisions are forced? If reading is an internal drama, which of our many minds should take precedence when we must strike a line and move on, when we must do something *other* than spin out one possible reading after another? This thing that enables us to decide is variously called "will," "desire," "logic," "thought," "reason," and "power."

Richards is not naive about the violence of interpretation or the struggle for power and precedence in interpretive communities.[2] He begins with what he takes to be the most common, but most "dangerous" and "baffling" answer to the question of what should guide us — the belief that usage fixes meaning, the notion that "a word when rightly used carries only one meaning (or exceptionally two or three), and that reading is essentially collecting these right meanings and a sort of adding them together" (235–36). (The clumsy prose is Richards'; the attitude, while not attributed to Adler, could be.) Richards' answer to his question is that the reader should be guided not by words alone but by the relations between words, not by single meanings but multiple meanings, not by sticking to one reading but by examining one's motives in choosing one interpretation over another, or as he puts it, "Our awareness of interdependence, of how things hang together, which makes us able to give and audit an account of what may be meant in a discussion — that highest activity of REASON which Plato named 'Dialectic'" (240).

As Richards acknowledges, this appeal to dialectic does not really answer his question, "What should guide the reader's mind?" It is, rather, only the substitution of a borrowed (and favored) term, "dialectic," for other, less favored terms: "logic," "thought," "desire," "will," "reason," or "power." If one reading may not be said to be more "reasonable" or "logical" than another, and if the resolution of disputes (rival interpretations) is not to be a matter only of will and power, what is the alternative of "dialectic," particularly as Richards names it?

For Adler, the answer to the question, "What should guide a reader's mind?" is always "the text." The text should guide. To read means to overcome the problems of presentation in books and to get it right, to get what the author said. It is true, you and I may differ over what a book says. "After all, a book is something different to each reader." For Adler, however, this does *not* mean that "anything goes":

> Though readers be different, the book is the same, and there can be an objective check upon the accuracy and fidelity of the statements anyone makes about it. (171)

Richards is also unwilling to say "anything goes." For one thing, there are errors and misreadings that can be corrected through instruction and application. Readers can learn how to pay attention to a text and how to pay attention to the ways they pay attention. With what Richards calls a "method" for attending to words, a reader's reading becomes less automatic, less routine. Readers can learn to put aside their desire to make a text too stable ("the easiest way to control a meaning is to pin it"). But there is a point at which Richards becomes impatient with the implications of his own performance as a reader — that is, the implication that a text is open for endless, brilliant readings. A reader's skill, in other words, can also become his problem. The potential for every word to mean many things can make it impossible to get past the first sentence or to say anything at all.

> There are no simple acts anywhere in our lives. But we do well to forget this except when forgetting makes us unjust, dogmatic, or unimaginative toward our own or others' meanings. (183)

At the level of practice, this is Richards' dilemma. It also points to the problem of maintaining a community of readers who might share their knowledge. We need to make things simple unless doing so makes us unjust, unimaginative, or dogmatic, but doing so will always make us unjust, unimaginative, and dogmatic. How then can one choose and still "balance enough possibles"? The answer, again, is "dialectic": "The art of remembering [that there are no simple acts] . . . is that supreme art of knowing, Dialectic." Dialectic, then, is both a way of handling texts and a way of handling one's relations to others, a way of being present without erasing the presence of others.

Dialectic is a term Richards can use but not command. Behind it lies the unresolvable point and counterpoint of his project — the swing between freedom and restraint, between open and closed systems, between the balance of possibles and the necessity of choice. These remain opposites he cannot combine into a new term, and (perhaps as a consequence) they are the root of his playfulness — as when, for example, he announces a list of 100 key words and produces 103; or when he creates a set of specialized quotation marks (a wonderful conceit), but then *uses* them to fix his words and clutter the page, until the text becomes almost unreadable. He resists order and requires it. He is both radical educator and fussy schoolmaster. He wants to celebrate ambiguity but not be misunderstood.

At the end of *How to Read a Page*, at the very point at which he questions the possibility of dialectic (since there is forever warfare within "the sphere of intellectual desire"), he expresses both a fond and a desperate wish:

> Can we not — as a parallel to the possibilities of World Communication which Basic English holds out — make an attempt in education which would measure up to our need? Can we not contrive that the fundamental *ideas* through which alone we can understand one another are studied in place of so much else which today leads us apart and into opposition? We might at least make the three or four books which best embody these ideas available in the most readable form. But this study must be by Dialectic not debate. Word-warfare on such great themes in this bomber-shrunk world is but incipient battle, prelude to oppression or surrender, and we have, most of all, to reconceive discussion itself. (241)

Richards is trying to imagine a world culture centered on three or four books written in Basic English (that is, the English language reduced to 850 words). Of course Richards is serious. But at the same time, his own extended argument has shown how such a proposal is crazy. These three or four books, he has taught us to say, cannot really be books at all. One would have to call them something else, perhaps "Great Books" — that is, books with important ideas that everyone can read and discuss without misunderstanding. This is the intellectually serious alternative to Adler's vision of a community of common readers sitting in a lovely room looking out onto a lovely quad and talking about great books. Richards is trying to imagine a world community bound together by a common culture, but it remains a naive Utopia given all that he has said about the nature of understanding and misunderstanding.

Richards desires a world guided by his own key words and ideas; the counterpoint to this is his claim that, most of all, we must "reconceive discussion itself" and replace debate with dialectic. This is the expansive Richards.

Adler, you will recall, could tell us only to change friends if the discussion got tough or unseemly or out of hand. Richards would have us change the scene and the relations between the actors. This new way of speaking, if it can be achieved, is what he would like to call "dialectic." This is his hope for the future. And this, it seems to me, is where teachers are right now: wondering still, while faced with violence in the classroom and out, whether we need to change our friends or reimagine what it means to talk together about books.[3]

NOTES

1. Chicagoans, like members of any community, put restrictions on key terms — in this case terms like "freedom" or "democracy." "Docile," for example, must be synonymous with "active" in Chicago: "A person is wrongly thought to be docile if he is passive and pliable. On the contrary, docility is the extremely active virtue of being teachable. No one is really teachable who does not freely exercise his power of independent judgment. The most docile reader is, therefore, the most critical" (238–39).

2. I don't agree with Geoffrey Hartman, in other words, that Richards was compelled to evade a "meditation on authority" (Brower, Vendler, and Hollander 162). The second half of *How to Read a Page* could be read as just such a meditation.

3. I am grateful to Matt Cooper and Christine Ross for their help as research assistants on this project.

WORKS CITED

Adler, Mortimer J. *How to Read a Book: The Art of Getting a Liberal Education.* New York: Simon and Schuster, 1940.

Berthoff, Ann E. *The Making of Meaning.* Portsmouth, NH: Boynton/Cook, 1981.

Booth, Wayne C. and Marshall W. Gregory. *The Harper and Row Reader.* New York: Harper & Row, 1984.

Brower, Reuben, Helen Vendler, and John Hollander, eds. *I. A. Richards: Essays in His Honor.* New York: Oxford UP, 1973.

Richards, I. A. *How to Read a Page.* New York: W. W. Norton, 1942.

Producing Adult Readers: 1930–50

T he selection of the right material for the right reader, then, is
a problem of no small consequence. Recreation for leisure hours,
intellectual progress, even literacy itself, depends in a large measure on how well the problem is solved by the reader himself or by
someone from whom he seeks advice and counsel.

> — WILLIAM S. GRAY AND BERNICE E. LEARY,
> *WHAT MAKES A BOOK READABLE: WITH SPECIAL*
> *REFERENCE TO ADULTS OF LIMITED READING ABILITY:*
> *AN INITIAL STUDY* (1935)

I

The right material for the right reader. This essay explores the large-scale
organization of reading in the United States before, during, and after World
War II but particularly during the depression, when unemployment or
"enforced leisure" created a new and, to some, dangerous population of adults
with time on their hands — time, it was felt, that might best be spent with a
book. There were adult readers, of course, before the *adult reader* became a key
term in a diverse program of research and instruction. For my purposes in this
essay, the "adult reader" is a figure of speech, a character in the professional
literature whose name is invoked to justify a research agenda, the expense of
public funds, or the organization of a curriculum.

This adult reader is not the common reader, since the adult reader had to
be conceived of as abnormal, needing special direction or assistance. The
adult reader, however, was still a reader, able to read words or sentences, able
to make some sense out of letters on a page. I will not, then, be reviewing programs for nonreading adults. I will be looking at those programs designed for

From *The Right to Literacy*, eds. Andrea Lunsford, Helene Moglen, and James Slevin
(New York: MLA, 1990) 13–29.

adults who were said to read poorly or randomly or not enough — to be the wrong readers reading the wrong books. In the words of one document,

> These include the adults who acquired laborious, inefficient reading habits in youth, who symbolize all books and reading matter by dull textbooks of a passing era, those who are deterred by the formal aspects and the literary traditions of libraries, those 40 (or 50)? million living in regions unserved by any library, those too busy and limited in time to tolerate the academic style and verbosity of a large portion of our books on serious topics, and especially that very large group of persons who simply do not know that there is matter in print that is of interest to them. (National Commission 3)

The negative references to "literary traditions" and "academic style and verbosity," a fairly common gesture in the professional literature of the 1930s and 1940s, represent the rhetorical front of a new constituency's efforts to claim reading as its subject — to take it, that is, from the institutionally established representatives of English. The field is thus divided, with an idealized educated reader on one side (a reader who goes to the library to select literary texts) and the adult reader on the other side (a reader who does not know what to read or how to read properly).[1] Both readers are figures that enable a certain conception of reading and instruction, of books and readers. The rejection of "literary traditions" by reading specialists was a rhetorical move whose effect was to clear a space for newly conceived programs of research and instruction: the "scientific" study of reading, a pedagogy based on efficiency and utility, the application of readability measures; the development of adult education programs, readers' advisory services, the Great Books series. All, in a sense, fill a space made possible by the definition of a different class of reader.

It was possible, of course, to name this difference in terms of a reader's position in relation to the usual channels for distributing books. There were readers who either literally couldn't get hold of books (they couldn't afford them or, as in the reference above, they lived outside regions served by libraries), or they were readers who couldn't imagine themselves being served by the existing channels of distribution. These would be readers who could get their hands on books but who couldn't imagine that books "belonged" to them or that they could manage them. Or the difference could be named in terms of class. In the 1930s particularly, the Affiliated Schools for Workers (later the American Labor Education Service) defined the adult reader as a person who, in most cases because of unemployment, had not only the time to read but also the motive — for retraining, for leisure, for understanding. And the workers' education movement produced materials — that is, teaching materials, reading lists, collections of workers' autobiographies — that are strikingly different from those produced through the universities and funded research programs directed at the adult reader. (See, for example, Hourwich and Palmer; *Annotated List;* Carter.)

In general, the representation of the adult reader as a worker or as a person needing newly conceived access to books was displaced by a more powerful representation of the adult reader as a reader lower on a developmental scale — a figure more powerful, that is, for the way it commanded and organized the field. The problem of reading was thus conceived of as a problem residing primarily in books (they were too hard) and in readers (they were poorly prepared) and not in a system of production and distribution. The argument I want to make is that during this period publishers, librarians, educators, and reading specialists constructed an abstraction called the adult reader. This figure functioned as a way of organizing a way of speaking, but it was also a way of organizing the market, since the adult reader was a potential consumer of those products controlled by publishers, librarians, educators, and reading specialists; the adult reader was a consumer, that is, of both books and education.

Let me set the scene for this brief history by referring to those challenges to the figure of the adult and the adult reader that preoccupied contemporary commentators. It was, the literature says over and over again, a period when education had produced a reading public unimaginable by earlier terms and standards — unimaginable in both its size and its heterogeneity. It was a time when publishing practices, schools, and libraries could bring more books to more people than ever before — a time, that is, of what was thought to be a great opportunity for the spread of culture (the culture of books and writing) and a time of great danger, since the reading public (suddenly imagined as a mass audience) could be shaped and moved by the production of reading material under no one's direct control. The wartime concern for propaganda as a technology for the control of hearts and minds was both a reflection of and a comment on the general awareness of the mass media and the masses. And it was, it was said, a time when the scientific approach to education would erase cultural stereotypes and force a new look at students and readers. It was no longer quite so easy to imagine what the other person was thinking or reading.

For my purposes I will divide the literature into three camps. There were those, like William Gray, who played a major role in the development of the scientific study of reading and reading pedagogy; those like I. A. Richards and Mortimer Adler, who were imagining the "proper" education of the educated public (worried about college graduates and undergraduates who lacked the proper understanding of "great books"); and those like Douglas Waples, researchers affiliated with library schools, receiving funding from the American Library Association and other organizations, and concerned with the use of libraries to direct adult reading (through reading lists and readers' advisory services). Waples, like Gray, was a member of the faculty at the University of Chicago, and, like Gray, he drew on the new techniques of the social sciences for studying individual and group behavior.

I will illustrate my argument by drawing primarily from Gray and his students and from Waples and the work funded by the American Library Association. Let me note in passing, however, a parallel set of texts, texts written out of a different tradition and from different institutional sites and yet with pragmatic how-to titles and an underlying concern for social order that make them quite similar to the work of the social scientists. I am referring to books like *How to Read* (Ezra Pound, 1931), *How to Teach Reading* (F. R. Leavis,

1932), *How to Read a Book* (Mortimer Adler, 1940), and *How to Read a Page* (I. A. Richards, 1942).[2]

In some ways the Leavis-Adler axis is the least interesting to those who have been reading recent critiques of English, English as the practice of university English departments. The figure of the reader here is a familiar one. The reader is a convenient abstraction constructed in terms of absence (what the reader didn't or couldn't do), and what the reader didn't or couldn't do is just what the scholar would have easily done, what the teacher would be happy or, at least, prepared to teach. The reader was a person who did not (or could not) read like Leavis, but Leavis would be happy to show him the way. It was the classic gesture of imperialism: to define the others in terms of what they lack, something we have, and to plan a program to provide for the needs of the impoverished.

When I turned to an alternative literature on reading — librarians' reports, reports of federal commissions, research by reading specialists — I found a similar pattern, authorized not by the powerful presence of a great reader (like Leavis) who could stand single-handedly for the culture but by the powerful rhetoric of social science research, which could speak for truths that were objectively there in the traces of human choice and behavior, which could tell a story that did not seem to be written by a single person or set of interests.

The project of constructing this figure brought together opposing schools, both progressive and conservative educators. The motive to construct the adult reader, in other words, was greater than the differing motives represented by differences in educational philosophy. It would be wrong, however, to assume that the governing motive here was simply economic, narrowly conceived as a desire to sell books or course credits. The project was driven also by the desire to imagine a unified culture, which could be read generously as a desire to extend education across divisions of race and class but which could also be read symptomatically as the dominant (literate) culture's desire to reproduce itself.

To tell this story as a story, I need to identify actors and agents. These are not the actors and agents identified by the researchers I have taken as my primary sources. The key agent in my account is something I loosely call English — not narrowly conceived as the practice of professional critics and university English departments but the more general field — including librarians, educators, publishers, and public policy makers who are concerned with the organization of reading and writing in American culture. When I refer to *English*, I am referring to a way of speaking about reading, writing, language, and culture and also to something more historically specific and present, scholarly disciplines made up of practitioners and their texts, and, in the mid-1930s, a variety of institutions: the United States Office of Education, the Modern Language Association, the National Council of Teachers of English, the University of Chicago and its graduate programs, the American Library Association, the Affiliated Schools for Workers, the Progressive Education Association, the American Council on Education, local teachers' groups, academic departments, the publishing industry — all concerned to organize reading and writing. In what I take as a complex and difficult reference, *English* stands for an organized attempt to produce readers and writers. It is, among other things, an expression of the literate culture's desire to reproduce itself, to match the right books with the right readers.

II

Perhaps the best way to begin a story about the construction of the adult reader is to begin with adolescence. I do not want to suggest that the development of the "adolescent reader" led to the construction of the adult reader, but the issues in adolescent literature are more clear-cut, both as they are represented in schooling and in the wider distribution circuits of the library and the marketplace; therefore, it is not difficult to show how the construction of the adolescent reader served interests and purposes other than those of actual adolescents who needed or wanted to read.

The adolescent reader is a familiar figure; today there are book lists at libraries, publication programs in the major publishing houses, book clubs, and sections of bookstores all labeled in the name of the adolescent or young adult reader. These do not contain all the books that adolescents can or do read, nor do they contain all the books by or about adolescents. Another principle of selection is at work here. Those books that are excluded are said to be too long or too difficult; some contain "inappropriate" content; some are determined to lie outside the interests of adolescents; some authors and publishers are seeking a wider audience. All these decisions are made through reference to the adolescent reader, a figure that could be said to be a product of developmental psychology or statistical measure but one that is also the product of a more generalized desire to reproduce a predictable image of adolescence. In other words, the programs designed to produce adolescent readers do not assist a "natural" fit of reader and text. Those prescriptions for matching the adolescent with the right books propose as normal a stereotype of the adolescent; they reorganize the distribution system so that certain choices become predictable and others unlikely.[3]

The figure of the adolescent reader is partly a product of the same progressive movement that produced the current concept of adult education. This was the movement to formalize a general education, one separate from vocational education or college preparation and designed to prepare the general population for full lives. In a particularly apt phrase from a resolution offered at the close of the 1944 United States Office of Education Conference on General Education, general education was referred to as "life adjustment training":

> If the vocational schools served 20% of the population and college prep another 20%, we do not believe that the remaining 60% of our youth of secondary school age will receive the life adjustment training they need and to which they are entitled as American citizens. (Applebee 144)

To provide teenagers with the experiences that would prepare them for life, English needed to define the common field of adolescent experience. The problems unique to adolescence would be represented in a literature designed to explicate and solve these problems — books to illustrate "normal" or "mature" responses to the difficult experiences of adolescence. A Baltimore librarian described her job this way: When students came into the library, she was to prescribe books "very much as physicians prescribe sulfa drugs, . . . by prescribing as best she can, and by keeping a sharp lookout for reactions" (Applebee 147).

The creation of an adolescent literature required the creation of a typical adolescent, one version of the right reader for these books. Here is a recent account of that adolescent:

> The "image" of the American Boy that emerges is of a clean-cut, socially poised extrovert, an incurious observer of life rather than a participant, a willing conformer, more eager to get than to give, a bit of a hypocrite but a rather dull companion — a well-adjusted youth not much above a moron. And the "image" of the American Girl? She is the one who likes the American boy. (Lynch and Evans 413)

The point I want to argue is that the new terms changed not only the production and the distribution of images but the production and the distribution of books. One set of books was substituted for another. Here, for example, is a 1937 report from the Tulsa school board to Tulsa parents:

> As you read the list of seventy four book titles which follow, you will not find therein the titles of outstanding works of literature excepting "A Message to Garcia," "The Gettysburg Address," and "The Declaration of Independence."
>
> The reason for this is explained in consideration of the criterion on which they were chosen: namely, what contribution does this book make toward:
>
> 1. Building and maintaining physical and mental health;
> 2. An understanding of the fundamental principles and institutions of a democratic society;
> 3. Knowledge of the interaction between man and the natural environment;
> 4. Individual guidance and counseling?
>
> The application of this criterion brought into our list practically none of the works of literature which are in themselves great works of art; and it did bring into our list many books that reflect the common problems of health, understanding, knowledge, and guidance. They are all well written (the poorest of them from a literary point of view is probably "Work of Art" by Sinclair Lewis); and when read by young people of the secondary-school age under the competent direction and clear understanding of an intelligent teacher, they should be of great educational value in the various areas to which they are recommended. (LaBrant 210)

It is interesting to consider why these criteria should rule out the earlier material in the high school curriculum ("outstanding works of literature"), material that at several points in the history of American education were said to provide health, understanding, knowledge, guidance, and counseling. In part, this was simply the result of the application of social science measurement to the canon. Surveys had shown that the kids hated great books and that neither their teachers nor their parents read them when they didn't have to. On those grounds it made sense to require students to read books that would work, that would produce the expected social or psychological effects. Great books were an inefficient way to produce the goals of general education. It is also possible to find arguments against "outstanding works of literature" based on democratic principles (great books had little to do with the experience of the majority of those in school). The wider the circle of readers, the more difficult it became to assume that reading would be valued generally or without question. As Lou L. LaBrant put it, "What is regarded by the teacher as a normal, desirable, and even necessary activity, is in the mind of the students' parents a luxury or perhaps sheer idleness" (190). In general, the work of both the reading specialists and the librarians is based on a rejection of those values represented by literature and by reading as the reading of literature. Partly, the specialists and librarians are staking a claim to reading as a subject by conceiving of it as separate from the study of literature, particularly as practiced in colleges and universities. It is against this representation of reading, in fact, that we should read the work of Leavis and others to preserve the canon as a means for propagating taste and sensibility.

The program to produce a new class of reader, whether adolescent or adult, was accompanied by a program to produce a new class of book — the adolescent novel or, for the adult market, the "readable book," a kind of no-nonsense democratic text, without the "academic style and verbosity of a large portion of our books on serious subjects." According to the American Library Association Commission on Adult Education (1924), "The dearth of books that are at once simple, informal, interesting, adult in tone, and reliable in content greatly limit the effectiveness of the adult education services of libraries" (National Commission 1).

For young adults in school full-time, as well as for adults in school at night, the new reading programs represented a desire to reject traditional conceptions of literary value while retaining reading as a value — valued, in particular, as a way to organize, guide, and inform a heterogeneous public, not the common reader but the masses, reading. This was the program: to fill leisure time and to produce a common sensibility — not a common culture in an Arnoldian sense but a set of shared goals and understandings. In place of outstanding works of literature, the curriculum and the libraries and the publishing industry were prepared to offer useful books, books of information, guidance, and self-help organized by "level."

When the figure of the reader was reconceived, the market was reorganized according to categories of age and mental development, and books were redistributed (and in some cases newly produced) to serve specialized audiences. This is a crude formula, but the general supply of reading material, certainly not undistinguished but divided along class lines (high and low), became redivided, with the reader's stage of development introduced as a factor. Older readers, readers who no longer needed primers or packaged material, were conceived of as a special audience requiring the right books to be the right readers. English, that is, both preserved and reproduced its construction of the adolescent by creating a genre called "adolescent literature" and by removing adolescents from a more general market. And the shift for adolescents was reproduced with adults. Readers or potential readers characterized primarily by their economic situation (unemployed workers, immigrants, adults with the time or the motive to seek out additional education) were reconceived in terms that erased their economic status. For educators, researchers, and publishers — all of whom had an interest in this newly conceived consumer — these readers' distinguishing differences were defined in terms of ability level, rather than their positions as members of a class, culture, or workforce.

III

Adults are not captive consumers like adolescents; adults are not necessarily in school, and, if they are in school, it is under different terms and with different expectations. They get their books from bookstores, friends, and libraries. And, significantly, much of the early research on reading was sponsored by library associations and library schools. Researchers argued that with the new methods of the social sciences, they would find and describe the real "adult reader," by survey, by case study, by interview, by tracking down all those readers who checked out a preselected sample of books in a given year. The search was on to find out what adults wanted to read and what they could read — to find the right books and the right readers.

The general assumption was that the increased number of readers and the increasing availability of books had made it increasingly difficult to imagine the reader as the relatively stable figure he once was.

> To prepare for all types of students — those from the prairies, towns, and industrial cities; from wealthy suburban homes, slums, and tenant farms; from religious and irreligious homes; from Catholic, Protestant, and Jewish environments; from black, white and yellow races; from families supporting and opposing trade unions; from provincial and sophisticated groups — and to attempt to inculcate in all an appreciation of literature, requires an almost infinitely wide and flexible program. (LaBrant 190)

To prepare for and to inculcate all types of students requires an almost infinitely wide and flexible program. The remainder of this essay considers how this program — infinitely wide and flexible — is translated, at least through adult education, into a program of the right books for the right readers. These terms mark the culture's desire and anxiety to both contain and control the various readers of a diverse society.

One response to the rigidity of prior programs was the creation of what, characteristically, was called "free reading." If the reading conventionally assigned to readers was neither free nor flexible and if, as studies had shown, neither students nor their teachers would read outside of class the sorts of books the curriculum assumed they should read, then perhaps the answer was to add on a reading program that was open — one in which students could read what they wanted to read. This, after all, is one way of reproducing the circumstances of adult reading. Readers, it was argued, read what they want to read. That, then, is what they should do in a program of instruction.

There is, of course, no such thing as free reading — not only because books are commodities and controlled by a variety of market forces but also because readers do not have clear, single motives. What was perhaps most surprising to the researchers who studied these new readers was the recognition that free reading did not produce the expected results: readers didn't know what they wanted to read, or they didn't want to read anything, or they chose books that scandalized those who oversaw their reading. The researchers learned that free choice and an open field did not produce the desired results — that is, the right people reading the right books. Here is Douglas Waples, one of the leading reading researchers of the 1930s and 1940s, working through the problematics of a reader's will:

> Most of us actually read what lies within easiest reach, what demands the least mental effort, and what concerns our special interests. Our reading is thus determined by accessibility, readability, and subject interests — in this order. Accessibility best explains why we seldom read on subjects we are most curious about. Mass reading is much more accessible. The records show that we seldom do read what we really like, except when, by some miracle, our favorite subjects are discussed in a congenial style in some publication we hold in our hands. . . .
>
> *Why* people read what they read, we will never know exactly. About all we can say is that whenever anybody reads anything at all, certain incentives have triumphed over various inhibitions. Whenever we decide not to read and so decide to do something else, our inhibitions have prevailed. . . . On a desert island, we would read the phone book if we happened to have one. . . . But since a wide variety of reading matter is easily accessible to most of us, it is readability that largely explains our selections. (Anderson 217–18)

What is most interesting here is how the question of accessibility, the first in importance, is translated into a question of readability; the key question becomes not how books are produced and distributed but how they are written.

In the face of what seemed to be random or uncontrolled reading, English set to work to organize a field that seemed to defy organization — by creating book lists, by surveying readers to see what they wanted (and needed), by standardizing response (or "comprehension"), by shaping adult taste (prohibiting or discouraging the reading of "cheap" novels, to use one of Waples's phrases), and by trying to stimulate the production of a new type of book, the readable book.[4] This, in some ways, tells the story of the development of the figure of the adult reader — from a person with limited access to books to a person with a limited ability to process text. And the story of adult education became the story of reading drills and comprehension exercises (to ensure that all readers agree), reading tests (to sort out levels of readers), readability formulas (to create levels of texts), and a newly created genre of readable writing. (The *Reader's Digest* is perhaps the most lasting example of this.)

One of the achievements of reading researchers in the 1940s was the development of formulas to measure readability, the most notable of which was developed by William Gray at the University of Chicago. Gray's formula is significantly different in its intent from Rudolf Flesch's better known formula for "plain" English. Flesch's index is part of an argument for a universally efficient language — clear prose for all people. Gray's formula was, initially, a diagnostic tool for teachers and librarians and, secondarily, a guide for would-be writers of adult books. He is not idealizing clear prose but arguing for a specific kind of simplified prose for the adult reader of limited ability. A librarian would use the formula (based on the number of clauses, the number of words in a clause, and so on) to guide readers toward a graded series of readers. Similarly, writers and publishers could use the formula to develop graded materials for adult readers. Here, for example, is an expression of the expectations created by Gray's work:

> The need for readable books is not yet met but is at least recognized. Publishers and educators are now convinced and experimentation in the production of the needed simple books on topic of current interest, addressed to adult minds, is under way in the "Readability Laboratory" recently established at Teachers College, Columbia University, under the direction of Professor Lyman Bryson, a member of the American Library Association Board on the Library and Adult Education. (National Commission 2)

As a device for organizing research and curriculum and as a device for thinking about the problems of reading, the concept of the readable book takes the available supply of books — books that are being read by adults, including those who are working class or with limited formal education or limited English — and defines many of them as "unreadable," inappropriate. This shift is the most surprising and has had the most lasting and negative effect on adult education, where readers are often directed away from the books that other adults read. There are enough examples of readers of all ages and classes taking inspiration from books that are difficult, books they cannot completely understand, to suggest that a move to easy or efficient books is neither inevitable nor necessarily preferable in assisting adult readers (or any reader, for that matter).

The abstraction, "adult reader," came to represent those who did not or could not read what they were supposed to read. There remained something monstrous (or mysterious) about these subjectivities that were not the recognizable products of the "standard" culture. In the 1930s and 1940s, largely through the influence of Gray and Waples, the survey became the standard instrument to probe these mysteries. As was the case with the construction of the typical adolescent, the process organized adult types according to fixed stereotypes of race, class, and gender. Here, for example, is a 1936 report:

> Whereas the women's list is dotted with such "cream-puff" items as *The Magnificent Obsession, Forgive Us Our Trespasses,* and *Imitation of Life,* the men's list impresses by its general virility. The women select heavily from fiction; the men compose their reading diet with more substantial stuff. Even the fiction they read is of a decidedly more vigorous sort. (Anderson 228)

To determine subject interests among prospective adult readers, Douglas Waples asked people to rate their interest in a variety of subjects, like public morality, and he surveyed the following groups: prisoners, post office employees, machinists, farmers, medical students, and high school teachers. He found that interest in public morals ranged from the prisoners (with the highest interest rate) to Vermont farmers (with the lowest). Waples concluded, "The prisoners' interest is self-explanatory. [!] The farmers' indifference suggests aloofness from urban frivolity" (Waples and Tyler 27). In *Who Reads What?* (1935), Charles H. Compton reports on a survey of seven hundred recent readers of Thomas Hardy, their names taken from the circulation records at the St. Louis Public Library. The list includes 96 salesmen and saleswomen.

> They are mostly department store clerks and Piggly Wiggly or neighborhood grocery clerks. The women generally call themselves sales ladies. There are a number of traveling salesmen and others who hit the front doors in disposing of their wares. It is incredible that these salesfolks who sell us sox and ties and BVD's, bread and butter, sugar and tea, can really understand Hardy — at least not in the way our wives do, who write papers on him for women's club programs. It must be a mere coincidence that those of Hardy's works which critics generally consider his greatest are also the most popular with these salespeople. (36)

Across the literature, one finds researchers fitting readers into prior types or predictable categories.

This process is seen perhaps most dramatically in the case studies of the period, in which individual cases are read in terms of English's powerful agenda. Here, for example, are excerpts from a case study reported by Ruth Strang, one of Gray's students. It is the case study of a "Negro" busboy living in Chicago, called by his initials, N. T., whose age is between forty-one and fifty and whose last grade of public education was grade 9:

> Reading is one of his three leisure time activities, the other two being attending the movies and playing an instrument. To these he devoted, on the average, fourteen hours a week. When interviewed he was reading *Mein Kampf,* which he had bought. During the last month he had read Wells's *Outline of History,* Coon's *Measuring Ethiopia,* and Voltaire's *Candide.* (51)

The researcher administered a test, written responses to set passages. The responses, she said, showed N. T.'s tendency to "include his own personal opinion and additional ideas which he attributes to the author but which were not included in the article." She says, "He makes no attempt to separate his summary of what the author said from his own comments." Her conclusion was that N. T. "need[s] help in getting a more adequate idea of what he reads and especially in selecting reading material which is within his range of ability to comprehend. For what does it profit N. T. to read if he gains from his reading only erroneous ideas?" (53).

This investigation into the practice of a reader became a measure of whether, to English, he was a reader or not. As a consequence, N. T. — who read Wells, Hitler, Coon, and Voltaire, all in a three-month period — is defined as a nonreader, someone who can best be served by the introduction of books he would find more "readable." He was the wrong reader reading the wrong books.

The measure of his failure as a reader, at least beyond the numerical measure of the comprehension test (or, perhaps, the researcher's inability to see an order in his reading — after all, what conventional program would bring together *Mein Kampf, Measuring Ethiopia, Candide,* and Wells's *Outline of History?*) was the degree to which N. T. failed to separate his beliefs from an author's. He did not, or could not, call attention to the difference between what he knew and what a book said. He identified with what he read; he let an author speak for him, saw himself as an equal partner in the conversation, or took as his own that which was said by another. What might be identified as the source of N. T.'s pleasure as a reader is, for English, a source of anxiety. He failed to achieve the kind of distance from the text that is, under various names, still one of the goals of literacy education, in which students are asked to talk about an author's devices or to read "critically," to resist becoming taken by or lost in what they read.

One can detect a similar anxiety in many of the examples Waples, Berelson, and Bradshaw offer in *What Reading Does to People: A Summary of Evidence on the Social Effects of Reading and a Statement of Problems for Research* (1940). For example:

> A still more satisfactory account, for our purposes, of what the *New Masses* does to its readers might be given in terms of the motives responsible for the reading — motives which the reading generally satisfies. It is safe to suggest that readers of the *New Masses* are most numerous among the "deprived" groups. They generally lack the security which larger incomes would provide. They lack the prestige enjoyed by other classes with higher social status, more respectable occupations, wider social contacts, and a generally larger share of the things that everyone wants. Hence, to say that an effect of reading the *New Masses* is an increase in the readers' sense of security and prestige through their identifications with the social platform of the Communist party is more explanatory than to say that they read the *New Masses* because they are communists or that the reading increases their loyalty to the Communist party. (20)

The concern expressed here is a concern for uncontrolled reading, heightened by the newly realized sense of the power of mass media, including print, to move a large and relatively unknown readership. Waples, Berelson, and Bradshaw, who believe they are opening up the possibilities for the study of the "social effects" of reading, are blunt about the social and political backdrop to their research. The opening pages of their book refer to necessary changes in social policy in a time of crisis, to "the international events of 1940" and the "domestic social experiments of the New Deal":

> Whether such changes occur with or without the violence and distress of international or civil wars depends in large part upon how the several agencies of mass communication — print, radio, and cinema combined — are used to clarify and to interrelate the interests of contending factions. Mass communications can be used to show where common interests lie, to encourage rational and deliberate changes; or they may be used by each faction to antagonize rival factions and to precipitate violence. (1)

And, they conclude, "Conditions beyond our control define the problems of adjustment to social forces which can be met by intelligent changes in the conditions within our control" (2).

IV

The selection of the right material for the right reader. These terms have served as the key terms in my account of reading research and instruction in the twenty-year period, 1930–50. Their force can be felt in current practice. Let me turn to a brief example, one that came to me through the Modern Language Association Literacy Conference in September 1988.

A handsome series of materials for adult new readers, called Writers' Voices, was recently developed by the Literacy Volunteers of New York City with an impressive advisory committee and funding and assistance from a long list of companies and foundations. In a sense, the series represents the cooperative efforts of concerned persons from business, education, and the community — the best we have to offer. Let me turn to one book in the series, an anthology containing selections from two books by Maya Angelou, *I Know Why the Caged Bird Sings* and *The Heart of a Woman* (Literacy Volunteers).

There are fifty-five pages of text in this book; only twenty-one of them contain selections from Angelou's two books. The rest of the pages are preface, preparation, questions, and apparatus. The first seventeen pages are made up of the following sections: "About *Writers' Voices*," "Note to the Reader," "About Maya Angelou," "Maya Angelou's Family Tree," "About Joe Louis," and "About the Selection from *I Know Why the Caged Bird Sings*." A reader is given seventeen pages of preparation for seven pages of *Caged Bird*.

The headnote for each of the books in Writers' Voices is a statement by a literacy student, Mamie Moore, from Brooklyn: "I want to read what others do — what I see people reading in libraries, on the subway, and at home." One could argue that Writers' Voices is one example of how the culture prevents Mamie Moore from doing what other readers do. She is not, after all, reading the paperback copy of *Caged Bird,* something people read in libraries, on the subway, and at home; she is reading a substitute version, one that is significantly different from the original and, in a sense, harder to read, since its opening seventeen pages argue that the reader cannot read the book, that the reader is not prepared.

If one steps outside the standard texts of reading pedagogy and adult education, outside their conception of the right book and the right reader, it is possible to see Writers' Voices as a carefully organized attempt to keep *I Know Why the Caged Bird Sings* out of the hands of new readers by giving them an alternative text and by making Angelou's words seem difficult, unapproachable (or unapproachable without the assistance of a specialist and special preparation). As an example of practice, Writers' Voices effectively reproduces the very problems it is designed to address and, in doing so, maintains the tradition I've charted in the 1930s and 1940s. This is not the result of bad faith or crass commercialism. Literacy workers are, after all, often volunteers.[5] It is, rather, the product of a way of thinking and speaking about reading, books, and the adult reader that deserves critical reappraisal. The habits of past practice are limiting the options available to literacy volunteers today.

The purpose of this brief history is to provide a context for current practice, a way of seeing certain terms and assumptions as situated in particular historical moments or specific academic projects. It is possible, I have argued, to see the problems of adult reading as problems of access, and it is possible to see the dominant programs for adult readers as limiting access to books, by taking readers out of the open market and by presenting reading as something to be done only through a program of assistance. To do this, however, we have to read against the figure of the adult reader as it is part of the legacy of adult education. When we read the tradition this way, it suggests that we (*we* as representatives of English) should be cautious of certain instincts, certain predictable gestures or conclusions, certain unconscious practices, like the practice of determining for others the right books — good books, readable books. We need to resist what seems to be an inevitable move — to define the sensibilities of others in terms of their differences from our own, to imagine that teaching inevitably involves giving others what we have and they lack — our books, our habits, our version of critical consciousness. Perhaps the money and the energy spent guiding readers might be better spent changing the ways we, as a society, produce and distribute texts, the material goods of a literate culture.[6]

NOTES

1. Here, as an additional example, is Douglas Waples and his colleagues. Waples was Professor of Research in Reading at the University of Chicago Graduate Library School and one of the original figures in the "scientific" study of reading:

> Certain values have been imputed to reading by the scholars and writers who have made their reputations by reading and criticizing the writings of others. It is not remarkable that those for whom reading is thus a vested interest should declare that reading is a good thing, that readers are wiser people than nonreaders, that those who read and approve what the contemporary critics approve are persons of superior taste, nor that those who read the more

abstruse and more scholarly works are persons of superior wisdom. (*What Reading Does to People* 23).

2. To this list I would add the volumes by Thompson and Rosenblatt. There is almost no reference back and forth between the Adler-Leavis list and the Gray or Waples groups. At best, there are a few references to Adler, whose book was on the best-seller list for more than a year.

3. I recently felt the force of this economy in my own family. When we set out on summer vacation, we brought books — some for ourselves and some for our children, including my adolescent son. For my son, we took books from the adolescent list at the library (a list also provided by his school): *Lord of the Flies, The Call of the Wild*. He said he wanted to read war books and, through my selection, took *Battle Cry* and *For Whom the Bell Tolls*. My wife and I took what we were calling three Pittsburgh novels: *The Car Thief, Second Brother*, and *An American Childhood*. These are all either set in our town or have an author who lives in Pittsburgh. The adult books could also be said to have been adolescent literature, however, since all have an adolescent as the central character, although with a presentation of crime or sexuality that could be deemed inappropriate for adolescents. My son read all the books except *The Call of the Wild, For Whom the Bell Tolls*, and *An American Childhood*.

4. It is interesting to consider how a positive term in a discussion of the distribution of books may become a term of moral disapprobation. One could argue that a wide range of cheap books widely distributed and skillfully presented is an appropriate and powerful way to deal with the problem of adult reading. The translation of the book as a commodity into the book as a cultural force (cheap books to "cheap" books) is one strategy in the construction of the adult reader.

5. The Literacy Volunteers of New York, however, is also in the business of selling books. Each volume in the Writers' Voices series is priced at $2.95, making one of their books only a dollar less than an inexpensive paperback. If you pay the additional $2.00 required to order a copy, it is more. My point is that Writers' Voices is competing for the book buyer's money and attention.

6. This project would not have been possible without the advice, consultation, and assistance of Chris Ross, who spent hours in the library reviewing material.

WORKS CITED

Adler, Mortimer Jerome. *How to Read a Book*. New York: Simon, 1940.

Anderson, Harold A. "Reading Interests and Tastes." *Reading in General Education: An Exploratory Study*. Ed. William S. Gray. Washington: American Council on Education, 1940. 217–70.

Annotated List of Materials for Workers' Classes. New York: Affiliated Schools for Workers, 1934.

Applebee, Arthur N. *Tradition and Reform in the Teaching of English*. Urbana: NCTE, 1974.

Carter, Jean. *Mastering the Tools of the Trade: Suggestive Material for Experimental Use in the Teaching of English in Workers' Classes*. New York: Affiliated Schools for Workers, 1932.

Compton, Charles H. *Who Reads What? Essays on the Readers of Mark Twain, Hardy, Sandburg, Shaw, William James, the Greek Classics*. New York: Wilson, 1935.

Flesch, Rudolf. *The Art of Readable Writing*. New York: Harper, 1949.

Gray, William S., and Bernice E. Leary. *What Makes a Book Readable: With Special Reference to Adults of Limited Reading Ability: An Initial Study*. Chicago: U of Chicago P, 1935.

Hourwich, Andria Taylor, and Gladys L. Palmer. *I Am a Woman Worker*. New York: Arno, 1974.

LaBrant, Lou L. "American Culture and the Teaching of Literature." *Reading in General Education: An Exploratory Study: A Report of the Committee on Reading in General Education*. Ed. William S. Gray. Washington: American Council on Education, 1940. 186–216.

Leavis, F. R. *How to Teach Reading: A Primer for Ezra Pound*. Cambridge: Minority, 1932.

Literacy Volunteers of New York City. *Selected from* I Know Why the Caged Bird Sings *and* The Heart of a Woman. By Maya Angelou. Writers' Voices. New York: Literacy Volunteers of New York City, 1989.

Lynch, James Jeremiah, and Bertrand Evans. *High School English Textbooks*. Boston: Little, Brown. 1963.

National Commission on the Enrichment of Adult Life, National Education Association. "Committee Report on Adult Education in the Library," No. 33. Washington: 1936.

Pound, Ezra L. *How to Read*. London: D. Harmsworth, 1931.

Richards, I. A. *How to Read a Page: A Course in Efficient Reading with an Introduction to a Hundred Great Words*. New York: Norton, 1942.

Rosenblatt, Louise. *Literature as Exploration*. For the Commission of Human Relations of the Progressive Education Association. New York: Appleton, 1938.

Strang, Ruth. *Explorations in Reading Patterns.* Chicago: U of Chicago P, 1942.

Thompson, Denys. *Reading and Discrimination.* London: Chatto, 1934.

Waples, Douglas, Bernard Berelson, and Franklyn R. Bradshaw. *What Reading Does to People: A Summary of Evidence on the Social Effects of Reading and a Statement of Problems for Research.* Chicago: U of Chicago P, 1940.

Waples, Douglas, and Ralph W. Tyler. *What People Want to Read About: A Study of Group Interests and a Survey of Problems in Adult Reading.* Chicago: American Library Assn. and U of Chicago P, 1931.

The Argument of Reading

I

It is almost impossible to find a recent account of English (or English as a school subject) that does not begin with a reference to the problem of the new criticism and its legacy in the American classroom. The new criticism is everywhere, we are told; its hold on practice seems firm in spite of the ways its key texts and key figures have been routed by recent developments in theory and critical practice. Here, for example, is Frank Lentricchia (in "Someone Reading") on the new criticism:

> The American New Criticism, the critical movement which made formalism famous in this country, and whose death has been periodically announced ever since the late 1950s, remains in force as the basis (what goes without saying) of undergraduate literary pedagogy, so that, having passed into the realm of common sense, the ideological effect of the New Criticism in the United States is to sustain, under conditions of mass higher education, the romantic cult of genius by dispossessing younger readers of their active participation in the shaping of a culture and a society "of and for the people" — by stripping those readers of their right to think of themselves as culturally central storytellers: an extraordinary irony for a critical method whose initial effect was entirely democratic — to make the reading of classics available to all, even to those of us whose early cultural formation did not equip us to read Shakespeare and Milton, but a predictable irony, in retrospect, when we remember that new critical formalist reading at the same time defined and valued itself as secondary reading of explication. So while the New Criticism taught us to read, it simultaneously taught us how to subordinate our reading powers and humble ourselves before the "creative" authority of superior primary writing. (323-34)

In this line of argument, the "new criticism" marked a potentially positive moment of intervention in the English curriculum, one that would redefine the

---

From *Argument Revisited, Argument Redefined: Negotiating Meaning in the Composition Classroom*, eds. Barbara Emmel, Paula Resch, and Deborah Jenny (Thousand Oaks: Sage, 1996) 199-213.

relationship between the student and the text (and, through this realignment, between the student and literary or literate culture — "the initial effect was entirely democratic" — students might have been represented as "culturally central storytellers"), but the potential of the moment was lost when the classroom exercise became not only formalistic (focusing on the features in the text rather than on the relationship established between the text and its readers) but also elitist (a celebration of the "genius" of the author and a necessary subordination of students and their writing before "primary writing"). The subject in the curriculum became someone else's reading and writing, someone bigger, better, more famous, more powerful, and this is the subject we continue to teach today, over and over, in literature and in composition.

Anyone who works in the field can think of local exceptions to this generalization, but it still has great explanatory power. Composition, in spite of its celebration of democracy, still marks the place in the curriculum (according to Susan Miller) where bad or immature or amateur student writing proves the value of the great writing taught down the hall. And when composition thinks and talks about reading, it is usually in terms of levels: beginning, intermediate, and expert. The goal is to improve students' reading by improving the level at which they can read and work, hence the speed reading/study skills add-ons to many courses of instruction; or to control the reading (with the assumption that students are beginning readers) so that the difficulty of the text, its complexity, is not allowed to get in the way of writing, hence the many readers that offer short, easy-to-read selections as the material for student essays.

This is a quick and convenient account of the place of reading in contemporary American composition, but let me use it for a minute as a point of reference. The problem in either case is defined as developmental rather than, say, ideological. This representation of the problem of reading finesses the wide view in Lentricchia's argument, that the problem is a general cultural problem, one that is reproduced in but not specific to learners. Good reading is not, in other words, simply a matter of development or maturity or experience. Behind Lentricchia's despair over the state of reading is the sense that schooled readers, even at their best, have learned a form of mastery ("the secondary reading of explication") that is itself the problem (defined at least partially as a humility before or subordination to the primary text of schooling).

I want to use this essay to think about the competing desires to deny and to recover reading in the introductory course in the English curriculum. The issue for me, at least for the moment, is not whether or what students should read, but *how*. I want to argue that the introductory course should be a course in "close reading," the fundamental method of the New Criticism. I want to argue that this reading is neither retrograde nor politically naive, and I want to think about close reading as a form of argumentation, the techniques and goals of which are disappearing from the undergraduate curriculum. There are composition courses and programs that make close reading part of the necessary preparation of a writer, but they are few and far between and they are becoming more and more invisible when composition talks to itself about key people, programs, ideas, and issues.

I would say, for example, that the course represented in Bill Coles's book, *The Plural I,* is a course in close reading. As, with some important differences, is the course alluded to in Mariolina Salvatori's chapter "The Argument of Reading in the Teaching of Composition." (This is a course I know well. I've sat in on it, even taught a version of it, as I have sat in on and taught a version of Bill Coles's course. This has been one of the great pleasures of working in my department. The work that Tony Petrosky and I have done similarly assumes a course where, for example, both assigned texts and student papers are used as occasions for lessons in close reading.)

In her chapter, Mariolina Salvatori begins with Bill Coles's concern that the presence of reading (or literature) in the writing classroom would make writing disappear as a subject and students' writing disappear as a text. She moves from this example to consider the ways reading might be (and has been) reconfigured as part of a writer's necessary preparation. Her account of reading, it seems to me, attempts to recover a form of close reading for the composition classroom — a reading that is recursive, that pays particular attention to the text, a reading that is argumentative and reflexive. Lentricchia refers to the problem of writing as the willed product of American literary culture, or literary culture as represented in schooling. The course Salvatori alludes to was designed to stand in opposition to the "common sense" of reading as it has prepared generations of students and teachers. The course asks students to pay particular attention to the text (including the text of their own reading, often the text they write), to make this the center of their attention, paying a particular and unnatural attention to the words on the page. The course puts a particular premium on irony — that is, the distance one can achieve from the very systems that produce one's reading. The goal is not the production of meanings nor a formal description of how a text works. The course teaches, rather, a way to pay a disciplined and difficult attention to one's own practice.

I would like to locate this kind of course in a history that links it with the New Criticism but differentiates it from those classroom practices enshrined in, say, *Understanding Poetry.* The impulses represented in the New Criticism, those acknowledged by Lentricchia — to center criticism in the work of students, to make all texts available to the largest number of people — these admirable desires are perhaps the positive legacy of the New Criticism and can be imagined separately from the less interesting products of the larger movement that carries its name.

II

One way I have of reading and understanding Mariolina Salvatori's work (and, I should add, one way I had of reading and understanding Bill Coles's work when I first came to Pitt) was through the work of Richard Poirier, both his written work and his teaching in graduate courses (where we worked not on great authors but on the problems of language as they were represented or worked out in certain literary texts, and worked on them through short written exercises designed to engage us most productively as readers with the works we were reading). I came to this sense of what it meant to work in English through Poirier's teaching and through what was then his recent book, *The Performing Self* (1971). In brief, the argument of that book was that one came into identity (or *presence*) as a language user through one's awareness of and struggle with the languages of the present and the past. These moments of contact were constant and continuous but could be realized most profoundly through the kinds of confrontation allowed by literature and brokered through the classroom. Poirier argued, for example,

> English studies cannot be the body of English literature but it can be at one with its spirit: of struggling, of wrestling with words and meaning. Otherwise English studies may go one of two ways: it can shrink, in a manner possibly as invigorating as that which accompanied the retrenchment of Classics departments; or it can become distended by claims to a relevance merely topical. Alternatively, it can take a positive new step. It can further develop ways of treating *all* writing and *all* reading as analogous acts, as simultaneously developing performances, some of which deaden, some of which will quicken us. (84)

What I have since come to learn is that through Poirier and Coles I was also learning to think about English through the terms and practices of two teaching programs of great significance to English in America, the composition program at Amherst and a staff-taught introductory literature course at Harvard called Humanities 6 (or Hum 6). In Poirier's account, which I will turn to in a minute, Hum 6 was a course that linked close work with written language to Emerson, Frost, Wittgenstein, Leavis, Richards, and, as its negative counterpoint, to Brooks and Warren's *Understanding Poetry* and that form of teaching we have learned to identify with the New Criticism.

Let me take a moment to work out Poirier's account of the course in the final chapter of his most recent book, *Poetry and Pragmatism* ("Reading Pragmatically: The Example of Hum 6"). Poirier argues that the problem with the recent histories of criticism (or of English studies) is that they tend to leave out critical works of "stunning individuality." Among these omissions are works in the Anglo-American critical tradition that promoted the kind of "linguistic skepticism" later defined as deconstruction. With this lost work, he includes examples of teaching:

> Without necessarily depending on any of these writers [Peirce, James, Dewey, Santayana, Cavel, Stein, Stevens, Frost], certain kinds of intense close reading were being pedagogically advanced, well before the post-World War II period, which without defining themselves theoretically — at the time that would have been thought inappropriate in undergraduate classrooms — or calling themselves skeptical, managed to inculcate in more than a few teachers and students a habit of enjoying the way words undo and redo themselves to the benefit of social as well as literary practice. (173)

The course he takes as an example, one that he taught as part of a staff at Harvard in the mid-Fifties, was an introductory literature course, "The

Interpretation of Literature," known to students and staff as Hum 6. This course began on a different campus as the sophomore follow-up to the Amherst freshman course, the course identified with Theodore Baird (for a discussion of Baird, see Gibson and Varnum, particularly Varnum's book on English 1–2). The sophomore course was created by Armour Craig, Baird, and Reuben Brower. Brower carried the course with him when he went to Harvard (as others like Bill Coles or Roger Sales carried an Amherst-like course to other campuses). Poirier was part of a staff that taught with Brower at Harvard, a staff that included Peter Brooks, Thomas Edwards, Neil Rudenstine, David Kalstone, Anne Ferry, Margery Sabin, and Paul De Man (who wrote in *TLS* that "my own awareness of the critical, even subversive, power of literary instruction does not stem from philosophical allegiances but from a very specific teaching experience [Hum 6]").

But it is the details, not the names, that make this story interesting. The sophomore course at Amherst, according to Poirier,

> appeared to be less daring than the Baird course, English 1–2, perhaps because it emphasized, as did courses then being given at other places, the close reading of texts or, in Brower's better phrase, "reading in slow motion." For him reading ideally remained *in* motion, not choosing to encapsulate itself, as New Critical readings nearly always ultimately aspire to do. It was different from Brooks and Warren, with their *Understanding Poetry* — importantly so. (180–81)

The differences are represented in their touchstones — Eliot for the new critics, Frost for the Harvard/Amherst group — and in their ideological commitments. New Criticism idealized religious, political, and poetic unity. For the Harvard/Amherst group, through Frost, the lesson to be taught was that order is linguistic, man-made, contingent, and temporary. And order was the product of work with language, with language that was already in play, and the goals of this work were not simply improved reading but an improved participation in the culture and in the world ("to the benefit of social as well as literary practice").

> Hum 6 was distinguished not so much by a commitment to a reading list as a commitment to assignments or "exercises." Any athlete or dancer or musician — or reader — must have learned *how* to exercise and when to get back to exercise in order always to know the rigors by which any degree of mastery is attained. Reading is an acquired talent with words, which is all that reading ever can be directly engaged with, and it involves the measured recognition that words can do unexpected and disturbing things to you. . . . Reading must be actively synchronized with the generative energies of writing itself. It is not enough to understand what is being said, since this is always less than what is being expressed. (Poirier 175–76)

And, Poirier adds,

> Obviously, reading/writing of this kind cannot occur in space; it occurs in time, word by word, sentence by sentence, responsive to opportunities as they open up, to resistances as they are encountered, to entrapments

which must be dodged, all of these latent in the words just previously laid down and in the forms, both large and small, that reading and writing often fall into. (176)

What distinguished the work in Hum 6 (and marked its separation from the Brooks and Warren brand of New Criticism) was its moral urgency, an urgency rooted in the sense that "words can do unexpected and disturbing things to you." Like the composition course represented in *The Plural I* (a course, we should remember, that makes immediate use of assigned readings, usually short passages, and that asks students to read their relation to the world and to knowledge and to language by learning to read their own essays closely), the literature course assumes that the stakes are very high indeed, that these introductory courses are places to work out in practice (to enact) what it might mean to be present in the world (or to be present as a language user in a discursive order not of one's own making). The course was ambitious and called for the best from both teachers and students, which is most likely why it is remembered so fondly and in such detail.

Hum 6 was, at the same time, unwilling to make grand claims for its significance. The course was "low-keyed" in comparison to the courses with which it competed, courses with titles like "Ideas of Good and Evil" or "The Individual and Society." (The course I took at Ohio Wesleyan in the Sixties was called "The Devil, Hero, and God.") Here, for the last time, is Poirier:

> Meanwhile, the people I have associated with this course, from the Hum 6 staff all the way back to Emerson, harbored no such illusions as are now abroad about the power of reading or of writing, especially in criticism. Reading and writing are activities which for them require endless scruple. That is how the activity of reading begins, how it is carried on, and why, so long as the words are in front of you, it should never end. It need never be broken off out of some guilty feeling that the activity of reading is not sufficiently political or socially beneficial. It is to be understood as a lonely discipline that makes no great claims for itself. Reading conducted under such a regimen can be subversive only to the extent that it encourages us to get under and turn over not systems and institutions, but only words. (193)

The importance of this qualification still holds. Those who work on reading and writing in introductory courses can easily be seen to be working with very little in comparison to colleagues whose students, at least putatively, are dealing with the "big" questions (say) of race, class, and gender. Doing this work up close and at the point of practice, working to revise a sentence or a phrase, working on how one reads a line, thinking about the consequences of phrasing it this way or that, and doing this work with students, produces gains that are small and local — and, to the profession, largely invisible. This, to me, is why the meeting of composition and cultural studies has been such a great disappointment. The cultural studies course has been quick to teach the critique of commodity capitalism; it has shown almost no interest in teaching students how to work with words (turning them this way and that) as a form of critical practice.

III

The value of Hum 6 is not simply that it seems to authorize or give precedence for the teaching I would like to promote in the Nineties. (Although it does.) The value is not just that Hum 6 connects my graduate training with my present work. (Although it does. And I will confess that it gives me pleasure to see Poirier fondly recalling a freshman course and acknowledging the ways it enabled professionals to think through critical issues.) Hum 6 also functions for me as an important point of reference in the history of composition. Hum 6 is not, of course, a part of our standard accounts of the field and its history. The full argument for its role in composition's history is a complicated one and belongs to a different chapter than this, but let me offer a quick sketch. I want to use Hum 6 (and its relation to the Amherst composition course English 1–2) to think about literature and composition, about competing definitions of "argument," and about the usual sources called on to authorize instruction in logic and argument as part of the English (as opposed to the philosophy) curriculum.

Poirier would have us begin with Emerson to think about linguistic skepticism as part of American thought. I want to make mine a genealogy of instructional practice and so I will begin with Richards and Leavis, the British sources of the New Criticism, who in the Twenties and Thirties radically redefined what it meant to *do* English in school. Our present moment is still driven by the desires and anxieties set into play by their work. Eagleton, in "The Rise of English," phrases it this way:

> No subsequent movement within English studies has come near to recapturing the courage and radicalism of their stand. In the early 1920s it was desperately unclear why English was worth studying at all; by the early 1930s it had become a question of why it was worth wasting your time on anything else. English was not only a subject worth studying, but *the* supremely civilizing pursuit, the spiritual essence of the social formation. Far from constituting some amateur or impressionistic enterprise, English was an arena in which the most fundamental questions of human existence — what it meant to be a person, to engage in significant relations with others, to live from the vital centre of the most essential values — were thrown into vivid relief and made the object of the most intensive scrutiny. (31)

This is a dauntingly seductive project, beginning with the belief that education, education in the use of language, could make people better — better able to live and better able to live together. Eagleton, finally, has not much sympathy for the project (which becomes for him associated with Leavis and the group he gathered at the journal, *Scrutiny*):

> The whole *Scrutiny* project was at once hair-raisingly radical and really rather absurd. As one commentator has shrewdly put it, the Decline of the West was felt to be avertible by close reading. Was it really true that *literature* could roll back the deadening effects of industrial labour and the philistinism of the media? (34)

As the argument went, it was not literature itself that would stem the tide; it was what one could learn, through proper instruction, by reading literary texts. And, the fear of mass media was not simply an expression of snobbery or class-consciousness. For a generation that had learned through World War I and during the period between the two world wars to understand propaganda and the effects of control through mass media, there was much at stake in teaching students to understand from the inside how language worked and to discriminate between "good" uses of language and "bad." Close reading became a means of investigation, a way to exercise discrimination in the face of commercial, political and cultural interests with a previously unheard-of power to penetrate daily life and produce the "common" sense of the citizenry.

Close reading was a method designed to examine how a text "worked" and to measure its goals or implications, its version of what it means to be present in the world, against an idea of the Good. This "good," as with any version of the good, was contingent and only partially examined. For Leavis it was represented by a "great tradition" of the English novel and an idealized version of Renaissance England. For the American New Critics, the Agrarians, the appropriate texts were modern, ironic and unsentimental; the place was a conservative, idealized rural South. I am not arguing for the Great Tradition or the works collected in *Understanding Fiction* or *Understanding Poetry*. As a seemingly necessary step in the argument, Leavis, among others, grounded his critical practice in a set of (what were taken as obviously or unquestionably) great examples — as in *The Great Tradition*. And it is for his examples that Leavis has become an object of criticism. William Cain, for example, says that Leavis

> is a powerful and admirable figure, but I hope I have made clear that his work is too flawed and over-bearing to serve as a model for critical and pedagogical performance. His emphasis on criticism and judgment (as opposed to mere "elucidation") and his concern for general "critical consciousness" (as opposed to academic specialization and disciplinary enclosure) are inspiring and important. But in other respects — his very narrow canon, over-valuation of Lawrence, dismissal of dissent — Leavis is too rigid and dogmatic to stand as the exemplary figure for English studies. (161)

As I say, I am not particularly interested in defending or critiquing Leavis's version of the canon. The examples I am seeking for English studies are not to be found in the library. And so the Leavis-figure important to Cain is less important to me. (Although I will add that words like *overbearing, rigid,* and *dogmatic* do not necessarily carry a negative valence when I cast characters for the scene of instruction. The notion that a dogmatic teacher/critic only be slavishly followed assumes a student/reader more passive and one-dimensional than I find convincing.) I am not interested in using critics for my examples but classes, assignments, textbooks, and methods. Again — I am not trying to recover Leavis, but close reading, for English studies. (A more extended and perhaps less enthusiastic account of Leavis's methods would begin with textbooks like Denys Thompson's *Reading and Discrimination* or E. G. Biaggini's *The Reading and Writing of English*.)

The point I would make is that in the opening moments and at their best, the new critics were polemicists and their interest in the classroom and its methods was political. That is to say, the point of close reading was to enable students to argue with the very forms of understanding produced by the texts they were reading (or writing), to enable them to argue with the forms of understanding they were meant to take for granted, that were meant to be beyond question, outside the interests of the reader or the writer or the class-room. The pedagogy was designed to make visible those productions of self-hood and society, those forms of reading, writing, and imagining produced by contemporary mass culture through literature, radio, film, and advertis-ing. Students, by reading, engaged in an argument with interests and points of view and habits and seductions latent in the words on the page and the "forms, large and small, that reading and writing often fall into." These last words are, again, Poirier's (176). They allow me to highlight the degree to which close reading, or at least one classroom use of close reading, is an exer-cise in argumentation. One learns to define oneself, at the immediate point of contact, with the arguments built into (hidden in) the "common sense" of the mass culture.

This tradition of argumentation has been the hallmark of a certain kind of "literary education." The tradition is not, however, the same thing as the study of literature — it belongs to particular programs or classrooms, partic-ular ways of doing English. You can trace it through the development of British and American culture studies (both as a critical practice and as a class-room practice, although not necessarily in either — for a discussion of the pedagogy of British Cultural Studies, see Richard Miller).

As I have tried to indicate through my essay, this tradition of argumen-tation has touched on the history of composition in the United States, partic-ularly through the work of those who taught at Amherst: Bill Coles, Roger Sales, Walker Gibson, and others, including, I think, some of their students and colleagues. The hallmark of this teaching is its method. Student essays are reproduced. They become *the* text or one of the primary texts of the course. Students learn to read their writing closely not to make corrections but to ask how the language works or doesn't work. Revision is a key in these class-rooms because writers are always working against the forces evident in their text. And, of course, the work is read against some version of the "good," often defined in terms of what it means to be a person, to engage in signifi-cant relationship with others, or to live from the vital center of essential val-ues. By teaching reading, the writing course, as I am imagining it, can teach students to engage in a complex, revisionary argument with the culture as it is present in their own sentences and paragraphs, in their shape and sound, in what they do, and in who or what they point to in allusion. This kind of attention to text and context has been preserved in certain forms of literary education.

This kind of attention is not, however, in the mainstream of composition instruction. Composition has been dominated by a different pedagogical tra-dition, one that puts almost no premium on close reading, where the student essay, the "product," is an irrelevant or sometimes embarrassing byproduct of the real work of the course, where student writing is read, if it is read at all, primarily for grading or correction or, and this is important, where it is read by the student and the teacher to prepare for the kind of revision that is *not* an argument with the text (and the forces latent in its language) but is rather an acceptance of those forces, a submission. That is to say, in most cases the goal of revision is to perfect or complete or shore up the essay that has begun to complete the work of the culture as it has been brought into play by individual students in a writing class. A reader reads not antagonistically, but to see the patterns that need to be filled or completed.

What happened to close reading in the composition course? Why is it missing? The reasons, of course, are overdetermined; the answers complicated. To mass produce copies of student papers is expensive and awkward. To read closely and carefully demands time and attention from the faculty; this labor is unprecedented and seldom rewarded. To devote class time to "inferior" prose seems wasteful. Within a certain structure of values, English is a system designed to *preserve* the distinction between "great" writing, which deserves close reading, and student writing, which does not.

Another way to think about this is to think about the position of criticism at a key moment in the construction of composition as a professional field. You can, for example, look at the reception of Brooks and Warren's rhetoric (or of Kenneth Burke) to see the ways composition was trying to stake its claim over and against what was loosely called "literature." The Conference on College Composition and Communication, its journals, and its key figures were eager to cast their lot with linguistics (the science of language) and rhetoric (the reading and elaboration of standard texts). In the reception of *Modern Rhetoric,* which was poorly read and poorly reviewed, one can see the shifts of attention and influence that produced (say) James Kinneavy and Edward P. J. Corbett, even Wayne Booth, as key figures in the recent history of composition, that made it inevitable that composition should turn to philosophy and rhetoric for its models of argumentation, and that made Amherst (or Bill Coles or Roger Sales) almost invisible, or visible only as strange and cranky outsiders. (Look, for example, in the index of Stephen North's *The Making of Knowledge in Composition.*)

Criticism and close reading, including the close reading of student "exercises," Emerson and Frost, Poirier and Brower, Amherst and Harvard — I like to imagine a moment when these could have been important points of reference in the development of composition. Let me be clear, I am not trying to argue against the ways argument is currently figured in the undergraduate curriculum. I think John Gage's work and the curriculum at the University of Oregon make a powerful case for how the introductory composition course can provide intellectual training in argumentation and can be a serious part of the undergraduate curriculum. Nor am I trying to imagine a lost Eden; I am aware of all the limits and difficulties of the kind of course I am associating with Harvard and Amherst. Teaching students to feel the negative pressure of "their own language," to argue with those versions of themselves that come most easily, happily, and naturally through the language and habits of contemporary culture and American schooling, is risky and difficult teaching; its moments of achievement are not nearly so evident as those available in other kinds of writing classes; its problems are often more so. I do, however, want to suggest that there are ways of teaching the introductory course that participate in a tradition of practice where literature and composition, reading and writing, do not necessarily function as opposing terms.

WORKS CITED

Bartholomae, David, and Anthony R. Petrosky. *Facts, Artifacts, and Counterfacts: Reading and Writing in Theory and Practice.* Portsmouth, NH: Boynton, 1986.

———. *Ways of Reading.* Boston: Bedford Books, 1993.

Biaggini, E. G. *The Reading and Writing of English.* New York: Harcourt, Brace and Company, 1936.

Brooks, Cleanth, and Robert Penn Warren. *Understanding Poetry.* New York: Harcourt, Brace and Company, 1938.

———. *Understanding Fiction.* New York: Harcourt, Brace and Company, 1943.

———. *Modern Rhetoric.* New York: Harcourt, Brace and Company, 1949.

Cain, William E. *The Crisis in Criticism: Theory, Literature, and Reform in English Studies.* Baltimore, MD: Johns Hopkins University Press, 1984.

Coles, William E., Jr. *The Plural I – and After.* Portsmouth, NH: Boynton, 1988.

Eagleton, Terry. *Literary Theory: An Introduction.* Minneapolis: University of Minnesota Press, 1983.

Gibson, Walker. "Theodore Baird." *Traditions of Inquiry.* Ed. John Brereton. New York: Oxford University Press, 1985.

Leavis, F. R. *The Great Tradition.* New York: New York University Press, 1960.

Lentricchia, Frank. "In Place of An Afterword – Someone Reading." *Critical Terms for Literary Study.* Ed. Frank Lentricchia and Thomas McLaughlin. Chicago: University of Chicago Press, 1990. 321–39.

Miller, Richard. *Representing the People: Theoretical and Pedagogical Disjunction in the Academy.* Diss. University of Pittsburgh, 1993. AAC9317985.

Miller, Susan. *Textual Carnivals: The Politics of Composition.* Carbondale: Southern Illinois University Press, 1991.

North, Stephen. *The Making of Knowledge in Composition.* Portsmouth, NH: Boynton, 1987.

Poirier, Richard. *The Performing Self: Compositions and Decompositions in the Languages of Contemporary Life.* New Brunswick, NJ: Rutgers University Press, 1992.

———. *Poetry and Pragmatism.* Cambridge, MA: Harvard University Press, 1992.

Thompson, Denys. *Reading and Discrimination.* London: Chatto, 1934.

Varnum, Robin. *Fencing with Words: A History of Writing Instruction at Amherst College During the Era of Theodore Baird, 1938–66.* Urbana, IL: NCTE, 1996.

Stop Making Sense:
An Interview with David Bartholomae

JOHN BOE AND ERIC SCHROEDER

WRITING ON THE EDGE: I'd like to start with my favorite question for a writer: How did you learn to write and care about writing, and what teachers influenced you along the way?

BARTHOLOMAE: When I was an undergraduate, no one would have ever accused me of being a good writer. I was not adept at it. I wasn't somebody who wrote a lot or wrote for pleasure. I was, however, going to become an English teacher because I was playing small-college football and my favorite football coach was an English teacher.

I think I probably learned the most about writing from the man who was the head of my graduate program at Rutgers, Richard Poirier. I was so enamored with the way he wrote that I wanted to write like that. He was formed out of the tradition of teaching at Amherst with Reuben Brower and a group of influential teachers, including Theodore Baird, Bill Coles, Tom Edwards, and Roger Sale. When Brower left Amherst for Harvard, Poirier went there to become part of the group teaching the Humanities 6 course. For this group, writing was fundamental to the teaching of literature, especially writing the short paper where you try to articulate a position in relation to a text. You would perform a short reading, and then your little short essay was itself close-read. Usually the attempt was not to make you stylish, but to get all the crap out, to make your thinking sharper and more focused, to make you think about the consequences of the positions you had taken. I took an introduction to graduate studies with Poirier and wrote a lot. In graduate school, I experienced both the discipline and the routine of having to write a lot. I remember the kinds of comments I would get on my papers. But what I remember most is just really wanting to write the way he did.

The other great writing lesson I had was that I wrote my dissertation in England. I had one of the last of the NDEA fellowships, and so my wife and I went to Oxford. I was still a student at Rutgers, but we just wanted to be

---

From *Writing on the Edge*, Fall 1999: 9–28. This interview was originally titled "Stop Being So Coherent."

there — they had all the research facilities, and I thought, "Well, if I can write my dissertation in Oxford, why write in New Brunswick, New Jersey?" It meant that I wrote my whole dissertation without any interaction with my committee, and when I brought it back, my chair just read about halfway through it and said, "You're going to have to revise this." And so I did; I really massively rewrote it, and I learned a lot. I learned a certain level of humility, but I also learned about the grace of revision from that experience, that things do get better if you go back to work on them.

WRITING ON THE EDGE: You seem to have had an unusual experience in graduate school, focusing so much on writing. For a lot of people in graduate school, there seems to be little attention paid to writing. I felt my writing atrophied in graduate school, compared with what I'd gotten out of my undergraduate experience at Amherst.

BARTHOLOMAE: You do hear that story a good bit, but it certainly wasn't my experience. When I was an undergraduate, I didn't take a composition course because I was exempted from it. And I don't remember really laboring over my writing. As far as academic prose is concerned, I did it painfully at the last minute and was always told that I had good ideas somewhere in there but the writing was awfully messy.

WRITING ON THE EDGE: What you say about the comments you would get on the papers reminds me of how you have described getting your own students to revise their papers, telling them, "We've marked your papers where we were interested, puzzled, or bored." I was really struck by the word "bored" because I think a lot of pedagogy these days discourages us from being that frank with students and telling them, "This is really boring." Were those the kinds of comments you were getting on your own writing?

BARTHOLOMAE: Those were exactly the kinds of comments. One feature I remember that is still a part of the way I mark papers is to be very frank, to let that frankness determine the kind of editorial conversation that you have with students, where you really treat them as adults and you say, "This is boring," or "This is uninteresting," or "This is a dead end, don't do it." In the first course I took with Poirier, he would cross whole sections of a paper out — which I also will do. He would just draw a line through those three paragraphs you wrote trying to warm yourself up. I remember once I was trying to be profound and waxing poetic — the comment in the margin was, "Don't do that again." And, of course, I knew exactly what he meant. I knew what I was doing, and I was trying to figure out whether that was going to be currency or not, and he said "Nope." So then I went back to the drawing board.

WRITING ON THE EDGE: Today we seem to coddle students so much that often they aren't ready for that kind of criticism.

BARTHOLOMAE: I do think that we coddle, but I also think they're ready for the criticism. Sometimes if I describe my teaching, people — both my graduate students at my own university or other teachers at the 4 Cs — will think my class is a kind of in-your-face boot camp, a sort of Robin Varnum version of what Amherst must have been like.

And what I have to tell them is that I think my classes are actually very friendly places. My students laugh a lot, I've won awards for my teaching, and I think my classrooms are popular places. But I think students like to be treated as adults. And they are trying to develop some scale of value to get a feeling for what it means to be an adult intellectual. I don't think it coddles them when you do that. One of the Amherst legacies for me is that I think part of what we have to do as educators (and particularly as people who work with language) is help students escape the crap of contemporary culture. There's so much nonsense and so much easy generalization and so much bogus authority that I think the only way you can deal with it is to say, "Don't do that."

My sense is that one of the great holes, one of the great silences in the profession right now, particularly in 4Cs, is around the whole question of value. You don't ever find sessions where people are arguing about whether this particular piece of student writing is good writing or not. And you can construe good any way you want; it can be good in aesthetic terms, or good in terms of its social use, or good in terms of its intellectual value, but those are real questions, and they're questions about which we really shouldn't even agree, but we don't even know the terms of the disagreement. The 4Cs promotion of writing has been to confer the status of the writer on everybody, which is a wonderful thing to do. It's to enable writing as much as possible and to be promoters of writing. But as a profession this has kept us from not only giving students a way of writing, some procedures that they can use to get started in writing, but also from raising questions of value. I think different programs promote very different kinds of writing, and I don't think we argue these questions of value.

My generation comes out of the tradition of training (actually an elitist one) where we were expected to argue whether this poem was better than this poem, or this novel was better than this novel, and why. And I felt and I feel that to be an important and productive exercise. Today we don't carry that practice into the classroom where we engage students with it. One of the things I like to do is to engage students in productive discussions as opposed to mean-spirited ones. In most of my classes I'll hand out copies of two student papers and ask the questions, "Given what these papers are setting out to do, which does it better? Where does the other fall short? How would you work on it to make it a better piece of writing?"

WRITING ON THE EDGE: Isn't that classroom activity very much out of the Amherst English 1 tradition? But a lot of people don't make student texts a central or almost any part of the writing course. Can you really teach writing doing that?

BARTHOLOMAE: I would say no. I would say that the person who really taught me to be a writing teacher was Bill Coles, who also came from Amherst. Although, over time, I learned to teach quite differently from Bill. One of the things that Bill said that remains a kind of watchword in our program is that the student's writing is the primary text in the course and that it must be; that must be where you begin and what you learn. You have to learn as a professional to read student writing, and students have to learn to read their own writing so that they can learn what work it represents, so they can learn how to work on it.

The corollary for me has been that teaching really begins once you have a draft, and then you begin the process of learning how to read it and revise it. Revision isn't something you do on the side or for extra credit; revision is the mode of instruction. It's "Here's this text; let's think about what this piece of writing does and what it doesn't do. And let's think about where it can go." I can engage the students in that process, and then I can say, "OK, now, go to work." And when I evaluate students, I will evaluate them, then, not on what they did on the first crack at it, but what happened in successive revisions. That's where I see them at work, and that's measurable. We can see what's different, and we can talk about it. And if it's the same paper all over again, I don't care how slick it is, they haven't done any work in the course. Or they're not yet learning how to do the work in the course as I imagine it.

WRITING ON THE EDGE: You argue in your introduction to *The Teaching of Writing* that "Writing and writing itself, not some substitute or stand-in, should be at the center of the curriculum." Is there any chance of this actually happening, or is this rather like hoping it would rain beer?

BARTHOLOMAE: I think if I lower the horizon a bit I can ask, "Can English departments at this point in our history make this commitment and make it legitimately?" I think it's possible. Will they? I doubt it, but I think it's possible. And I think there is something to struggle for and to work for.

WRITING ON THE EDGE: Another thing you acknowledge getting from Amherst is the use of sequences. One of the things I love about *Ways of Reading* are the carefully constructed sequences of assignments. Can you talk a little bit about sequences? They don't seem hugely popular in our profession, but it seems to me they ought to be.

BARTHOLOMAE: I agree they ought to be. I'll tell you an interesting application of sequences. I've had a long involvement now with the John S. Knight Writing Program at Cornell, which is a very interesting undergraduate program staffed largely by graduate students from all over the campus, but also with significant faculty involvement, and faculty from all across the curriculum. The faculty who run the program with Jim Slevin, who has played a central role as a consultant, were trying to figure out how to engage these graduate students with a writing course in productive ways. And their solution to this pedagogical problem was to have them write sequences. Not to ask them how to do one writing assignment, but to ask them to organize a sequence of writing assignments. Let's say there were going to be two books at the center of the course; then the problem is how you organize the engagement with those books in such a way that you're not only covering the material but students are learning to write. Where do you begin, then what comes next, then what comes in response? And you watch these graduate students suddenly think through the reading of these two books of anthropology not as learning the field or covering the field, but as taking you into a way of reading, a way of writing, that marks somebody's young professional entrée into a community (a community of scholars I would say, not a community of anthropologists). The Cornell program gives out an award for the best assignment sequence. The sequences are brilliant, really wonderful!

I don't impose sequenced assignments on the world, but I can't imagine being a responsible teacher without, in advance, charting out the work of the course as a progressive engagement with X, Y, and Z. And that's whether I'm doing a graduate seminar or a freshman course or a class for majors.

WRITING ON THE EDGE: You also write about the need to write impossible assignments, assignments that interfere with the students' writing.

BARTHOLOMAE: You need to give students a productive place to begin. That's very difficult. Say you've asked them to read *Middlemarch,* and you want them to write something; it's the first writing assignment and you don't even know where to begin. My shorthand for the course is that I want to point them toward something that they don't know how to do: that's what makes the course a course, pointing them toward some way of working with that text that they cannot imagine. To do that you really do two things: You help them to imagine what they can't imagine, and you interfere with the habits that they already have. My students think in writing about *Middlemarch* they can talk about Dorothea and Casaubon as if they were real people. So if I'm going to write a sequence, I'm going to ask them to think about where and how the book seems to invite identification. I want them at some later point to get to thinking about strategies of representation in a novel like that — in particular, the way in which the narrator teaches you how and why to distance yourself rather than to simply identify with the people who are in front of you.

To get from the one place to the other, they have to do a lot of work. Some of it's just regular: They've got to learn how to work with a block quotation, they've got to learn how to write about a novel by both working with small pieces and doing some kind of summary. But there's also the interference part. I have to keep saying, "Remember, you're writing about an author, a reader, and a text. Some of your sentences have to be not about Dorothea, but about a reader, or about George Eliot, a writer, or about the novel and how it's working." You can set the task that specifically; that is, in the subject position of your sentence, there must be some reference to either the writer or the reader. Students learn to do a certain kind of reading that then puts them in a position to imagine — which in my rhythm of teaching is usually two drafts later — that they're no longer saying that they hate Casaubon and they also hate Will Ladislaw, but they're thinking about how and why a novel or an author is orchestrating a set of expectations and identifications and then thwarting them or satisfying them.

That's a long way of saying that I do think that you have to figure out in advance what you want students to do, and it should be something that they can't imagine. It's your job to help organize the work so it could be imaginable. That to me is organizing their work rather than telling them what to say. And one of the things you need to do along the way is interfere. It's not that students have been badly taught; it's just that they're moving now to this college-level literature class and a different way of thinking about reading — or in a composition class you're trying to get students to feel the flexibility of let's say the essay as a genre, rather than just rely on what they take to be its fixed structure. So you've got to say, "Stop being so coherent, stop proving every point; search for the example that doesn't fit, stop searching for the example that fits." I like to teach students to write parenthetically so they get a feel for what it means to say something and to say something else simultaneously.

WRITING ON THE EDGE: Along with difficult or impossible assignments, you're known for giving students impossible readings, things that the teacher doesn't fully understand. I love the recent piece in *College English* where Lynn Bloom reviews all the textbooks and says, "The one exception to all my explanations again is *Ways of Reading*." Is it good news or bad news that you're the one exception?

BARTHOLOMAE: It was good news for me! But it wasn't a surprise. *Ways of Reading* actually came out of a tradition of teaching. One of the things that I brought early in my career to my own table as a teacher was a sense that the fundamental purpose of the freshman course should be to allow students to be engaged with those works that were generally valued inside the academy. And usually the freshman composition course and its readers didn't do that. Instead, the standard anthology took pieces that students could work on with ease, and so the course, the students, and everything associated with it was thought of with contempt because its materials were not of the value of the work that you were writing about as a graduate student or that you were arguing about with your colleagues. They would read E. B. White, and we would read Empson! I felt all along that it was our job to give students works of value and teach them how they could use them. That assumed that you have to allow students to do things they couldn't do well in order to prepare them to do them well later.

A classic example is the course that Tony Petrosky and I did, the basic reading and writing course at Pitt. This course was for the small percentage who tested below Basic Writing, kids who were identified as being unable to succeed in school. We had them reading Margaret Mead and organized the course so they'd come up with a theory of development. The course was being evaluated by the college; someone from the Psych Department and someone from the History Department concluded, "God, this course is great! It really does give students an engagement with primary texts, gives them a feel for the excitement of intellectual life." And then they both had this moment of horror and said, "But then they can get it all wrong! They won't get the right theory of adolescent development until they know so and so, they won't get the history right until they read so and so." And we said, "Yes, but that's not what this course is about. It is not about covering the canonical texts and theories. It is about reading and writing, about using primary texts and articulating theories."

So *Ways of Reading* has proven to be a powerful pedagogical tool. Tony and I are also quite proud of it as an anthology of contemporary nonfiction, showing the range and the variety and the ambition of the genre. It's not a cross-curricular reader; it really is trying to represent what to us are not only really interesting but also teachable examples of nonfiction, nonfiction that's trying to do a kind of work that is adventuresome, in many cases unconventional, often compelling and memorable.

On my campus we have a group of people who do what's called creative nonfiction, the nonfiction in the Phillip Lopate anthology or published in the journal *Creative Nonfiction*. It's a writing that I know how to admire, but it's not a writing that I'd be interested in teaching. And then you have the writers in the composition texts, the canon Lynn Bloom identifies. The argument Tony and I make to the creative nonfiction crowd is that as you think about creative nonfiction, you want to also think about Roland Barthes or Stanley Fish or Paul Auster or John Wideman or Adrienne Rich, people who have done remarkable things with the genre of the essay — in other words nonfiction — but not in that more belletristic tradition. And yet their work has been left out of the educational anthologies, which have tended to go for more tightly organized and conventionally formed works.

WRITING ON THE EDGE: You make it harder not just on the student but also on the teacher. You don't get to teach the old E. B. White chestnuts, the stuff you can talk about in your sleep. Instead you have to deal with something you really don't understand.

BARTHOLOMAE: I think it allows you to say to a class, "Well, let's figure out what this is, what is the meaning of this?" That's a real project, one you can do with some pleasure.

WRITING ON THE EDGE: In that basic course, one of the metaphors you use is trying to get students to invent a discipline — so that they wouldn't have to borrow one of ours. But isn't there a problem when they get into disciplines because often nobody in those disciplines explains to the student how the discipline works? They assume that the students come in with the methodology. Elsewhere you say the problem with us as English teachers is we make them invent our discipline. Why don't we or how should we teach disciplinarity?

BARTHOLOMAE: Or should we teach disciplinarity? That's a hard question, and I can answer it on behalf of English (I don't think I have an answer on behalf of the undergraduate curriculum), which is that, traditionally we teach disciplinarity in the junior and senior years when you declare a major and you do a kind of focused work. I actually believe that. What I don't believe is that the first step is the foundational course as represented by Psych 101: 250 kids in a room memorizing terms that they don't sense the application for. On our campus, the foundational course is a small English course where you have material to work on, and in working on it you learn that there are tools that you need, tools like an ability to imagine the essay form, or having a vocabulary with terms like "narrator" or "sonnet" or "audience."

Should we teach students disciplinarity? I have actually quite mixed feelings. I think my primary commitments have always been to general education and to the introductory course. As a department chair, however, I have become more and more concerned about our failure as an English department to know very much about our majors, about their ambitions, desires, and career trajectories. We have about 450 English majors, but the numbers who go on to graduate school, who move toward an M.A. and Ph.D., are minuscule — maybe six a year. One of the things that we as a faculty have been trying to do is to come to a better sense of how to construct our required senior seminars, to make them capstones that allow students to move out into the world with some sense of their own orientation to what they have been trained to do or what they might be expected to do, to have a seminar, for example, that might actually point toward that much larger percentage of students who want to be certified to be English teachers. Their senior seminar probably should be constructed differently than it would be for those who need to be able to do the critical and theoretical work to write the kind of paper that they could use to get into our graduate school, as opposed to the senior seminar that would prepare somebody to think about how or why to teach *Huckleberry Finn* to 14-year-olds, or the *Scarlet Letter*; or what the language issues are; or to learn about Ebonics while preparing to go into the city and try to teach standard English in a world where English is not standard, where English is quite varied and its varieties are compelling.

One of the things that I sense in my own department is that we don't prepare students very well to go into the world of work. We and the community say that the English major is important because you learn to solve problems, to work with texts, to communicate. But the forms of that communication now are far beyond what we're prepared to teach students. We don't have the facilities or the expertise as a department to allow those of our majors for whom PowerPoint presentations and document design could be crucial to be prepared when they go to work for Westinghouse. I think we should do that. As a department, one of the problems we're working with right now is how you find the space and the money to be able to provide the equipment you would need to do this, and where you find the faculty expertise. Then there's the traditional set of arguments among the faculty about whether that's worth doing or not, about to what degree we are in the service of the culture, preparing students for particular vocational careers, and to what degree we are simply standing as the icebreaker, where we, the world be damned, are gonna teach them film studies or whatever.

WRITING ON THE EDGE: At the 4 Cs you often hear the argument that preparing for the real world means collaborative writing. As a person who's collaborated so much with Anthony Petrosky, do you encourage and teach your students to write and work collaboratively?

BARTHOLOMAE: No, never once.

WRITING ON THE EDGE: Isn't there a contradiction since you do it so much and the real world does it so much?

BARTHOLOMAE: I have had students work collaboratively to prepare presentations. I'm teaching a course with *Middlemarch* in it, so I'll get a team of students and send them off to, let's say, find out something about nineteenth-century medical practices, and they'll come back and report. But collaborative writing as it's talked about in 4Cs, I don't do it. It could be that I'm just lazy, that I have patterns and habits to my teaching, but I think I probably would also be willing to say that I choose not to teach collaborative writing. I have fifteen weeks. Among the things that I want to work with, I can't do everything. And I think you can learn to collaborate with somebody as the need arises. The things I know I need to teach take priority over that.

WRITING ON THE EDGE: You say we need to admit that we train people for Westinghouse and such, which makes a lot of sense. But in a review of Susan Miller's *Textual Carnivals,* you say that composition is irrefutably counterhegemonic. You say a composition course should be part of the general critique of traditional humanism, which seems to contradict sending people out to work for the corporation. How should we go about being counterhegemonic and subverting traditional humanists as composition teachers: to the ramparts! The sixties! [*Laughter*]

BARTHOLOMAE: There's nothing worse than having your own sentences come back! [*Laughter*] I don't know that I would say that as strongly anymore. One of the things is, if you have children between the ages of 16 and 25 — and I have three of them — you get a very different attitude toward resistance. [*Laughter*]

One of the reasons I love composition is it teaches you how and why to resist the forces of the country as you feel them in your sentences, like that easy generalization the kid writes that says that corporations like Westinghouse are the enemy of the people and are corrupt because capitalism is corrupt. Whether that's a political position that I want to promote or not is irrelevant to my teaching. But as a sentence, it doesn't begin to take its own terms seriously, or to examine its assumptions, or to imagine a rhythm of the syntax that would allow some moment of reflection on its own terms. I always say to kids who write these sentences, "How do you know that?" Or, "How do you get to speak for the United States of America?" That's what I think of as appropriately counterhegemonic.

I do think that the person who goes to Westinghouse and rises will probably rise because of her writing. Yet she's going to write in very conventional forms. The history of writing shows us how to value work within conventions. And, in the workplace, we all know that somebody can do something inside of a memo that leads you to say, "There's a live person in there. There's a mind at work." "Who is that person?" your manager says. And that comes not because you're completely redefining nuclear energy but because inside the immediate project people are working on, you have a way of participating. You can participate as a writer in such a way that you not only get the work done well, but you get it done thoughtfully, with some sense of style and presence.

Somebody asked me once what the relationship was between *Ways of Reading* and Paris 1968. I said, "There is absolutely none." I know I was a great disappointment because it was at a time when some of the critiques of the book were that it seemed to promote or call for some kind of social activism. And yet because of its attention to reading and writing it was finally quietist. I have been involved with campus activism in one way or another so that I know there is no more cynical gesture than to imagine that in a required fourteen-week course you can teach somebody to have a political consciousness. I just don't believe that can happen. But I do think we can teach somebody to work on sentences. And I think that practice can be political. So that's how I've slipped my way out of the sentence about counterhegemonic. [*Laughter*] Susan Miller made me do that. [*Laughter*]

WRITING ON THE EDGE: Early on in one of your pieces you talk about the tyranny of the thesis. It seems to me that in freshman writing, we're often putting students in the box, teaching them that if they do these steps, have a thesis statement, they'll write well.

BARTHOLOMAE: To be a writer means to be aware of the box as a box. As a teacher, I know that I can produce the effect of the thesis-driven paragraph. And the culture has been determined to produce that effect over time. I wish actually that there were more flexibilities built in at earlier stages. I think it's not only a matter of giving young writers a kind of form that they can inhabit in order to get work done, but in turn it's the kind of work that they do. And the tyranny of the thesis is that you're stuck proving the commonplace. You begin with whatever comes into your head, and if you're smart enough you find everything you need to prove it. And you leave out everything that's interesting because it doesn't quite fit. Then you say it again. So one of the things that I like to do is to surprise my students early on by asking them to please not be so coherent. The rhythm of the course is such that for the course to work, there has to be a point where students really are writing much worse than they were, with less control and facility and ease than they were when they came in. And it happens even at the level of the sentence. They start to try to put together sentences, and they can't pull them off because they now have complexity. And in some ways, that's the point during the course when you teach students semicolons, and dashes, and parentheses, and how in fact to marshal together all these things that they want to do.

I teach the parenthesis. If we taught the parenthesis with the same vigor as a nation that we teach the topic sentence, we'd have a whole different world; our children would be different. They'd be able to say something in their funny voice as well as their serious voice, or think of a qualification while they were thinking of the assertion. So I like to teach the parenthesis. And I like students to feel that part of the way they should imagine themselves as writers is in a somewhat difficult and at times prickly and always potentially experimental relationship to the forms that they're given to do their work in.

WRITING ON THE EDGE: The lesson of how students need to move backwards to move forward seems a particularly difficult one for new writing teachers to learn because it's so ingrained into teacher training now that what you're doing is trying to measure progress in student writing. What advice do you give to a new teacher about that?

BARTHOLOMAE: I would never say it's moving backwards to move forward. I would say that moving forward is always going to have to involve putting students in positions where they become less adept and sometimes less comfortable and less happy with you and the class. I think one of the really hard things about a writing class which is small and fairly intense and where you're responsible for organizing this work over time is that if you do your job well, there is a point that's sort of scary, where students aren't writing very well and they feel very much at sea and you have to be able to know how to pull that together by week fourteen. Sometimes it feels as though the bottom is falling out. But that's progress.

WRITING ON THE EDGE: In your basic reading and writing course, you are co-teaching with one of your colleagues. How do you get an institution to support two faculty members teaching the lowest of the low at the university, when most universities will dump that on graduate students? Most universities would see that as an incredible squandering of resources. Doesn't that course make up half the students' semester load?

BARTHOLOMAE: If they had a 15-course load, it was 6 credits out of the 15. Well, how did we do it is actually in the introduction and the dedication to *Facts, Artifacts, and Counterfacts*. There was a dean, Robert Marshall, who remains a dear friend, who essentially said to the faculty, "It is wrong for us to bring students here and to not prepare them and then to fail them, when we know in advance they need additional help." So he was willing to invest the energy and the resources of the institution. That was quite a long time ago now. But the tradition of teaching and the success of the teaching on campus has been such that it's never been questioned. As a matter of fact, I can't imagine that it ever will be questioned. That course and its missions and its commitment of resources has defined part of the culture of writing and teaching on our campus, and it's something everybody's proud of. It's true that only our very best teachers get to teach the basic writing course. We do have graduate students teach it, but they tend to be the ones who have done a lot of teaching and who feel a real commitment to the program. And we still have tenure-stream faculty teaching the course.

WRITING ON THE EDGE: It seems to me like this is a success story that none of the rest of us wants to hear! Because it runs counter to practice nearly everywhere else. Is there any hope for the rest of us? Can we get your dean?

BARTHOLOMAE: Or is it something that could be done now in this climate? I don't know that it was an accident of history; I think there are places where it could be done. But no individual should feel that he or she failed for being unable to pull it off because it does require that amazing moment of a coming together of a sort of larger institutional commitment: The guards are asleep at the gates, and you sneak in and get something started, and then nobody can stop it!

WRITING ON THE EDGE: I want to switch to a couple of questions about your famous debate with Peter Elbow. Among the many sparkling things you said was the following, which seems true to me: "The argument that produces archetypal criticism produces cognitive psychology, free writing, and new journalism. I've got Bruner, Linda Flower, Peter, Tom Wolfe, and John McPhee all lined up in this genealogy, this account of the modern curricular production of the independent author, the celebration of the point of view as individual artifact, the promotion of sentimental realism, the true story of what I think, feel, know, and see." I thought this was a very perceptive, Leavis-like line you put these people in I, but I wondered, you know . . .

BARTHOLOMAE: [*Laughs*] It got me in a heap of trouble!

WRITING ON THE EDGE: I couldn't imagine trouble with the line so much as with the tone with which the line was treated.

BARTHOLOMAE: The tone was partly a product of the ritual of the debate, and of the moment. My department has a very old, very large, very active creative writing program. We offer an MFA, and we are in some ways now the center of creative nonfiction — which I called sentimental realism. My colleague Lee Gutkind, who edits the journal *Creative Nonfiction*, asked me to come to his seminar and to speak to students about sentimental realism and to account for the tone of that sentence. So that passage did get me in a heap of trouble!

I was in front of people for whom Tom Wolfe or his current equivalents are heroes. I mean that is exactly who they're trying to write themselves to be. And so I had to explain what I meant. I'm not against what they do, which I'll stick with calling sentimental realism. But I stick with the desire to not take for granted the cultural value that's given to the celebration of point of view.

WRITING ON THE EDGE: Of what view?

BARTHOLOMAE: Of point of view. Of my point, here I am, front and center, I'm experiencing this and I'm going to tell you about it. I understand the cultural value of that work, I understand why that dominates the best-seller list right now, I understand the pedagogical advantage. I think Peter's strongest argument is in the pedagogical advantage of inviting young people into that moment and anointing them as writers, to allow them to feel the authority of their own immediate experience and point of view. I understand all of that. I just don't take it to be the mission of the required first-year course. And that was what I said to the seminar, that I was speaking for a course that's required at schools all across the country. Anybody who is a program director or in some way administratively responsible must think about the rationale behind that requirement. You are beholden in some way to rationalize what you are doing in the required course to those who are requiring it.

My sense of that introductory course is that it is, in fact, to introduce students to doing a certain kind of intellectual work in the four years they're in college that in a way has to do not with their priority but with their secondarity, that is, the way in which they are in relation to somebody else. Let's say it's Adrienne Rich or something else they've read, let's say Robert Coles. I think it's then absolutely central that you ask students, "Where do you speak in relation to Adrienne Rich or Robert Coles?" I think Adrienne Rich in speaking does not want students to be silent. But she does want to be heard. And she wants to say something that they need to listen to. And it may very well run counter to their expectations and challenge the very sense of authority that allows them to imagine the world being constructed in a certain way. Here is a common situation in my class. A student is reading Adrienne Rich, she's talking about patriarchy, and the student, a guy, wants to write about how much he loves fishing with his dad. He loves fishing with his Dad, you know! And it's important that he loves fishing with his dad! But if he's going to read Adrienne Rich, he's got to think about fishing with his dad as part of a set of patriarchal rituals that serves the culture in certain ways. That's what I think the course is.

I think we teach students to do that so that they can have a four-year education and it will be a good one. So I said to the creative nonfiction seminar, "You know, the required composition course is one course in a four-year curriculum. If want to go on and be creative writers, we offer a creative writing major as well as a literature major. They can spend the next three years as journalists doing journalism or in the nonfiction track writing nonfiction and learning to love Tom Wolfe or Barry Lopez or whomever. I don't have to do it all. So I argue in the name of the required course.

WRITING ON THE EDGE: Peter Elbow got the last word in the debate, saying to you, "You assume discourse means argument and that difference means opposition." Is this a fair attribution?

BARTHOLOMAE: Yes, I think it is, in the spirit that I think Peter offers it. I've been trying to imagine opposition not as it's represented by resistance or as it's enshrined in sort of a new-left cultural politics, but opposition as in the questioning of common sense, not doing what comes naturally, calling attention to the terms that underlie what you do — argument not as polemic, not as stridency, but argument as in questioning the relationship to other people's texts but also to your own. I do think that writing instruction does require struggle, where you do put yourself in a questioning relationship to the culture that's given you its forms and its assumptions. You learn as a writer how to be present inside of all of that. But there's a part of Peter that wants to make me quibble — to say, opposition as I understand it is not the same thing it meant to Jim Berlin, or those who feel that writing courses are going to bring down postmodern capitalism — that's not part of my vocabulary, not my goal.

WRITING ON THE EDGE: Can you talk a little about reading and how we teach students to do the kind of reading that you're advocating, because it does seem that we have to reshape the way they think about texts. It seems that rereading plays an enormous role in this. And it's one of those things we rarely ask students to do.

BARTHOLOMAE: Rereading is a form of revision. The course that I teach — whether it's a composition course or a literature course or something else — not only says to a student go back and revise this paper, but in order to go back and revise this paper, go back and reread what you've been working on.

I'll give students something hard to read like *The Pedagogy of the Oppressed*. They'll write a paper, their first paper, and the good students will just sum it all up. And you say to a student, "How did you do that? What allowed you to do that?" Inevitably they'll say, "Well, you know, I just ignored all the stuff I didn't understand in chapter 4." And of course they did! Because they're trained in the rhetoric of mastery — you don't show your weak hand, you show your strong suit. So I think that the pedagogical rule is, "Go read chapter 4 and do a paper now. Bring those things that you don't understand to the front. And you're allowed to write a sentence that says, 'Well I don't completely understand what Paolo Freire means by problematization. I think he might mean the following.'" A moment of translation can then take place: "When

Freire says X, Y, and Z, I think what he's saying is the following." That's a very productive moment, when a student begins to speak for the parts of the text that can't be quickly summarized, or that don't fit with what the student has been prepared to know or understand. I think you have to give people things that are worth reading and that are teachable and where there's some work to be done.

One of my rules of thumb is that I tend to not want to talk about something in class until students have written about it. That is, you need to prepare students to take the plunge, take the responsibility for the first attempt to say what something means or say why it's interesting before you begin to organize it for them. It makes the teaching more fun. If I go in and tell everybody what I think is going on in Paolo Freire, I'll get twenty-two papers all saying the same thing, and that's not my goal. I'm really interested in getting students to feel that they can be the readers of something that they don't feel prepared to read. I think students need to understand that it isn't about memory — that books are themselves mnemonic devices, that that's why we love them. You can make marks in them, and then you open them up again; you don't have to remember, you can go back and look at it. Students need the ability to write the sentence that acknowledges the text as a problem.

I remember learning this from Mariolina Salvatori, who's one of the best teachers I've ever seen, who assigns what she calls the difficulty paper. She was a part of the group that did *Facts, Artifacts, and Counterfacts*. She learned early on that one of the things you have to have students do is articulate their sense of difficulty so that it's not shameful, but it's strategic and productive. Difficulty becomes not, "I can't do it." Instead, students explain what it is that makes it difficult. And in doing that, they're in a position to begin to imagine difficulty as part of the text's strategy, and its fundamental existence in relation to them, what their next move is going to be. Difficulty becomes part of the intellectual landscape you're negotiating, rather than something shameful that you have to hide. So that's another way to allow students to experience reading.

Many of us still enjoy reading things that we're not prepared to read. As you get older, certain things you can read very quickly, like dissertations. I've served on a lot of dissertation committees in our Spanish Department. My wife is a Spanish teacher and is fluent in Spanish, so I'll bring a dissertation home. And her Spanish is great, and I can read Spanish, but it is stumbling. I can read the dissertations in two hours, because, you know, they're dissertations.

WRITING ON THE EDGE: Since dissertations are easy, what do you like to read that's hard, that challenges you? Confuses but attracts you?

BARTHOLOMAE: I find that I take much of my own reading pleasure now from reading contemporary fiction and poetry. Tony and I are doing a book that will be a literature anthology and textbook. It does not try to cover the genres or to cover a period or a national literature. But its argument is that one of the ways of imagining the one required literature course students take is that it should situate them in relation to their own contemporary literary culture. So they should know who Sonia Sanchez is and be able to think of that work in relation to their own reading and writing; they should participate in that particular cultural moment. I don't think that English departments generally define the responsibility of the required literature course in that way. What we're asking is that if students across the country are going to take one required literature class, what should be in it? I'm more and more convinced that what should be in it should be primarily serious literature written in the last ten years. And from that, students can come to an understanding of literary culture and literary value. Then if they want to do historical work or additional work, they can. So I find myself reading a lot more literature with enormous pleasure. I'm more and more interested in the writers we bring to campus, not as display but as part of my own academic calendar. Before somebody comes to town, I want to read their work, I want to go to the reading, I want to have some sense of what's going on, who that person is, what's happening. That's what I like to read. And, of course, Tony and I are always reading new nonfiction as we work toward a new edition of *Ways of Reading*.

WRITING ON THE EDGE: Going back to our earlier discussion of students and their reading and rereading, it seems that one of the problems we run into is that of coverage. In one quarter or semester we have to do so much work, and if we're asking students to reread and we're asking them to rewrite, then it seems to me the university could look at that course and say that you hadn't covered a lot of material.

BARTHOLOMAE: That's right. They would. I think that part of an English department's commitment should be to coverage. I couldn't imagine an English major who hadn't also done the *Norton Anthology* course, to get the sweep of British literature from Chaucer to Woolf. But I think of the general education course as having a different responsibility. One of the courses that I like to teach is a course called American Literary Traditions that fulfills the general education requirements, and most of the students are not English majors. My understanding of my responsibility in that course is not to cover all of American literature, but to give them some sense of the terms of the title. Why American? What is literature? And how do you understand tradition? So I'd rather do eight books that would allow me to put things in interesting pairs, where I would teach Robert Frost and Philip Levine. Or I would teach *Walden* and teach Gretel Ehrlich's *The Solace of Open Spaces* in order to think about how this literature functions in the service of something that you call America, and if you read *Walden* and *The Solace of Open Spaces*, what do you know about a tradition? Or read Emily Dickinson, and a woman whose poetry I admire very much, Lynn Emanuel. It's fun to get figures who work as a conversation with each other. I don't see coverage as the role of a general education course.

WRITING ON THE EDGE: What happens when you get students who are juniors and seniors and haven't done general education and they have to do general education?

BARTHOLOMAE: In the real world, not everybody does things in order. I think that's the fundamental dilemma of teaching, that you can't get everybody to start on the same page, and you can't get everybody to end on the same page, and you can't get everybody to move at the same speed all the way through. I would say the skills of close reading are part of the general education imperative: Students who are juniors and seniors who haven't learned that, must.

I actually have a kid in my class this semester who's a senior engineering major, who is a pretty good student and pretty smart kid. He's really struggling in the course because he has to work closely with the material that he's writing about, and he's not prepared to do that. It scares him. What he can do is write a very glib paper about man's inhumanity to man, and I'm not buying it, and I haven't been buying it, and I keep saying, "You have to take me to one of the poems from Philip Levine's *The Simple Truth* to show me the way in which Levine is engaging this question that you want to write about: man's inhumanity to man." It's hard for him to want to do that. Because he thinks his education is over, he thinks that all he needs to do in this course is fulfill his goddamn requirement, and he wants me to get off his goddamn back. "I'm an engineer, I've already got a job, and you're telling me . . ."

WRITING ON THE EDGE: "You're gonna keep me from graduating?!"

BARTHOLOMAE: "I like you, I admire your career, but this is what I'm teaching, and goddamnit you're gonna do it!"

WRITING ON THE EDGE: This phrase just leapt out at me when you wrote about how much work the basic reading and writing course can be; you said underlying the teaching of such a course are "patience and violence." Violence?

BARTHOLOMAE: Oh, absolutely. I mean, that's what makes it such hard work. In the basic reading and writing course, I'd say the majority of students are working class and minority kids for whom a variety of behaviors — and by that I don't just mean reading and writing, but ways of sitting, ways of being in class — have developed over time, in very hostile relations to white guys my age who wield authority. In that teaching I have to be a very enabling presence. But I also have to be the white guy who's in the position of authority.

WRITING ON THE EDGE: You the man.

BARTHOLOMAE: I am! And I can't not be, I mean, that's a given. Actually, I think even pedagogically and linguistically, I have to be. So it's not only a matter of getting into the political sense of what it means to standardize the English of these kids who come in, whose English isn't standard, but also just the violence of scenes that I will never forget. For instance, we ask students to speak in sentences in class. And I think it's my job to engage everybody. So let's say we've got a young man whom I want to speak, and he'll say something like, "Yeah." I say, "I want you to not just say that you think something, but I want to hear it; I want you to try it out on us. We all want to hear it." And I'll wait. That silence is very scary. My feeling is that I must will him into a conversation that he both wants to have and doesn't want to have. So it's a very violent course to teach. And you're putting conditions on people's work, work has to come in on time, things have to be corrected, certain subjects aren't allowed, and all of that is hard.

I know it's sort of chic now to talk about violence in relation to the middle-class kid in your class, or violence in relation to those in minority positions generally, but I do a lot of teaching where I'll have minority kids in classes. I understand how I'm in a position of power that engages acts of violence. There's a very different feel in the basic reading and writing class. It's very volatile. Kids do stomp out. And women who teach the class have been some-times treated in ways that are frightening for them. At an urban university, one of your commitments is to bring kids in who just aren't prepared to sit in "polite conversation." And we are absolutely committed to that. To pretend that it's not sometimes weird and violent is just a lie.

Introduction: Ways of Reading

WITH ANTHONY PETROSKY

M AKING A MARK

Reading involves a fair measure of push and shove. You make your mark on a book and it makes its mark on you. Reading is not simply a matter of hanging back and waiting for a piece, or its author, to tell you what the writing has to say. In fact, one of the difficult things about reading is that the pages before you will begin to speak only when the authors are silent and you begin to speak in their place, sometimes for them — doing their work, continuing their projects — and sometimes for yourself, following your own agenda.

This is an unusual way to talk about reading, we know. We have not mentioned finding information or locating an author's purpose or identifying main ideas, useful though these skills are, because the purpose of our book is to offer you occasions to imagine other ways of reading. We think of reading as a social interaction — sometimes peaceful and polite, sometimes not so peaceful and polite.

We'd like you to imagine that when you read the works we've collected here, somebody is saying something to you, and we'd like you to imagine that you are in a position to speak back, to say something of your own in turn. In other words, we are not presenting our book as a miniature library (a place to find information) and we do not think of you, the reader, as a term-paper writer (a person looking for information to write down on three-by-five cards).

When you read, you hear an author's voice as you move along; you believe a person with something to say is talking to you. You pay attention, even when you don't completely understand what is being said, trusting that it will all make sense in the end, relating what the author says to what you already know or expect to hear or learn. Even if you don't quite grasp everything you are reading at every moment (and you won't), and even if you don't remember everything you've read (no reader does — at least not in long,

From *Ways of Reading: An Anthology for Writers*, 6th ed., eds. David Bartholomae and Anthony Petrosky (Boston: Bedford/St. Martins, 2002) 1–18.

complex pieces), you begin to see the outlines of the author's project, the patterns and rhythms of that particular way of seeing and interpreting the world.

When you stop to talk or write about what you've read, the author is silent; you take over — it is your turn to write, to begin to respond to what the author said. At that point this author and his or her text become something you construct out of what you remember or what you notice as you go back through the text a second time, working from passages or examples but filtering them through your own predisposition to see or read in particular ways.

In "The Achievement of Desire," one of the essays in [*Ways of Reading*], Richard Rodriguez tells the story of his education, of how he was drawn to imitate his teachers because of his desire to think and speak like them. His is not a simple story of hard work and success, however. In a sense, Rodriguez's education gave him what he wanted — status, knowledge, a way of understanding himself and his position in the world. At the same time, his education made it difficult to talk to his parents, to share their point of view; and to a degree, he felt himself becoming consumed by the powerful ways of seeing and understanding represented by his reading and his education. The essay can be seen as Rodriguez's attempt to weigh what he had gained against what he had lost.

If ten of us read his essay, each would begin with the same words on the page, but when we discuss the chapter (or write about it), each will retell and interpret Rodriguez's story differently; we will emphasize different sections — some, for instance, might want to discuss the strange way Rodriguez learned to read, others might be taken by his difficult and changing relations to his teachers, and still others might want to think about Rodriguez's remarks about his mother and father.

Each of us will come to his or her own sense of what is significant, of what the point is, and the odds are good that what each of us makes of the essay will vary from one to another. Each of us will understand Rodriguez's story in his or her own way, even though we read the same piece. At the same time, if we are working with Rodriguez's essay (and not putting it aside or ignoring its peculiar way of thinking about education), we will be working within a framework he has established, one that makes education stand, metaphorically, for a complicated interplay between permanence and change, imitation and freedom, loss and achievement.

In "The Achievement of Desire," Rodriguez tells of reading a book by Richard Hoggart, *The Uses of Literacy*. He was captivated by a section of this book in which Hoggart defines a particular kind of student, the "scholarship boy." Here is what Rodriguez says:

> Then one day, leafing through Richard Hoggart's *The Uses of Literacy*, I found, in his description of the scholarship boy, myself. For the first time I realized that there were other students like me, and so I was able to frame the meaning of my academic success, its consequent price — the loss.

For Rodriguez, this phrase, "scholarship boy," became the focus of Hoggart's book. Other people, to be sure, would read that book and take different phrases or sections as the key to what Hoggart has to say. Some might argue that Rodriguez misread the book, that it is really about something else, about British culture, for example, or about the class system in England. The power and value of Rodriguez's reading, however, are represented by what he was able to *do* with what he read, and what he was able to do was not record information or summarize main ideas but, as he says, "frame the meaning of my academic success." Hoggart provided a frame, a way for Rodriguez to think and talk about his own history as a student. As he goes on in his essay, Rodriguez not only uses this frame to talk about his experience, but he resists it, argues with it. He casts his experience in Hoggart's terms but then makes those terms work for him by seeing both what they can and what they cannot do. This combination of reading, thinking, and writing is what we mean by *strong reading*, a way of reading we like to encourage in our students.

When we have taught "The Achievement of Desire" to our students, it has been almost impossible for them not to see themselves in Rodriguez's description of the scholarship boy (and this was true of students who were not minority students and not literally on scholarships). They, too, have found a way of framing (even inventing) their own lives as students — students whose histories involve both success and loss. When we have asked our students to write about this essay, however, some students have argued, and quite convincingly, that Rodriguez had either to abandon his family and culture or to remain ignorant. Other students have argued equally convincingly that Rodriguez's anguish was destructive and self-serving, that he was trapped into seeing his situation in terms that he might have replaced with others. He did not necessarily have to turn his back on his family. Some have contended that Rodriguez's problems with his family had nothing to do with what he says about education, that he himself shows how imitation need not blindly lead a person away from his culture, and these student essays, too, have been convincing.

Reading, in other words, can be the occasion for you to put things together, to notice this idea or theme rather than that one, to follow a writer's announced or secret ends while simultaneously following your own. When this happens, when you forge a reading of a story or an essay, you make your mark on it, casting it in your terms. But the story makes its mark on you as well, teaching you not only about a subject (Rodriguez's struggles with his teachers and his parents, for example) but about a way of seeing and understanding a subject. The text provides the opportunity for you to see through someone else's powerful language, to imagine your own familiar settings through the images, metaphors, and ideas of others. Rodriguez's essay, in other words, can make its mark on readers, but they, too, if they are strong, active readers, can make theirs on it.

Readers learn to put things together by writing. It is not something you can do, at least not to any degree, while you are reading. It requires that you work on what you have read, and that work best takes shape when you sit down to write. We will have more to say about this kind of thinking in a later section of the introduction, but for now let us say that writing gives you a way of going to work on the text you have read. To write about a story or essay, you go back to what you have read to find phrases or passages that define what for you are the key moments, that help you interpret sections that seem difficult or troublesome or mysterious. If you are writing an essay of your own, the work that you are doing gives a purpose and a structure to that rereading.

Writing also, however, gives you a way of going back to work on the text of your own reading. It allows you to be self-critical. You can revise not just to make your essay neat or tight or tidy but to see what kind of reader you have been, to examine the pattern and consequences in the choices you have made. Revision, in other words, gives you the chance to work on your essay, but it also gives you an opportunity to work on your reading — to qualify or extend or question your interpretation of, say, "The Achievement of Desire."

We can describe this process of "re-vision," or re-seeing, fairly simply. You should not expect to read "The Achievement of Desire" once and completely understand the essay or know what you want to say. You will work out what you have to say while you write. And once you have constructed a reading — once you have completed a draft of your essay, in other words — you can step back, see what you have done, and go back to work on it. Through this activity — writing and rewriting — we have seen our students become strong, active, and critical readers.

Not everything a reader reads is worth that kind of effort. The pieces we have chosen for this book all provide, we feel, powerful ways of seeing (or framing) our common experience. The selections cannot be quickly summarized. They are striking, surprising, sometimes troubling in how they challenge common ways of seeing the world. Some of them (we're thinking of pieces by Michel Foucault, Clifford Geertz, Adrienne Rich, and Virginia Woolf) have captured and altered the way our culture sees and understands daily experience. The essays have changed the ways people think and write. In fact, every selection in the book is one that has given us, our students, and colleagues that dramatic experience, almost like a discovery, when we suddenly saw things as we had never seen them before and, as a consequence, we had to work hard to understand what had happened and how our thinking had changed.

If we recall, for example, the first time we read Susan Griffin's "Our Secret" or John Edgar Wideman's "Our Time," we know that they have radically shaped our thinking. We carry these essays with us in our minds, mulling over them, working through them, hearing Griffin and Wideman in sentences we write or sentences we read; we introduce the essays in classes we teach whenever we can; we are surprised, reading them for the third or fourth time, to find things we didn't see before. It's not that we failed to "get" these essays the first time around. In fact, we're not sure we have captured them yet, at least not in any final sense, and we disagree in basic ways about what Griffin and Wideman are saying or about how these essays might best be used. Essays like these are not the sort that you can "get" like a loaf of bread at the store. We're each convinced that the essays are ours in that we know best what's going on in them, and yet we have also become theirs, creatures of these essays, because of the ways they have come to dominate our seeing, talking, reading, and writing. This captivity is something we welcome, yet it is also something we resist.

Our experience with these texts is a remarkable one and certainly hard to provide for others, but the challenges and surprises are reasons we read — we hope to be taken and changed in just these ways. Or, to be more accurate, it is why we read outside the daily requirements to keep up with the news or conduct our business. And it is why we bring reading into our writing courses.

WAYS OF READING

Before explaining how we organized this book, we would like to say more about the purpose and place of the kind of strong, aggressive, labor-intensive reading we've been referring to.

Readers face many kinds of experiences, and certain texts are written with specific situations in mind and invite specific ways of reading. Some texts, for instance, serve very practical purposes — they give directions or information. Others, like the short descriptive essays often used in English textbooks and anthologies, celebrate common ways of seeing and thinking and ask primarily to be admired. These texts seem self-contained; they announce their own meanings with little effort and ask little from the reader, making it clear how they want to be read and what they have to say. They ask only for a nod of the head or for the reader to take notes and give a sigh of admiration ("yes, that was very well said"). They are clear and direct. It is as though the authors could anticipate all the questions their essays might raise and solve all the problems a reader might imagine. There is not much work for a reader to do, in other words, except, perhaps, to take notes and, in the case of textbooks, to work step-by-step, trying to remember as much as possible.

This is how assigned readings are often presented in university classrooms. Introductory textbooks (in biology or business, for instance) are good examples of books that ask little of readers outside of note-taking and memorization. In these texts the writers are experts and your job, as novice, is to digest what they have to say. And, appropriately, the task set before you is to summarize — so you can speak again what the author said, so you can better remember what you read. Essay tests are an example of the writing tasks that often follow this kind of reading. You might, for instance, study the human nervous system through textbook readings and lectures and then be asked to write a summary of what you know from both sources. Or a teacher might ask you during a class discussion to paraphrase a paragraph from a textbook describing chemical cell communication to see if you understand what you've read.

Another typical classroom form of reading is reading for main ideas. With this kind of reading you are expected to figure out what most people (or most people within a certain specialized group of readers) would take as the main idea of a selection. There are good reasons to read for main ideas. For one, it is a way to learn how to imagine and anticipate the values and habits of a particular group — test-makers or, if you're studying business, Keynesian economists, perhaps. If you are studying business, to continue this example, you must learn to notice what Keynesian economists notice — for instance, when they analyze the problems of growing government debt — to share key terms, to know the theoretical positions they take, and to adopt for yourself their common examples and interpretations, their jargon, and their established findings.

There is certainly nothing wrong with reading for information or reading to learn what experts have to say about their fields of inquiry. These are not, however, the only ways to read, although they are the ones most often taught. Perhaps because we think of ourselves as writing teachers, we are concerned with presenting other ways of reading in the college and university curriculum.

A danger arises in assuming that reading is only a search for information or main ideas. There are ways of thinking through problems and working with written texts which are essential to academic life, but which are not represented by summary and paraphrase or by note-taking and essay exams.

Student readers, for example, can take responsibility for determining the meaning of the text. They can work as though they were doing something other than finding ideas already there on the page and they can be guided by their own impressions or questions as they read. We are not, now, talking about finding hidden meanings. If such things as hidden meanings can be said to exist, they are hidden by readers' habits and prejudices (by readers' assumptions that what they read should tell them what they already know), or by readers' timidity and passivity (by their unwillingness to take the responsibility to speak their minds and say what they notice).

Reading to locate meaning in the text places a premium on memory, yet a strong reader is not necessarily a person with a good memory. This point may seem minor, but we have seen too many students haunted because they could not remember everything they read or retain a complete essay in their minds. A reader could set herself the task of remembering as much as she could from Walker Percy's "The Loss of the Creature," an essay filled with stories about tourists at the Grand Canyon and students in a biology class, but a reader could also do other things with that essay; a reader might figure out, for example, how both students and tourists might be said to have a common problem seeing what they want to see. Students who read Percy's essay as a memory test end up worrying about bits and pieces (bits and pieces they could go back and find if they had to) and turn their attention away from the more pressing problem of how to make sense of a difficult and often ambiguous essay.

A reader who needs to have access to something in the essay can use simple memory aids. A reader can go back and scan, for one thing, to find passages or examples that might be worth reconsidering. Or a reader can construct a personal index, making marks in the margin or underlining passages that seem interesting or mysterious or difficult. A mark is a way of saying, "This is something I might want to work on later." If you mark the selections in this book as you read them, you will give yourself a working record of what, at the first moment of reading, you felt might be worth a second reading.

If Percy's essay presents problems for a reader, they are problems of a different order from summary and recall. The essay is not the sort that tells you what it says. You would have difficulty finding one sentence that sums up or announces, in a loud and clear voice, what Percy is talking about. At the point you think Percy is about to summarize, he turns to one more example that complicates the picture, as though what he is discussing defies his attempts to sum things up. Percy is talking about tourists and students, about such things as individual "sovereignty" and our media culture's "symbolic packages," but if he has a point to make, it cannot be stated in a sentence or two.

In fact, Percy's essay is challenging reading in part because it does not have a single, easily identifiable main idea. A reader could infer that it has several points to make, none of which can be said easily and some of which, perhaps, are contradictory. To search for information, or to ignore the rough edges in search of a single, paraphrasable idea, is to divert attention from the task at hand, which is not to remember what Percy says but to speak about the essay and what it means to you, the reader. In this sense, the Percy essay is not the sum of its individual parts; it is, more accurately, what its readers make of it.

A reader could go to an expert on Percy to solve the problem of what to make of the essay — perhaps to a teacher, perhaps to a book in the library. And if the reader pays attention, he could remember what the expert said or she could put down notes on paper. But in doing either, the reader only rehearses what he or she has been told, abandoning the responsibility to make the essay meaningful. There are ways of reading, in other words, in which Percy's essay "The Loss of the Creature" is not what it means to the experts but what it means to you as a reader willing to take the chance to construct a reading. You can be the authority on Percy; you don't have to turn to others. The meaning of the essay, then, is something you develop as you go along, something for which you must take final responsibility. The meaning is forged from reading the essay, to be sure, but it is determined by what you do with the essay, by the connections you can make and your explanation of why those connections are important, and by your account of what Percy might mean when he talks about "symbolic packages" or a "loss of sovereignty" (phrases Percy uses as key terms in the essay). This version of Percy's essay will finally be yours; it will not be exactly what Percy said. (Only his words in the order he wrote them would say exactly what he said.) You will choose the path to take through his essay and support it as you can with arguments, explanations, examples, and commentary.

If an essay or story is not the sum of its parts but something you as a reader create by putting together those parts that seem to matter personally, then the way to begin, once you have read a selection in this collection, is by reviewing what you recall, by going back to those places that stick in your memory — or, perhaps, to those sections you marked with checks or notes in the margins. You begin by seeing what you can make of these memories and notes. You should realize that with essays as long and complex as those we've included in this book, you will never feel, after a single reading, as though you have command of everything you read. This is not a problem. After four or five readings (should you give any single essay that much attention), you may still feel that there are parts you missed or don't understand. This sense of incompleteness is part of the experience of reading, at least the experience of reading serious work. And it is part of the experience of a strong reader. No reader could retain one of these essays in her mind, no matter how proficient her memory or how experienced she might be. No reader, at least no reader we would trust, would admit that he understood everything that Michel Foucault or Adrienne Rich or Ralph Waldo Emerson had to say. What strong readers know is that they have to begin, and they have to begin regardless of their doubts or hesitations. What you have after your first reading of an essay is a starting place, and you begin with your marked passages or examples or notes, with questions to answer, or with problems to solve. Strong readings, in other words, put a premium on individual acts of attention and composition.

STRONG READERS, STRONG TEXTS

We chose pieces for [*Ways of Reading*] that invite strong readings. Our selections require more attention (or a different form of attention) than a written summary, a reduction to gist, or a recitation of main ideas. They are not "easy" reading. The challenges they present, however, do not make them inaccessible to college students. The essays are not specialized studies; they have interested, pleased, or piqued general and specialist audiences alike. To say that they are challenging is to say, then, that they leave some work for a reader to do. They are designed to teach a reader new ways to read (or to step outside habitual ways of reading), and they anticipate readers willing to take the time to learn. These readers need not be experts on the subject matter. Perhaps the most difficult problem for students is to believe that this is true.

You do not need experts to explain these stories and essays, although you could probably go to the library and find an expert guide to most of the selections we've included. Let's take, for example, Adrienne Rich's "When We Dead Awaken: Writing as Re-Vision." This essay looks at the history of women's writing (and at Rich's development as a poet). It argues that women have been trapped within a patriarchal culture — speaking in men's voices and telling stories prepared by men — and, as a consequence, according to Rich, "We need to know the writing of the past, and know it differently than we have ever known it; not to pass on a tradition but to break its hold over us."

You could go to the library to find out how Rich is regarded by experts, by literary critics or feminist scholars, for example; you could learn how her work fits into an established body of work on women's writing and the representation of women in modern culture. You could see what others have said about the writers she cites: Virginia Woolf, Jane Austen, and Elizabeth Bishop. You could see how others have read and made use of Rich's essay. You could see how others have interpreted the poems she includes as part of her argument. You could look for standard definitions of key terms like "patriarchy" or "formalism."

Though it is often important to seek out other texts and to know what other people are saying or have said, it is often necessary and even desirable to begin on your own. Rich can also be read outside any official system of interpretation. She is talking, after all, about our daily experience. And when she addresses the reader, she addresses a person — not a term-paper writer. When she says, "We need to know the writing of the past, and know it differently than we have ever known it," she means us and what we know and how we know what we know. (Actually the "we" of her essay refers most accurately to women readers, leading men to feel the kind of exclusion women must feel when the reader is always "he." But it is us, the men who are in the act of reading this essay, who feel and respond to this pressure.)

The question, then, is not what Rich's words might mean to a literary critic, or generally to those who study contemporary American culture. The question is what you, the reader, can make of those words given your own experience, your goals, and the work you do with what she has written. In this sense, "When We Dead Awaken" is not what it means to others (those who have already decided what it means) but what it means to you, and this meaning is something you compose when you write about the essay; it is your account of what Rich says and how what she says might be said to make sense.

A teacher, poet, and critic we admire, I. A. Richards, once said, "Read as though it made sense and perhaps it will." To take command of complex material like the selections in [*Ways of Reading*], you need not subordinate yourself to experts; you can assume the authority to provide such a reading on your own. This means you must allow yourself a certain tentativeness and recognize your limits. You should not assume that it is your job to solve the problems between men and women. You can speak with authority while still acknowledging that complex issues *are* complex.

There is a paradox here. On the one hand, the essays are rich, magnificent, too big for anyone to completely grasp all at once, and before them, as before inspiring spectacles, it seems appropriate to stand humbly, admiringly. And yet, on the other hand, a reader must speak with authority.

In "The American Scholar," Ralph Waldo Emerson says, "Meek young men grow up in libraries, believing it their duty to accept the views, which Cicero, which Locke, which Bacon, have given, forgetful that Cicero, Locke, and Bacon were only young men in libraries when they wrote these books." What Emerson offers here is not a fact but an attitude. There is creative reading, he says, as well as creative writing. It is up to you to treat authors as your equals, as people who will allow you to speak too. At the same time, you must respect the difficulty and complexity of their texts and of the issues and questions they examine. Little is to be gained, in other words, by turning Rich's essay into a message that would fit on a poster in a dorm room: "Be Yourself" or "Stand on Your Own Two Feet."

READING WITH AND AGAINST THE GRAIN

Reading, then, requires a difficult mix of authority and humility. On the one hand, a reader takes charge of a text; on the other, a reader gives generous attention to someone else's (a writer's) key terms and methods, commits his time to her examples, tries to think in her language, imagines that this strange work is important, compelling, at least for the moment.

Most of the questions in *Ways of Reading* will have you moving back and forth in these two modes, reading with and against the grain of a text, reproducing an author's methods, questioning his or her direction and authority. With the essay "When We Dead Awaken," for example, we have asked students to give a more complete and detailed reading of Rich's poems (the poems included in the essay) than she does, to put her terms to work, to extend her essay by extending the discussion of her examples. We have asked students to give themselves over to her essay — recognizing that this is not necessarily an easy thing to do. Or, again in Rich's name, we have asked students to tell a story of their own experience, a story similar to the one she tells, one that can be used as an example of the ways a person is positioned by a dominant culture. Here we are saying, in effect, read your world in Rich's terms. Notice what she would notice. Ask the questions she would ask. Try out her conclusions.

To read generously, to work inside someone else's system, to see your world in someone else's terms — we call this "reading with the grain." It is a way of working *with* a writer's ideas, in conjunction with someone else's text. As a way of reading, it can take different forms. In the reading and writing assignments that follow the selections in this book, you will sometimes be asked to summarize and paraphrase, to put others' ideas into your terms, to provide your account of what they are saying. This is a way of getting a tentative or provisional hold on a text, its examples and ideas; it allows you a place to begin to work. And sometimes you will be asked to extend a writer's project — to add your examples to someone else's argument, to read your experience through the frame of another's text, to try out the key terms and interpretive schemes in another writer's work. In the assignments that follow the Rich essay, for example, students are asked both to reproduce her argument and to extend her terms to examples from their own experience.

We have also asked students to read against the grain, to read critically, to turn back, for example, *against* Rich's project, to ask questions they believe might come as a surprise, to look for the limits of her vision, to provide alternate readings of her examples, to find examples that challenge her argument, to engage her, in other words, in dialogue. How might her poems be read to counter what she wants to say about them? If her essay argues for a new language for women, how is this language represented in the final poem or the final paragraphs, when the poem seems unreadable and the final paragraph sounds familiarly like the usual political rhetoric? If Rich is arguing for a collective movement, a "we" represented by the "we" of her essay, who is included and who excluded by the terms and strategies of her writing? To what degree might you say that this is a conscious or necessary strategy?

Many of the essays in [*Ways of Reading*] provide examples of writers working against the grain of common sense or everyday language. This is true of John Berger, for example, who redefines the "art museum" against the way it is usually understood. It is true of John Edgar Wideman, who reads against his own text while he writes it — asking questions that disturb the story as it emerges on the page. It is true of Harriet Jacobs, Paul Auster, and Virginia Woolf, whose writings show the signs of their efforts to work against the grain of the standard essay, habitual ways of representing what it means to know something, to be somebody, to speak before others.

This, we've found, is the most difficult work for students to do, this work against the grain. For good reasons and bad, students typically define their skill by reproducing rather than questioning or revising the work of their teachers (or the work of those their teachers ask them to read). It is important to read generously and carefully and to learn to submit to projects that others have begun. But it is also important to know what you are doing — to understand where this work comes from, whose interests it serves, how and where it is kept together by will rather than desire, and what it might have to do with you. To fail to ask the fundamental questions — Where am I in this? How can I make my mark? Whose interests are represented? What can I learn by reading with or against the grain? — to fail to ask these questions is to mistake skill for understanding, and it is to misunderstand the goals of a liberal education. All of the essays in this book, we would argue, ask to be read, not simply reproduced; they ask to be read and to be read with a difference. Our goal is to make that difference possible.

READING AND WRITING: THE QUESTIONS AND ASSIGNMENTS

Strong readers, we've said, remake what they have read to serve their own ends, putting things together, figuring out how ideas and examples relate, explaining as best they can material that is difficult or problematic, translating phrases like Richard Rodriguez's "scholarship boy" into their own terms. At these moments, it is hard to distinguish the act of reading from the act of writing. In fact, the connection between reading and writing can be seen as almost a literal one, since the best way you can show your reading of a rich and dense essay like "The Achievement of Desire" is by writing down your thoughts, placing one idea against another, commenting on what you've done, taking examples into account, looking back at where you began, perhaps changing your mind, and moving on.

Readers, however, seldom read a single essay in isolation, as though their only job were to arrive at some sense of what an essay has to say. Although we couldn't begin to provide examples of all the various uses of reading in academic life, it is often the case that readings provide information and direction for investigative projects, whether they are philosophical or scientific in nature. The reading and writing assignments that follow each selection in this book are designed to point you in certain directions, to give you ideas and projects to work with, and to challenge you to see one writer's ideas through another's.

Strong readers often read critically, weighing, for example, an author's claims and interpretations against evidence — evidence provided by the author in the text, evidence drawn from other sources, or the evidence that is assumed to be part of a reader's own knowledge and experience. Critical reading can produce results as far-reaching as a biochemist publicly challenging the findings and interpretations in an article on cancer research in the *New England Journal of Medicine* or as quiet as a student offering a personal interpretation of a story in class discussion.

You will find that the questions we have included in our reading and writing assignments often direct you to test what you think an author is saying by measuring it against your own experience. Paulo Freire, for example, in "The 'Banking' Concept of Education" talks about the experience of the student, and one way for you to develop or test your reading of his essay is to place what he says in the context of your own experience, searching for examples that are similar to his and examples that differ from his. If the writers in this book are urging you to give strong readings of your common experience, you have access to what they say because they are talking not only to you but about you. Freire has a method that he employs when he talks about the classroom — one that compares "banking" education with "problem-posing" education. You can try out his method and his terms on examples of your own, continuing his argument as though you were working with him on a common project. Or you can test his argument as though you want to see not only where and how it will work but where and how it will not.

You will also find questions that ask you to extend the argument of the essay by looking in detail at some of the essay's own examples. John Berger, for example, gives a detailed analysis of two paintings by Frans Hals in "Ways of Seeing." Other paintings in the essay he refers to only briefly. One way of working on his essay is to look at the other examples, trying to do with them what he has done for you earlier.

Readers, as we have said, seldom read an essay in isolation, as though, having once worked out a reading of Virginia Woolf's "A Room of One's Own," they could go on to something else, something unrelated. It is unusual for anyone, at least in an academic setting, to read in so random a fashion. Readers read most often because they have a project in hand — a question they are working on or a problem they are trying to solve. For example, if as a result of reading Woolf's essay you become interested in the difference between women's writing and men's writing, and you begin to notice things you would not have noticed before, then you can read other essays in the book through this frame. If you have a project in mind, that project will help determine how you read these other essays. Sections of an essay that might otherwise seem unimportant suddenly become important — Gloria Anzaldúa's unusual prose style, Rich's references to Woolf, the moments when Harriet Jacobs addresses the "women of the North." Woolf may enable you to read Jacobs's narrative differently. Jacobs may spur you to rethink Woolf.

In a sense, then, you do have the chance to become an expert reader, a reader with a project in hand, one who has already done some reading, who has watched others at work, and who has begun to develop a method of analysis and a set of key terms. You might read Jacobs's narrative "Incidents in the Life of a Slave Girl," for example, in the context of Mary Louise Pratt's discussion of "autoethnography," or you might read the selections by Gloria Anzaldúa, W. E. B. Du Bois, Ralph Ellison, and John Edgar Wideman as offering differing accounts of racism in America. Imagining yourself operating alongside some of the major figures in contemporary thought can be great fun and heady work — particularly when you have the occasion to speak back to them.

In every case, then, the material we provide to direct your work on the essay, story, or poem will have you constructing a reading, but then doing something with what you have read — using the selection as a frame through which you can understand (through which you can "read") your own experience, the examples of others, or the ideas and methods of other writers.

You may find that you have to alter your sense of who a writer is and what a writer does as you work on your own writing. Writers are often told that they need to begin with a clear sense of what they want to do and what they want to say. The writing assignments we've written, we believe, give you a sense of what you want (or need) to do. We define a problem for you to work on, and the problem will frame the task for you. You will have to decide where you will go in the texts you have read to find materials to work with, the primary materials that will give you a place to begin as you work on your essay. It would be best, however, if you did not feel that you need to have a clear sense of what you want to say before you begin. You may begin to develop a sense of what you want to say while you are writing — as you begin, for example, to examine how and why Anzaldúa's prose could be said to be difficult to read, and what that difficulty might enable you to say about what Anzaldúa expects of a reader. It may also be the case, however, that the subjects you will be writing about are too big for you to assume that you need to have all the answers or that it is up to you to have the final word or to solve the problems once and for all. When you work on your essays, you should cast yourself in the role of one who is exploring a question, examining what might be said, and speculating on possible rather than certain conclusions. If you consider your responses to be provisional, examples of what might be said by a bright and serious student at this point in time, you will be in a position to learn more, as will those who read what you write. Think of yourself, then, as a writer intent on opening a subject up rather than closing one down.

Let us turn briefly now to the three categories of reading and writing assignments you will find in [*Ways of Reading*].

QUESTIONS FOR A SECOND READING

Immediately following each selection are questions designed to guide your second reading. You may, as we've said, prefer to follow your own instincts as you search for the materials to build your understanding of the essay or story. These questions are meant to assist that process or develop those instincts. Most of the essays and stories . . . are longer and more difficult than those you may be accustomed to reading. They are difficult enough that any reader would have to reread them and work to understand them; these questions are meant to suggest ways of beginning that work.

The second reading questions characteristically ask you to consider the relations between ideas and examples in what you have read or to test specific statements in the essays against your own experience (so that you can get a sense of the author's habit of mind, his or her way of thinking about subjects that are available to you, too). Some turn your attention to what we take to be key terms or concepts, asking you to define these terms by observing how the writer uses them throughout the essay.

These are the questions that seemed "natural" to us; they reflect our habitual way of reading and, we believe, the general habits of mind of the academic community. These questions have no simple answers; you will not find a correct answer hidden somewhere in the selection. In short, they are not the sorts of questions asked on SAT or ACT exams. They are real questions, questions that ask about the basic methods of an essay or about the issues the essay raises. They pose problems for interpretation or indicate sections where, to our minds, there is some interesting work for a reader to do. They are meant to reveal possible ways of reading the text, not to indicate that there is only one correct way, and that we have it.

You may find it useful to take notes as you read through each selection a second time, perhaps in a journal you can keep as a sourcebook for more formal written work.

ASSIGNMENTS FOR WRITING

[*Ways of Reading*] actually offers three different kinds of writing assignments: assignments that ask you to write about a single essay or story, assignments that ask you to read one selection through the frame of another, and longer sequences of assignments that define a project within which three or four of the selections serve as primary sources. All of these assignments serve a dual purpose. Like the second reading questions, they suggest a way for you to reconsider the stories or essays; they give you access from a different perspective. The assignments also encourage you to be a strong reader and actively interpret what you have read. In one way or another, they all invite you to use a story or an essay as a way of framing experience, as a source of terms and methods to enable you to interpret something else — some other text, events and objects around you, or your own memories and experience. . . .

"Assignments for Writing" ask you to write about a single selection. Although some of these assignments call for you to paraphrase or reconstruct difficult passages, most ask you to interpret what you have read with a specific purpose in mind. The work you are to do is generally of two sorts. For most of the essays, one question asks you to interpret a moment from your own experience through the frame of the essay. This, you will remember, is the use that Rodriguez made of Richard Hoggart's *The Uses of Literacy*.

Other assignments, however, ask you to turn an essay back on itself or to extend the conclusions of the essay by reconsidering the examples the writer has used to make his or her case. Adrienne Rich's essay "When We Dead Awaken: Writing as Re-Vision" is built around a series of poems she wrote at various stages in her career. She says that the development represented by these poems reflects her growing understanding of the problems women in a patriarchal society have in finding a language for their own experience. She presents the poems as examples but offers little detailed discussion of them. One of the assignments, then, asks you to describe the key differences in these poems. It next asks you to comment on the development of her work and to compare your account of that development with hers.

In her essay, Rich also says that writing is "renaming." This is an interesting and, one senses, a potentially powerful term. For it to be useful, however, a reader must put it to work, to see what results when you accept the challenge of the essay and think about writing as renaming. Another assignment, then, asks you to apply this term to one of her poems and to discuss the poem as an act of renaming. The purpose of this assignment is not primarily to develop your skill as a reader of poems but to develop your sense of the method and key terms of Rich's argument.

A note on the writing assignments: When we talk with teachers and students using *Ways of Reading,* we are often asked about the wording of these assignments. The assignments are long. The wording is often unusual, unexpected. The assignments contain many questions, not simply one. The directions seem indirect, confusing. "Why?" we're asked. "How should we work with these?" When we write assignments, our goal is to point students toward a project, to provide a frame for their reading, a motive for writing, a way of asking certain kinds of questions. In that sense, the assignments should not be read as a set of directions to be followed literally. In fact, they are written to resist that reading, to forestall a writer's desire to simplify, to be efficient, to settle for the first clear line toward the finish. We want to provide a context to suggest how readers and writers might take time, be thoughtful. And we want the projects students work on to become their own. We hope to provoke varied responses, to leave the final decisions to the students. So the assignments try to be open and suggestive rather than narrow and direct. We ask lots of questions, but students don't need to answer them all (or any of them) once they begin to write. Our questions are meant to suggest ways of questioning, starting points. "What do you want?" Our own students ask this question. We want writers to make the most they can of what they read, including our questions and assignments.

MAKING CONNECTIONS

The connections questions will have you work with two or more readings at a time. These are not so much questions that ask you to compare or contrast the essays or stories as they are directions on how you might use one text as the context for interpreting another. Mary Louise Pratt, for example, in "Arts of the Contact Zone" looks at the work of a South American native, an Inca named Guaman Poma, writing in the seventeenth century to King Philip III of Spain. His work, she argues, can be read as a moment of contact, one in which different cultures and positions of power come together in a single text — in which a conquered person responds to the ways he is represented in the mind and the language of the conqueror. Pratt's reading of Guaman Poma's letter to King Philip, and the terms she uses to describe the way she reads it, provides a powerful context for a reader looking at essays by other writers, like Harriet Jacobs or Gloria Anzaldúa, for whom the "normal" or "standard" language of American culture is difficult, troubling, unsatisfactory, or incomplete. There are, then, assignments that ask you both to extend and to test Pratt's reading through your reading of alternative texts. In another assignment, you are asked to consider different ways of writing "history," writing about the past, by looking at the work of two very different writers: John Edgar Wideman, a fiction writer who turns his hand to "real life" when he writes about his brother and his family, and Patricia Nelson Limerick, a professional historian who writes not only about the American West but also about the writing of the American West, about how the American West has been written into popular culture and the popular imagination.

The purpose of all these assignments is to demonstrate how the work of one author can be used as a frame for reading and interpreting the work of another. This can be exciting work, and it demonstrates a basic principle of liberal arts education: students should be given the opportunity to adopt different points of view, including those of scholars and writers who have helped to shape modern thought. These kinds of assignments give you the chance, even as a novice, to try your hand at the work of professionals.

THE ASSIGNMENT SEQUENCES

The assignment sequences are more broad-ranging versions of the making connections assignments; in the sequences, several reading and writing assignments are linked and directed toward a single goal. They allow you to work on projects that require more time and incorporate more readings than would be possible in a single assignment. And they encourage you to develop your own point of view in concert with those of the professionals who wrote the essays and stories you are reading.

The assignments in a sequence build on one another, each relying on the ones before. A sequence will usually make use of three or four reading selections. The first is used to introduce an area of study or inquiry as well as to establish a frame of reference, a way of thinking about the subject. In the sequence titled "The Aims of Education," you begin with an essay by Paulo Freire. Freire, a Marxist educator, takes a standard account of education (in which students are said to be "given" knowledge by a teacher) and, as he says, "problematizes" that account, opens it up to question, by arguing that such classrooms only reproduce the powerlessness students will face in the larger society. The goal of the sequence is to provide a point for you to work from, one that you can open up to question. Subsequent assignments ask you to develop examples from your own schooling as you work through other accounts of education in, for example, Adrienne Rich's "When We Dead Awaken," Mary Louise Pratt's "Arts of the Contact Zone," or Susan Griffin's "Our Secret."

The sequences allow you to participate in an extended academic project, one in which you take a position, revise it, look at a new example, hear what someone else has to say, revise it again, and see what conclusions you can draw about your subject. These projects always take time — they go through stages and revisions as a writer develops a command over his or her material, pushing against habitual ways of thinking, learning to examine an issue from different angles, rejecting quick conclusions, seeing the power of understanding that comes from repeated effort, and feeling the pleasure writers take when they find their own place in the context of others whose work they admire. This is the closest approximation we can give you of the rhythm and texture of academic life, and we offer [*Ways of Reading*] as an introduction to its characteristic ways of reading, thinking, and writing.

Postscript: Teaching Composition

In 2000, my dear friend and colleague Mariolina Salvatori was appointed a Carnegie Scholar as part of a Carnegie Foundation initiative in support of "the scholarship of teaching and learning." Mariolina has written extensively on pedagogy, past and present, and from her work with the Carnegie program crafted her own working definition of the "scholarship of teaching." Frustrated by anecdotal accounts of the classroom (and the authority they have traditionally carried) and concerned about the limits of classroom observation (for example), she argues in a recent edition of the journal *Pedagogy* that the scholarship of teaching must be held to the same standards as other forms of scholarship in the field, that it must reconfigure teaching from an "amateur" to an "expert" activity, and, finally, that

> It needs to present teaching as intellectual work — work that can be theorized, work whose parameters and conditions of possibility can be analyzed as well as evaluated in accordance with formally articulated standards, work that is interpretable within a framework of disciplinary knowledge and modes of inquiry. (304)

The essays I've gathered in Part Two represent what I might offer as my evolving sense of the "scholarship of teaching," from early accounts of our program and my courses, to more generalized engagement with the teaching practices of the field (like "sentence-combining"), to broader national and commercial pedagogical projects, like the Great Books program or public literacy initiatives.

I came to the latter through the MLA Literacy Conferences; I attended the first and chaired the second (in 1990). I also had a distant involvement with another, very different conference, "The Linguistics of Writing," chaired by my colleague Colin MacCabe (with whom I once team-taught a memorable section of freshman English). I didn't attend the conference, but I saw the film (if you can imagine such a thing), "Big Words, Small Worlds," directed by Ian Potts, written and presented by David Lodge, featuring Stanley Fish, Raymond Williams, and Jacques Derrida (among others), and with a brief commentary by Jean Luc Godard — if you haven't seen it, it is a hoot — and

I read the book version, *The Linguistics of Writing: Arguments between Language and Literature*. I felt at the time (and feel now) that this should have been a key text in composition in the United States. It has not been (and largely, I think, because we have been less willing to let language and literature scholars be in productive conversation), although an essay by Mary Louise Pratt, "Linguistic Utopias," has gotten a fair amount of play in composition circles, and I think this is due to her presence as the keynote speaker at the second MLA Literacy Conference and the publication of that address, "Arts of the Contact Zone," in *Profession 91* and then in *Ways of Reading*.

I have also included one of two interviews I chose for this book. The interview tells a story I've told many times. It is a story common to people of my generation. I had almost completed my PhD before I ever taught a course and ever had the chance to contemplate what it might mean to have a career in English. I had no preparation for this course, other than the standard notion that I should teach something I was interested in — which I did and to a group of first-year students who had no way of understanding how or why they should be engaged with my interests, who were as unprepared as I was for what we were assigned to do together. The problem of that moment has driven all of my teaching. How do we promote and value productive engagement with the texts we value? And how do we do this for first-year students, students who are inevitably and necessarily unprepared as readers and writers? Both *Facts, Artifacts, and Counterfacts* and *Ways of Reading* address these questions, the first for students identified as "basic writers" and the second for a more general audience. (I should quickly add that *Ways* has been successfully used in basic writing programs at community colleges.)

It was my idea (and not Bedford/St. Martins's) to include a section from *Ways of Reading*. I think of the textbook as part of my scholarly and professional work. As anyone who works in this genre knows, writing seriously for a student audience presents extremely interesting and difficult writing problems. Still, as I say at the end of Part One, it is a very rare and special reader who reads not only the scholarship but also the textbook. I wanted this volume to insist on a connection that has been present to me at every moment.

As I say in the Preface, this part, "Teaching Composition," gathers essays that speak to the teaching of writing, not simply my teaching but also "our" teaching (if such a unity can be imagined) as seen from a variety of vantage points and perspectives. We don't wake up one day, as Stanley Fish says of literary criticism, and invent the teaching of writing or the teaching of composition. We work within the sway of all that precedes us and informs our practice. I. A. Richards, Mortimer Adler, Reuben Brower, Richard Poirier — these names reference traditions of teaching that I find strangely absent from most accounts of the history of composition and important both for what they tried to do and how their teaching might inform the present.

"Teaching Composition" begins with accounts of my own teaching (and learning) and it ends with the introduction to the textbook *Ways of Reading*. It seems appropriate to conclude with a reference to the teaching I am doing now. Below, I include the course description I wrote for my composition students in the Fall 2003 term. These were students in freshman composition (once called General Writing at the University of Pittsburgh, now called Seminar in Composition).

WORK CITED

Salvatori, Mariolina Rizzi. "The Scholarship of Teaching: Beyond the Anecdotal." *Pedagogy: Critical Approaches to Teaching Literature, Composition, and Culture.* 2.3 (2002): 297–310.

A COURSE DESCRIPTION

Introduction. The subject of this course is writing. Writing, as I think of it, is an action, an event, a performance, a way of asserting one's presence. It is a way of asserting one's presence but, paradoxically, in a language that makes the writer disappear. (No matter what you write, the writing is not yours; it is part of a larger text, one with many authors, begun long ago.) And its end is outside your control. In spite of what you think you are saying, your text will become what others make of it, what they say you said.

One of my goals in this course is to arrange your work to highlight your relationship (as a writer) to the past and to the words of others (to history, literature, and culture). This is the reason for the assigned readings, and this is the primary role reading will play in this writing course. You will be asked to read a series of assigned texts and to write in response to what you have read. I want to foreground the ways in which your writing takes place in relation to the writing of others. My goal, as your teacher, will be to make that relationship interesting, surprising, and productive. These meetings between the past and the present, writing and a writer, those places in your essays where you work with someone else's words and ideas represent, to my mind, the basic scene of instruction; they are the workplaces, the laboratories, the arenas of what is often called a "liberal" education.

The Course. I have asked you to think of a writing course as the representative workplace of a liberal arts education. You might also think of our course as a studio course, like a course in painting or sculpture or musical composition. You will be practicing your art by working on specific projects. I will be looking over your shoulder, monitoring your progress, and, at various points in the semester, assessing work you gather together in a portfolio.

In this sense, the course is a course where you practice writing. You can expect to write regularly, at least one draft or essay each week. You will need to develop the habits and the discipline of a writer. You will need a regular schedule, a regular place and time for writing. There is nothing fancy about this. You need to learn to organize your time so that there is time for writing, so that it becomes part of a routine.

You'll need to learn to work quickly but also to keep your attention inside sentences for hours at a time. This requires discipline, a kind of physical training I can best describe as athletic. Writers need to be able to sit in one place and to think inside of sentences for long periods of time. While you will have to set your own goals, I would suggest setting aside six hours a week in three two-hour sittings. These are writing times, periods when you are sitting in one place and working closely with words, yours and others'. You should do nothing else during these sessions. You should work in the same place at the same time every week.

I can insist on this kind of care and attention, but I can't teach it. I can, however, teach you ways of working on your writing. I have come to believe that the most important skill I can teach in a writing course is reading — the ability to read your own writing closely and to make critical judgments about the quality of your prose. In this sense, the composition course is like most other courses in the English department. It teaches close reading and critical understanding. There are also important differences, however. In a literature course, a course on Shakespeare, say, or the Victorian novel, even though you may have papers to write, your primary focus is on Shakespeare's language or the language of Victorian fiction. You work to better understand what these writers are doing in their writing, and the value of their writing is pretty much taken for granted. In a writing class, it is your work that is the center of critical attention, not Shakespeare's or Thomas Hardy's, and the question of value is front and center. A writing course is a course in practical criticism, and the pressing questions are directed to your prose — to what you are doing, to where the writing is going, to what it is worth.

Revision/Practical Criticism.   You will be evaluated in this course on the quality of your work as a writer. The evidence that you have learned to read closely and critically will be present in your writing — and particularly in revisions. There is more to writing, in other words, than first thoughts, first drafts, and first pages. A writer learns most by returning to his or her work to see what it does and doesn't do, by taking time with a project and seeing where it might lead. To that end, this course will be organized so that you will work a single essay through several drafts; each essay will be a part of a larger project. When I assess your writing I will be looking primarily at the progress from draft to draft.

The Required Reading.   Each semester I choose three or four books to serve as the center of the course. All of them are interesting in their own right, all of them are currently commanding the attention of serious readers, and all of them could be said to offer a lesson in writing. I tend to choose books that I would like to read slowly and carefully and in the company of smart and interesting undergraduates.

This semester the assigned readings are: *The Simple Truth*, Philip Levine; *A Thrice Told Tale*, Margery Wolf; *Houdini's Box*, Adam Phillips; and *Mao II*, Don DeLillo. They are all in the bookstore. I require a Handbook. I have ordered copies of *A Pocket Style Manual*, Diana Hacker. If you have a different Handbook, check it out with me. It is probably fine.

The books I have chosen are all about writing. They are, of course, acts of writing and as enacted arguments there is much we can learn from them. But they also take writing as their subject. I would like you to think of them as textbooks, as books with lessons for writers.

As I choose books for the course, I am deliberately looking for books that are difficult, books that you are *not* prepared to read (at least as I imagine your preparation as readers). I want you to learn how to work with difficult materials (something not comfortably or quickly read or understood), and I want you to see how writing assists that work. I choose works in different genres: poetry, nonfiction, fiction. I want to use the course to raise questions about the category of "literature," about its uses (and the uses of writing more generally) in contemporary intellectual projects, and about the relationship between a nation's literary culture and the training of writers in the nation's schools.

Routines.   I have planned for 14 weeks and divided the semester into three units, each ending with a portfolio review.

You should plan to read each book at least *twice*; the first reading should be completed before we begin to discuss the material in class. The first time through you should read quickly, to get a general sense of what the writer is doing, what the piece is about. Then you should read through a second time, this time working more closely and deliberately with the text, particularly with those sections that seem difficult or puzzling or mysterious. You should read with a pen or pencil, marking the text in a way that will help you when you go back to it (particularly when you go back to it as a writer). If you can't bring yourself to write in your book, you should begin to develop a system using note cards or Post-it notes.

Each week you will write one essay and/or revise one essay, both as stages in a larger project. Each week you should prepare two copies of everything you have written, one for me and one for another reader. One copy of *everything* you write for this course must be gathered together in your portfolio. Keep the second copies in a separate, backup folder. To monitor your progress, I will review your portfolios at three points in the term — around the fifth week, the tenth, and at the end of the term. Your final grade will be based on my final reading of the portfolio. It will be an assessment of your work in the course over the term. I will be particularly interested in the development I see in revision and across the portfolio. I will be looking for evidence of your involvement with the course and of your willingness and your success in working on your writing. I will *not* add together and average the grades from the earlier reviews.

I will also read individual essays carefully each week and write comments on them. I will not grade individual papers; I edit them. I write comments to suggest problems, changes, new directions, ideas I have if you plan to revise. My comments offer a writing lesson. I expect you to read them as such. If you don't, you are missing part of the course. (And if you want to write back to my comments, you can.)

I spend a lot of time on these comments, and I will expect you to take time to read what I have written. If you find that I have written much on your paper, you should take this as a sign of love, not of desperation. It means I was interested, engaged. I know that my handwriting can be a problem. I will not be embarrassed if you ask me to decipher what I have written. I will, however, be heartbroken if you simply skip over what is hard to read.

The best way to read my comments is to start at the beginning of your essay, reread what you have written, and stop to read my comments along the way. This is how I write the marginal comments, while I am reading. They show my reactions/suggestions at that moment. The final comment is where I will make a summary statement about your essay. Be warned: I tend to be blunt and to the point. If I sound angry, I probably am not. I want to get your attention, I want to be honest, and I see no reason to beat around the bush.

If your work seems thoughtless or quickly done, I will notice. I have taught writing for many years, and I know when writers are working hard and when they are fooling around. I will tell you if I think you are fooling around.

I will not put grades on individual essays. I will grade your performance over 14 weeks, but I see no reason to grade each and every piece you write. In many cases, I will be asking you to extend yourself and to do what you cannot do easily or with grace. It would make no sense for me to grade everything you do. (Please see the separate handout on Error and Plagiarism. I will expect you to consistently and successfully proofread all papers, including first drafts.) I will be available to answer questions or to look at an essay immediately before and after class.

Class Participation. I will regularly reproduce your papers (with names removed) and use them for class discussion. Much of our class time will be spent discussing copies of your essays. This is as important to your education as the time you spend alone working on your writing. As I think of class discussion, it is work. The goal is for individuals to pool their resources, to question each other, to look carefully at a text and, as a result, to reach a point where they can say things (or do things with a text) they could not say (or do) on their own.

Our discussions will be focused on a particular problem or line of inquiry. They are not simply a chance to chat or to say whatever is on your mind. I see it as my job to direct the discussion, to ensure that it is productive and reasonably efficient. If I seem pushy at times, it is because I am doing my job as a professor. I will try to keep an eye out for quiet spots in the room, but participation is a matter of attention and initiative. If you feel that others are dominating the conversation, it is up to you to break in.

I expect you to attend all classes. If you are absent, you are not taking the course, and I will ask you to drop or give you a failing grade. If you must be absent, please let me know in advance or immediately after. If for reasons of medical or family difficulties you miss more than two classes, I will most likely advise you to seek a special withdrawal from the Dean's office. Similarly, all written work must be completed on schedule. Because you will be writing every week, and because one week's work will lead to the next assignment, you cannot afford to fall behind. I will not accept work that is late. If you are not doing the writing, you are not taking the course, and I will ask you to drop or give you a failing grade.

Writing Groups. I will form you into groups of two or three. Few writers work alone; they rely on friends and colleagues to listen to ideas, to read drafts, and to help with copyediting. You will be responsible for commenting on your partner's essay and draft each week.

End of Term. I will not return the final folders. And I will not put comments on the work in the final folders. You will have heard plenty from me throughout the semester, and the end of a semester is a busy and distracting time for all of us. This does not mean, however, that I am not interested in talking with you about your work. If you would like to review the folder or individual essays, come see me first thing at the beginning of the next semester. There is no final exam.

Materials. You will need a sturdy folder with pockets to hold your work and everything I hand out in class. You should have a dictionary at your desk. I do not advise a thesaurus. At this stage of the game, there are no such things as synonyms. As writers, you will need to struggle for the particular meanings of words.

PART THREE

The Profession

Freshman English, Composition, and CCCC

P ROLOGUE

When I was invited to run for office in CCCC, like all candidates I had to put together a short statement of principle or belief for the ballot — a kind of mini-stump speech where I would set out my sense of the organization and its mission. This was a hard piece to write — "what I believe" in 200 words — and particularly hard for me since (frankly) I thought no one ever read them, that when the ballots came in the mail, people looked at the pictures, read the c.v., and pitched the rest.

And so I was taken by the number of people who have since come up to speak to me about what I wrote. I said, in brief, that I felt a great debt to CCCC, that at an early point in my career, when I felt like I was looking in as an outsider on the vast and austere corridors of adult professional life, CCCC provided a sense of community that made me believe I could get started — that there was, in fact, work for me to do, that it was good work, and that I could do it in good company. My graduate program did not give me this sense of vocation. My department could provide only a portion. No other professional organization seemed so open.

I said in that document that I felt CCCC was the organization that made work in composition possible — and in saying that, I felt its truth in the context of my personal history. I did not mean — although I could have been saying — that CCCC had or should have the authority to order or authorize work in composition, that it should determine the canon, approve methods, say Yes to some and No to others, accredit programs, unify a field that was various and disparate. I meant that CCCC (and in particular the annual meeting) seemed to me to provide the terms and context that allowed people to get to work, and to work with energy and optimism, not cranking out just one more paper, not laddering their way up to the top, not searching for difficult texts and dull readers, not bowing and scraping before another famous book or another famous person, but doing work that one could believe in, where

From *College Composition and Communication,* 40.1 (1989): 38–50.

there was that rare combination of personal investment and social responsibility, where we felt like we could make things happen, not just in our own careers, but in the world.[1]

I can be more precise: I had just finished a dissertation on Thomas Hardy and I could not imagine writing another paper on Hardy or the Victorians or the subjects I had presumably mastered in graduate school. I had also established a basic writing program, and the writing of my students and the problematic relationship between their work and the work of the academy, these seemed to hold all of the material I needed to make a career. I felt that in the ways people talked to each other at meetings, and that in the ways they talked about their subjects — writing and teaching — there was clearly room being made for me to get started on that career.

I was surprised at the number of people who spoke to me about those words and who said, in effect, that in saying what I did I was speaking for them. This set me to thinking about history and about generations: the people who founded CCCC; the generation of men and women, many of them now retired or on the eve of retirement, who reshaped its language and agenda in embattled times, in the 60's and 70's; and my generation, like the organization, just now reaching middle age.

I have spent much of the last year reading over the documentary record of CCCC — articles, essays, speeches, papers, secretary's reports, accounts from the "roving reporter" who, for several years, was assigned to take notes and report to the membership on the annual convention. I found it a wonderful experience. The documents are rich and various. I have been "in" composition for some time, but I had little sense of its history, particularly the history represented by the people and issues that filled the rooms of our meetings and the pages of our journal. I wanted to account for CCCC as an agent, since I had experienced it so sharply as a force in my own career. What follows is a preliminary version of that account, where CCCC stands as an organized and organizing way of speaking and thinking, with both stated and unstated projects, including the necessary project of defining and protecting its claim to a subject, what we have variously called "required English," "freshman English," and "composition."

FRESHMAN ENGLISH

CCCC was born out of the need to have a certain kind of discussion that existing venues were not making possible (not NCTE, not MLA). In fact, 4C's could be said literally to begin in a conversation that would not fit into the 1948 annual meeting of NCTE.

In 1948, NCTE featured a series of sessions on "College Undergraduate Training" at its national convention in the Stevens Hotel in Chicago. One session, on "Three Views of Required English," was chaired by John Gerber (who was to become the first chair of CCCC) and during the session one of the speakers, George Wykoff (who would become the second chair of CCCC) set aside his prepared remarks (a description of his institution's freshman course) to speak about the usefulness and value of composition. Wilbur Hatfield referred to Wykoff's impromptu remarks as "a clarion call to the profession to alert itself to improving the climate for the teaching of freshman English."[2]

The story goes that the resulting discussion was so lively and contentious that the session went well over its allotted time and threatened to keep the participants from the annual banquet, where James Michener, who had just won the Pulitzer Prize for *Tales of the South Pacific,* was scheduled to speak. The group was hesitant to let the conversation end; they complained that they were not given adequate time and wouldn't be silenced until Gerber suggested that they continue the discussion at a special conference the following spring. A committee of seven petitioned the Executive Committee of NCTE to sponsor a special 2-day conference on freshman English.[3] The proposal was approved, and the next spring — in Chicago, in 1949 — 500 people met to talk and read papers at a conference on "College Freshman Courses in Composition and Communication."

This was the first meeting of CCCC, even though the organization had not yet been given a name or official status. At this meeting participants unanimously passed a resolution supporting the formation of a permanent organization devoted to freshman English. Gerber presented this request to NCTE — this time requesting a separate annual meeting, a separate governing body, and a journal. After much discussion, this request was approved by NCTE at its November meeting in Buffalo in 1949.

And so CCCC became part of the council, but also a semi-independent entity. Here is John Gerber commenting on the moment in "CCCC Facts — 1956":

> In true progressive fashion [CCCC] was told to do the things that would make it happy and well adjusted and not to do the things that would make it unhappy. Also, it was told that at the end of three years it might be annihilated if it had not been good. (117)

It turned out to be good enough, and at the end of its three-year trial period it was given a second three-year term; following that trial period, NCTE changed its constitution to make the conference a permanent entity. At this point CCCC established a procedure for elections and appointed a representative executive committee, drawing equally from universities, liberal arts colleges, teachers colleges, technical schools, and junior colleges. By 1950 it had a membership of 550, representing 48 states, Hawaii, and the District of Columbia.

This is the history, in brief. But it doesn't provide a satisfactory answer to the question "Why?" Why was it necessary to imagine freshman English as separate — as different enough from the other English, or the other Englishes represented in the curriculum, to require a separate professional organization?

For one thing, those responsible for freshman English felt the need to respond to two pressures, both of which threatened their interests. The first was, in John Gerber's terms, "the common enemy . . . the senior professor of literature" (*Loomings* 7). This figure is almost too familiar — this senior professor of literature. The terms we now commonly use to define college English would give prominence to the word "literature" in Gerber's statement. Against literature, that is, freshman English asserted itself as composition.

I think we need to read this differently, however. While it is true that the organization, with its need to name itself and its subject, displaced freshman "English" with freshman "composition and communication," there was much debate in the early meetings over whether composition or communication or something else altogether was the proper subject for CCCC. And the motive here was largely to make a place for a new set of interests, not merely to erase the old ones.

I think that the key word in Gerber's sentence is "senior" — the "*senior* professor of literature." The "common enemy," that is, was a version of English represented by an attenuated humanistic tradition that placed literature (a Norton-anthology-like unified body of texts) as an unquestionable center of value, and that placed the professor, who could demonstrate acceptable ways of using and responding to those texts, as the primary representative of English.

The other pressure was the pressure of numbers — the numbers of students, many of them GI's, swelling colleges and universities after the war, placing dramatic and unprecedented demands on introductory courses (courses they were said to be "unprepared to take") and requiring the creation of a new faculty to do a teaching for which their English PhD's had not prepared them. There were also, then, economic and culture forces poised to redefine English in post-secondary education.

Given these threats to the freshman course, and given the desire to do something with English and do something for students for whom the old English was an inadequate or inappropriate form of instruction, there was good cause to band together, pool information and resources, and (1) develop an agenda to give status and recognition to those teaching freshman English, (2) revise the graduate training of prospective teachers of English, and, most importantly, (3) work on developing this course, freshman English, a course without a proper subject or history — one whose name, freshman English, was an open term, indeterminate and, therefore, both inspiring and frightening.

In the documents that mark the first 15 years of CCCC, you hear this refrain over and over again: no one knows, on any given day on any given campus, what goes on in freshman English; it's there as a force on every campus, it carries a common name, but it refers to everything, anything — no one knows what it is. There was no way of speaking about reading and writing at the introductory level, where it was not yet shaped into English, no way to fix the discourse, to give the institution the feeling that it had this course in control. Everyone knew what went on in "The American Novel" or "18th Century British Literature," but this other English course was a black hole. And this was simultaneously CCCC's greatest problem — to give standards, unity, and definition to this course — and its greatest attraction, since it put its members in a position to make up English as they went along.

COMPOSITION

Having emptied English, the organization had to try to fill it again. In this gesture what came to be called "composition" participated in a project that has come to characterize modern English studies. The CCCC project paralleled developments in criticism — and in particular the New Criticism, whose beginning moment was similarly a rejection of the senior professors of literature. Criticism, as a new way of imagining how to do English, was similarly going to revive pedagogy and relocate English in the immediate experience students had with texts (that is, in the practice of reading).

This is the history I imagine, that since the 1940's there has been a continuing struggle to displace the old humanism — with its entrenched theories of knowledge, culture, and pedagogy — and to replace the English of the senior professors with a new English. The opposing term for composition, then, is not literature but a version of literary study threatened not only by composition but by other critical movements in the discipline: women's studies, black studies, film studies, gay studies, critical theory, culture study, studies of working-class language and literature, pedagogy. CCCC provided a site where English was open for negotiation (or renegotiation).

Let's look briefly at the two opening talks of the first CCCC convention. I don't mean to suggest that these two talks fully represent the issues occupying the organization. Nor do I want to suggest that these two figures shaped the organization and its concerns. I want to take this moment, one that was shaped and enabled by CCCC, and use it as an example of the possibilities for representing "English" in this new place, under the aegis of this new professional organization. I'm interested in the speakers as speakers, not figures in an intellectual history.

The speakers were Richard Weaver and James McCrimmon. McCrimmon, the first to speak, cast this session as a debate (it is hard to tell whether Weaver was aware of this in advance and whether he was a willing participant), and in doing so he identified Weaver as a representative of that "English" that the new organization was poised to question or replace.[4] His point of reference was Weaver's recent *College English* article, "To Write the Truth" (10 [Oct. 1948]: 25–30). Weaver anticipated an argument in his talk, but it was not the argument he got from McCrimmon.

Weaver's talk, "Composition as a Liberal Art," was grounded in the commonplaces of the humanistic tradition. (It has a familiar ring; the language is current in today's debate on the academy and the humanities.) Weaver argued that a proper education in language can lead to a unified culture, a refined, moral sensibility, and a perception of eternal truths beyond language. Against this he posed a composition course interested only in mechanical matters, skills. He said, "And as there is a big difference between filling in blanks in a workbook and forging out of one's own chaotic thought a coherent piece of discourse, it is easier to teach the limited skill than the larger art of composition." The failure to teach the larger art was a failure of will and vision — teachers were not willing to comment on the substance of students' papers; they were not willing to take responsibility for showing students "the direction in which truth lies"; they were willing to be concerned with form and technique alone.

Surely, he said,

> it is a sign of the depth of the intellectual crisis that many have not made up their minds as to whether our colleges and universities should be centers of knowledge or centers of skepticism. I do not mean here skepticism in the sense of departing from a dogma or differing with a popular canon; I mean that skepticism which is the despair of knowledge — a feeling that one cannot know even the proximity of truth, but must, if he is a teacher, find his work in the mere churning of opinion.

And it is the study of language, he said, that can

> keep us from succumbing completely to that absurdity called "educating for a changing world." The very fact that languages carry a burden of tradition and reflect an aspiration toward logical order makes them a means of coherence and an instrument of stabilization. The work of scholars is the safeguard of continuity.

McCrimmon, on the other hand, was trying to speak for an English that took as its subject, and as its source of value, the instability of language, particularly as exemplified by the varieties of English present in the work of students.

> I think it is both absurd and detrimental to our purpose to demand that all college writing should be done at a formal level. If we judge usage by the standard of appropriateness to the occasion rather than by an absolute standard, I think we will find that what we have lost in pedantic certainty we have gained in pedagogical effectiveness.

McCrimmon cast his argument against the notion of a single, unifying English. Can Weaver, he said, mean anything more than that "we should teach students to speak and write what has been asserted to be the truth by Plato, or Aristotle, or Thomas Aquinas, or perhaps some less remote authority?"

> If this assumption — that Truth is what the Elect say it is — is sound, the answer to what ails Freshman Composition is simple. That answer is that the course has got out of the control of the Elect and can only be saved by returning it to their control. If you believe that, you should reject the whole corpus of linguistic research, since that science is chiefly responsible for the linguistic relativism which Mr. Weaver so much deplores. If you agree with Mr. Weaver, you should denounce Bloomfield and Curme and Fries and Perrin and all other scientific grammarians, for their leadership has led us all astray. You should even withdraw from the National Council of Teachers of English, or at least purge the present membership, because the NCTE must be a most subversive organization.

On the one hand you have an argument for an idealized English with the power to unify and stabilize the culture; on the other hand, you have an argument for preserving and valuing linguistic difference.[5]

Weaver, in the *CE* article, had argued that

> Adam helped to order the universe when he dealt out these names, and let us not overlook what is implied in the assertion that the names stuck. There is an intimation of divine approval, which would frown upon capricious change.

The early work of Hayakawa and Korzybski enabled McCrimmon to imagine that the notion of a proper meaning, like the notion of a proper utterance, was available to systematic critique. If there was no necessary relationship between words and things, then there were no absolute meanings, meanings must somehow be negotiated — and that, the ways meanings and languages are negotiated individually and collectively, was what CCCC was prepared to take as its subject.

Language as an abstraction, language as practice; an idealized English, common English: these were the fundamental oppositions at play in these two speeches. This opposition is played out in any number of talks and papers in the opening years of CCCC. I could, for example, have organized a similar discussion by turning to the keynote speeches for the second meeting of CCCC: Kenneth Burke's "Rhetoric — Old and New" and Rudolf Flesch's "Let's Face the Facts About Writing." CCCC enabled the expression of a fundamental anxiety about "required English," a useful anxiety that produced new ways of speaking about language, writing, and pedagogy.

The history of CCCC includes the story of repeated attempts to reconstruct a unified field, to discipline this unruly discourse, to translate anxiety into security, and to replace the senior professors of literature with senior professors of composition. There has been too much pain and disappointment for me to say this lightly, but I think it is fortunate that these attempts have largely failed.

CONFERENCE ON COLLEGE COMPOSITION AND COMMUNICATION

Chairs' addresses, like this one, customarily end by taking the long view — making proposals for future action or future direction. And since I have been exploring where we began, it seems only proper that I should offer my hopes about the future. I don't have time today to offer my reading of other key moments in CCCC history. I can't, that is, move from the 40's to the 80's except by a leap. I would, however, like to offer my sense of where we are now and where we are going.

What I would like to do is to reflect on how we talk about who we are and what we do, and how we have come to talk about these things as we do; I am interested in the terms we use to constitute our subject, the terms we take for granted and the degree to which we take them for granted. Today I'll stick to the three terms of our name — composition, communication, conference. These terms are our legacy; we must not betray those who have given them to us. They are also our problem, our burden, since they resist reflection and change.

Communication

This term has an interesting history. The official union of speech and writing (represented by the words composition and communication in our title) can be attributed to several factors — the existence of model freshman English courses that combined public speaking and media studies with composition and literature; the Navy V - 12 program, which forced colleges and universities during the war to combine instruction in speech and written communication in freshman courses in officer training programs; and the "communications" movement, one of whose key figures was Harold Allen, the third chair of 4C's and a member of the original committee of seven who founded the organization.

Many articles in the early journals were devoted to explaining the communications course — what it was and how it worked — and there was some debate over its appropriateness. In 1948 (as in 1988), there was reason to wonder what the word meant and why it was in our title. With slightly different timing, we could have been the Conference on Composition and Linguistics or the Conference on Composition and Semantics. And if these had been our names, we would be a very different organization today.

My sense is that the best way to think of the term "communication," and the best way to think of its function in our title, is to think of it as a fortunate device, a term that keeps us from ever completely knowing our subject. Because of it, we can never simply study composition; there is always also this something else that we know is there but that we can't define. The undefinable term is evidence of our anxiety about composition as a subjectless activity, to be sure. At one time communication was the thing to be added to composition to make it respectable — to make freshman English a subject and not just the place where students worked on papers. But it was, and remains, a guarantee that there will always be a missing term, a structural presence to call into question any attempts to unify the field.[6]

Recently we have seen "communication" removed from the construction "composition and ____ " and replaced with the word "rhetoric." Characteristically, we call upon rhetoric when we want to identify our interests with some form of language study that is removed from the immediate scene of freshman English. We become rhetoricians, not just composition teachers. Rhetoric gives composition a literature, a body of theory, even a critical and scholarly project. It makes the field easier to imagine. "Rhetoric" not only displaces the term "communication"; it offers the possibility of a coherent pair.

I am continually amazed, however, by the degree to which we speak and write as though we had control of the rhetorical tradition — as though it were ours and we could name its key figures and projects. At the moment, rhetoric is very much out of our control. It seems, in fact, to defy every discipline's desire to keep order. All across the humanities and the human sciences, those undertaking critical or philosophical projects have become rhetoricians studying the discourse of their disciplines, or they are looking at the role of language in the way people negotiate power relationships, in the ways they establish knowledge and community.

I can only regret the degree to which the organization has tried to draw the line and keep this literature out of view. (I think it has much to do with the ways we are trying to preserve and honor the work of the second generation of composition scholars, those who opened the field to the classical and so-called "modern" rhetorical tradition.) Three years ago Maxine Hairston argued in "Breaking Our Bonds and Reaffirming Our Connections" that if we do not struggle to maintain our own disciplinary boundaries, we would lose our identity and disappear (*CCC* 36 [Oct. 1985]: 272–82). I am nervous about our sudden obsession with disciplinary boundaries. I regret graduate courses or graduate programs with reading lists designed to define composition and rhetoric as a set or self-contained field. I believe that to tell our graduate students to read Blair, Campbell, and Whately but not Foucault, Pratt, and Jameson is to assert the worst and most paranoid kind of disciplinary influence. It means that we will jeopardize their role in the general project that is reforming English. And it closes the field to those with interests beyond a limited version of the rhetorical tradition.

Composition

As CCCC organized its interests, it changed the name of its subject from "required English" or "freshman English" to "composition and communication." The problem of English, by this progression, is displaced from an institutional site (a curriculum designed to produce unwilling readers and writers) or students (freshmen whose English was not yet mature) to a generalized academic subject (something located beyond either the institution and its practices, or students and theirs).

This change of terms was meant to will an academic respectability, but also to signal a conventional scholarly project for CCCC. This project never materialized, however, and largely because the membership was unwilling to turn attention away from the institution and from students. At one point, in the late 50's, there was even a proposed amendment to the CCCC constitution intended to focus the organization's efforts "upon a discipline rather than a course or a particular group of teachers." The amendment was defeated.[7]

Composition stands, then, for both an abstract subject and something materially present, a course and its students. The early work of CCCC was based on a recognition of this as a productive doubleness, a recognition that the most pressing general issues in the study of language could be represented in the work of students — that, in fact, one could study English by studying the work of students — and that students, by reflecting upon their own practice, could be brought into contact with the proper subject of English.

This was not an easy move to make, to be sure, since it also marked most dramatically the difference between freshman English and the other English. To put students' work at the center was to put Milton or Shakespeare on the margins. Now that the canon is generally under siege, and the study of culture is achieving a position of status in the academy, it is easier (not so dangerous) to imagine that composition could be the center of a professional life.

If "communication" signifies our doubt, then "composition" stands for our certainty. It is what we know, the subject we command, often so well that it is difficult to imagine it again as a subject open for question or negotiation.

It is also, in a familiar construction, half of the equation "literature and composition." There is literature and there is composition and we can either bridge the gap or show the bastards the door.

This is not, I have tried to argue, a useful construction. It is not as though there were now two solid, monolithic Englishes in a battle for power. To be sure, there are departments where composition and composition faculty are under siege. There are departments where black studies, film studies, women's studies, and critical theory are under siege, to name a few similarly situated areas of scholarship. And there are success stories. There are departments where faculties of various backgrounds are teaching a variety of introductory courses — courses where student writing is central, courses where the subjects are open to negotiation and revision, courses that are neither literature courses nor composition courses but courses in something else, something that can't be named in just those terms.

CCCC's contribution to this work is derived from its historical concern for pedagogy and the classroom, for composition, for both the material and the psychological conditions affecting the production of text, and from its history as a community committed to valuing (rather than mocking) the common (and unconventional) things people do with language.

Conference

Finally, I come to the word conference — the word that stands for us, the 2,500 assembled in St. Louis, but also the 6,500 who are at home. Conference is a strange label for a professional organization, but in some ways apt for us, since we take such strength and pleasure from the act of meeting and talking. This is not, need I add, generally true of professional organizations.

We are at the point now where it has become possible and fashionable to speak of composition as a mature discipline. In 1956, in retrospect, Gerber said that the conference had reached a bumptious, ebullient adolescence. Thirty-three years later, when we are 39 years old, we have passed into a solid, if not completely respectable middle age.

We are financially stable, having experienced an unprecedented period of growth for a professional organization in the humanities. And we are big. From a first-year total of 297 members, we now have around 9,000. From a convention of 500 in Chicago, we now bring 2,500 people to St. Louis. In fact, we seem in disturbing ways to be getting too big to provide the sense of good-natured, knowable community that had been our hallmark in the past. While it was once possible to have a sense of everything going on at a meeting, the program has now become huge and diffuse, in some ways impossible for any single individual to comprehend. And we can point to scholarly achievements to announce our maturity: faculty holding distinguished chairs, publication series at major presses, several journals publishing an incredible range of research. We have even reached that pinnacle of disciplinary status, we now produce more words than any single person can possibly read. We cannot be kept up with.

I love, for example, to pick up the *Longman Bibliography* and page through it. To an outsider it must look like the strangest and most idiosyncratic collection of books and articles ever assembled. There is an order, to be sure, an order I admire, but it is not the kind of order we usually associate with academic life. We may be a discipline, but we are surely not disciplined in any usual sense of the term.

One way of defining maturity, then, is in terms of the literal growth of the profession. We are so many, we offer such a rich variety of voices and projects, we have established our niche in academe.

Much of the recent talk about our maturity laments this richness, seeing in it a failure to establish a philosophical or methodological center. In *The Making of Knowledge in Composition*, Stephen North asks, "Can composition really muster enough coherence to justify an autonomous academic existence, or is that just wishful thinking?" (Boynton/Cook, 1987, 374) What we need, some would say, is order: a canon, a set of texts to define the best that has been thought and said.

I have watched several of my contemporaries work on bibliographies or anthologies designed to provide necessary background to prospective students in composition. I know where these reading lists come from and I understand their order. At the same time, I know that I have read few books on these lists, or if I have read them I read them only recently. And I know that these collections of books and articles had little to do with what I take to be the essential parts of my preparation for the field, since much of that preparation came while I was doing work that was not "in" the field at all.

People of my generation have begun to call for a disciplined, ordered field, something that was not there for us when we got started, when we were in a position to believe that we were making it up as we went along, striking unusual connections, poking in strange places for sources and methods, finding subjects where no one else had bothered to look.

Here, then, is the point I want to argue. I am suspicious of calls for coherence. I suspect that most of the problems in academic life — problems of teaching, problems of thinking — come from disciplinary boundaries and disciplinary habits.

Our meetings have been devoted to possibility, with no great respect for tradition or precedent, and we are the recipients of that legacy — fractious, prone to argument, not likely, as Robert Gorrell once said, to "lapse into the lethargy of agreement." We form ourselves into small collectives — caucuses and special interest groups: these collectives fix our commitment to CCCC by establishing a place that is and is not the whole.

In our organizational history as in our research there has been a concerted effort to preserve diversity in academic life — to bring attention to those who would otherwise be ignored. And yet now, as we enter our 40's, we seem to be desperately trying to become respectable, to make the mistakes of middle age.

In 1963, a group charged with observing and evaluating the annual meeting reported with chagrin, "We still speak with many voices. We need to know what relationship these voices have to our central purpose."[8] As I see it, our central purpose has been to make room for these many voices, to imagine a multivocal, dialogical discipline that reflects in its actions its theoretical opposition to a unifying, dominant discourse. To propose a unifying tradition, a canon, disciplinary boundaries — to do this is to turn our backs on our most precious legacy, which is a willed and courageous resistance to the luxury of order and tradition. The charge to this generation and the next is to keep the field open, not to close it; to provide occasions for talk, not lecture and silence; to acknowledge our roots in English, not deny them; to resist the temptations of rank and status; and to offer the invitation to others to find their work in CCCC.[9]

NOTES

1. I am not, as I'll argue later, trying to set up an opposition between literature and composition as areas of professional activity. I am making a claim for the kind of context CCCC, at its best, creates for teachers and scholars. Paula Johnson wrote: "Literary scholarship does not strive to effect anything, except maybe an advancement in academic rank for the scholar. Composition research, on the other hand, tries to do something to what it studies. The social analogue is plain: the leisured elite and rude mechanicals." ("Writing Programs and the English Department," *Profession '80*, New York: MLA, 1980, 15.) This is a formulation whose terms I do not accept. Composition has become, certainly always was, also a way for some to do little more than advance a career (with CCCC providing place and time). And literary studies has (perhaps always) provided the occasion for individuals to do something with a subject, with the materials and conditions of its production, with the scene of instruction. I don't accept the easy terms of Johnson's formulation. I remain committed, however, to the formulation: there are forms of professional life that are deadening; there are forms that make useful work possible.

2. For much of this early history, I have relied on the secretary's report, CCCC (October 1950); the following *CCC* articles by John Gerber: "The Conference on College Composition and Communication" (March 1950), "Three-Year History of the CCCC" (October 1952), "CCCC Facts — 1956" (October 1956); Gerber's *Loomings* (ED 103 893); my own correspondence with Harold Allen (1/27/88; 2/24/88); and a fine dissertation by Nancy K. Bird, "The Conference on College Composition and Communication: A Historical Study of Its Continuing Education and Professionalization Activities, 1949–1975" (Virginia Polytechnic University, 1977). Wykoff's statement is taken from "The Chicago Convention," *College English* (February 1949): 283. The 1948 meeting was preceded by a meeting in 1947 sponsored by NCTE and the Speech Communications Association devoted to the new communications skills courses designed for returning veterans. This meeting was not a success, although some of the participants were involved in the 1948 meeting.

3. The seven were: John Gerber, Carlton Wells (Michigan), Harold Allen (Minnesota), T. A. Barnhart (St. Cloud State), Mentor Williams (Illinois Institute of Technology), George Wykoff (Purdue), and Frank Bowman (Duke). The NCTE executive committee named a separate committee and authorized it to sponsor two conferences (in 1949 and 1950) on Freshman English. This committee consisted of John Gerber, George Wykoff, Harold Allen, Mentor Williams, John Cowley (Iowa State Teachers College), Clyde Dow (Michigan State Normal), Karl Dykema (Youngstown), Ada Roberts (Culver-Stockton), Ernest Samuels (Northwestern), and Samuel Weingartner (Wright Junior College).

4. Both talks can be found in the "Report of the Conference on College Freshman Courses in Composition and Communication, April 1 and 2, 1949," in the NCTE archives.

5. Let me make it clear that McCrimmon was offering a doctrine of linguistic relativism appropriate to the post-war economy. He was not looking to destabilize the class system but to make room for new candidates for the rising middle class: "If my student should later use his acquired skill to win for himself and his family a comfortable standard of living, I am not at all embarrassed. But then I am less afraid of materialism than is Mr. Weaver — an admission which may be charged either against my philosophy or my nationality."

6. Among my list of key moments in CCCC history are the attempts to remove "communication" from our title.

7. See "Report of the Committee on Future Directions," *CCC* (February 1960): 3–7.

8. "Report of the Evaluation Committee," *CCC* (December 1963): 202. The authors include Robert Hogan, then Executive Director of NCTE; Priscilla Tyler, Chair of CCCC; and Louise Rosenblatt.

9. I'm grateful to Chris Ross for her help with the research on this project. Mike Rose and Steve Carr read an earlier draft and suggested a number of important changes. The project owes an obvious debt to Gerald Graff's *Professing Literature: An Institutional History* (Chicago: University of Chicago Press, 1987).

The Tidy House: Basic Writing in the American Curriculum

T he unrecognized contradiction within a position that valorizes the concrete experience of the oppressed, while being so uncritical about the historical role of the intellectual, is maintained by a verbal slippage.

— GAYATRI SPIVAK
"CAN THE SUBALTERN SPEAK?"

Remember, in Foucault's passage in his *History of Sexuality:* "One must be a nominalist." *Power* is not this, *power* is not that. *Power* is the name one must lend to a complex structure of relationships. To that extent, the subaltern is the name of the place which is so displaced from what made me and the organized resister, that to have it speak is like Godot arriving on a bus. We want it to disappear as a name so that we can all speak.

— GAYATRI SPIVAK, IN AN INTERVIEW WITH
HOWARD WINANT, "GAYATRI SPIVAK ON THE
POLITICS OF THE SUBALTERN."

1

I found my career in basic writing. I got my start there and, to a degree, helped to construct and protect a way of speaking about the undergraduate curriculum that has made "basic writing" an important and necessary, even an inevitable, term. This is a story I love to tell.

I went to graduate school in 1969 under an NDEA fellowship (NDEA stands for National Defense Education Act). The country had been panicked by Sputnik; the Congress had voted funds to help America's schools and children become more competitive. The money was directed toward math and science, but NCTE (National Council of Teachers of English) wisely got its

From *Journal of Basic Writing,* 12.1 (1993): 4–21.

foot in the door and saw that at least a token sum was directed toward the humanities, and English in particular, and so NDEA helped send me to Rutgers to graduate school. You could think of it this way — I went to graduate school to save the world from communism.

Because I was an NDEA fellow, I went to graduate school but I never had to teach, at least not until I was well into my dissertation. And so, in 1973, when the money ran out and in order to see what the job might be like, I asked my chair if I could teach a course. He agreed and I found myself teaching Freshman English for the first time.

I did what I was prepared to do. I taught a course where we asked students, all lumped into a single group, "Freshmen," to read an essay by Jean Paul Sartre, and I gave them a question to prompt their writing: "If existence precedes essence, what is man?" This was my opening move. By some poor luck of the draw, about half of my students were students who we would now call "basic writers." I knew from the first week that I was going to fail them; in fact, I knew that I was going to preside over a curriculum that spent 14 weeks slowly and inevitably demonstrating their failures. This is what I (and my school) were prepared (by "English") to do. I want to cast this moment, in other words, as more than an isolated incident. I want it to be representative.

One student wrote the following essay (you can visualize the page — the handwriting is labored and there is much scratching out). The writer's name is Quentin Pierce:

> If existence precedes essence main is responsible for what he is.

> This is what stinger is trying to explain to us that man is a bastard without conscience I don't believe in good or evil they or meanless words or phase. Survive is the words for today and survive is the essence of man.

> To elaborate on the subject matter. the principle of existentialism is logic, but stupid in it self.

Then there is a string of scratched out sentences, and the words "stop" and "lose" written in caps.

Then there is this:

> Let go back to survive, to survive it is neccessary to kill or be kill, this what existentialism is all about.

> Man will not survive, he is a asshole.

> STOP

> The stories in the books or meanless stories and I will not elaborate on them This paper is meanless, just like the book, But, I know the paper will not make it.

> STOP.

Then there are crossed out sentences. At the end, in what now begins to look like a page from *Leaves of Grass* or *Howl*, there is this:

> I don't care.

> I don't care.

about man and good and evil I don't care about this shit fuck this shit, trash and should be put in the trash can with this shit

Thank you very much

I lose again.

I was not prepared for this paper. In a sense, I did not know how to read it. I could only ignore it. I didn't know what to write on it, how to bring it into the class I was teaching, although, in a sense, it was the only memorable paper I received from that class and I have kept it in my file drawer for 18 years, long after I've thrown away all my other papers from graduate school.

I knew enough to know that the paper was, in a sense, a very skillful performance in words. I knew that it was written for me; I knew that it was probably wrong to read it as simply expressive (an expression of who Quentin Pierce "really was"); I think I knew that it was not sufficient to read the essay simply as evidence that I had made the man a loser — since the document was also a dramatic and skillful way of saying "Fuck you — I'm not the loser, you are." I saw that the essay had an idea, "existentialism is logical but stupid," and that the writer called forth the moves that could enable its elaboration: "To elaborate on the subject," he said, "let's go back to survive."

The "Fuck You" paper was a written document of some considerable skill and force — more skill and force, for example, than I saw in many of the "normal" and acceptable papers I read: "In this fast-paced modern world, when one considers the problems facing mankind. . . ." I know you know how to imagine and finish that essay. It has none of the surprises of the fuck you essay. It would still, I think, be used to classify its student as a "normal" writer; the other would identify a "basic" writer.

I could see features in the fuck you essay that spoke to me in my classroom. I did not, as I said earlier, know how to read it. I didn't know how to make it part of the work of my class. I failed the "basic writers" in my Freshman English class and I went to my chairman, Dan Howard, a man whom I admired greatly, and I told him I would never do this again. I would never teach a course where I would meet a group of students, know that some would fail, watch those students work to the best of their ability and my preparation and then fail them. It was not the job for me. I would rather be a lawyer. (This is true, not just a joke; I took the law boards.)

He said, "Why don't you set up a basic writing program" and gave me my first full-time job. A year later I went to Pitt, again to work with a basic writing program. The one decision I made was that I was not going to get rid of Jean Paul Sartre. I wanted to imagine a course where students worked with the materials valued in the college curriculum. I did not want to take those materials away from them. I wanted, rather, to think about ways of preparing unprepared students to work with the kinds of materials that I (and the profession) would say were ours, not theirs, materials that were inappropriate, too advanced. And so we set up a seminar, with readings and a subject or theme to study (so that basic writing students, we said, could work firsthand with the values and methods of the academy); we did this rather than teach a "skills" course that could lead, later, to "real" work.

I felt then, as I feel now, that the skills course, the course that postponed "real" reading and writing, was a way of enforcing the very cultural divisions that stood as the defining markers of the problem education and its teachers, like me, had to address. In its later versions, and with my friend and colleague Tony Petrosky, the course became the course reported in *Facts, Artifacts, and Counterfacts*. I am thrilled to see that there will be talk about this kind of course here at the conference today. There are versions of the course being taught in the most remarkable variety of settings — city schools, rural schools, Indian reservations, high schools, colleges for the deaf. The course is still being taught at Pitt, with wonderful revisions. The two features of the course that have remained constant are these: difficulty is confronted and negotiated, not erased (the Jean Paul Sartre slot remains); students' work is turned into a book (the fuck you paper becomes an authored work, a text in the course).

Now — as I said, this is a story I love to tell. It is convenient. It is easy to understand. Like basic writing, it (the story) and I are produced by the grand narrative of liberal sympathy and liberal reform. The story is inscribed in a master narrative of outreach, of equal rights, of empowerment, of new alliances and new understandings, of the transformation of the social text, the American university, the English department. I would like, in the remainder of my talk, to read against the grain of that narrative — to think about how and why and where it might profitably be questioned. I am not, let me say quickly, interested in critique for the sake of critique; I think we have begun to rest too comfortably on terms that should make us nervous, terms like "basic writing." Basic writing has begun to seem like something naturally, inevitably, transparently there in the curriculum, in the stories we tell ourselves about English in America. It was once a provisional, contested term, marking an uneasy accommodation between the institution and its desires and a student body that did not or would not fit. I think it should continue to mark an area of contest, of struggle, including a struggle against its stability or inevitability.

Let me put this more strongly. I think basic writing programs have become expressions of our desire to produce basic writers, to maintain the course, the argument, and the slot in the university community; to maintain the distinction (basic/normal) we have learned to think through and by. The basic writing program, then, can be seen simultaneously as an attempt to bridge AND preserve cultural difference, to enable students to enter the "normal" curriculum but to insure, at the same time, that there are basic writers.

2

Nothing has been more surprising to a liberal (to me) than the vehement (and convincing) critique of the discourse of liberalism, a discourse that, as I've said, shaped my sense of myself as a professional. I have been trying to think about how to think outside the terms of my own professional formation, outside of the story of Quentin Pierce and my work in basic writing. I am trying to think outside of the ways of thinking that have governed my understanding of basic writers, of their identity as it is produced by our work and within the college curriculum.

To do this counterintuitive thinking, the critique of liberalism has been useful to me. Let me provide two examples as a form of demonstration.

Here is Shelby Steele, in the preface to *The Content of Our Character*, talking about how he writes. I like to read this as an account of the composing process, the composing process NOT as an internal psychological drama (issue trees, short-term memory, problem-solving, satisficing) but as an accommodation of the discursive positions (the roles or identifications) that can produce a writer and writing. It is also a program for a liberal rhetoric, a way of writing designed to produce or enforce the ideology of liberalism (in this case, the argument that differences of race and class don't matter):

> In the writing, I have had to both remember and forget that I am black. The forgetting was to see the human universals within the memory of the racial specifics. One of the least noted facts in this era when racial, ethnic, and gender differences are often embraced as sacred is that being black in no way spares one from being human. Whatever I do or think as a black can never be more than a variant of what all people do and think. Some of my life experiences may be different from those of other races, but there is nothing different or special in the psychological processes that drive my mind. So in this book I have tried to search out the human universals that explain the racial specifics. I suppose this was a sort of technique, though I was not conscious of it as I worked. Only in hindsight can I see that it protected me from being overwhelmed by the compelling specifics — and the politics — or racial difference. Now I know that if there was a secret to writing this book, it was simply to start from the painfully obvious premise that all races are composed of human beings. (xi)

It is a remarkable statement and enacts, in the paragraph, the link between an attitude (a recognition of common humanity, looking beneath surfaces) and the discursive trick, the "sleight of word," to steal a phrase from Gayatri Spivak, the displacement this position requires/enables in the act of writing. The attitude that all men are equal produces a text where the overwhelming specifics — and the politics of racial difference — disappear. It is a figuration that enables a certain kind of writing. It is, I think, a writing we teach in basic writing (the control of the overwhelming details, the specifics; the erasure or oversight of the problems — personal, social, historic — that produce basic writing), just as it is a writing we perform, in a sense, in the administration of basic writing programs, making certain "overwhelming specifics" disappear.

When I first came upon this book, I knew that I was supposed to be critical of Steele (that he was a conservative, an old-fashioned humanist); I knew I was supposed to be critical before I could perform or feel the critique. Actually, I'll confess, I loved his book and what it stood for. It evokes sympathies and identifications I have learned to mistrust.

Here is a different statement about writing, one that is harder to read (or it was for me), this time by Patricia Williams, from her remarkable book,

The Alchemy of Race and Rights. It is not, directly, a critique of Steele, but it speaks a version of writing and the writer that stands opposed to his. It is not, I should say quickly, what we would have once called a "Black power" statement on race and writing — that is, it does not simply reverse Steele's position (Steele argues that he must forget he is Black) to argue that a writer must remember, discover her Blackness, to let race define who, as a writer, she essentially is. Williams' argument is not produced by the same discourse.

Williams' position is different; it sees subject positions as produced, not essential, and as strategic. Williams' book thinks through what it is like to write, think, live, and practice law as a Black woman — that is, to occupy positions that are White and Black, male and female, all at once.

She recalls a time when, back to back, a White man and a Black woman wondered aloud if she "really identified as black." She says:

> I heard the same-different words addressed to me, a perceived white-male-socialized black woman, as a challenge to mutually exclusive categorization, as an overlapping of black and female and right and male and private and wrong and white and public, and so on and so forth.

> That life is complicated is a fact of great analytic importance. Law too often seeks to avoid this truth by making up its own breed of narrower, simpler, but hypnotically powerful rhetorical truths.

> Acknowledging, challenging, playing with these *as* rhetorical gestures is, it seems to me, necessary for any conception of justice. Such acknowledgment complicates the supposed purity of gender, race, voice, boundary; it allows us to acknowledge the utility of such categorizations for certain purposes and the necessity of their breakdown on other occasions. It complicates definitions in its shift, in its expansion and contraction according to circumstance, in its room for the possibility of creatively mated taxonomies and their wildly unpredictable offspring. (10–11)

And over and over again in her book, she offers this as the figure of the writer:

> But I haven't been able to straighten things out for them [her students] because I'm confused too. I have arrived at a point where everything I have ever learned is running around and around in my head; and little bits of law and pieces of everyday life fly out of my mouth in weird combinations. (14)

There is a double edge to this comparison. On the one hand, Williams represents the critique of liberalism and its easy assumptions, say, about the identity of African Americans and White Americans, or Workers and Owners, or Men and Women. It defines sympathy as something other than the easy understanding of someone else's position; it makes that sympathy, rather, a version of imperial occupation, the act of the taking possession of someone else's subjectivity. The pairing also represents how writing and the writer might be said to be figured differently when one reconfigures the relationship of the individual to convention, the writer to writing, including the conventions of order and control. Williams' writing is disunified; it mixes genres; it willfully forgets the distinction between formal and colloquial, public and private; it makes unseemly comparisons. In many ways, her prose has the features we associate with basic writing, although here those features mark her achievement as a writer, not her failure.

Here is a simple equation, but one that will sum up the thoughts this leads me to: to the degree to which the rhetoric of the American classroom has been dominated by the topic sentence, the controlling idea, gathering together ideas that fit while excluding, outlawing those that don't (the overwhelming, compelling specifics); to the degree that the American classroom has been a place where we *cannot* talk about race or class or the history of the American classroom, it has taught both the formal properties and the controlling ideas that produce, justify, and value the humanism of Shelby Steele, that produce Patricia Williams' text as confusing, unreadable (which, in a classroom sense, it is — our students are prepared to find her writing hard to read and his easy), and it produces basic writing as the necessary institutional response to the (again) overwhelming politics and specifics of difference. It is a way of preserving the terms of difference rooted in, justified by the liberal project, one that has learned to rest easy with the tidy distinction between basic and mainstream. In this sense, basic writers are produced by our desires to be liberals — to enforce a commonness among our students by making the differences superficial, surface-level, and by designing a curriculum to both insure them and erase them in 14 weeks.

In her recent work, Mary Louise Pratt has argued against the easy, utopian versions of community that have governed the ways we think about language and the classroom. In linguistics, for example:

> The prototypical manifestation of language is generally taken to be the speech of individual adult native speakers face-to-face (as in Saussure's famous diagram) in monolingual, even monodialectal situations — in short, the most homogeneous case linguistically and socially. The same goes for written communication. Now one could certainly imagine a theory that assumed different things — that argued, for instance, that the most revealing speech situation for understanding language was one involving a gathering of people each of whom spoke two languages and understood a third and held only one language in common with any of the others. It depends on what working of language you want to see or want to see first, on what you choose to define as normative. (38)

If you want to eliminate difference, there are programs available to think this through. In the classroom, similarly, she argues, teachers are prepared to feel most successful when they have eliminated "unsolicited oppositional discourse" — that is, the writing they are not prepared to read — along with parody, resistance, and critique, when they have unified the social world in the image of community offered by the professions. Who wins when we do that, she asks? and who loses? Or, to put it another way, if our programs produce a top and bottom that reproduces the top and bottom in the social text, insiders and outsiders, haves and have nots, who wins and who loses?

This is not abstract politics, not in the classroom. Pratt acknowledges this. In place of a utopian figure of community, she poses what she calls the "contact zone." I use this term, she says,

> to refer to social spaces where cultures meet, clash, and grapple with each other, often in contexts of highly asymmetrical relations of power, such as colonialism, slavery, or their aftermaths as they are lived out in many parts of the world today. (34)

She extends this term to classrooms and proposes a list of both the compositional and pedagogical arts of the contact zone. Imagine, in other words, a curricular program designed not to hide differences (by sorting bodies) but to highlight them, to make them not only the subject of the writing curriculum, but the source of its goals and values (at least one of the versions of writing one can learn at the university). Pratt lists the various arts of the contact zone. These are wonderful lists to hear as lists, since they make surprising sense and come out of no order we have been prepared to imagine or, for that matter, value.

These are, according to Pratt, some of the literate arts of the contact zone: autoethnography (representing one's identity and experience in the terms of a dominant other, with the purpose of engaging the other), transculturation (the selection of and improvisation on the materials derived from the dominant culture), critique, collaboration, bilingualism, mediation, parody, denunciation, imaginary dialogue, vernacular expression. (Imagine these as the stated goals of a course.) And these are some of the pedagogical arts: exercises in storytelling and in identifying with the ideas, interests, histories, and attitudes of others; experiments in transculturation and collaborative work and in the arts of critique, parody, and comparison (including unseemly comparisons between elite and vernacular cultural forms); the redemption of the oral; ways for people to engage with suppressed aspects of history (including their own histories); ways to move *into and out of* rhetorics of authenticity; ground rules for communication across lines of difference and hierarchy that go beyond politeness but maintain mutual respect; a systematic approach to the all-important concept of *cultural mediation.* (Imagine these as exercises.)

Now — the voice of common sense says, basic writers aren't ready for this, they can't handle it, they need a place to begin. But this sense makes sense only under the sway of a developmental view of language use and language growth (and "developmentalism" — cherishing and preserving an interested version of the "child" and the "adult" — this, too, is inscribed in the discourse of liberalism). Thinking of development allows one to reproduce existing hierarchies but as evidence of natural patterns — basic writers are just like other writers, but not quite so mature. One could imagine that oppositional discourse, parody, unseemly comparisons, if defined as "skills," are the equal possession of students in *both* basic writing and mainstream composition courses. In fact, one could argue that "basic writers" are better prepared to produce and think through unseemly comparisons than their counterparts in the "mainstream" class. Pratt rejects the utopian notion of a classroom where everyone speaks the same language to the same ends; she imagines, rather, a classroom where difference is both the subject and the environment. She gives us a way of seeing existing programs as designed to hide or suppress "contact" between cultural groups rather than to organize and highlight that contact.

Now of course education needs to be staged, and of course tracking makes strategic sense; of course one needs a place to begin and a place to end or to mark beginnings and endings, but it is not impossible to think beyond our current sense of beginnings and endings (of basic writing and the courses that follow), beyond placement exams that measure the ability to produce or recognize the conventionally correct and unified text.

There is caricature here, I know, but one could imagine the current proportion of students in basic writing courses and mainstream courses redistributed by an exam that looked for willingness to work, for a commitment to language and its uses, for an ability to produce a text that commands notice, or (in Pratt's terms) for the ability to produce opposition, parody, unseemly comparisons, to work outside of the rhetoric of authenticity, to produce the autoethnographic text. Or we could imagine not tracking students at all. We could offer classes with a variety of supports for those who need them. These might be composition courses where the differences in students' writing becomes the subject of the course. The differences would be what the course investigates. We would have, then, a course in "multiculturalism" that worked with the various cultures represented in the practice of its students. There would be no need to buy an anthology to find evidence of the cultural mix in America, no need to import "multiple cultures." They are there, in the classroom, once the institution becomes willing to pay that kind of attention to student writing.

There is caricature here, but so is there caricature in our current accounts of *the* basic writer and his or her essential characteristics. There is a great danger in losing a sense of our names as names — in Patricia Williams' terms, as rhetorical gestures, useful for certain purposes but also necessarily breaking down at the very moment that we need them.

Or — to put it another way. Basic writers may be ready for a different curriculum, for the contact zone and the writing it will produce, but the institution is not. And it is not, I would argue, because of those of us who work in basic writing, who preserve rather than question the existing order of things.

3

Developmentalism. Certainly the most influential conduit for this discourse in American composition is James Britton. He has been given the kind of saintly status given Mina Shaughnessy. He seems to represent (in his sympathy for the other, for children, for diversity, for growth and empowerment) a position beyond positions. This is, of course, a sleight of hand, and a problem, one we share in producing when we read Britton generously. (And let me be quick to say, I understand all the good reasons why we might read him generously.)

As a way of thinking outside of Britton, both about writing and about children, but also about professional work and about the consequences of such thinking, I want to turn to a comparatively unknown book, *The Tidy House*, one that could be thought of as a countertext to *The Development of Writing Abilities*. It is written in a similar time and place, in the late 60s and early 70s in Britain. It looks at the same subject: writing and schooling.

In Steedman's words, this is what *The Tidy House* is about:

> In the summer of 1976, three working-class eight-year-old girls, Melissa, Carla, and Lindie, wrote a story about romantic love, marriage and sexual relations, the desire of mothers for children and their resentment of them, and the means by which those children are brought up to inhabit a social world.

> This book, which takes its title from the children's narrative, offers an account of their story, and suggests what interpretations we, as adults, can make of it. Their story, which is structured around two opposing views of childcare held by their two central female characters, served the children as an investigation of the ideas and beliefs by which they themselves were being brought up, and their text can serve us too in this way. (1)

I'll confess that I have been very much taken by this book. It is beautifully written, sensible, evocative, surprising. And it powerfully suggests the roads not taken by composition studies and its professionals.

The book begins with the girls' story, called "The Tidy House." It is written all in dialogue. Here, for example, is the children's account of what adults say to each other in bed at night when they are making babies:

What time is it?

Eleven o'clock at night.

Oh no! Let's get to bed.

Ok.

'Night, sweetheart, See you in the morning.

Turn the light off, Mark.

I'm going to.

Sorry.

All right.

I want to get asleep.

Don't worry, you'll get to sleep in time.

Don't let us, really, this time of the night.

Shall I wait till the morning?

Oh stop it.

Morning.

Don't speak.

No, you.

No. Why don't you?

Look, it's all over.

Thank you, Mark.

Mark kissed Jo, Jo kissed Mark. (43–44)

Steedman's work on this story leads her to women's accounts of their lives in the working-class neighborhood of the girls, to Henry Mayhew and the words of girls from the streets of London in the 19th century, to domestic education and the historical uses of children's writing. And, in Steedman's career, it has led to interests in history and autobiography, in the production of "the child" in England.

Steedman saw in the students' story a history of social practices, practices that not only argue about educability and appropriateness but about how girls become women and what it means to live within one's class. Teachers are not prepared, she argues, to see history and culture in the classroom or in the work of its children.

> It is almost impossible for a teacher to look at a room full of children and not see them in some way as being stretched out along some curve of ability, some measuring up to and exceeding the average, some falling behind. This is the historical inheritance we operate with, whether we do so consciously or not, and it has been a matter of "common sense" and common observation rather than a matter of theory to know as a teacher that children of class IV and V parents are going to perform relatively badly compared with children of higher socioeconomic groups. (5)

And, "What teachers know as a result of this history, and as a matter of 'common sense,' is that, in general, ability groupings turn out in practice to make rough and comprehensible matches with social class divisions."

For Steedman, as both a teacher and a social historian, the fundamental question is how these young writers, given their positions as girls and as working-class girls, can negotiate, understand, and critically confront those versions of themselves that are written into the social text. An uncritical schooling, an education in language divorced from its social and political contexts, would effectively preserve the narratives of class and gender within which these children find themselves (within which they write "their" story). For Steedman, the writing done in school gives both the professional and the student access to a history and attitudes and feelings shaping their particular moment. Writing is the way history, class, and culture become manifest in the classroom, in an environment that pretends to stand outside of time.

What Steedman suggests is not just a direction for research but a different version of professional responsibility, where as professionals who manage writing in institutional settings we might see that writing as material for an ongoing study of American life and culture. It is a telling irony that on my campus, where young working-class women write, scholars go to archives to "discover" working-class writing by women.

To learn to read her students' story, Steedman went to a record of children's voices from the eighteenth century to the twentieth. To learn to read her students' stories, Mina Shaughnessy went to her heart — to the remarkable sympathy which would allow her to understand the work of students distinctly different from her in culture and sensibility. Shaughnessy's text, in a sense, is the quintessential liberal reflex; it demonstrates that beneath the surface we are all the same person; it writes her students' lives, needs, desires into a master text that she commands. Basic writing, as an extension of that moment, preserves that project: fitting students into a version of who they are as writers that we tend to take for granted, that seems to stand beyond our powers of revision and inquiry, because it is an expression of our founding desires to find, know, and help (to construct, theorize, and preserve) basic writers.

4

So what in the world have I done here. I find myself characterizing basic writing as a reiteration of the liberal project of the late 60s early 70s, where in the name of sympathy and empowerment, we have once again produced the "other" who is the incomplete version of ourselves, confirming existing patterns of power and authority, reproducing the hierarchies we had meant to question and overthrow, way back then in the 1970s.

We have constructed a course to teach and enact a rhetoric of exclusion and made it the center of a curriculum designed to hide or erase cultural difference, all the while carving out and preserving an "area" in English within which we can do our work. Goodness.

Now, at the end of my talk, it seems important to ask, "Do I believe what I have said?" If this has been an exercise in reading against the grain of the discourse that has produced basic writing (and, I said, my work as a professional), do I believe this negative, unyielding rereading?

The answer is yes and no, and sometimes yes and no at the same moment. Let me conclude, then, with a series of second thoughts (or "third thoughts" as the case may be).

If you look back over the issues of the *Journal of Basic Writing* (or at programs and courses), there is a record of good and careful work. I couldn't begin to turn my back on all that or to dismiss it as inconsequential. We can all think immediately of the students who have been helped, of college careers that have begun with a basic writing course. Good work has been done under the name of basic writing by both students and professionals. I cannot get over, however, my sense of the arbitrariness, the surrealism, of the choices represented by the sorting of students in actual basic and mainstream classes. Looking at the faces, working with the writing — the division never makes anything but institutional sense. There are cases to prove that the idea is a good one. There are cases to prove that the idea is all wrong.

And there are problems of error — of controlling the features of a written text — that stand outside of any theorizing about basic writing as a form of resistance. It seems to me finally stupid to say that every nonstandard feature of a student's prose is a sign of opposition, can stand as "unsolicited oppositional discourse." If I think back to Quentin Pierce's essay, some of the "errors" could be read as oppositional, but not all of them and not all of them for the same reasons. At the same time, the profession has not been able to think beyond an either/or formulation — either academic discourse or the discourse of the community; either argument or narrative; either imitation or expression. Part of the failure, I think, is rooted in our inability to imagine protocols for revision, for example, that would negotiate rather than preserve the differing interests of students and the academy. We do not, for example, read "basic writing" the way we read Patricia Williams' prose, where the surprising texture of the prose stands as evidence of an attempt to negotiate the problems of language. I want to be clear about this. Williams is a skillful, well-educated writer. The unconventional nature of her prose can be spoken of as an achievement. She is trying to do something that can't be conventionally done. To say that our basic writers are less intentional, less skilled, is to say the obvious. But we would say the same thing of the "mainstream" writers whose prose approximates that of Shelby Steele. Their prose, too, is less skilled, less intentional than his. It is possible, it seems to me, to develop a theory of error that makes the contact between conventional and unconventional discourses the most interesting and productive moment for a writer or for a writing course. It is possible to use the Steele/Williams pair to argue that when we define Williams-like student writing as less developed or less finished than Steele-like student writing, we are letting metaphors of development or process hide value-laden assumptions about thought, form, the writer, and the social world.

Let me think back to Quentin Pierce. Do I believe in the course represented in *Facts, Artifacts, Counterfacts* — do I believe it is a reasonable way to manage his work as a reader and writer? Yes. I believe deeply in that course. At my school, it changes every time it is taught — with different readings, better writing assignments. But in principle, I believe in the course. Someone else will have to produce its critique. I can't. At the same time, I should add that a similar course is being taught at a variety of levels of our curriculum at the University of Pittsburgh. It is also the mainstream composition course and an introductory course for majors. There are differences that could be called differences of "level" (for the students more accustomed to reading and writing, we choose assigned readings differently; the course moves at a different pace; sentence level error is treated differently). It is, however, the same course. And the students who are well-prepared could easily be said to need extra time and guidance in learning to see the limits of the procedures, protocols, and formats they take for granted — the topic sentence, reading for gist, the authority of the conclusion. The point is that while I believe in the course, I am not sure I believe in its institutional position as a course that is necessarily prior to or lesser than the mainstream course. Do I believe

Quentin is served by being called a basic writer and positioned in the curriculum in these terms. I'm not sure I do.

I don't think we can ignore the role of the introductory writing course in preparing students to negotiate the full range of expectations in the university (as it reproduces the expectations of the dominant culture), including linguistic convention, correction, etc. Does this mean a separate course? No. Does it mean we identify and sort students in useful, even thoughtful ways? No.

There was much talk at the Maryland conference about abolishing basic writing and folding its students into the mainstream curriculum, providing other forms of support (tutorials, additional time, a different form of final evaluation). Karen Greenberg and I argued this point at the open session. I am suspicious, as I said then, of the desire to preserve "basic writing" as a key term simply because it is the one we have learned to think with or because it has allowed us our jobs or professional identities. I think it would be useful, if only as an exercise, to imagine a way of talking that called the term "basic writing" into question (even, as an exercise, to treat it as suspect). Would I advocate the elimination of courses titled "basic writing" for all postsecondary curricula beginning next fall? No. I fear what would happen to the students who are protected, served in its name. I don't, in other words, trust the institution to take this as an intellectual exercise, a challenge to rethink old ways. I know that the institution would be equally quick to rely upon an established and corrupt discourse (of "boneheads," of "true college material," of "remediation"); it would allow the return of a way of speaking that was made suspect by the hard work and diligence of those associated with basic writing. As Shaughnessy told us, the first thing we would need to do to change the curriculum would be to change the way the profession talked about the students who didn't fit. Will I begin to formally question the status of basic writing at my own institution? Yes. In a sense, this was already begun several years ago by graduate students in our department, and by my colleague, Joe Harris.

I suppose what concerns me most is the degree to which a provisional position has become fixed, naturalized. "Basic writing," the term, once served a strategic function. It was part of an attempt to change the way we talked about students and the curriculum. We have lost our sense of its strategic value. "Basic writing," it seems to me, can best name a contested area in the university community, a contact zone, a place of competing positions and interests. I don't want to stand in support of a course designed to make those differences disappear or to hide contestation or to enforce divisions between high and low. It seems to me that the introductory curriculum can profitably be a place where professionals and students think through their differences in productive ways. I'm not sure more talk about basic writing will make that happen.

WORKS CITED

Britton, James. *The Development of Writing Abilities.* London: Macmillan Education, 1975. 11–18.
Pratt, Mary Louise. "Linguistic Utopias." *The Linguistics of Writing.* Eds. Nigel Fabb, et al. Manchester: Manchester UP, 1987.
———. "The Arts of the Contact Zone." *Profession 91.* New York: MLA, 1991.

Spivak, Gayatri Chakravorty. "Can the Subaltern Speak?" *Marxism and the Interpretation of Culture.* Eds. Cary Nelson and Lawrence Grossberg. Champaign: U of Illinois P, 1988.

——. "Gayatri Spivak on the Politics of the Subaltern." Interview by Howard Winant. *Socialist Review* 20.3 (July–Sept. 1990): 81–87.

Steedman, Carolyn. *Past Tenses: Essays on Writing, Autobiography and History.* London: Rivers Oram Press, 1992.

——. *The Tidy House.* London: Virago, 1982.

Steele, Shelby. *The Content of Our Character.* New York: St. Martin's, 1990.

Williams, Patricia J. *The Alchemy of Race and Rights.* Cambridge: Harvard UP, 1991.

What Is Composition and (If You Know What That Is) Why Do We Teach It?

A DISCLAIMER

I will not be presenting a theory paper here. Nor do I want to argue for a particular kind of program or set of practices. I have no desire to be comprehensive. I have, however, been "in" composition for some time; more recently, I have done a good bit of traveling to evaluate departments and programs. I would like to offer something like a report from the field and to write about some places where composition has shown its face in interesting or surprising ways. I need to be clear: the composition I am talking about is not a consensus or a specific professional (or "disciplinary") agenda; it is not in the control of composition professionals; it is not represented by the conflicts that take place at meetings or in journals. It is, rather, a set of problems produced by a wider, more diffuse set of practices and desires, usually brought into play by instances of language change or variety (or by the possibility that writing might change or be various). In a sense, the history of composition has been the record of institutional and professional responses to challenged standards, challenges to a standard of writing produced by writers who were said to be unprepared. Composition marked the people and places charged to prepare those students and/or to defend and rationalize their "unauthorized" writing.

I am interested in composition as it is represented in both its institutional and more broadly cultural setting. When I refer to composition, I mean the institutionally supported desire to organize and evaluate the writing of unauthorized writers, to control writing in practice, and to define it as an object of professional scrutiny. Composition, then, refers to what goes on across the grades and across academic departments. It refers to curricular agendas (stated and unstated), to daily pedagogical encounters of all sorts and varieties, to the marketing of careers and materials, to institutional arrangements and negotiations, sponsored research, the importing and exporting of theory and method (where, for example, writing is organized or valued off campus

From *Composition in the 21st Century*, eds. Lynn Bloom, Donald Daiker, and Edward White (Carbondale: Southern Illinois UP, 1996) 11–29.

through a vague memory of what English teachers thought and said) — an array of often competing desires for order and control, sometimes meeting out in the open, sometimes not; sometimes meeting on shared terrain and even terms, often not. Composition is not, then, the same thing as the combined desires and practices of the members of the Conference on College Composition and Communication on any given day. It is not summed up in the journals, and it has an off-and-on-again relationship with the "key figures" in the field.

CURRICULUM

Let me begin with a local example, an excerpt from a student essay that won first prize in the University of Pittsburgh's undergraduate writing competition. I want to use it to think for a minute about the sources and uses of writing, particularly writing in schooling, where schooling demands/enables the intersection of tradition and the individual talent and provides the point of negotiation between a cultural field and an unauthorized writer. As you read this piece, notice the traces of at least two sources: a student and an academic discipline.

> Initially, such early steel entrepreneurs like Andrew Carnegie and Henry Clay Frick used the technique of vertical integration to control all factors of steel production. This necessitated the construction of massive bureaucratic organizations to take advantage of economies of scale in the procurement of the required natural resources and the subsequent production of the steel itself. Each organization was a textbook bureaucracy, with its fixed areas of managerial jurisdiction and supervisory hierarchies consisting of numerous layers of management personnel. At the same time, in order to achieve strict control over these new, huge bureaucratic operations, management adopted techniques which minimized human variability and uncertainty in the production process. Most of these techniques were derived in large part from Frederick W. Taylor's philosophy of "scientific management." Taylor believed that standardization of work procedures and division of labor in mass-production industries would enable firms to achieve optimal levels of output and increased revenues. For example, on the question of organizing work Taylor expressed the following views: "All possible brainwork should be removed from the shop. . . . Each man [should receive] complete written instructions describing in detail the task which he is to accomplish. This task specifies not only what is to be done, but how it is to be done and the time allowed for doing it. . . ." Taylor's philosophy was quite influential in the early 1900s and, consequently, the steel industry implemented many of his principles. The firms enacted bonus and wage incentive plans designed to appeal to the greed of the "economic man," defined jobs within very narrow boundaries, and instituted highly detailed shop rules and procedures which the floor supervisors were instructed to enforce through a system of rewards and punishments.

It is easy to see why this was an award-winning essay. For a moment, I would like to turn its success against itself and against those practices it represents. For a moment, I would like to think of this essay as too good, too finished, too seamless, too professional. This is not a hard critique to imagine — instead of talking about writing in the disciplines, we can talk about writing and discipline, as in discipline and punish, the reproduction of disciplinary boundaries and disciplinary authority. It has become easy to get this kind of critical purchase on the texts of contemporary life.

In this sense, you could think of the essay as providing the terms of its own critique: the writing is an example of the techniques of vertical integration as they are part of the university curriculum. The writing is Taylorized, organized to minimize human variability and uncertainty in the production process. "All possible brainwork should be removed from the shop." "Rules and procedures are enforced through a system of rewards and punishments."

I do not want to dismiss the accomplishment represented here, either on the part of the student, or his teacher, or the institution. But I do want to open up the essay to question. The best way to do that is for me to imagine other possible narratives, other histories that are being displaced here. Here, for example, is the story I might tell. The writer, since this is Pittsburgh, is the son of an unemployed steelworker — or the daughter of a middle manager in what is now USX, a multinational corporation no longer primarily making steel. They would also have other stories to tell about management and labor in the steel industry, and other ways of telling the story, but that story and those methods are silenced by the "official" disciplinary history, one couched in the rhetoric of "objectivity" or one that deals in terms of Great Men and Great Ideas.

There are dangers here. I am clearly idealizing the student who is silenced. Or the danger is that I will paint a portrait of too complete a victim (a writer for whom this essay is simply shameful, a loss, a writer who has no control, no sense of himself or herself as a writer). But with these dangers in mind, let me push ahead.

Because we have had students write family histories and neighborhood histories, and because we teach some of the published and unpublished narratives of life in the Monongahela Valley, I am aware of the ways in which a nexus of knowledge and desire that I will (problematically) name "the student" could be excluded from this narrative of "The Adversarial Relationship Between Management and Labor in the American Steel Industry." I want to insist upon the ways in which, at least in this document, the historical narrative excludes this writer as a source and defines her position, rather, as someone who assembles materials according to a master plan.

But there are other narratives suppressed by this master narrative of industrial organization. I am increasingly drawn to the metaphor of space in talking about writing. Some sentences create spaces a writer has to fill; some sentences are careful to hide or overlay a writer's space, the space where the writer needs to come forward to write rather than recite the text that waits to be written. Here the key space for me comes both before and after the block quotation. There is the student who, having read Taylor, says, "Huh? What made this so powerful? so convincing? How was this read in the Monongahela Valley?" or the student who says, "This is terrible! How did they get away with that? Why would anyone have bought this argument?"

But there is also another silence represented by those spaces: it is, in Gerald Graff's terms, the silence the disciplines maintain in the face of students, like parents hiding their fights from the children. That is, one can imagine in those spaces all of the second thoughts that belong, not to the student working with the material, but to the discipline and its work — other readings of labor relations in the early periods of the steel industry; other ways of doing history, with numbers or with diaries and newspapers and letters, let us say, rather than with great men and great ideas. One could imagine a different text, one much less finished; and one could imagine that this counter-text would imply a different form or goal to a writer's education: for an undergraduate to ask difficult questions about the "official" work of history, and to ask these questions from the inside, while doing it; for the official work of history to maintain space for second thoughts, including the musings or sidetracks of an amateur; for a writer to produce a text that is, in a sense, less finished and less professional. It is hard to imagine, for example, the institution sending this student back to this essay with any other motive than to perfect it — to make it even more perfectly what it already is. It is rare to find an individual, either inside or outside an English department, teaching protocols for revision whose goal is to call the discourse into question, to undo it in some fundamental way. The problem here is not departmental or disciplinary. It is derived from a larger conception of the academy and intellectual labor, particularly as it involves students. As a faculty, we do not have a way of saying to a student, "Make that essay a little worse, not quite so finished, a little more fragmented and confused," and to say this in the name of learning. The institution is designed to produce and reward mastery, not to call it into question.

And what about composition professionals — those of us "in" composition? I would like to say that the turn toward criticism and critical theory was leading to work in this direction, but I do not think that is the case. The essays on Mikhail Bahktin or Hélène Cixous in our journals make only the faintest connection to the history paper (even the "composition" paper). This is partly an intellectual problem — what *is* the connection? And it is partly the legacy of the liberal tradition in composition. The structures of support produced in the name of composition (tutorials, the composing process, journals, Writing Across the Curriculum) allow us to identify with the student as an individual without taking notice of or responsibility for the forms of knowledge being produced through their writing.

Here is a brief second example. I include it because it is more familiar to English teachers. This, too, was a prize-winning essay in a university writing contest. The excerpt comes from a paper on Dylan Thomas's poem "Fern Hill":

> Through the structure of the last stanza, Thomas reveals that there is no peaceful sleep for the narrator. The dream parallels the nightmare of reality. Time has indisputably flown with the fields. The choice of the verb "wake" completes the tragic mood. Its harsh, clipped sound recalls other meanings: "to hold a funeral," or "to keep a vigil over." The masterful duality in the sleep sequences works toward one goal: to appeal to

the basic human fear of death and loss. It is horrifically successful. The contrast between the peaceful sleep of the child and the uneasy half-asleep older man is extremely saddening.

This was the unanimous first choice by every judge except the one from the English department, for whom the piece was the worst example of a student reproducing a "masterful" reading (that is, reproducing a reading whose skill and finish mocked the discipline and its values). It is too good and finesses key questions: what, you want to say to the writer, allows you to believe that you can speak for all readers of the poem? Or — "sad and horrific," "the nightmare of reality" — come on, it is just a poem. The poem may appeal to these emotions, but it is another thing to say that the poem creates them. Or — in whose interests is this story of youth and age and death? Why do we tell it over and over again?

It is not hard for us to think about how to get a critical purchase on this text. But, imagine what it would take to explain your position to your colleague in chemistry when he says that this sounds just like an English paper is supposed to sound, "you know — flowery." How would you explain to your colleague that he is exactly right and that is exactly why the paper, even if it marks some kind of achievement, does not deserve a ribbon?

But this is not a one-sided dilemma. In the story I am telling, the problem with the English paper was replicated with papers from other disciplines. The rest of us loved the lab report the chemistry professor said was just mechanical, uninspired. The rest of us loved the case study of the underground economy of a Mexican village that the sociologist said was mostly cliché and suffering from the worst excesses of ethnography.

Our inability to talk with each other about writing, about the student text and what it represents — as that writing reflects on the fundamental problems of professional writing, writing that negotiates the disciplines, their limits and possibilities — our inability to have that kind of discussion leads us (or our institutions) to give awards to papers we do not believe in and to turn away from the papers we do, papers most often clumsy and awkward but, as we say to each other, ambitious, interesting, a sign of a student for whom something is happening. In spite of our positions as critics, as teachers we are trapped within a discourse of error that makes it impossible to praise the student paper that is disordered and disorderly.

The chemistry professor and the English professor do not have these conversations because they are not prepared to and because they want to respect disciplinary boundaries and because they want to keep certain secrets secret. Their silence is a version of the silence in composition, where we are extraordinarily hesitant to argue about what writing is good and what is bad, what is worth doing and what is not; where we can talk for hours about empowering writers without raising the fundamental questions of power as they are represented in discourse. We move the furniture in the classroom, collaborate on electronic networks, take turns being the boss, but we do not change writing. It is still the same old routine.

But I want to focus attention on the students' writing, the Taylor essay and the Dylan Thomas essay, and to think about what achievement they represent. Here, as a way of working toward that discussion, is Paul Bové on Stephen Toulmin, one of the key figures in composition's "new" rhetoric:

> We might say that Toulmin's expansion of reason is one of the latest forms of error, that always found among traditional intellectuals as they tell stories about and to themselves and their masters. . . . Toulmin's own thinking leads us nowhere near these questions, for as a traditional intellectual there is no reflective origin to be found in his work. He makes no effort to understand his own position within the regime of truth, that is to say, the space within which he practices is taken for granted, assumed to have natural status within the discourses of truth and judgment. The result, in part, is that his work goes on untroubled by any implications it might have within the apparatus of power/knowledge, especially as this affects those less empowered by this very apparatus. In effect, I take Toulmin to exemplify intellectual irresponsibility, a disregard for extension of the regime of truth across society and national borders, and a carelessness toward interrogating one's own intellectual function within such an apparatus. ("Rationality," 66)

Now for a moment, I would like to imagine Bové providing the terms for a practical criticism. I would like to imagine how an instructor might be prepared to write at the end of the student's essay something along these lines: "Next time, don't be so careless about interrogating your intellectual function within the regime of truth." How would one phrase this so that it could be read? What sort of context would make the ensuing work both possible and valued? If composition is in any way going to be a critical practice, instructors will need to be prepared to imagine such forms of commentary.

I want to force this equation of Toulmin and the two student writers because I think it is not a comparison any member of the academy is prepared to make. I want you to imagine that one important way of saying "don't be careless" to student writers is as that term is used by Bové. I want you to imagine that the same critique can (and should) be applied to the student writer. It is too convenient to say that students, because they are students, do not share in the general problems of writing (like writing history or writing literary criticism, like the problem of the writer's relationship to the discourse that enables his or her writing). It enables us to produce thousands of writers (and professors) who think that writing is trivial unless it comes prevalued through channels of publication. The version of writing we sell shrinks from the comparison of Stephen Toulmin and a freshman; it gathers its authority from the representation that writing problems are unique to beginners, to students.

I want to use Bové as a way of capturing a simple word, "carelessness," and deploying it in the critique of writing untroubled by its relationship to "tradition" and to discursive habits and their status in the distribution of knowledge/power in the institution. That is, we can imagine that the goal of writing instruction might be to teach an act of criticism that would enable a writer to interrogate his or her own text in relationship to the problems of writing and the problems of disciplinary knowledge. (This is not, needless to say, the same thing as promoting Writing Across the Curriculum.)

Let us think for a moment in utopian terms about the future of student writing. Composition — or, those professionals willing to work on student writing — has a particularly valuable (or, perhaps "novel" or "unexploited") way of imagining criticism as something to be learned in practice, perhaps learned at the point of practice. This is different from studying the work of critics or theorists. Composition — or, the space within English studies where student writing is a central concern — is positioned to promote practical criticism because of its historic concern for the space on the page and what it might mean to do work there and not somewhere else.

CRITICISM

So, since this is a book about the next century, what is the future for this kind of work? How might we imagine the role of composition in the 21st century?

Here is Bové again, this time at the end of his book *Intellectuals in Power: A Genealogy of Critical Humanism*:

> Critical scholarship should seize the power function of "truth" and sophistically enlist it for political work intended not only to reveal the dark side of humanism's oppression but also to knock the underpinnings from humanism and the dominant regimes it supports. Criticism must be negative, and its negation should be of two sorts: invested with knowledge and the skills to produce more, it should destroy the local discursive and institutional formations of the "regime of truth," but this local negation will be most effective when aimed at necessary conditions for the extension of that regime, at those nodal points upon which humanism rests its own power and banks its own reserves. But this "negation" must have a "positive" content; it must carry out its destruction with newly produced knowledge directed not only against the centers of the anthropological attitude but, with an eye to its utility, to others in one's own locale and elsewhere. (309–10)

The project of critical scholarship, as it is defined here, could be said to be opposed to composition. That is, if we take composition to stand for the most common representation of writing in the required composition course, where the writer is figured as an individual agent making decisions governed by genre and convention and by a desire to be correct, then the composition course could be seen as one of those nodal points "upon which humanism rests its own power and banks its own reserves."

The "negation" of composition, or what is labeled composition, goes on daily in the workings of English departments — in personnel decisions, in the ebb and flow of goodwill and status that is part of a department's everyday life. This is news to no one, although in the last decade the terms of the negation have changed as the source of the critique has passed across areas in the department, roughly from literature to theory. Given the potentially shared institutional histories and ideological programs, the failure of an alliance between "theory" and "composition" is, for some at least, disappointing. It is possible, in other words, to see both as similar attempts to reimagine what it means to "do" English. Their presence as areas of professional definition in English was initially defined in opposition to the traditional use and status of literature and the forms of reading and writing promoted by a "literature" faculty. Both were renegotiating (with other new areas in English studies) the representation of high and low, the understanding of language as a problem in the undergraduate curriculum, the fragility of the traditional figure of the "author," and "official" accounts of the production and reproduction of knowledge, including disciplinary knowledge.

Composition has almost been nonexistent, however, in recent critiques and histories of English studies. When composition is figured into these accounts, it is figured negatively, said to represent a naive understanding of the problematics of language (see for example J. Miller), and to actively promote a purely functional literacy in service of or sponsored by late or postindustrial capitalism (as in Ohmann). The most recent version of this account is written into the introduction to Wlad Godzich's *Culture of Literacy*. According to Godzich, the 1980s featured both the spread of theory and, with Reaganomics and the recession, a push toward the "new vocationalism" — "a utilitarian conception of the university which foreshadowed its current transformation into a production site for the new force of production in a postindustrial society: knowledge" (1). These phenomena unfolded, according to Godzich, "in curious ignorance of each other, not least because they occupied different habitats: theory, the elite research institutions which continued to recruit students from milieux for the most part unaffected by the new illiteracy; composition, the rest, including the large land-grant universities" (1–2). Writing programs established their autonomy by promoting "a new differentiated culture in which the student is trained to use language from the reception and conveyance of information in only one sphere of human activity: that of his or her future field of employment" (5).

Godzich argues that composition profited when university resources were reallocated in the 1980s, getting funds and faculty lines at the expense of literature and theory. It is true, I think, that over the last 20 years federal and local monies have supported composition as an area of research and curriculum development and that composition "faculties" (although broadly defined to include nontenure-stream instructors) have increased.

It is useful, however, to also see this phenomenon as a coherent expression of *English's* desires; it is not simply the clever or lucky advancement of one subgroup at the expense of another. While I cannot cite figures and it would be unethical to name names, I have seen records of hiring patterns in departments that I think are representative. What these patterns show is that the effect, and in some ways the intent, of growth in English departments has been to divert money from tenure-stream faculty lines in order to provide increased funding for graduate study through the creation of a larger pool of teaching and research assistants. The growth in composition has been accompanied by a growth in the size of graduate programs, programs of literature and theory and cultural studies. It is not unusual to find a department, at least in large universities, where the faculty teaches only majors and graduate students. English, then, has spent its money on the graduate rather than the undergraduate curriculum, providing specialized courses for the faculty to teach and turning introductory courses and general education over to teaching assistants and fellows. I was recently on a campus where both a dean and a department chair acknowledged this as part of the ways decisions were made to allocate salary monies. The history department had spent its money on assistant professors, the English department on TAs and, to a lesser degree, part-timers. Specialization within the field and the values determining appropriate work for the professoriat have produced "composition" as it is realized in the formation of careers and the organization of resources in relation to the lower-division courses. The creation of the slot for the "critical theorist" and the slot for the "composition specialist" has both produced a curriculum that relies on part-timers and graduate students in the writing courses. The movement toward specialization has also determined who gets to use and practice criticism in the academy.

While I would argue with some other details in Godzich's account (composition, at least as it is represented by what goes on at professional meetings, was preoccupied with theory in the 1980s, not ignorant of it), what I have wanted to suggest is the importance of distinguishing between the various material practices, institutional pressures, habits, and conventions that govern writing and schooling. Godzich argues that in the 1980s, programs and careers were made in the name of what could be called the "new vocationalism." It is important to note, however, that the interests being served by the reallocation of resources in the 1980s included those that could be lumped under the name "critical theory," by "freeing" faculty from basic instruction and providing graduate students to take the seminars taught instead. It is misleading to imagine that the conflict was between critical theory and composition (as it was once misleading to argue that it was between literature and composition). The lines of interest separated those committed to basic instruction (across programs of composition, literature, and cultural studies) from those interested in "advanced" work. While it is true that some of those courses in basic instruction were promoting only instrumental uses of language, it is not a useful way of generalizing composition. (At least it is not useful if one wants to imagine the potential for English departments' involvement with introductory and general education. It is, of course, possible to argue that English departments should only serve to produce English majors and/or Ph.D.'s.) An argument like Godzich's forces the profession to overlook courses, programs, and projects developed in opposition to the institutional and cultural pressures to promote a functional literacy.

Composition as Reaganism or last-gasp humanism is a convenient reading of the 1980s. Without attention to the "local," it can be said to have both historical and empirical truth. Composition, however, has radically divergent relations to the "regime of truth" (and, I would say, has had such divergence since it became a school subject in the 19th century). My desire, however, is not to make a case for composition as "critical scholarship." As I understand what composition is, it could not be composition and be identical with this project. Composition — that is, the term I want to preserve to enable a certain kind of thinking about writing, local and institutional — is concerned with how and why one might work with the space on the page, and, in this sense, it is not the same thing as Theory. It is, rather, a way of committing professional time and energy to the revision of the Taylor essay — both as it is the product of institutional goals and practices (composition, then, is a commitment to study, critique, and change writing in the schools) and as the product of a particular writing at a particular point in time (composition, then, is a commitment to intervene in and direct the practice of individual writers). Composition would take its work to be revision; the form of composition I am willing to teach would direct the revision of the essay as an exercise in criticism (even, I think I would say, cultural criticism — that is, I would want students not only to question the force of the text but also the way the text positions them in relationship to a history of writing).

This binds composition to the ordinary in ways that are professionally difficult. It takes as its subject the writing of the Taylor essay rather than Toulmin, and this buys less in the academic marketplace. And it ends with revisions that are small, local, and difficult to value. It assumes the direct intervention in specific projects where (from a certain angle of vision) the gains are small. If it teaches criticism, it is practical criticism (or criticism-in-practice). Composition produces hundreds of thousands of writers every year; if there is composition in the 21st century, by the midcentury it will have produced millions. In this sense, the stakes are high. The worst that could happen, to my mind, is that English would give up its stake in a direct intervention with the production of writing.

CAREER

Composition currently serves as a term that justifies and produces certain career paths in English. This is commonplace; people talk regularly about the number of composition jobs on the job list. I am not sure this is simply a matter of a growing demand for writing teachers. It is (or it might also be said to be) a way the profession is choosing to allocate its resources — maintaining the viability (and exclusivity) of some careers by choosing to cluster a certain set of curricular responsibilities under the name "composition" (and, in composition, producing the category of the "specialists" that, in turn, justifies the use of part-time or adjunct teachers to do the daily work of instruction).

There was a time, for example, when it was possible to make the argument that everyone in English should teach composition, that it was part of everyone's mission and preparation. Composition — that is, the set of career interests represented by the term — assisted the division of the labor pool by arguing that not everyone could teach composition, not everyone was prepared, that it required a certain kind of training and orientation. I have never been convinced by this argument (having never been trained in composition, at least as that training is now defined in graduate programs across the country). I see composition as a professional commitment to do a certain kind of work with a certain set of materials with a general commitment to the values and problems of English. (And, therefore, I see composition courses properly housed in an English department.) The route "into" composition, then, was once like the route into film studies or women's studies, and like these, composition has become professionalized, so that the routes of entry have become more predictable, "disciplinary," and formalized.

It seems clear to me that composition professionals continue to provide rationale for the argument that establishes their identity and necessity in the English department by promoting the disciplinary status of the field. I find it hard to support or endorse this, even as I want to support the common enterprise. I refuse to encourage graduate students to define a professional identity solely through CCCC and the composition journals. It is, however, getting harder and harder for me to maintain this position, not because of a changed sense of what it means to be professionally committed to composition, but because of the battering people are taking when they try to work outside of disciplinary boundaries that organize the field of English.

The most surprising thing I have noticed as I travel and monitor the development of composition as an area of professional identification is the consistency, virulence, and direction of the attack on composition and those in it. Composition has never been a route to status in the profession. The surprising thing is the degree to which the programs most visibly under attack are those distinguished by the seriousness of their commitment to research and theory. (The criticism of programs at Texas, Syracuse, Carnegie-Mellon, and Pittsburgh is public knowledge.)

These programs have differing ideological commitments, and the attacks have come from both the right and the left. What is most striking is that it is the more thoughtfully organized and highly funded programs (in terms of commitment to faculty) that are being called into question, and this by English, not from the outside. It is not, in other words, a case of the faculty in political science questioning why the composition program is not teaching students how to write term papers. It is faculty in English attacking composition programs on ideological grounds. In fact, a visible and critically oriented program is more likely to be criticized than one whose approach to writing is fairly old-fashioned (teaching topic sentences as the key to writing) or simply poorly run. That is, it is not inconsistent to find "careless" programs housed in high-powered, critically aware English departments. Or, it is not uncommon to find English departments more troubled by an ambitious composition program than a mediocre one.

Now, there are many ways to explain this. When programs make themselves visible and invite ideological critique, they get what they ask for. There are also material bases to the conflict, as I have argued above. It could be said that what is at stake are the hearts and minds and bodies of graduate students. This, too, is what composition is; it is the term used to justify or to front the widespread support of graduate study in English. It is a rare English department that hires, promotes, or rewards graduate teaching assistants with an eye to their participation in the undergraduate curriculum. The more faculty involved with a composition program, the greater the potential conflict over the understanding and distribution of support for graduate study. Composition asks for a commitment of time (the time spent teaching and preparing to teach) that can easily seem to graduate students and graduate faculty as time that has nothing to do with their professional goals or professional preparation.

If I speak, now, as the traveler who has visited and evaluated departments and programs, the second most surprising thing I have noticed in the profession is the production of a kind of career I once could never have imagined. And that is the career of the composition specialist who never teaches composition. I may date myself by my surprise at this, but it seems to me to be increasingly common to find a specialist whose professional identity keeps him or her from the scene of instruction that defines his or her specialty. Composition has produced and justified a career that has everything to do with status and identity in English and little to do with the organization, management, and evaluation of student writing, except perhaps as an administrative problem.

These careers are not inevitable. I am going to use my career as an example (I will be either the chump or the hero of this story), but I have in fact taken my cue from others and could point to similar cases at a variety of institutions. There are senior faculty "in" composition who regularly teach the introductory composition course, and by regularly I mean every term. To the degree to which I am speaking for myself, I want to make it clear what I want this to stand for. I teach the course every year, often every semester. This is not a sacrifice. It is not a statement about solidarity with the masses (either the TAs or the students). It is not a commitment to teaching (as opposed to research). It is, rather, a fundamental commitment to a certain kind of intellectual project — one that requires me to think out critical problems of language, knowledge, and culture through the work of "ordinary" or "novice" or student writers. It is a way of working on the "popular" in relation to academic or high culture.

Courses

Here, at the end of this paper, I find myself trying to articulate a position for composition between critical negation and carelessness. Or, to put it another way, I want to try to imagine a way for composition to name a critical project, one that is local, one whose effects will be necessarily limited, but one, still, of significant consequence. I think of the question this way — what does it mean to accept student writing as a starting point, as the primary text for a course of instruction, and to work with it carefully, aware of its and the course's role in a larger cultural project?

Let me think this through by means of a final example, a student paper:

> A few summers ago, I accompanied my church youth group on a mission trip to St. Croix, in the Virgin Islands. We were to clean up

damage from a hurricane which passed through the summer before. To tell you the truth, I really wasn't looking forward to working, but rather I was excited to visit the Virgin Islands. But, by the end of my trip, I would not have traded my experience for anything in the world.

Our group flew from Philadelphia to Puerto Rico, and then to St. Croix. After arriving from a long plane trip we were driven to the place which for the next couple of weeks we would call "home." We stayed on an old plantation which was located in the lower class part of St. Croix. The plantation was surrounded by a 15 foot high stone wall, but on the other side of the wall were the slums. As we entered the driveway leading to the plantation, adults as well as children lined up. They all watched carefully, probably trying to figure out why we were on their island.

On the first day of our journey, we started by picking up trash and tree limbs which had fallen to the ground from the hurricane the year before. It was so incredible how much damage was done and how it appeared that the hurricane had just passed. This task took several days to accomplish, even in a small area. There were just so many things covering the ground it was just unbelievable.

From day to day, we came in contact with lots of people who had lived on the island for many years. Quickly, we learned how many of the islanders felt about people from the "States." Once, while we were working, a group of islanders approached us and inquired why we were there. They asked why we were intruding on their land when we had a land of our own which was better. It was almost as if they were afraid that we were trying to take their island from them. I could tell by their voice of inquiry that they felt threatened. Even after we tried to explain that we were trying to help them in a time of need, they still wanted to know what we expected in return. At this point in time, I felt shut out. They would not except that the only reason that we were there was to help them.

Over the weeks we accomplished several tasks. These tasks included digging up five foot in diameter tree stumps, rebuilding roofs of homes which were blown off, picking up trash, and helping run a coffee shop for the homeless and less fortunate. All of these tasks were time consuming and entailed much work. As we went to the different locations, I found the chance to talk to a lot of the islanders. They seemed very anxious to know my reasons for helping them. I explained that all my work was volunteer and that I liked to help others. Slowly they started to except [sic] the fact that I, as well as the others, just wanted to befriend them. I witnessed their feelings starting to change toward us and soon they appreciated the work we had done.

As our time of service came to an end, I looked back on the huge difference which we had made on the island. After these several weeks, the islanders came to realize that we did not expect anything in return for our work, except their friendship. In the beginning, this concept was hard for them to understand, but as they watched the changes occur, they learned to appreciate our help. In fact, by the end, the many people which at one time had questioned our existence were the ones to tell us how sad they were to see us leave. They graciously thanked us over and over for our help. Their appreciation was unbelievable. They just constantly asked how they could pay us back. They praised the work which we had done and expressed their undying gratitude.

This change in our position in such a short amount of time was incredible. We went from being the unacceptable in their community to the heros of the community. We were once looked down and frowned upon, but after working hard to prove our position we were more than accepted. Our efforts proved to change our position in that particular society and we became well respected guests on the island. (unedited student paper)

In the spirit of the Conference on Composition in the 21st Century, I want to end by provoking discussion, so let me end quickly and without taking responsibility for conclusions. I recently taught an introductory composition course where students wrote travel narratives, at least for starters, and read Mary Louise Pratt's *Imperial Eyes*. I chose Pratt's book because I thought it a good introduction to the problems of writing as they preoccupy the professoriat, and I chose it because it was difficult. Part of the point of the course was to teach students how and why they might work with difficult texts. The course was divided into three sections. The first dealt with revision, the second with a writer's use of Pratt's book, the third with sentences (revision exercises asking students to translate their sentences into and out of a style that might loosely be called "Pratt-like," somewhat in imitation of the exercises in Joseph Williams's *Style: Ten Lessons in Clarity and Grace*).

I used Pratt in the course as an example of a writer working on a project similar to the students' (learning how to articulate a critical reading of travel narratives) but also to help make the point that writers need to understand the degree to which their writing is not their own. In this case, students were invited to see their writing as part of a tradition that began with travel narratives of the 18th and 19th century and that implicated them in the same general cultural project, here taking possession of worlds not their own. This is part of what a writer needs to know in order to revise. Or, to put it another way, this historical perspective is as important for composition, it seems to me, as seeing today's textbooks or classroom rhetorics in relation to their 18th- and 19th-century counterparts. I say this not to argue against the current work on composition's history. I do, however, want to argue that the profession has not yet found a way to make composition a name for a critical/historical study of student writing.

I want you to imagine, then, a course that takes the St. Croix essay as its central text. The question for the writing teacher, then, is "What next?" As I am imagining composition, the job of the teacher is to prepare students to work on that text. It is not, as it might be in other courses, to set it aside. I want to make this point because I have seen many courses, often offered as "cultural studies" composition courses, that provide a knowledge of the problems of writing only by erasing student writing. In such courses, for example, students would learn to produce arguments about American imperialism or arguments against the "missionary" narrative; they would perhaps summarize

Pratt's argument. The central work of the course would not, however, be work on the very discourse within which the students, as writers, operate. They would not revise the essay because the essay would be seen as irredeemably corrupt or trivial. And, of course, the results of that revision would be up for grabs — the final product may be more of the missionary narrative, not less. In fact, I can say from experience that students who learn how to produce the critique of the narrativizing of the other will, when they write a narrative, easily produce the very discourse they have learned to critique. Students learn to be critical of their writing (to understand how and where they are implicated in questionable ways of speaking) long before they learn to change it. (This is demonstrated, I think, in William E. Coles's *The Plural I.*)

The course put the St. Croix narrative (with some others also written by students) as primary texts. (The St. Croix narrative can stand for all of the narratives the students wrote. It is the narrative that ordinarily writers cannot *not* write.) The problem for the course was how to imagine its revision, particularly if revision was to be made possible by and to enact a critical reading of the text, and where that critical reading was not merely a critique of the formal properties of the text — where a writer would have to ask about and think about, say, the history of North American relations with St. Croix. Through this discussion, students were to imagine the revision of their own opening essays.

In a strange displacement, revision is not usually taught as criticism. In fact, as a result of the "writing process movement," criticism was removed from the writing course, where it was seen as counterproductive (a "barrier" to writing) and characterized in the figure of the maniacal English teacher with the red pencil. There was, then, a "correction" of writing that was deliberately blind to questions of value. The process movement, for example, produced forms of evaluation, like holistic scoring, where the evaluative judgment was comparative (one could not appeal to considerations outside the boundaries of what most writers would produce) and where readers were taught *not* to read closely.

Within the terms of the process movement, the primary goal was the efficient production of text. Students learned to produce writing; questions of value seldom, if ever, came up, at least as value is imagined as social value. And within this field of vision, revision was primarily addition and subtraction — adding vivid details, for example, and taking out redundancies. The result (or the goal) was to perfect and, by extension, preserve the discourse. Within these protocols for revision, the missionary narrative may become more finished, but it will remain the missionary narrative. Details can be added, but they will have the status of the details in the essay (as local color). It would be inappropriate to ask questions of the discourse as a discourse: What is its history? Whose interests are served? What does the scene of the plantation mean? What does it mean in terms of the history of St. Croix? What does it mean that it is offered as background and color? Why don't the people of St. Croix get to speak? How might one *not* write a missionary narrative and yet still tell the story of a missionary trip to St. Croix? The writing process curriculum, at least as I have characterized it here, produces good writing without asking questions about "the good."

A course in practical criticism (and I can only begin to suggest its difference) would teach students to question the text by reworking it, perhaps attending to detail in one week, perhaps breaking or experimenting with the narrative structure the next, perhaps writing alternative openings or endings, perhaps writing alternative scenes of confrontation, perhaps adding text that does not fit (a report on the history of St. Croix or a report on the documents preparing students for the trip), perhaps adding different voices or points of view, perhaps writing several versions of who the writer or the St. Croixians might be said to be. In every case, the product would be an essay that was, in a certain sense, less skillful or less finished or less masterful than the original. The key point for me is that a course in practical criticism must return students to their writing. In the context of my example, it requires the ability to understand both Pratt's argument and her way of reading; it assumes (and exercises) the ability to produce a critical reading of the St. Croix essay; but its final work, for each student, is multiple revisions of the travel narratives they have begun.

I have tried to place composition in the context of the curriculum, of debates about the place of criticism in the academy, of careerism, and of a course, one where freshman writers could be thought of as continuous with European travel writers of the 18th century. I want to at least suggest the possibilities for a practical criticism (as opposed to a critical scholarship), one that investigates the problems of writing at the point of production and that investigates representations of writing as a mode of learning. That is what I think composition is or might properly be. It is, I believe, a good field to work in, but you have to be willing to pay attention to common things.

WORKS CITED

Bové, Paul A. *Intellectuals in Power: A Genealogy of Critical Humanism*. New York: Columbia UP, 1977.
——. "The Rationality of Disciplines: The Abstract Understanding of Stephen Toulmin." *After Foucault: Humanistic Knowledge, Postmodern Challenges*. Ed. Jonathan Arac. New Brunswick, NJ: Rutgers UP, 1988. 42–70.
Godzich, Wlad. *The Culture of Literacy*. Cambridge: Harvard UP, 1994.
Miller, J. Hillis. "Composition and Decomposition: Deconstruction and the Teaching of Writing." *Composition and Literature: Bridging the Gap*. Ed. Winifred Bryan Horner. Chicago: U of Chicago P, 1983. 38–56.
Williams, Joseph M. *Style: Ten Lessons in Clarity and Grace*. 6th ed. New York: Longman, 2000.

Composition, 1900–2000

B y 1900, composition as a university subject was already a century old. Writing instruction and the writing of regular "themes" were part of the university curriculum in the United States throughout the nineteenth century, with goals and methods perhaps best represented in Blair's *Lectures on Rhetoric and Belles Lettres* (1783), Newman's *A Practical System of Rhetoric* (1827), Parker's *Aids to English Composition* (1844), Boyd's *Elements of Rhetoric and Literary Criticism* (1844), and Quackenbos's *Advanced Course of Rhetoric and English Composition* (1855). Composition courses, usually required, are among the most distinguishing features of the North American version of university education. They represent a distinctively democratic ideal, that writing belongs to everyone, and a contract between the institution and the public — a bargain that, over time, made English departments large and central to the American university and to the American idea of an undergraduate education.

It is useful to highlight 1900, however, since the turn of that century is usually understood as the period when, under the influence of the German model, the university was remade in its modern form, with a focus on research and with the creation of departments, including English departments. In 1900 it was still taken for granted that English departments had a fundamental commitment to the teaching of writing (and this was primarily a faculty commitment), although as the curriculum was divided into required courses and electives, that commitment was (unfortunately) translated into a required freshman composition course, and questions were raised about the opportunities for research and professional advancement in the area defined by the practice of written English. At the beginning of the twentieth century, discussions in the professional literature and at professional meetings raised questions that abide today: Who should teach these courses, and what is the appropriate preparation? What *is* a composition course, and what is its content? Is there any evidence that writing courses work? Are they worth the considerable investment of time and money?

From *PMLA* Dec. 2000 (Special Millennium Issue): 1950–55.

The MLA, it is important to note, was part of the conversation. In 1901, 1902, and 1903, the Pedagogical Section, at the prompting of Fred Newton Scott, published a series of reports in *PMLA*. (Scott was a member of the English department at the University of Michigan; in 1907 he would become president of the MLA and in 1911 president of the National Council of Teachers of English [NCTE]. The reports can be found, with an excellent introduction, in John Brereton's book *The Origins of Composition Studies in the American College, 1875–1925*.)

A committee of the Pedagogical Section sent out questionnaires on topics related to composition. The 1901 questionnaire surveyed opinions on rhetoric as an area of graduate study. A "decided majority" (188) endorsed the advanced study of rhetoric, although there were familiar queries about what the term *rhetoric* represented: was the goal to improve the writing and teaching of graduate students? or to open up new areas of research? The report concluded that "the term Rhetoric as heretofore generally employed, may well be enlarged in meaning so as to include much more than practical composition and that the field thus opened will afford abundant opportunity for investigation by the serious student" (201–02).

In 1902 the committee asked, Are composition courses worth the time and effort? Wouldn't student writing be equally served through readings in great literature? The responses are interesting (and, again, remarkably familiar in temper and argument). On the whole, the answer to the first question was yes, writing did improve through direct instruction, and this instruction required a course in composition and not literature. From Harvard: "We find a marked difference between the work of the freshman and sophomore classes in English composition, a difference which shows that the writing of the same man before the course in freshman composition and after it, is technically of very different quality. With one exception all the members of the department who teach English composition agree in this opinion" (212).

The last of the reports, in 1903, asked departments to consider two positions, one arguing that the appropriate goal of composition was "the art of writing clearly and correctly about ordinary matters and with such limitations as you expect in a good business letter"; the other represented in the following (quite remarkable) passage by J. F. Genung (at Amherst College): "I have always regarded rhetoric as dealing, in all its parts and stages, with real literature in the making, and composition, however humble its tasks, as veritable authorship. . . . To put the student frankly on the basis of authorship, . . . is to impart immensely greater reality to his study of rhetoric" (218). As I read these options, the committee was trying to phrase a crucial and difficult question — not whether students should write themes or short stories, composition or literature (a line taken, unfortunately, by several respondents), but whether, as Genung argues, student writing can be taken seriously as writing, as something more than an exercise in correctness and more than a submission to standard forms and expectations. Can student writing be used to raise fundamental questions of literary value (what is good writing? what is its history? what are its uses?), and is there, as a consequence, a justifiable equivalence in courses conventionally defined as literature and courses conventionally defined as writing? Is composition a serious course of study in English, or is it trivial and remedial? Can professionals take this subject as their own, or is it shameful, unacademic? These are fundamental questions, asked at a key moment in the history of English as a university subject.

In 1903 the respondents came down on the side of putting students "frankly on the basis of authorship." Unfortunately, the next half century in English was not driven by a conception of composition as "veritable authorship." As English departments grew into literature departments and as the number of students grew (and the problems of managing small, labor-intensive courses increased), the composition course was viewed as a burden and a drain and made mechanical and trivial enough to justify the scorn with which it was usually treated. The appropriate authors to be studied were major figures in the emerging canons of English and American literature. Composition fell out of sight of the MLA and most of the other significant venues of professional discussion.

In a brief history like this one, the next significant date is 1949, the year of the first meeting of the Conference on College Composition and Communication. CCCC (or "the Four Cs"), with the sponsorship of the NCTE, provided an annual meeting and a journal — and, over time, awards and book displays and a bibliography and public recognition and special-interest groups and networks of scholars, teachers, and publishers — for those in composition who sought not only a community of scholars and teachers but professional distinction and identity. The CCCC was created to provide what was not available in the MLA and the NCTE. The emergence of composition as a field in English coincides with the development of other area studies: women's studies, film studies, gay and lesbian studies, African American studies. CCCC and the men and women whose work led the field in the fifties and sixties provided the context for the emergence in the seventies of composition as a defined field with a research agenda, professional alliances, internal debates and consensuses, a varied and distinguished literature (recognized through national awards, including the MLA Mina P. Shaughnessy Prize), and newly developed programs of undergraduate and graduate study, including basic and advanced courses and specialized PhD programs.

So — what is the state of composition in 2000? The core issues remain the same: who does the teaching, what is the proper preparation, what is the appropriate content for these courses, and are they worth the time and expense? I am often asked, is the teaching better? Are students writing better than they used to? I don't know that it is useful or possible to try to answer these questions. On both sides of the desk, the quality of the work rises and falls with the recognition and rewards that go to those who give it serious time and attention.

Perhaps the best way to focus on composition in 2000 is to return to MLA documents: the *MLA Job Information List* and two remarkable reports, the *Final Report of the MLA Committee on Professional Employment* (1997) and the *Report of the ADE Ad Hoc Committee on Staffing* (1998).

As late as the first half of the seventies (when I was in the job market), *composition* was rarely used to describe a tenure-track slot, let alone to describe a required area of PhD preparation. By the mid-eighties, composition was the big news in an otherwise discouraging job market. In 1986 24 percent of all the listings in the *MLA Job Information List* were for positions in composition and rhetoric. This is compared with 15 percent for British literature and 10 percent for American literature (including multiethnic literatures). In 1999, of the 898 jobs in the *List*, 25.4 percent were in composition and rhetoric, 22 percent in British literature, and 21 percent in American literature (including multiethnic literatures).

The MLA and ADE reports make visible, however, the other side of the composition job market. They document the withdrawal of *all* tenure-stream faculty members from all lower-division teaching and, in particular, from the teaching of composition. And they document the institution's necessary reliance on non-tenure-stream faculty members (with lower pay, higher teaching loads, and reduced benefits) to teach the required courses. Both documents deserve close reading — the arguments are carefully researched, and hard-edged — and both deserve discussion on every campus, with particular attention to the recommendations, which I do not have space to list here.

The MLA report argues:

> Over a half century [. . .] higher education deliberately and as a matter of public policy gathered a student body that, from one point of view, would be described as "increasingly ill-prepared." Over the same half century, however, the institutions of higher education cultivated with equal deliberateness a particular kind of faculty ambition for which the best working conditions and salaries and the highest professional reputation were ever more closely linked to intellectual capacities expressed through specialized research. (35)

The distinction between advanced research and lower-division teaching, perceived as "routine service," was institutionalized through the use of adjunct faculty members in the teaching of lower-division courses. The ADE report indicates that this problem is not unique to research departments or to PhD-granting universities. The "percentage of faculty members holding full-time and part-time non-tenure-track appointments remains roughly the same across all types of institutions and departments, whether or not they have graduate students and whether or not they make use of graduate students as teaching assistants." The ADE report argues that "[l]ower-division courses, and especially writing courses, are where the adjuncts are. Reclaiming tenure-track lines inescapably means reclaiming the lower-division sector of the curriculum as one where members of the professorial-rank faculty can, do, and must teach" (4, 25).

The figures from the *MLA Job Information List*, in other words, do not indicate that more composition courses are being taught by tenure-stream faculty members; they simply indicate that more tenure-stream faculty members have credentials in composition. There is neither the money nor the institutional will (nor, to my mind, good reason) to hire specialists to teach all the thousands of writing courses offered each semester around the country. (Let me be clear about this — while I feel English departments should include faculty members whose careers are linked to the field and to the success of a composition program and its students, I do not believe that composition specialists are the only, or even necessarily the best, teachers of composition. In fact, every program in the country produces evidence to the contrary every year, as teachers without the professional credential, including part-time faculty members and graduate students, win teaching awards, generate outstanding evaluations, and produce prizewinning students.) Certainly, one of the most important achievements in composition at the end of the twentieth century was the successful promotion and development of writing across the curriculum, which brought a broader range of faculty members to the teaching of writing.

The growth of the professional status of composition as a field and the remarkable increase in the number of jobs has had no significant effect on the problems of staffing or on the conditions of employment for the vast majority of those who teach composition courses — that is, part-time faculty members and full-time adjuncts. (I leave graduate teaching assistants off the list because I think there have been improvements in their employment conditions, and I think these improvements are linked to the work of composition professionals. There are many who would disagree.) A skeptic might argue that there is a link between the growth of composition as a field and the increased reliance on part-time, non-tenure-stream instructors, that the English profession's response to the felt pressure to *do* something about composition was to do the predictable, to create and endorse a research agenda and field expertise. This isolated the problem and made it easier for faculty members in general to say that they were not prepared to teach or take responsibility for composition. And, in fact, one of the most significant developments of the nineties has been the creation of composition programs outside English departments and existing departmental structures, programs with faculty members outside the tenure stream, programs that can employ graduate students and ABDs from an even wider pool.

Do I have a prediction? Only that the problem of staffing will dominate the next decade. One solution — and this argument is gaining increased support inside the composition community — would be to eliminate the composition requirement. (See, for example, Sharon Crowley's *Composition in the University*.) I sense a similar will (although for different reasons) outside composition programs. Cutting the requirement will, of course, affect the size of English departments and, particularly, their graduate programs. I don't know that colleges and universities are going to be able to get out of the historical commitment to teach writing to everyone; I don't know that parents and legislators are going to let us off the hook. I agree with those who argue that English departments must increase the participation of tenure-stream faculty members in lower-division courses, review and reduce the size and number of PhD programs, and regularize and improve the working conditions of non-tenure-stream faculty members, who will certainly continue to be present in the composition curriculum. If the requirement remains and if composition programs are not going to be spun out of the departmental structure altogether, I think two things will have to happen. Institutions will need to reimagine the locations, rewards, and identities of those involved in writing instruction (bringing writing across the curriculum to the lower-division, for example). And institutions will need to direct the production and promotion of student writing beyond the individual course — imagining a writing requirement, for example, that is not solely a matter of work in a single class.

I would love to believe that our institutions could learn to make these accommodations by following the example of developments in English. Departments might begin by assessing the resources directed to the major and to graduate education (where larger course sizes are possible and reasonable) and by conceptualizing the lower-division courses without necessarily adhering to program boundaries — without beginning with the assumption that certain courses "belong" to composition, literature, creative writing, film, linguistics, and so forth. Changes in English departments, however, will require a new politics. The divisions within English severely limit our ability to argue locally and nationally for the importance of our work. The interests of English are greater than the interests of our various field identifications, and, although the interests of English are difficult to articulate or to name, they certainly include work on behalf of "literature in the making."

WORKS CITED

ADE Ad Hoc Committee on Staffing. *Report of the ADE Ad Hoc Committee on Staffing. ADE Bulletin* 122 (1999): 7–26. Dec. 1998. 29 June 2000 <http://www.ade.org.ade/ bulletin/n 122/122007.htm>.
Brereton, John, ed. *The Origins of Composition Studies in the American College, 1875–1925: A Documentary History*. Pittsburgh: U of Pittsburgh P, 1995.
Crowley, Sharon. *Composition in the University: Historical and Polemical Essays*. Pittsburgh: U of Pittsburgh P, 1998.
MLA Committee on Professional Employment. *Final Report of the MLA Committee on Professional Employment. PMLA* 113 (1998): 1154–87. Dec. 1997. 29 June 2000 <http://www.mla.org/ reports/profemp/profemp_frame.htm>.

Literacy and Departments of Language and Literature

As a member of the MLA executive Council, I participated in the discussions that led to this* conference and felt moved by my colleagues and their sense of urgency, particularly as expressed by Rosemarie Scullion and Sylvia Molloy. At the time of our council meetings, however, I was thinking mostly about staffing issues and the various reports and resolutions related to the use of graduate student and non-tenure-stream labor — some of them useful, some of them not very useful at all. And there I felt a real sense of urgency — and I remember thinking that there might be a way these issues converged.

I thought, for example, that if students could be persuaded to see literature courses taught in translation by my colleagues in the foreign language and literature departments as possible choices in satisfying the general education literature requirement, then fewer students would be coming to English and I would be able to cut sections of courses taught by part-time or adjunct faculty members — courses with titles like Short Story in Context, Introduction to Poetry, Women and Literature, Literature and the Contemporary, courses that could easily be taught by specialists in the foreign language departments using texts in translation. This would bring a larger number and broader range of undergraduates to the foreign language and literature departments, it would remind students that literatures are available to them in translation, and it would make a small dent in the large number of adjunct faculty members in English.

That students do not elect literature courses offering French, German, or Italian fiction in translation is as much a matter of how we administer these requirements as it is evidence of students' determined choice. When they look for literature courses, students by default will turn to English in the catalog. They don't think to look under *S* for Slavic or *H* for Hispanic. Or students say to their advisers, "I need a literature course on Tuesday and Thursday at 9:00," and their

---

*From *PMLA* 117.5 (2002): 1272–78. This conference refers to the 2000 MLA Conference on The Relation Between English and Foreign Languages in the Academy.

advisers turn to English in the catalog. Still, excellent lower-division courses, using the national literatures in translation, are offered by other departments.

As part of my preparation for the conference, I met with the chairs of the foreign language departments at my university. I was curious what areas of our relations they would want to highlight for review. (I should add that there is no formal structure that would have us meet regularly. There is a humanities council — the chairs of all the humanities departments — but it rarely meets and has proven to work best only in times of crisis. The Committee of Foreign Language and Literature Department Chairs meets regularly. It is possible that I will be invited more regularly to those meetings — that we might see ourselves more specifically as departments of language and literature.)

The quick conclusion at the meeting was that we should develop a regular procedure for cross-listing courses between English and the other departments. This would bring their courses to students' attention; I hope, in fact, that it will mean that I will need to offer fewer lower-division literature courses (and have a smaller adjunct faculty). And this kind of cross-listing may make it easier for all of us to imagine that we are not in competition for students and therefore easier to design courses that can turn more freely to literature in translation — so that a thematically or generically organized literature class in the English department (or even a period course) could turn more quickly to include work in translation — something we now do rarely and with a sense that we are poaching.

We survey our majors every year in the spring. Among the questions we ask are questions about what is missing from the curriculum. Every year our students ask for single-author courses, courses in Joyce, Faulkner, Woolf, or Wharton. This year, for the first time, a very significant number asked for courses in Latin American and Russian literature. As it stands, these courses are available to students but not as electives in service of the major. If we were to cross-list upper-division courses as well, students would have the option of including these courses as part of their formal preparation as literature majors. And this could work both ways — we could, in fact, see more majors from the foreign language departments in our upper-division courses.

And, finally, we talked about possible certificate programs in literature. I doubt we would rename this a Certificate in Comparative Literature, since that assumes a program of study I don't know that we can or should revive. It may be the case, however, that while film studies, cultural studies, and women's studies include literature, literature is not necessarily at their center; perhaps there is a reason on our campus to find a new context for literary study.

And so I suppose the best way to represent myself on this panel is as an English department chair, thinking as English departments do — that they are at the center of the universe of languages and literatures, not quite sure what is happening around them, confident that they have everyone's best interests in mind, and seeing the other departments as possible solutions to problems at home. In preparing for this conference, I read through several years of the *ADFL Bulletin*, where English is most often represented as an imperial power — big, rich, powerful; blind, intransigent, self-interested — annexing the world's literature, then film, then culture itself as its domain.

I would like to think about the language and literature departments as departments, and as departments related to other departments through the peculiar lines of authority and accountability defined within colleges. I will use my own department and university as a case in point. My guess is that we are relatively typical. Where we are not, I hope the differences too will help to prompt discussion. My argument is that the best way to imagine the possible relation between English and foreign languages in the academy is to imagine the possible relations between departments. We are not, after all, imperial powers. We have no armies, we have little budget that we actually control; when we clash it has been over who gets to teach a particular novel in translation; when we collaborate it is often to overcome bizarre administrative barriers to team teaching or to cross-listing courses. I know that the origins of English studies (and American studies and Latin American studies and Russian studies, to name a few) were linked to the project of the nation and were funded, at least in part, in service of the nation; still, I can't see the strategic advantage of mapping local politics to global politics if our topic is the relation between English and foreign languages *in the academy.*

If anyone had asked me six months ago, I would have said that the relations between English and foreign language faculties on my campus are deep, regular, and highly articulated. When I arrived at the University of Pittsburgh in 1975, there was a comparative literature program that offered a certificate to majors in English or the other language and literature departments. It was very much tied to a particular faculty member and to an NEH grant; when the faculty member retired and the grant money dried up, the program died. In its place, however, other faculty members have developed several very innovative and successful interdisciplinary programs: women's studies, film studies, cultural studies, Latin American studies, medieval and Renaissance studies, Atlantic studies, urban studies, and, on the horizon, global studies; in English, we have a program in children's literature and we have developed a joint major with Africana studies. If anything, I would have said, we are spreading ourselves too thin, we are too promiscuous in our relations, we have too many partners.

All these programs bring together teachers and students from the various language and literature departments. The curricula — and the extracurricula of lectures, colloquia, and publications — all have developed common points of reference in relation to histories, theories, texts, and pedagogies. As an administrative achievement, I think it is safe to say that several of these programs would not exist and would not thrive without having been underwritten by the English department and its faculty. That is, the English department provides faculty members, space, and staff support. The directors of several of these programs are, or have been, members of the English department faculty. In the large programs closest to our interest — women's studies, film studies, cultural studies — the greatest percentage of courses are taught by members of the English department. In film studies, for example, which offers a major, eighty percent of the major courses taken by graduating seniors are in English; English provides the student advising.

And this is, of course, as it should be. We are a very large faculty compared to the other departments, and so we can afford to lend people to the programs. And it is very much in the interests of individual professors to teach in these programs — the courses serve their research agendas; faculty members greatly value the opportunity to be in regular conversation with students and colleagues from across campus.

Still, ours is a peculiar accounting system. When a senior faculty member teaches in cultural studies (and it is often the senior faculty members who are in demand), the dean gives me at the most $3,000 to hire a part-time or adjunct faculty member to take his or her place in the English department curriculum. I trade a very significant scholar and teacher, and a significant salary, for a part-time faculty member who will teach an introductory-level course in film, composition, or literature.

Two recent MLA reports — the 1997 "Final Report of the MLA Committee on Professional Employment" and the 1998 "Report of the ADE Ad Hoc Committee on Staffing" — both argued that in order to address the increased use of non-tenure-stream instructors in introductory and general education courses, tenured or tenure-stream (T/TS) faculty members must commit to teaching courses in the lower division of the curriculum. In the academic year 2001–02, the English department at the University of Pittsburgh had 851 majors. In the same year, only 25% of all our courses were taught by T/TS professors (below the national average for English departments, 30.7%). It has occurred to me more than once that the growth of these important areas of interdisciplinary cooperation in language and literature has been at the expense of the introductory, general education courses in English and underwritten by my department's willing cultivation of a relatively underpaid and underprivileged body of adjuncts. For an English department chair, staffing is a pressing issue, perhaps the most pressing issue on a chair's desk. And on many campuses, certainly on mine, staffing pressures are compounded by increased enrollments. I know that it often appears as though English departments are doing everything they can to attract students, but I don't believe this to be the case. We get no bonuses for increasing the number of majors (ours increased by 55% in the last two years) or for increasing the numbers of sections we teach; these numbers are a problem — more than an annoyance, an ethical problem and, increasingly, a problem defined as one between labor and management.

If I were to follow the recommendations of the MLA reports, if I were to raise the percentage of T/TS faculty in the lower division (or, for that matter, in the upper division), perhaps the first route I would have to take would be to no longer sign off on faculty teaching in interdisciplinary programs. These programs, I would have to say, are a luxury we can no longer afford.

Let me be clear. I have no intention of doing this or of denying faculty members access to our newly developed interdisciplinary programs. I want to illustrate, though, the degree to which interdisciplinary programs in language and literature are underwritten by English, at least on my campus, and to suggest some of the costs.

I would have said, then, that there was considerable cooperation between the language and literature departments on my campus, and that the joint projects were largely successful — at least at the level of program development and faculty and student satisfaction. I was very interested, however, to read the accounts of the development of one area of interdisciplinary activity, cultural studies, as reported in the Winter 2002 *ADFL Bulletin*, particularly as it included questions of language and literacy. Cultural studies as an area of scholarly concern brings popular culture and everyday language to the table. And, in doing so, it troubles the order of language and literature. Let me briefly outline the arguments in articles by Russell Berman, professor of German studies and comparative literature at Stanford, and Michael Holquist, professor of comparative literature at Yale. Berman argues the following:

> Languages are embedded in culture and are born in culture, but the critical discourse of cultural studies has paid scant attention to the intersection of language and culture. Surprisingly perhaps, it appears that much of the cultural studies movement ignores linguistic multiplicity. This may reflect either a theoretical blind spot, that is, an assumption of language as fundamentally transparent, or a disciplinary predisposition to select primarily anglophone material. Is cultural studies ultimately as much an English-only project as American studies always had been? (5)

He argues that foreign language scholars are better prepared and better positioned for the project of cultural studies:

> Teaching foreign languages implies a direct and special engagement with the material of the other culture — its language — which indicates how close the foreign language field is tied de facto to the project of cultural studies. In other words, the historical advantage of foreign language curricula, the institutionalized inclusion of culture as a topic of inquiry, has to be opened up to the wider discussion of culture in literary scholarship. (6)

And he concludes:

> The transformation of the discussion of culture has implications for curriculum, pedagogy, and institutional structure, as well as for research. It is urgent that foreign language departments build on their historical advantage [. . .] in order to strengthen their positions within the university [. . .]. (7)

I would have taken this as a fact — that cultural studies has changed curriculum, pedagogy, and institutional structures, and that it has strengthened the position of foreign language departments within the university. I suppose that the question that remains concerns the position of language in cultural studies. This is the issue taken up by Holquist. He too raises the question of declining enrollments in foreign language departments (with the exception of Spanish). He argues that while cultural studies fits easily into the traditional structures of teaching in English (the Shakespeare course is more popular than ever),

[t]he situation looks quite different in language departments, where teachers of foreign language feel less like successful imperialists than they do like beleaguered natives [. . .]. That is to say, the turn to cultural studies has been no less marked in foreign language departments than in English departments, but this move carries with it a danger to their academic missions that teachers of English are spared. As the number of students enrolled in German studies or French studies grows, the role of the German language or the French language in such programs is diminished. We may be keeping up our enrollments, but there is a danger that by doing so we have jettisoned our main task. (16)

He asks us to remember philology, the philology of Kant, Wolf, and Humboldt, because its aim was to "remember language" (19). And he concludes:

Remembering languages in all their specificity and difference is the most effective way to expose students to a world in which tectonic shifts in politics, economics, and culture are indeed producing radical new effects, while at the same time making them aware that we still have not shaken off the need to order the world in signs, a need that is as old as history itself. (19)

I was surprised and taken by this line of argument — partly because it had such a familiar ring to it. It is often forgotten — and often forgotten by English departments — that English departments, too, are departments of language and literature. The imperative for language instruction is there historically — the teaching of writing was part of the original charge to English in the formation of the university in the United States — and it continues today in the public imagination and in the almost universal requirement for writing instruction in the freshman year and, increasingly, in courses across the curriculum in the later years. It has been my impression that foreign language departments see language instruction in the introductory curriculum as a problem and as undesirable work while asserting at the same time that close attention to language practices in almost every other setting is absolutely central to scholarship and pedagogy. To the degree that this is correct, English and foreign language departments share contradictory structures of value.

Holquist's eloquent statement echoes the terms by which composition programs have tried to define (and to explain) themselves in English departments. On the one hand, in the face of the pressure to study literature, someone else's writing, composition programs remind students (and their teachers) that the important problems of language and writing reside in their writing too — problems concerning identity, authority, gender, class, representation, standardization, and knowledge. Composition courses, at their best, provide the occasion for students to "[remember] languages in all their specificity and difference" by turning attention to language in use and language in context, including the context of the students' writing in relation to the linguistic values and the language projects valued in a university. On the other hand, composition programs are struggling against the pressure (from the culture, generally, but also from various parts of the institution) to mount courses that are prevocational and instrumental, to teach a simplified writing by forgetting language.

Wlad Godzich alludes to this pressure in his introduction to *The Culture of Literacy*:

> The new writing programs, lacking either tradition or intellectual legitimation, sought to gain acceptance, and thus a legitimacy of sorts, by becoming responsive to what their practitioners saw as society needs, and what were in fact the impulses provided by these market forces. In the spirit of the "New Vocationalism," these programs took to defining literacy as the mastery of specific codes of linguistic usage defined by the career objectives of the students. Their ascendancy [. . .] was an indication that the traditional programs in English and in the other literatures had somehow failed, or, at the very least, could no longer be relied upon to ensure the literacy of students. (12)

And he says, "The literacy programs that already exist evince a profound distrust of interpretation and other critical functions in relation to language, and proclaim mastery and competence as their goals" (14).

Godzich is quick to generalize about composition courses and composition programs without demonstrating any knowledge of the particulars. I have spent much of my career working with undergraduate writing programs, and I have a great respect for the attempts to create introductory courses committed to presenting "interpretation and other critical functions in relation to language." This is difficult work, important and not without risk, as indicated, for example, by the controversy surrounding the freshman course at the University of Texas and the effects it had on various careers. It is true that more and more undergraduate composition programs are being developed outside English departments (and so outside any accountability to literature — whatever that term might mean locally), and it is true that English departments are developing writing tracks in the major, and there is great pressure and temptation to make these largely vocational. On some campuses, these newly defined tracks in the major are seeking connections to ESL and to translation programs. I would say that Godzich is correct, then, in his assessment of the forces running through and around composition in the university. He is wrong, however, in assuming that the "vast bulk" of these programs are blindly complicit (5).

One of the most encouraging developments in English has been a renewed sense of a possible coherence between the lower division and the upper division and between composition and literature, as the project of cultural studies has allowed professionals to articulate a common set of concerns. There are undergraduate programs in English departments where students are learning about writing in history and in culture by studying the effects (and consequences) of history and culture in the work of recognized authors, but also and at the same time in students' own sentences in paragraphs, in their own poems, stories, or essays. Those responsible for writing programs have a long and substantial record of efforts to manage, promote, and theorize an attention to students' language that is critical and reflective. That is, to use Holquist's terms, within the broad and contested array of composition courses and composition programs, there are those working primarily to "expose students to a world in which tectonic shifts in politics, economics, and culture are indeed producing radical new effects, while at the same time making them aware that we still have not shaken off the need to order the world in signs, a need that is as old as history itself" (19). It has been important to express these goals and to train new teachers and to develop curricula with those goals in mind.

Holquist, I know, was not speaking only of lower-level language instruction, but then neither am I. I find it impossible to think about the upper-division or more advanced areas of study without thinking at the same time of the lower division, of general education, and of the role of language study generally in an undergraduate education. As a professional, and as a department chair, I have been unwilling to think of the lower division, or of general education courses, as separate from the central concerns of English. In her paper at the April conference, Claire Kramsch expressed the hope that foreign language programs and composition programs might find a new route to imagining their shared interests and projects. If this is to happen within our current departmental structures, it will come through the arguments a new alliance might make concerning the necessary conjunction of language and literature — in pedagogy, curriculum, and scholarship. (Outside our current departmental structures, one could imagine a comprehensive department of language, as there are now literature departments defined without regard for national language boundaries.) There are surprising (or perhaps not-so-surprising) points of commonality to be found in the literature on composition pedagogy and the literature on the teaching and learning of foreign languages. It is, in fact, interesting to note that much of the work in composition, including efforts to imagine the genre of student writing and to imagine the trajectories of student learning, have drawn on research in second-language learning. Without a full sense of its sources, composition teachers and scholars speak regularly of L1 interference, of interlanguages, of the necessity and logic of error; they speak of students writing in a university setting as students who have crossed boundaries, who work in contact zones; the pedagogy makes much use of dialogue, practice, imitation, and translation. If you look to the composition journals, Mary Louise Pratt would certainly rank in the top ten in citations. In relation to an imagined standard of academic discourse, students are figured as either a Richard Rodriguez or a Gloria Anzaldúa, depending on the language politics of the writer or teacher.

Frankly, I don't quite know where to go with this observation beyond noting the connections. At the conference, Claire Kramsch suggested, for example, that English and foreign language departments could combine efforts to improve resources directed at teacher training. I am trying to think of something bolder, and Kramsch (and her colleagues) provide the terms for this. In his article "Reconciling the Language-Literature Split through Literacy," Richard Kern draws on the important work of Kramsch, Widdowson, Swaffar, Arens, Mueller, Berman, Jurask, and Byrnes to argue for a literacy-based curriculum in foreign languages. In such a curriculum, he says, reading and writing are defined not "as peripheral support skills but as a crucial hub where language, culture, and thought converge." The study of language would provide the occasion to "create, interpret, and reflect on discourse in order to better understand how meanings are made and received, both in their own culture and in a foreign culture" (22). There will, of course, be different levels of engagement at different levels of the curriculum, but the introductory course is not different in its commitment to remembering language in a critical and cultural context. Kern says, "[W]e still want to teach students to do things with words, but we also want them to reflect on how things are done in their native language and culture as compared with the ways they are done in the new language and culture" (23). And he says, "The point is not just to give students something to talk about for the sake of practicing language but also to engage them in the thoughtful and creative act of making connections among grammar, discourse, and meaning; between language and content; between language and culture; between another culture and their own" (24).

This has been the project of composition, at its best, for the last four decades. It is remarkable to see the degree of shared language and mission. And, at its best, composition has been necessarily situated in English departments and in productive (if difficult) conversation with literature, film, linguistics, and cultural studies.

To shape change, to do something as departments of language and literature that we cannot yet quite imagine, will require us to remember language. This was certainly a thread in the lectures and discussions throughout the MLA "Conference on the Relation between English and Foreign Languages in the Academy." Since I can't help but think as a department chair, I wonder if the lower-division language courses Kern proposes could serve to satisfy the almost universal composition requirement. Perhaps. I think everyone will benefit by bringing the foreign language and literature departments more fully into the requirement structure of general education.

But there are larger issues at stake here: the coherence of the curricula in languages and literatures, and the values we bring to our teaching and scholarship. While I am not confident that the problems of staffing language courses and meeting the demands of composition requirements can be solved by an interdisciplinary effort, it certainly might be useful to join forces in imagining how to solve the conceptual and (local) political problems of teaching and valuing language and literacy in relation to literature.

WORKS CITED

Berman, Russell A. "Foreign Languages and Foreign Cultures." *ADFL Bulletin* 33.2 (2002): 5–7.
"Final Report of the MLA Committee on Professional Employment." *PMLA* 113 (1998): 1154–77.
Godzich, Wlad. *The Culture of Literacy*. Cambridge: Harvard UP, 1994.
Holquist, Michael. "Why We Should Remember Philology." *ADFL Bulletin* 33.2 (2002): 16–19.
Kern, Richard. "Reconciling the Language-Literature Split through Literacy." *ADFL Bulletin* 33.3 (2002): 20–24.
"Report of the ADE Ad Hoc Committee on Staffing." *ADE Bulletin* 122 (1999): 7–26.

Reading and Writing in the Academy:
A Conversation with David Bartholomae

Q. It seems that you followed a standard graduate school path for your time when you wrote a literary dissertation for a Ph.D. Could you tell us how you got interested and involved in the research on writing — the bulk of your research since graduate school?

A. In some ways it's a story about circumstances. I had gone to Rutgers on a NDEA fellowship and was pretty far along in my program before I finally got a chance to teach. The course was composition, and in it were a number of students who I could tell from the very beginning weren't going to pass. Today we would call them "basic writers." At that time, we had no training in teaching composition and there was little supervision. We just basically taught whatever we wanted to teach. Under these circumstances, all I was prepared to do was to offer a course that would fail these kids. I afterwards went to the chair of my department, a man named Dan Howard, whom I liked very much, and told him that I was very unsettled by this experience. I never wanted to do it again. He said that he too was concerned about this problem and he told me how to do something about it. So I spent a year helping to set up a writing workshop and a basic writing program at Rutgers. I was trying to help those that our regular courses wouldn't do anything for. And I found it very interesting.

But Rutgers was a very interesting place at that time, and even though we got absolutely no training in composition and there was really, in some ways, open contempt for the introductory composition course, it was a graduate program that produced a lot of people who have made their careers in composition and its issues. Linda Flower was in the program at that time and so were Donald McQuade, Bob Atwan, Bruce Herzberg, Pat Bizzell, and John Brereton, among others.

Q. That's odd. Do you have any idea why that came about?

A. I think one of the reasons was the approach to literary studies. We were not trying to package and sell great authors or produce precious interpretations of texts or do literary history, but to think about the problems of

From *Issues in Writing* 6.1 (1993/1994): 4–23. Interview conducted by Roberto Stokes and David Holborn.

language as they were present in various literary texts. The reason I wrote a dissertation on Thomas Hardy is that I was interested in the question of the relationship of an essentially working-class person to a middle-class genre, the novel. The novel contained a sense a language, a set of conventions and attitudes that excluded other languages, conventions, and attitudes. So in a way I looked at Thomas Hardy as a basic writer. What was said about Hardy in the early reviews is what's often said about basic writers. That is, there's something very powerful in the writing, but that he writes so badly. He's clearly not refined or properly educated. I was interested in trying to figure out the critics' responses to Hardy, and Hardy's use of the genre, its cultural capital. So I found myself in my graduate training being prepared to think about language as a problematic and a social problematic, and to think about writers not as geniuses but as offering particularly rich instances of a more generalizable writing problem. In a sense, it was exactly the kind of preparation that made us start to think about basic writers and their work.

When I went on the job market. I had a kind of two-roads-in-the-woods experience. I was offered two jobs, a job at Boston University as a Victorian scholar and a job at Pittsburgh as the assistant director of the composition program, where I would be expected to do something to develop basic writing. I had to think about exactly where I wanted my career to go. I went again to Dan Howard, the chair. Basically he said I should remember that I would be doing this work for the rest of my life, that I should look around at my colleagues and think about what I see in their work and their lives that I hated and admired. That made it clear for me. I was intrigued by the problems that were present in the basic writing courses that I was teaching, and would have almost rather die than write one more word about Thomas Hardy.

Q. In your address to the College Composition and Communication Conference when you were chair in 1988 you made a reference to the conflict between the senior professor of literature and the composition specialist as being the very cause of the organization's existence. Do you still see this as an important conflict and one that drives organizations like the 4 Cs?

A. I'm going to give a roundabout answer. My memory of the 4 Cs talk is that what I was trying to do was to characterize not a historical reality, but a way in which the participants represented their positions. There was clearly a time — it was in 1946 — when people felt that MLA and NCTE weren't providing the forum that they needed, and they formed a new organization, the 4 Cs. Their way of representing their position was in relationship to what *they* said were senior professors of literature who weren't really interested in writing and teaching and in the kinds of students that were entering the university right after the war. I think there was probably truth to that then, and still today. I do a lot of traveling, evaluating both English department and composition programs, and it is certainly true that one of the prevalent ways in which English departments are defined is in terms of a literature program and a literature faculty and a composition program and a composition faculty, and they are seen as somewhat at odds.

What I was also trying to say in my 4 Cs address was that this construction — literature or composition — was not useful or inevitable. It might be better to think about attitudes toward language, attitudes which (with historical accuracy) we might label conservative and liberal. That is, there were certain conservative attitudes toward language that were represented both in the literature curriculum *and* in composition. There were those who were interested primarily (I used Weaver to represent this position) in conserving cultural values in the writing class, and those who (under the sway of what they were calling the new linguistics or the new science of language) were interested in valuing language variety and language change, represented at the time, at least as I stated it in my address, by McCrimmon, but probably more powerfully by Kenneth Burke.

In many departments, my own included, the really significant lines are drawn between faculty, whether they are in literature or creative writing or composition, who are willing to promote criticism and experimentation in the work of undergraduates as opposed to those who take a more conservative position in what they will and will not allow students to do. And the unfortunate thing is that because we institutionally organize ourselves in terms of literature programs and composition programs and nationally in terms of Modern Language Association and 4 Cs or literature and composition, we don't make the kinds of local and national alliances that we might make if in fact we were cutting the pie differently.

So that I felt then as I feel now that there are battle lines, or at least lines of tension, drawn between literature and composition, but that this is unproductive. The fundamental issues have to do with attitudes toward language instruction, what it means to call attention to language, or to the role of the academy in relationship to the culture and its literate values. There are people with common goals in literature and composition and yet we make it difficult to work together. There are profound differences in philosophy and practice within the composition community, and yet we are forced to argue as a monolith.

Q. Is it possible at Pitt to bridge the composition and literature programs?

A. It has been. There is a Pitt narrative, a kind of utopian narrative, that says it's a place where there have never been strong divisions between literature and composition. Most of us, both in our backgrounds and in our teaching, imagine ourselves involved in English rather than as a member of the literature faculty or composition faculty. So that you could look at introductory literature courses and they would look a lot like composition courses. And you could look at introductory composition courses and in some ways they would look like literature courses, that is, attention is given to assigned texts and to reading. That's the product of a faculty who, no matter where we are contractually in relationship to the department, are interested in writing and reading and don't draw fine lines between whether we're dealing with Hawthorne or with Emerson or with Gretel Ehrlich or with a student paper or a student short story. Ideally and at our best, it's a place that has tried very hard not to think in terms of those divisions but to think in spite of them. But at the same time we're also part of the world. There are times when we act like the rest of the world, and I think quite stupidly, and set up a whole different set of hierarchies and manage our goals and resources differently.

I've been very happy at Pitt; it's been a great place to work, and the happiest I've been has been through work that I've done with colleagues. For instance, this last semester I just finished team-teaching an introductory composition course with Colin McCabe, who's one of the directors of the British Film Institute and a major figure in cultural studies. There was something in the structure of the department that made it possible for senior faculty members to cross what would be seen by many as a big professional divide to teach together an introductory composition course by choice, out of an interest in the work.

Q. Could I follow up on this team-teaching description that you began to offer. How did that work in practice? What did each one of you do? How did you decide, for example, on a syllabus, on the pedagogy, on various things that might happen in class? Were you both in class at the same time leading discussions?

A. The class was one where we were both in the room at the same time. As a writing teacher, you're really in class in two ways. We would both comment on all the students' papers, so that the students would always get two sets of comments for their next revision. In class, we would take turns leading, with the other person sitting with the students as part of the discussion, so that if I were taking a particular line in relationship to a student paper, Colin would be with the students either arguing with it or arguing against it, whatever the case may have been.

As far as the development of the course was concerned, this one had an interesting history. Colin would come in from the perspective of the British tradition. He really hadn't been in a composition course, and yet having been interested in language as well as literature for most of his career, he was very interested in what he saw as a characteristically American democratic experiment — making everybody a writer. Part of his goal was to learn about it, and he felt, and I think rightly and with great generosity, that one of the ways to figure out what this was all about was to be there. The initial shape of the course was the shape as I and my colleagues had been teaching it for some time. A large part of it is teaching students revision, how to revise, how to think about revision, not as a cleaning something up or preserving something that's written, but as a way of raising questions about discursive practice. We had a book for the course, a difficult book. Part of the course was to teach students how to imagine difficulty positively as an intellectual experience. It was a book by Benedict Anderson called *Imagined Communities*. Colin very much wanted the students to work on sentences, so he introduced some materials from the British curriculum. He is rooted in classical training where, at least in a certain part of traditional British education, you take Latin sentences or Latin poems and translate them into English. On that model we used Joe Williams' book *Style*. It has a lot of translation exercises where the students translated their sentences into and out of Benedict Anderson-like sentences and other models. Colin was interested in getting students to think about syntax in relationship to both meaning and, in a sense, history and politics. He was not sure quite how to do that in a classroom where the language to describe syntax wasn't immediately available to everybody. We hit upon doing it through these translation exercises, and it was very interesting.

Q. While we are on the subject of collaboration, let me ask you about your frequent written collaboration with your colleague Anthony Petrosky. How does that work? Do you actually compose together? Or does one write a chapter and the other revise, and so on?

A. Since we've worked together so long, we've developed a system. We'll meet and talk things through, and then one of us will draft and one will revise. We don't sit together to write. We don't sit down together and talk out loud and bang sentences out. We usually meet and talk something through and then one of us will write a draft and the other will go to work on it. Then we'll meet and work from there.

Q. You were talking before about the line not being between composition and literature but rather between different ways of looking at language. So often when I read and listen to you talk, it seems that your approach — using student writing as text, for example — would work well at the introductory level, but that there would be more problems at the advanced level, say in a junior-senior course in the English novel. Would you agree that your approach is better suited to the introductory level?

A. It's an interesting question. People often say to me that the kind of work I'm imagining is too hard for students in an introductory course. So I have to argue that it's not too hard. Usually I'm arguing that students can work on serious intellectual projects in an introductory course. You are wondering if it is appropriate, for example, to spend time studying student writing in an advanced, "content" course. In my department, there are a number of courses at a more advanced level that follow the pattern that you've described as being a part of this introductory course. There's a lot of attention to writing, a lot of close work on revision, and what it comes up against is everybody's expectations about coverage. For example, we teach a course for our majors called Introduction to Critical Reading, and one of the difficult decisions in the evolution of that course was giving up the idea that the way to prepare a potential English major was to cover 200 years of American literature or 400 years of British literature so that people would know who comes first, Milton or Wordsworth. We made the decision that we would spend a lot of time working on a very limited number of texts, and a good bit of the work on those texts begins with students writing about them.

Let me give an example from a recent section I taught. *Uncle Tom's Cabin* was one of the books that we used. We were not interested in a general discussion about *Uncle Tom's Cabin* or Harriet Beecher Stowe or the nineteenth-century novel, but in looking at three student papers on *Uncle Tom's Cabin*, using these as examples of how the book was read. We were concerned with what these readers noticed in the book and how they accounted for what they noticed, how they made what they noticed significant as a way of thinking about the roots or agenda of that reading. Part of my work was to direct the revisions of these readings through a revision of the essays. It is only after this that students begin to look at the criticism on *Uncle Tom's Cabin*. In the course I am recalling, students read essays by James Baldwin, Jane Tompkins, and Jean Fagan Yellin. The students were asked to write about how and why and where these readings differed from each other but also from theirs, from the students'. So that when the students looked at Jane Tompkins or James Baldwin, it was not to go to the experts to finally get *Uncle Tom's Cabin* right. The published essays were a vehicle for students to think about those "professional" readings as readings and how they differed from their own. The point of this course was not to cover a lot of material, but to think at that higher level about problems of reading and writing. I've done the same thing in a senior seminar, where the purpose was to get senior English majors ready to go on to graduate school. I don't try to cover more material but to stop and think again about how they are prepared as readers, what it means to be "Englished" by an English department. One of the very powerful things to do for senior English majors, I think, is to look at their writing, that is, how they literally have learned to produce English, against some of the prose of contemporary literary critics who are more experimental, less bound to the old prejudices about structure and conclusion. I like to give them a way of reading somebody like Stanley Fish or bell hooks, let's say, not as sources of information, but as examples of writers using the resources of nonfiction to work out certain kinds of problems.

Q. You began that response by saying something about people criticizing you for the difficulty of the reading in your introductory classes. I recall reading a review of *Facts, Artifacts, and Counterfacts*, your book with Tony Petrosky that outlines and provides the rationale for a course in basic reading and writing, where the reviewer made essentially that point — that your chosen works were too difficult for basic readers and writers. How do you respond to that? How is it you can work with such difficult texts in a course designed for basic writers and readers?

A. I have two responses. One, it's in the nature of the course; from the time that Tony and I started thinking about writing courses and putting materials together for students, both for basic writing classes and then later for other composition classes, we actually took as our goal to put before students the very materials that they were said to be unable to read. It had to do with our sense of what education is all about, which is learning to work with materials that are marked or designated as not yours, as beyond you. And it was a political decision. For generations students were given things to read that were simple and stupid, material that didn't really have to be taught. This confirmed the faculty's assumption that it was the kids who were simple and stupid, that they couldn't do interesting work. It was a kind of self-fulfilling prophecy. Our goal was to take the kinds of texts that the academy was interested in, and valued, and liked to talk about, texts by Freud or Marx, let's say, and put these on the desks of basic writers. The fundamental opening move of the courses that we taught was to get students to see, in fact, that learning to work with this material is really learning to think about reading and writing, about how to begin to work with these texts. They did not need to listen to lectures or take a course in Marx or Freud *before* they could read their work. We wanted to put primary texts into the hands of freshmen. And we wanted to design courses and assignments to allow students to begin with those texts — to begin reading and writing, to begin an intellectual or academic project.

This was the concept behind the structure of the course reported in *Facts, Artifacts, and Counterfacts* and it is certainly what lies behind *Ways of Reading*.

Q. What informs the way you advise students to tackle their reading? For example, what reading research has caused you to look at reading in the ways that you do?

A. We started this a long time ago, back in the late 70s. We were responding to most of the reading research that had produced the classroom protocols for introductory courses. Much of this involved skimming and scanning exercises. There was a variety of reading research that basically told students how not to read, and yet how to strip mine books to get a certain level of information from them. The book became a source of information rather than an example of somebody thinking something through. At the time, there were two people we were reading who helped us to imagine a different form of instruction. One was Frank Smith, who was providing a very different view of reading as an interactive process. But more than Frank Smith was Frank Kermode, whose book, *Genesis in Secrecy*, was of particular interest to us. It gave us a way of imagining reading as, in a sense, a compositional activity. That's how we justified to ourselves what we were doing. The fact of the matter is that when we started we were actually at war with the reading researchers and reading specialists on our own campus, who wanted to have a course that was really a study skills course which told students how not to read their textbooks.

Q. In that response you offered a negative metaphor for a certain kind of reading; you called it "strip mining" the text. Can you offer a positive metaphor for reading or writing, one that resonates for you or one that you might have offered to your students?

A. I find it useful to talk about writing as revision. Revision is where the real work of a writing course takes place. By revision I don't simply mean what you do when you go back to work on a draft, but what you do when you always imagine yourself in a critical questioning relationship to the prior text. In this sense, even a first draft can be revisionary. If, when you sit down, let's say, to write an essay on *Uncle Tom's Cabin*, you realize that you're not going to invent literary criticism but that you're working in the context of disciplinary assumptions about what you're supposed to do, even at that moment the writing can be considered revisionary. The reason this conception is so powerful for me is that it stands opposed to another perspective that I find to be extraordinarily destructive and this is the one that holds that you have to say something original, or do something original, or have an original thought.

What the revisionary view says is that you're always working at both conscious and unconscious levels in relationship to prior texts, to other people's sentences as well as other people's paragraphs, and other people's larger projects, and other people's ideas when you begin to work with *Uncle Tom's Cabin*. Getting students to understand this at the level of practice makes the composition course a course in American culture or American schooling or American history.

Recently, in an introductory composition course that I taught, I had students write travel narratives, and then we worked with Mary Pratt's book *The Imperial I*. The course asked students to see that in a very real sense, the travel narratives that they wrote were in line with or actually in many ways produced by travel narratives written in the 18th and 19th centuries. Students learned to imagine that when they were revising paragraphs or working on sentences they were working on the textual legacy of the European appropriation of Africa and South America. "Good writing" in a travel narrative is not then a simple matter.

As far as reading is concerned, Tony Petrosky and I felt it important to provide negative metaphors, metaphors students could use to revise the ways they thought about reading. Students think they are supposed to remember everything that they read. We wanted to help students understand that reading is not represented by what you can remember but what you can do with the text. It's hard for me to think outside of the terms of our textbook *Ways of Reading*. There the positive alternatives are "strong readings," which are really the measure of what somebody is able to do with the text.

Q. In your book *Facts, Artifacts, and Counterfacts,* you speak of a course intended for basic writers, and yet you seem to have a certain ambivalence about that term "basic writer." Do you have any misgivings about putting basic writers together in the same class and separating them from the rest of the students?

A. Yes. I gave a talk a year ago at the National Basic Writing Conference in Garrison, Maryland. This paper was recently published in the *Journal of Basic Writing*. I argued that it was time to think about the consequences of using the term "basic writing" as though it were inevitable rather than strategic or provisional. What I wanted to say was that there was a time, when Mina Shaughnessy coined the term, when the phrase "basic writer" opened up a kind of intellectual and institutional space where we could work with such students without considering them stupid or bone-headed or failures or intractable or impossible, where we could think of them as a different kind of writer. That allowed us to think of a pedagogy that would be based on the difference represented by this different kind of writer. It was an extraordinarily powerful, and, in the best sense of the word, liberating moment.

What's happened is that this opening gesture has now become a way of institutionalizing a set of divisions that the initial argument was meant to make disappear. That is, the gesture was to allow this group of students access to the university and to break down a division between high and low, good and bad, or correct and incorrect. Now, basic writing has become a fixed slot in the curriculum, one that has to be filled each fall and winter with a predetermined number of bodies. There are now basic writing careers and expertise, institutional interests in preserving basic writing, in literally maintaining and producing the very hierarchy of haves and have-nots that the term once allowed us to call into question.

It seems to me that it is time for honorable institutions to take stock again of what we do when we give these tests that separate out the basic writers. We produce an underclass in our own curriculum, and we ought to think about the effects of the tracks that we lay down. I say this cautiously because I know that there's a lot of important good work that goes on under the name "basic writing." There are opportunities and careers made for students through basic writing classes that would not be made if we just got rid of them. If we propose to eliminate basic writing courses, I fear we would play into the hands of the more cynical forces in the institution, those looking to cut costs and cut corners. The institution would love to pretend that the need is not there, that we have "solved" the writing problem, which means that kids who have writing problems will be ignored. Of course, that's not what you want. And yet there are a lot of places — on my own campus, at Chico, at Ohio State — where people are starting to imagine what will happen if we eliminate basic writing as an organizing term and yet continue to make a commitment to the variety of writers and tasks represented by the student body and the college curriculum.

What it comes down to is this: I'm very nervous about taking what was strategically a powerful term, "basic writing," and turning it into something that will be a part of our landscape forever and ever, therefore insuring that there will always be basic writers.

Q. Is it fair to say that your ideas grow out of a very sharply defined political background, that there's a certain political content to much of what you say?

A. I think it's fair to say that. Like many people, part of my interest in composition in the 70s came out of a sense of responsibilities that were formed in the late 60s and early 70s. This period allowed a sentimental and idealized missionary version of oneself. While all of the profession is, in a sense, politicized now, there is a certain set of political interests that have been worked out in my career. I tend to be a pragmatist. I'm not interested in writing papers about theory or theorists. I'm interested in small, local and — for many — mundane sites: the writing assignment, the silences in students' papers, comments that might enable revision. What are the consequences of organizing students' reading and writing time over a 14-week semester? Or what's at stake in asking a student to revise a paper not to make it better, that is, more perfect, more self-contained or rhetorically powerful, but to make that paper in a certain sense worse, that is, less sure of itself, calling its own premises into question. This view asks a student to consider that the paper's careful organization is a problem rather than a triumph. These are the sorts of political questions that I am most interested in, ones that deal with local decisions about how reading and writing are organized and ordered.

Q. In "Inventing the University," you speak of students' need "to appropriate or be appropriated by a specialized discourse." It seems to me appropriating a discourse is clear, but what do you mean by a student being appropriated by a specialized discourse?

A. If you were an English major in college you know that there was a way in which we learned to produce readings of poems and novels. It had nothing to do with our own immediate interest and desire. It had nothing at all to do with how one naturally or rationally or inevitably read, but it had to do with a certain set of discursive practices. That is, you looked for repeating patterns and motifs. You saw those as a sign of order, accomplishment, and achievement. You knew that there had to be some underlying set of countervailing pressures or tensions. You did this with everything you read. And in that way your own disciplinary status came into being; your identity as a reader and your reading habits had been appropriated by something you at the time couldn't have named, couldn't have spoken of with any clear authority. You just thought you were getting smarter or reading better. You didn't realize that a profession was reproducing itself through the way you sat down to write your paper on *Tess of the D'Urbervilles* or "After Apple-Picking." But it was that.

In "Inventing the University," what I wanted to do was to write an essay that described the role of writing in post-secondary education. I wanted to say, here's how to imagine students, not as individual agents or entrepreneurs, but as part of an educational process that is producing large numbers of readers and writers every year. These subjects that are being produced are really fairly homogeneous. They may read and write different things, but if you travel a lot and go from campus to campus, the one thing you can't help but notice is that everybody pretty much learns to do the same thing. They've been appropriated by a set of values, a certain attitude toward the world, a certain relationship to the regime of truth. They've learned to value knowledge only if it's construed in certain ways, for example, moving from introductions to conclusions, making examples fit a thesis. You could imagine large numbers of students trying to find examples that don't fit their thesis, but we don't do it that way. We do it the other way around. Those interests are appropriating individuals as they come through the educational system. I was trying to describe that in the essay, trying to place writing and the writing curriculum in terms of this larger, more generalized cultural project.

I was trying to suggest that we need to think about the writing class not simply as a free or democratic place, a place in our complete control, a place where students could "own" their writing. At the time I wrote the essay, the writing class was constantly being thought of as a kind of democratic free space where students were empowered with their own language. I wanted to make an argument that to my way of thinking it was not a free space and the students were not empowered with their own language. It was a place filled with prior interests and agendas. Students can learn how to work within those interests and agendas or be appropriated by a discursive project that they certainly didn't invent. They don't invent the discourse, whether its argument or the personal essay, an analysis of *Moby Dick* or a loving description of their grandmother's house in Maine. All of these things are highly ritualized by the culture the students entered.

Q. Who has influenced you the most in the development of your ideas?

A. The first was Richard Poirier, the director of my graduate program. Three of his books had a great influence on me: *A World Elsewhere*, on American

Literature; his book on Frost, *Robert Frost: The Work of Knowing*; and *The Performing Self*. At the time, Poirier was for me a very compelling mind and writer. I was interested in the kinds of problems he imagined to constitute the study of English. I have come to understand that what he really represented was the very best of a tradition, a version of the new criticism influenced by F. R. Leavis and conceived to elaborate the relationship between the practice of writing and the practice of life, including social life. The thing that made Leavis so very powerful was the pressure to think about reading and writing, reading and writing as the practice of discrimination, and the quality of life. This was not, at its best, simply a matter of snotty refinement. It had to do with a larger cultural project, one poised against the brutality and ugliness of the emerging mass culture.

Leavis is now almost always criticized for being elitist, and of course there are ways in which he was. But he enabled more than a generation of students to imagine that reading, writing, and teaching would be part of a politically committed professional life. This was very powerful in my graduate education; it was one of the reasons why I moved eventually into composition. Composition also allows you to imagine that you are doing this work for the common good, for democracy, or for social change, that there is more to professional life than the pursuit of a career.

Then I read Raymond Williams (I was writing my dissertation on Thomas Hardy). Williams was essential for me in maintaining a sense of commitment to the idea of common good without the elitist overtones in Leavis. Turning to mass communication and film, to working-class issues, and the issues of popular culture allowed me to imagine Leavis' concerns more broadly conceived. After Williams came Bill Coles, who was my first boss and great mentor, and whose work is in some ways in a direct line with this Leavis-Poirier axis. When I met Bill Coles it was astounding that we had almost the same way of reading and talking about a student paper. Bill would ask students, in effect, "What kind of person do you become if you talk like that? What is your world, if you imagine the world in those terms?" That was the analytic that Bill carried into student writing. It was the analytic that I can remember learning to use in relationship to a literary text as a graduate student. When I heard him speak, it was as though we had been talking together for a long time. Bill's teaching and writing remain for me the daring, powerful legacy of close reading.

And then I read Mina Shaughnessy's work. When I was doing the work at Rutgers, Shaughnessy was far along in the project at CUNY, and I remember getting a copy of *Errors and Expectations* in manuscript through Susan Miller. I read *Errors and Expectations* then as I read it now: it's an attempt to do a kind of socially responsible close reading of a corpus that had been unread, the texts of basic writers. In a sense, it made clear to me how I was going to do what I was going to do. Leavis, Poirier, Williams, Coles, Shaughnessy — these were the figures, the sources of influence that I feel most strongly about thanking in an interview.

Q. Sometimes you say that the problems of teaching and the problems of thinking come from disciplinary boundaries, and yet you frequently talk of the need for students to appropriate a specialized discourse. Is there a contradiction here?

A. I think so. But you should remember that when I said that students need to appropriate specialized discourses, I didn't say they ought to. I wasn't describing an ideal, a utopia. I was trying to be descriptive. I was saying that given the way the university now works, students will have to appropriate a specialized discourse to be students. They are compelled by the structure of their education to major in something and the values of that major will govern the assessment of their performance.

But if you sit down in a history course to work on the history of Pittsburgh during the Vietnam War, there are a lot of things that you could do that could be interesting and intellectually profitable, but could very well not be good History, at least as it is conventionally construed in History classrooms. So I was describing a force or inevitability that wasn't my wish or desire, but that represents the way the academy works right now. In that sense, I have a dual response to your question. On the one hand, being appropriated by discourse means that students become trained in the disciplines without being able to ask any questions about these disciplines and their discursive order. In that sense it seems like a limiting form of education, and a writing course ought to prepare students to both understand what's at stake and to revise prose.

At the same time, I'm not absolutely critical of the American academy. I think that disciplinary knowledge has often been productive and powerful. If you look at *Ways of Reading*, you can see the way Tony and I worked out some of the issues from "Inventing the University." For instance, you'll notice that *Ways of Reading* is not a cross-curricular reader. We don't take a social science essay, a natural science essay, and a humanities essay. In fact, most of the work that we chose comes from figures like Michel Foucault or Clifford Geertz or John Wideman or Adrienne Rich — writers whose work really could be said to call into question the very limits of disciplinary structures of knowledge that the university takes for granted. That is, Foucault writes outside as well as inside of assumptions about history; Wideman outside as well as inside certain assumptions about culture; Geertz outside as well as inside of the tradition of ethnography or anthropological report. I never felt that ideally what we should do is to make students good little disciplinary soldiers, good history majors or good English majors. But I think the university is structured in such a way that they will inevitably be measured in relationship to the good disciplinary soldier, the good English major, the good history major. The value of composition in relation to this is that the composition course can provide an understanding of reading and writing, of the role of the reader and writer, to enable the kind of questioning that disciplinary instruction does not.

Q. Much of your writing that I've read presents this dual view you've just spoken of, the need for a specialized discourse yet a conflict with a more generalized discourse — what you sometimes call dissonance — and the need for a negotiation between the two. Do you think the same kind of conflict exists in writing outside of the classroom, for instance, in communities of technical writers or business writers?

A. If I answer a question about technical or business writing, I do so in almost complete ignorance. I don't do a lot of work with people outside the academy. But I was once a writing coach at a newspaper, and I learned that every journalist seems to see himself or herself in an antagonistic relationship with the editor. The editor comes to stand for a certain set of requirements as to length, objectivity, and so on. The journalist thinks she would write better if only the editor would let her, so sometimes she tries to sneak things in that she hopes the editor won't notice.

In my own experience as a university administrator, a program director, I know about this kind of tension. I can remember that the thing I used to like about memo writing was to try to find a way to remind my colleagues that I was still alive. On the one hand, the memo had to get information across, but at the same time, I'd always try to get a joke in there somewhere or let people know that I was breathing as well as telling them how they were supposed to handle grades at the end of the term.

I'm sure that everyone who writes as part of his business knows that one of the ways that he's going to get ahead is to be a good memo writer. But being a good memo writer has little to do with the requirements of the genre and everything to do with how you make your mark on that genre, or are noticed, or are clever, or better at it than other people.

The other way in which I imagine the productive role of conflict in workplace writing can be illustrated by the experience I had with Tony Sarmiento, the education officer for the AFL-CIO who I met on the planning committee for the MLA Literacy Conference. Tony represented the union in relation to onsite training, including literacy instruction. Tony has a very strong sense of the ways in which something that seems relatively simple, like lunchtime literacy instruction at Nabisco or Levi Straus, has everything to do with the desire to either mask or prevent some types of conflict from emerging in the workplace. The kind of writing that was being taught was a kind of writing that enabled people to be better functionaries within the corporate structure. Instruction that masked or suppressed conflict, from the union's perspective, was a problem.

But I also think of conflict as a positive concept in terms of students' relationship to their own writing as they struggle to get something written, whether that conflict represents a large cultural project or something more local. The student struggling to write the travel narrative is like Clifford Geertz struggling with the limits of ethnography, or Salman Rushdie, in his book on Nicaragua, trying to not simply take the third world and represent it as a folkloric or impoverished other. The conflicts are large. The individual moment gives you access to a conflict that is larger than the individual moment. I want students to know what it means to struggle with a particular sentence, be thoughtful about that sentence, and get a sense of where it comes from.

My feeling is that the work of somebody like Tony Sarmiento in relationship to workplace writing is to get writers at a variety of levels to be aware of their position as writers in relationship to the discursive orders of power and knowledge in corporate culture. As I understand the best programs in technical writing, they're not producing technical writers as functionaries but as people who are very good at reading the linguistic and cultural requirements of the workplace.

Postscript: The Profession

The first essay in this part was my Chair's address to the 1988 CCCC Convention; the second was a keynote address to the Fourth National Basic Writing Conference (in *The New Republic*, James Traub labeled this meeting "the p.c. assault" on the teaching of remedial English); the essay "What Is Composition" was written for a millennial conference whose primary sponsor was the WPA (the council of Writing Program Administrators); and the final two short pieces — "Composition: 1900–2000" and "Literacy and Departments of Language and Literature" — were published first in *PMLA* and were prompted by my presence on the Executive Council of the MLA. I've had the opportunity to work with most of the major national organizations in the profession (also including the National Council of Teachers of English (NCTE) and the Associated Departments of English (ADE) and with that has come the temptation (and the occasions) to make the Big Statement on behalf of my colleagues and the field. Most of these pieces are utopian. On such occasions, a speaker describes a world elsewhere, a world of desire — or at least that was my strategy. The three lectures were revised as essays and these, too, were meant to provoke controversy and to imagine a future. It is clear that all three had some effect, since they are often cited or used as a point of reference in thinking about key issues or about the history of the field. And the final piece in this section is an interview first published in *Issues in Writing* where the questions pushed in the direction of professional issues.

The 1988 CCCC Chair's address was written as a reply to Maxine Hairston's 1985 Chair's address. Hairston called for composition to break free from English departments:

> I think the time has come to break those bonds — not necessarily physically, although in some cases that may be a good idea — but emotionally and intellectually. I think that as rhetoricians and writing teachers we will come of age and become autonomous professionals with a discipline of our own only if we can make a psychological break with the literary critics who today dominate the profession of English studies. (273)

It is worth noting that Hairston is less sure about the necessity of a "physical" break — that is, creating independent writing programs (like the current program at her former institution, the University of Texas). The issue at the time had to do with the traditions of scholarship that would prepare not only writing teachers but those PhDs in rapidly growing numbers who would choose to identify themselves professionally with "composition."

I argued that English *was* an appropriate home for composition. After recalling her Chair's address, I said:

> I am nervous about our sudden obsession with disciplinary boundaries. I regret graduate courses or graduate programs with reading lists designed to define composition and rhetoric as a set or self-contained field. I believe that to tell our graduate students to read Blair, Campbell, and Whately but not Foucault, Pratt, and Jameson is to assert the worst and most paranoid kind of disciplinary influence. It means that we will jeopardize their role in the general project that is reforming English. And it closes the field to those with interests beyond a limited version of the rhetorical tradition.

I was not thinking at the time about the administrative difficulties faced by Directors of Composition, many of them untenured (as I was when I was first the WPA at Pitt) and facing a variety of obstacles in English departments, nor was I thinking about the working conditions of most of those who were teaching composition courses — graduate teaching assistants and part-time or adjunct faculty. Actually, I suppose the accurate thing to say is that I was most certainly *thinking* about these things, since they were on the minds of all those who were administering programs, but I did not think to bring these issues into professional discussion. That was a blindness, mine and the times, quite brilliantly addressed by the framers and signers of the Wyoming Resolution, who forced these issues onto conference agendas and made us realize that intellectual issues are related to material conditions, and particularly in a field whose subject includes a course and a curriculum.

At the time I wrote the Chair's address, I was concerned with research and scholarship and their relationship to teaching, and I was concerned with how research and scholarship in composition could best be sponsored, valued, and rewarded. I was arguing against the turn to rhetoric and the turn to cognitive psychology as the necessary foundations or models for scholarly work in composition, and I was arguing against the contempt for literature (as an institution) and literary scholarship that was the legacy of the CCCC generation before mine, for whom "lit-er-a-ture" (pronounced as if at a tea party) was used as a negative epithet. I felt then, as I feel now, that literary training can be an appropriate training for a teacher of composition. This just seems obvious to me. Literary training prepares one to read closely, to assign value to acts of writing, to think about writing in relation to history and culture. And I was arguing that traditions of literary scholarship could be extended to work on pedagogy and student writing. I was drawing on (and pointing to) the Amherst program as a reference for imagining such work; others have now begun to write about the program and its faculty.

In some ways, history has shown that English Studies *has* provided a useful reference point for composition. Any review of the current literature would show that literary theory has become an important point of reference, and more and more scholars are pursuing a form of literacy studies that takes them to a history of writing and teaching in the United States, which takes them as well to the history of American literature and literary culture. (The currents seldom flow in the opposite direction. When scholars *in* literature write about composition — I am thinking about John Guillory in *Cultural Capital* — the examples they select from our books and articles are seldom current or representative of the best work.) And it is becoming more and more common (and particularly on my campus) for composition courses to assign literary texts not just as subjects but as models for writing. (Contemporary poets are, to my mind, the most interesting sentence writers at work today; students can learn much about sentences by turning to the poets.)

At the same time, the present situation in composition is not what I had hoped for, with so many undergraduate writing programs breaking off from English departments to become "independent" or "free-standing." In an eloquent essay, "Meet the New Boss, Same as the Old Boss: Class Consciousness in Composition," Joe Harris notes that arguments (like mine) on behalf of the future disciplinary status of composition (should it be aligned with English Studies or with Rhetoric, for example) shift attention "away from present and real labor practices — who does what work for what pay. . . ." He says that:

> recent attempts to define a place and identity for composition have spoken much more to scholars than teachers — with Maxine Hairston exhorting us to "break our bonds" with literary studies, David Bartholomae countering that we need to continue "to acknowledge our roots in English," and Sharon Crowley recently urging us to renounce our "ethic of service." But while I, too, am concerned with how scholarly work in composition gets valued (or not), the crucial questions for me are these: Who does the actual teaching? What institutional structures best allow us to shape how writing gets taught to undergraduates? I am less worried, that is, about the status of composition as a discipline than about whether composition programs treat instructors fairly and teach undergraduates to write well. (56)

This is a tough choice. Do you turn your energies to the working conditions of composition teachers? Do you turn your energies to developing and securing composition's status within the structures of value represented by English Studies? Or, in a different mode: Do you turn your energies to maintaining composition's position within the disciplinary structure of the modern American university?

I wasn't thinking in these terms in 1988, although I have been thinking a good bit about them since. I'll say from the outset that I do not have a solution to the problem of the very high percentage of composition courses taught by adjunct and part-time faculty, faculty with lower pay, less support for teaching and preparation for teaching (including research), fewer rewards for a job well done, and (in some institutions, although not my own) little say in the courses they teach or the curriculum that surrounds them.

I don't have a solution, but I am concerned that we are identifying ourselves with the terms of an argument, one that circulates among deans and provosts, that is not in the best interests of either teachers or students of composition. You can hear these terms in Harris's sentences, where he assumes a separation between teaching and research, and between a writing faculty and the institutional structures that provide power, money, and status in the university: "recent attempts to define a place and identity for composition have spoken much more to scholars than teachers." The concern I have with Harris's formulation is that it assumes a division between scholars and teachers, and it assumes that there is no connection between the status of the discipline (or disciplinary status) and fair employment practices and effective teaching: "I am less worried, that is, about the status of composition as a discipline than about whether composition programs treat instructors fairly and teach undergraduates to write well."

Now I know very well that English departments are divided between a tenured/tenure stream "research" faculty and a "teaching" faculty made up of teaching assistants, full-time adjuncts, and part-time faculty. Harris, I believe, is correct in focusing on the divisions of rank and privilege as one of the key problems facing composition as a field. He and others (including various committees and task forces within the MLA) have made important suggestions for how these divisions might be addressed. In "New Boss/Old Boss," Harris issues the following challenges: We need to improve the working conditions of all teachers of writing; we need to reconfigure the first-year course to lessen the demands it places on staffing; and tenured/tenure stream faculty need to teach first-year writing. I agree with all of these proposals. I worry, however, that by trading on a convenient distinction between teachers and scholars, the program to improve the working conditions of all teachers of writing will deny teachers the motive or opportunity for scholarly engagement in their field and undercut composition's newly achieved place within the research agenda of the American university.

Before saying more, let me say that I believe the opportunities to improve the working conditions for teachers of writing are greater within English than outside. There are many, I know, who have given up on this hope. Let me give it one more try.

It is convenient and sometimes satisfying to think that composition teachers are the only ones who value undergraduate teaching. I do not believe this is true. I think good and careful teaching goes on all over the university. Having spent many years chairing a department, working with faculty across the curriculum, working with deans and provosts, and evaluating departments and writing programs across the country, I have come to understand that the "institutional structures that shape how writing gets taught to undergraduates" value *both* teaching and research. There is confusion and ignorance and a conflicted agenda, to be sure, but at root the question is not either/or. Therefore, I don't see how attempts to move composition to a teaching-only site, outside of a recognized department and free of the pressure to provide research incentives and tenure stream representation will provide better working conditions.

In cases, this may be so, but in general an English department can (and should) argue for the same contractual arrangements available to a program housed somewhere else. And the department can provide research opportunities, long-term security, intellectual oversight (which I believe to be essential for any curriculum), and, for what it is worth, a level of status within the institution to a degree not otherwise possible to programs outside of the departmental structure. The general success of the new wave of independent programs cannot be measured until several years from now; they will have to bear the test of time, including the time when current faculty turn over and new faculty must be recruited. I don't predict that they will be any more successful than programs in English in ensuring that faculty are treated fairly and students are taught well. And, without a research agenda and ties to research, I do not see how, over time, they can distinguish themselves from other academic support units on campus, which means that they will be low on the pecking order when budgets are shuffled, space is assigned, and resources are either increased or cut.

And there is evidence, I think, of improvement in the working conditions of teachers of writing within English departments. As I said above, I travel regularly to evaluate English departments and undergraduate writing programs. One thing I have noticed, and particularly in the research institutions, is a general improvement in the pay and working conditions of nontenure stream faculty, achieved (according to the logic I noted above) in the name of the creation of a "teaching faculty," faculty holding the title "lecturer" or "senior lecturer" and given renewable three- or five-year contracts. They teach a heavier load (eight rather than six, or six rather than four courses per year) on a different pay scale — yearly increments are keyed to the tenure stream scale with starting salaries below starting salaries for assistant professors. The positions are advertised and competitive. Those hired are recent PhDs, and in some cases MFAs. The review is careful and rigorous. The faculty have access to departmental governance and enjoy most of the perks of the tenure stream, including travel funds. They do not have access, however, to sabbatical leave and other forms of research support, since for legal reasons (and to protect tenure) the institution must be very careful to maintain the distinctions between support for teaching and support for research. The model is drawn from the sciences, where lecturers and senior lecturers have handled introductory and general education courses for decades.

A program like this is outlined in an article in the American Association of Colleges and University's publication, *Peer Review*: "Full-Time, Non-Tenure Track Appointments: A Case Study" written by Miles Brand, the former president at Indiana University. Brand announces with considerable satisfaction that he significantly improved the working conditions of the part-time faculty at Indiana by turning part-time lines into full-time nontenure-stream (NTS) lines. The additional funds this required came through a tuition increase supported by the Board of Trustees, who justified the increase on the grounds that it would "improve the quality of instruction." This was the selling point — that NTS faculty would improve the quality of undergraduate instruction.

These funds were used solely in support of NTS contract lines. Behind the quick approval of the Board of Trustees, I suspect, is the lore that the "research" faculty do not teach particularly well and do not care much about lower division instruction.

The move to turn lower division teaching over to full-time NTS faculty is not unique to Indiana. There are many campuses (including my own) where staffing in composition is following the pattern of the independent writing programs. And, in fact, within English departments, there are cases where key administrative positions once held by tenure track faculty are being turned over to NTS lecturers — positions such as director of composition or writing center director. And the move to create (or shore up) an NTS "teaching" faculty in English is in no way unique to composition. Lecturers are being hired to teach specialized areas, such as journalism and professional writing. And lecturers are being hired to teach and sometimes administer the lower division literature courses in service of general education.

That the creation of full-time NTS lines is a national trend is supported by the research of two faculty from the University of Michigan (Edie Goldenberg and John Cross), who had received funding from the Mellon Foundation to interview the "decision makers" on four Research One campuses in order to better understand the increased use of NTS faculty as part of institutional will and in order to better understand whether this is a problem or a solution to a problem. (See their article in *Peer Review*, "Why Hire Non-Tenure-Track Faculty?," although I believe that the recent reports are not yet published.) Their findings suggest that the Indiana story is a sign of the future. (I don't know if Indiana was part of their research.) Goldenberg and Cross argue, however, that there are differences from campus to campus (urban campuses have a greater pool of qualified NTS candidates) and from discipline to discipline (the largest growth in the use of full-time NTS faculty is in the Humanities departments).

It is, they find, certainly the case that full-time NTS faculty produce savings, although they note that few administrators identify cost savings as the original or primary motivation. The original motivation was said to be covering faculty on leave; providing faculty with special or real-world knowledge (a journalist, for example); providing postdoc opportunities for graduate students. In fact, most deans (they report) had only a vague and imprecise sense of the size of the part-time faculty (although they knew exactly the size of the tenure/tenure-stream [T/TS] faculty). Whether cost was the motive, the instructional budgets had been based for decades on the use of NTS faculty (usually part-time). These decisions had been made at the departmental level (or so it seemed to the deans). Whatever the case, budgets had long assumed that substantial numbers of lower division courses would be taught at a lower cost, and so new revenue sources would be needed to create a substantial number of new full-time lines (whether NTS or T/TS). Their conclusion is that once an institution makes use of NTS faculty, there is no going back and no conversions to T/TS lines.

Are we improving the working conditions of writing teachers by creating additional full-time NTS lines? Yes. But I want to register my concern about the trade-offs. If those positions do not provide support and rewards for research — that is, for professional engagement with a field that supports, interrogates, and authorizes that teaching—then everyone suffers over time: the field, the curriculum, the faculty member, the students. If teaching (or administration) becomes something other than intellectual work, then you get what you ask for: routine engagement with accountability to nothing more than a registrar and an advisory committee. Accepting the distinction between a teaching and a research faculty assumes that T/TS faculty should most properly be teaching majors and graduate students. This is how the distinction will be played out in the curriculum. And this division of labor will constitute an ugly argument — that the lower division is necessarily or appropriately uninformed by current work in research and scholarship. And finally, accepting the distinction between a teaching and a research faculty gives a formal solution to our long-standing anxiety about the relationship between teaching and research. Composition has done more than any other area in English to establish the possibilities for exchange — for a teaching based on research and for a research that acknowledges teaching. One of the most important recent developments across English Studies has been a concern for scholarship to speak to a broad audience, to resist the pressure (or the temptation) to follow the model of the sciences, and to write only for a small community of specialists. The separation of the research faculty from the concerns of general education will make it less likely that the research will speak to the concerns of a broad audience.

Furthermore, as my own dean has reminded me, although converting part-time to NTS lines makes good sense, these conversions work against any argument he could make to the provost for additional T/TS lines in English. Here is how I understand the case. In the Humanities (or in the current climate), a chair's most persuasive argument is that there are courses that must be taught and a T/TS person is the best person to teach them. It is less persuasive to argue that you need a scholar to cover a particular research area or to develop a particular area of strength. I cannot imagine a future where all composition courses are taught by TS faculty; in fact, I don't believe such a situation is desirable. I do believe that general education in English should be part of the research and scholarly agenda of English, and so I regret the trend to separate these programs (their oversight and administration) from faculty who are provided with the highest levels of research support. I think it is possible to create tenure track positions for a larger contingent of faculty in English with concerns for general education (and composition), and I think it is possible to improve the working conditions of those who teach these courses from outside the tenure stream. I believe that support for research and professional development must be part of that package of reform.

I think contract categories and working conditions will be an important part of the work of composition over the next decades. And I think the other key problem facing composition as a field will be to develop a robust and compelling research agenda. And I think these are linked. Without appropriate faculty status and the research support it brings, those writing the scholarship of composition will be working from a disadvantage. Without a record of substantial research, it will be hard to make the case for appropriate faculty status. It will most certainly be the job of the faculty in composition to teach the academy to understand and to value variant forms of discourse, including the writing of students. The employment of teachers, the valuing of student writing, and the future of scholarship in composition — I think these are related concerns. And I think everyone will lose if composition fails to make its case and to secure the advances of the last twenty years. And I continue to believe that English departments are in the best position to support this work.

WORKS CITED

Brand, Miles. "Full Time, Non-Tenure-Track Appointments: A Case Study." *Peer Review* 5.1 (2002): 18–22.

Cross, John G., and Edie N. Goldenberg. "Why Hire Non-Tenure-Track Faculty?" *Peer Review* 5.1 (2002): 25–28.

Hairston, Maxine. "Breaking Our Bonds and Reaffirming Our Connections." *College Composition and Communication* 35.1 (1985): 272–82.

Harris, Joseph. "Meet the New Boss, Same as the Old Boss: Class Consciousness in Composition." *College Composition and Communication* 52.1 (2000): 43–68.

Acknowledgements (continued from page iv)

David Bartholomae. "Against the Grain." From *Writers on Writing*, edited by Tom Waldrep. Copyright © 1985 by Tom Waldrep, Director, Center for Academic Excellence and Director, The Writing Center, Medical University of South Carolina, Charleston, SC 29401. Reprinted by permission of Tom Waldrep.

——. "Inventing the University." From *When a Writer Can't Write: Studies on Writer's Block and Other Composing Process Problems*, edited by Mike Rose. © 1985 by The Guilford Press. Reprinted by permission of the publisher.

——. "Writing Assignments: When Writing Begins." From *Fforum*, Fall 1982. Copyright © 1982 Regents of the University of Michigan. Reprinted with the permission of Sweetland Writing Center, University of Michigan.

——. "The Argument of Reading." From *Argument Revisited, Argument Redefined: Negotiating Meaning in the Composition Classroom*, edited by Emmel et al. Copyright © 1996. Reprinted by permission of Sage Publications, Inc.

——. "Writing on the Margins: The Concept of Literacy in Higher Education." From *A Sourcebook for Basic Writing Teachers*, edited by Theresa Enos. Copyright © 1987 by Theresa Enos. Reproduced with the permission of The McGraw-Hill Companies.

——. "The Study of Error." From *College Composition and Communication*, October 1989. Copyright 1989 by the National Council of Teachers of English. "Freshman English, Composition, and CCC." From *College, Composition and Communication*, February 1989. © 1989 by the National Council of Teachers of English. Reprinted with permission.

——. "Teaching Basic Writing: An Alternative to Basic Skills." From the *Journal of Basic Writing*, Volume 2, Number 2, Spring/Summer 1979. "The Tidy House: Basic Writing in the American Curriculum" from *Journal of Basic Writing*, Spring 1993, Volume 12, Number 1. Copyright © 1979, 1993 by *Journal of Basic Writing*, The City University of New York. Reprinted by permission.

——. "Producing Adult Readers: 1940-50" From *The Right to Literacy*, 1990. "Composition, 1900-2000." From the *PMLA Special Millennium Issue*, December 2000. "Literacy and Departments of Language and Literature." From *PLMA*, October 2002. Copyright © 1990, 2000, 2002 by the Modern Language Association. Published by the Modern Language Association of America.

——. "Wistful and Admiring: The Rhetoric of Combination." From *Sentence Combining: A Rhetorical Perspective*, edited by Donald Daiker, Andrew Kaerk, and Max Morenberg. "Released into Language: Errors, Expectations, and the Legacy of Mina Shaughnessy." From *The Territory of Language: Linguistics, Stylistics, and the Teaching of Composition*, edited by Donald McQuade. "What Is Composition and (If You Know What That Is) Why Do We Teach It?" From *Composition in the 21st Century: Crisis and Change*, edited by Lynn Z. Bloom, Donald A. Daiker, and Edward M. White. Copyright © 1985, 1986, 1996 by the Board of Trustees, Southern Illinois University. Reprinted by permission.

John Boe & Eric Schroeder. "Stop Being So Coherent: An Interview with David Bartholomae." From *Writing on the Edge*, Fall 1999. Copyright © 1999 Eric Schroeder & John Boe. Reprinted with the permission of the writers.

Wade Mahon. "Reading and Writing in the Academy: A Conversation with David Bartholomae." From *Issues in Writing*, Fall 1993/Winter 1994. Copyright © 1993 by Wade Mahon. Reprinted with the permission of the author.

Anthony Petrosky. "Introduction: Ways of Reading." From *Ways of Reading*, by David Bartholomae and Anthony Petrosky. Copyright © 2002 by Bedford/St. Martin's. Reprinted by permission of the publisher.

Richard Poirier. From *The Performing Self: Compositions and Decompositions in the Languages of Contemporary Life* by Richard Poirier. Copyright © 1992 by Richard Poirier. Reprinted by permission of Rutgers University Press.

INDEX